MONROE COLLEGE LIBRARY

32468000012600

WITHDRAWN FROM MONROE COLLEGE LIBRARY

D1255937

EUROPEAN HISTORICAL DICTIONARIES
Edited by Jon Woronoff

Historical Dictionary of the Republic of Moldova

Andrei Brezianu

European Historical Dictionaries, No. 37

The Scarecrow Press, Inc.
Lanham, Maryland, and London
2000

REF
DK
509.37
.B74
2000

SCARECROW PRESS, INC.

Published in the United States of America
by Scarecrow Press, Inc.
4720 Boston Way
Lanham, Maryland 20706
http://www.scarecrowpress.com

4 Pleydell Gardens, Folkestone
Kent CT20 2DN, England

Copyright © 2000 by Andrei Brezianu

All rights reserved. No part of this publication may be reproduced,
stored in a retrieval system, or transmitted in any form or by any
means, electronic, mechanical, photocopying, recording, or otherwise,
without the prior permission of the publisher.

British Library Cataloguing in Publication Information Available

Library of Congress Cataloging-in-Publication Data

Brezianu, Andrei.
   Historical dictionary of the Republic of Moldova / Andrei Brezianu.
      p.   cm.   —   (European historical dictionaries ; no. 37)
   Includes bibliographical references.
   ISBN 0-8108-3734-X
   1. Moldova—History—Dictionaries. I. Title. II. Series.
   DK509.37.B74   2000
   947.6—dc21   99-051306

⊗ ™ The paper used in this publication meets the minimum requirements of
American National Standard for Information Sciences—Permanence of
Paper for Printed Library Materials, ANSI/NISO Z39.48–1992.
Manufactured in the United States of America.

Contents

Editor's Foreword

The Republic of Moldova is one of the smallest fragments of the former Soviet Union. When the opportunity came for successor states to renew their independence in 1991, few seized it with greater joy. For Moldova, in various shapes and forms, had been dominated by others over most of its recorded history. A remote outpost of the Roman Empire in ancient times, it narrowly escaped being absorbed in the Ottoman Empire and was forcibly inserted in the Russian Empire, then more tightly integrated in the Union of Soviet Socialist Republics, while suffering excessive influence or intrusion from the Habsburg Empire (in the late 18th century), the German Reich (in the 1940s), and all along from Romania—the only land with which it had any generic affinity. The new state's relaunch was not entirely auspicious, being itself plagued by the presence of a breakaway region. Yet, despite numerous evident problems, Moldova has succeeded in establishing a working government and administration, shifting from a command to a free market economy, and adjusting to the pressures of much larger neighbors.

This story of domination and independence, a struggle far harsher and longer than most smaller European states have encountered, can be gleaned from the *Historical Dictionary of the Republic of Moldova*. It reaches back to the earliest times and stretches into Moldova's most recent period. It covers not only the political aspects, but also the economic, social, cultural, religious, and linguistic features that make Moldova rather distinct. This is done, first, in a chronology that follows the country's progression over time, then in an introduction that presents the main characteristics of the country, and, finally, in a dictionary that provides specifics on crucial persons, places, institutions, and events. The bibliography, much of which is inevitably not in English, itself enhances the value of this quite unique book.

There are exceedingly few people who could have written this volume since, for obvious reasons, Moldova is not that well known abroad, and all too many local authorities were more interested in presenting a skewed view. It is therefore fortunate that a sympathetic author undertook the task,

Andrei Brezianu, who is still at pains to provide the facts as well as they can be ascertained. Dr. Brezianu, who knows the country and the language, studied and then taught at the University of Bucharest before moving to the United States, where he has also taught and has worked as a consultant on linguistics, a broadcaster with the Voice of America, and an independent scholar and researcher. One can well imagine that one of the high points of his career came recently when he was able to lecture as a visiting professor at the Free International University of Moldova, located in a Moldova that was finally free.

Jon Woronoff
Series Editor

Acknowledgments

I am indebted to several individuals and experts who gave their time, research materials, and expertise to provide data and fresh perspectives for this dictionary. The actual collection of current information in this book was greatly assisted by the recommendations and professional advice of Grant Harris of the Library of Congress; the up-to-date material provided by Moldovan journalist Dinu Popa, now a resident of California; and the fine help offered by Iurie Reniţă of the embassy of the Republic of Moldova in Washington, D.C. To them and to all those who helped complete this work, I wish to express my gratitude.

I would also like to express my special and particular indebtedness to Moldovan scholar and author Dr. Vasile Nedelciuc, whose precious help as this dictionary was being written was constant and substantial. Thanks to his contributions, this book contains accurate information introducing the reader to many of contemporary Moldova's personalities, current issues, public fora, and political bodies; Dr. Nedelciuc's contributions are marked by his initials, V. N.

Preface

The Republic of Moldova is one of the areas of the former Soviet Union where—in addition to classic totalitarian oppression—the strategies of semantic deceit, at work for decades, have resulted in creating a high concentration of cultural and political delusion and intellectual confusion. To various degrees, this still thwarts a full understanding of the complex plight of this small area of the former Soviet Union's crucible.

The main goal of this historical dictionary is to offer an annotated work of reference, giving methodical access to the basic data about Moldova, past and present. This broad construct, discussing events, places, people, and issues, endeavors to provide factual insights into the social, economic, cultural, ethnic, and linguistic structures that account for the current specificity of Moldova's identity and manifold fragilities, as well as its other peculiarities in the post-Soviet context. This amalgam of facts and issues has been articulated and incorporated into an approach aimed at clarifying every relevant aspect of Moldova's recent and more distant history, including such vexed questions as the country's name; the Cyrillic versus Latin alphabet issue; the nation's three-pronged relationship to its neighbors (two individually distinct regions of Ukraine and one historic twin region of Romania); its two rival Orthodox Churches; the economic and political sequels of the trans-Nistrian ideological split; and, last but not least, Moldova—never a Soviet republic by choice—as a contracted sample, illustrative of some of the defining traits of the recent East-West divide in the history of Europe.

Note on Spelling and Pronunciation

Romanian, which is the principal language in Moldova, uses the Latin alphabet. A number of letters in the Latin alphabet used in the writing of Romanian are marked with diacritics to denote specific phonemes (**ă, î/â, ş, ţ**), while several consonants are spelled in two ways (**c/ch, g/gh**), depending on the phonemes they respectively denote:

- **ă** represents a sound similar to the English vowel sound in words like h**u**rt, d**i**rt
- **î** and **â** denote the same sound, which has no near equivalent in English: **î** is used when the sound occurs at the beginning of a word; **â** is generally used when the sound occurs in the interior of a word—**î/â** lies somewhere between the vowel sounds of the English words r**ee**d and r**u**de
- **ş** is very similar to the initial consonants in English words like **sh**epherd and **sh**eriff (**sh**)
- **ţ** is similar to the sound at the end of the English word ha**ts** (**ts**)
- **ch** is a digraph used before **e** and **i**, the same as in Italian, to denote the sound **k**, as in the English word **c**ard
- **c** when followed by **e** and **i** is pronounced like the first sound in the English word **ch**eese
- **g** when followed by **e** or **i** is pronounced like the English sound **g** in the word **g**eneral
- **gh** is used before **e** and **i** to denote the sound **g** as in the English word **g**arden

Six place-names found in this dictionary are apt illustrations of these phonetic-alphabetical situations:
Chi**ş**in**ă**u, **Cuci**urgan, **Ce**tatea Alb**ă**, **Gi**ur**gi**ule**ş**ti, R**â**bni**ţ**a (or R**î**bni**ţ**a), and Un**gh**eni.

Block-letter entries in the alphabetical listing of the dictionary have ignored diacritics; they are found instead, whenever applicable, in the body of the various entries.

Before Moldova's declaration of independence, the Slavonic alphabet was applied by the Soviet authorities to obfuscate the visible Romance aspect of the Romanian language spoken in Moldova. For reasons of consistency, in the bibliography of this dictionary, titles of works published under the Soviet rule in the Romanian language in Cyrillics have been transliterated according to the Western bibliographical practice—that is, using Roman equivalents of Russian Cyrillics instead of the normal Roman alphabet of Romanian.

Note on Toponyms

The official name of the country that is the subject of this dictionary is Moldova, the vernacular form for the anglicized, traditionally accepted form Moldavia (adjective: Moldavian). To avoid clumsy rewriting of old quotations and forced modification of fundamental terms, "Moldova" and "Moldavia," "Moldovan" and "Moldavian" appear alternately in this work. In the aftermath of the 19th-century incorporation of half of Moldova into the Russian Empire, most of Moldova's place-names underwent changes, beginning with the name of the Nistru River (Russian form: Dniestr) and of Chişinău, designated the chief city of the province under the Russianized name of Kishinev. Other toponyms with two or more different forms reflect the 16th-century Turkish conquest and subsequent occupation of a number of Moldova's key strongholds, for example, Tighina (Turkish: Bender; Russian: Bendery) or Cetatea Albă (Turkish and Russian: Akkerman). Ukrainian forms—for instance, Chernovtsy or Bilhorod Dnistrovsky over-lapping with the historic place-names Cernăuţi or Cetatea Albă—reflect some of the territorial alterations that occurred under Soviet rule after 1940. In the alphabetical section of this dictionary, the entries are listed in keeping with the current local and original usage, with foreign or subsequent equivalents being offered as synonyms immediately following the preferred spelling.

Abbreviations and Acronyms

ADR	Alianţa pentru Democraţie şi Reforme / Alliance for Democracy and Reforms
BMDP	Blocul pentru o Moldovă Democratică şi Prosperă / Bloc for a Democratic and Prosperous Moldova
BNM	Banca Naţională a Moldovei / National Bank of Moldova
CDM	Convenţia Democrată din Moldova / Democratic Convention of Moldova
CIS	Commonwealth of Independent States
CSCE	Commission on Security and Cooperation in Europe (U.S.)
ECBS	Economic Cooperation at the Black Sea
EU	European Union
FPCD	Frontul Popular Creştin Democrat / Christian Democrat Popular Front
FPM	Frontul Popular din Moldova / Popular Front of Moldova
GAU	Guarantee Administration Unit
GDP	gross domestic product
GUAM	Georgia, Ukraine, Azerbaijan, Moldova (economic cooperation group)
IMF	International Monetary Fund
KGB	Komitet Gosudarstvennoy Bezopastnost / Committee for State Security
MASSR	Moldavian Autonomous Soviet Socialist Republic
MNR	Moldavian Nistrian Republic
MSSR	Moldavian Soviet Socialist Republic
MUE	Mişcarea Unitate-Edinstvo / Unity-Edinstvo Movement
MVD	Ministerstvo Vnutrennikh Del / Ministry of Internal Affairs (Russian)
NATO	North Atlantic Treaty Organization
NGO(s)	nongovernmental organization(s)
NKVD	Narodny Komissariat Vnutrennikh Del / People's Commissariat of Internal Affairs
OSCE	Organization for Security and Cooperation in Europe

OSTK	Obedenionye Soiuz Trudovykh Kolektivov / United Council of Workers Collective
PCDM	Partidul Comuniştilor din Moldova / Party of Moldova's Communists
PDAM	Partidul Democrat Agrar din Moldova / Democratic Agrarian Party of Moldova
PFD	Partidul Forţelor Democratice / Party of Democratic Forces
PMDP	Partidul pentru o Moldova Democratică şi Prosperă / Party for a Democratic and Prosperous Moldova
PSD	Partidul Social Democrat / Social Democrat Party
PSDM	Partidul Social Democrat din Moldova / Social Democrat Party of Moldova
PSDU	Partidul Social Democrat Unit / United Social Democratic Party
PSM	Partidul Socialist din Moldova / Socialist Party of Moldova
US	Unitatea Socialistă / Socialist Unity
USSR	Union of Soviet Socialist Republics

The Republic of Moldova in 1999, featuring the restoration of Moldova's pre-Soviet territorial and administrative division into traditional districts (*judeţe*)—namely, Bălţi, Cahul, Chişinău, Edineţ, Lăpuşna, Orhei, Soroca, Tighina, Ungheni, and the autonomous territorial unit of Gagauzia. A tiny *judeţ* by the name of Taraclia does not appear on this map. It was formed in late 1999 to accommodate the calls of the local population of the former *raion* of the same name, who wished to be administratively separate from the larger *judeţ* of Cahul. The final name and status of the Nistru east-bank *judeţ* of Dubăsari is to be established pending the settlement of the dispute about that territory's claim to separate autonomy.

Historical Moldova in the 18th century, as featured in Demetrius Cantemir's German version of *Descriptio Moldaviae*, Frankfurt & Leipzig, 1771. Courtesy of the Rare Books Division, Library of Congress, Washington, D.C.

Chronology

A.D. 101–106   The Roman conquest of Dacia by Emperor Trajan. Intensive colonization of the new province. An underground process of popular Christianization starts taking root in the colony alongside Romanization.

ca. 130–160   Eastern frontier of the empire fortified by Hadrian, Trajan's successor. Building of a Roman *vallum* (bulwark) the vestiges of which are popularly known in Moldova today as "Valul lui Traian." Rome controls the mouths of the Danube River.

271–275   The Roman army retreats from Dacia. The frontier of the empire is reset along the lower course of the Danube down to the Black Sea.

275–602   Successive waves of migrating tribes invade the former Roman colony and start mingling with the sedentary Romanized population left behind by the departed imperial administration. The Danube frontier of the Roman Empire crumbles.

ca. 600   Beginning of the Slavic tribes' southward migration and gradual assimilation by the Romanized population of the former colony.

679–680   Bulgarian tribes move across the southern part of present-day Moldova along the shores of the Black Sea. First Bulgarian attacks on the Byzantine Empire.

681   Byzantine-Bulgarian Treaty. A Bulgarian czardom is established south of the Danube. Its center of gravity becomes increasingly Slavonic, thus driving a growing wedge between the Greek Byzantine Empire and the former Romanized territories north of the river. Formation of the individuality of the Romanian language in the family of the Romance languages.

864–865   The Bulgarians adopt Christianity amid controversies anticipating the historic schism between the Latin Church of Rome and the Greek Orthodox Church of Byzantium. Bulgarian ruler Boris chooses allegiance to the Church of Byzantium, deciding for Old Slavonic instead of Greek as the official language of liturgy. The decision carries momentous cultural consequences for the future of the region, due to, among other things, the upcoming dominance of Slavonic literacy throughout southeastern Europe and, later on, Russia.

940–965 Maurocastron (later Cetatea Albă) first mentioned as a port city on the Black Sea overlooking the mouth of the Nistru River.

1241 The great Tatar invasion. Most of the lands between the Carpathian Mountains and the Nistru River remain under Tatar occupation.

1330 Foundation by Basarab I of the independent voivodate of Wallachia (Bassarabskaya Zemlya ["Land of Bassarab"] in later Russian documents).

1334 First mention of Baia—as "civitas Moldaviae"—in a Latin document. Supplanting the vernacular "Moldova," the Latin form "Moldavia" prevails in official documents, diplomatic correspondence, geographical descriptions, and treatises and will become the accepted norm in English. (For etymology, see MOLDOVA, ETYMOLOGY.)

1343–1345 Tatar hordes menacing Transylvania's eastern borders in Moldavia are driven back and dispersed by Hungary's King Louis I of Anjou, with help from the Crown's Transylvanian vassals. One of them, Maramureş Voivode Dragoş (ca. 1352–1353), becomes the first appointed ruler of the boundary province of Moldavia, which starts attracting emigration from the neighboring principality, Transylvania. Under Dragoş and his immediate successors, Sas and Balc, Moldavia is organized as a defensive outpost, vassal to the Hungarian Crown.

1359 Moldavia established as an independent principality by Wallachian Transylvanian Voivode Bogdan. He renounces his Maramureş domains in the northern Carpathians, leaves his native land with an army of faithfuls, rejects the vassalage of the Hungarian Crown, secures power in the new province across the mountains, and proclaims himself independent prince of the new country, also called Bogdania in foreign documents. (The vernacular form in uninterrupted use is Moldova.) Bogdan I dies in 1365. His son and successor, Laţco (ca. 1365–1375), makes overtures toward the Church of Rome.

1371 Roman Catholic bishopric established in Siret, the capital of the principality.

ca. 1375–1391 Reign of Petru I Muşat. Moldova's capital moved to Suceava.

1377 Moldova's right of coinage asserted. First silver grossi minted by Petru I Muşat.

1387 Petru Muşat recognizes the king of Poland, Wladislaw II Jagello—whose sister he marries—as overlord.

1392 Defining Moldova's boundaries, Roman I, Petru Muşat's son, proclaims himself "By the grace of God the almighty, great ruler of Moldova's land from the Mountains to the Sea."

1400–1432 Reign of Alexander the Good.

ca. 1400 Construction of the fortress of Hotin overlooking the banks of the Nistru River.

1401 Cetatea Albă bishop confirmed metropolitan of Moldova by the patriarch of Constantinople. Metropolitan see moved from Cetatea Albă to the northern capital, Suceava.

1408 Tighina mentioned as a border checkpoint overlooking the banks of the Nistru River.

1420 Vărzăreşti Monastery, north of Nisporeni, referred to in a votive document. First raid of the Turkish fleet against Moldova's borders. Unsuccessful naval attack on the Black Sea fortress of Cetatea Albă.

17 July 1436 The village of Chişinău on the Bâc River is first mentioned in a public record.

25 June 1441 First mention of Adunarea Ţării (later on Sfatul Ţării), the principality's convocational General Assembly.

29 May 1453 The fall of Constantinople and the end of the Byzantine Empire. The Ottoman Empire seizes full control of the Black Sea, a "Turkish lake" for the next three centuries.

1454 New Turkish raid on Cetatea Albă.

1455 Sultan Mehmed II gives an ultimatum to Moldova's Prince Petru Aron demanding a yearly tribute in exchange for peace.

1456 The Ieni-Derbend Agreement. Moldova becomes tributary to the Ottoman Empire. Petru Aron consents to pay the sultan an annual tribute of 2,000 gold pieces in exchange for the Ottoman pledge that "No lands or estates of Moldova will be alienated."

1457–1504 Reign of Stephen the Great. Moldova stops paying tribute to the sultan.

1466–1469 Erection of the votive church of Putna.

1467 Hungarian attempt to regain suzerainty over Moldova. King Matthias Corvinus crosses into Moldova from Transylvania and seizes Baia, Bacău, Roman, and Târgu Neamț.

December 1467 Battle of Baia. Stephen the Great defeats Matthias Corvinus and foils Hungary's attempts to regain Moldova as a vassal principality.

ca. 1468 Construction of the fortress of Orhei on the west bank of the Nistru River.

1469 Battle of Lipnic. A Tatar invasion is crushed by Stephen the Great in combat near the banks of the Nistru River.

ca. 1471 Construction of the Soroca fortress on the west bank of the Nistru.

1474 Stephen the Great's plea for a common crusade against the Turks. Pope Sixtus IV calls Stephen the Great "Athlete of Christ."

January 1475 A huge Turkish army invades Moldova. Stephen the Great engages the Turks south of Vaslui in a swampy area surrounded by forests. The sultan's troops are trounced by the numerically inferior Moldovans.

1476 Joint offensive by the Turks and the Tatars attacking from the east bank of the Nistru River. Suceava and Cetatea Albă are attacked from the north by the Tatars, while the Turks march in from the south. In the battle of Valea Albă, Stephen's troops are defeated, but the bulwark fortresses of Suceava and Neamț and the new forts along the west bank of the Nistru prove impregnable and resist the invaders' assaults. Hit by an outbreak of cholera and running short of supplies, the Turkish army retreats.

1479 Construction of the fortress of Chilia at Moldova's southern border, on the Danube.

1484 New Turkish attack on Moldova. The key fortresses of Chilia and Cetatea Albă are captured. Moldova's seashore and southern defenses crumble.

1485 In a last-ditch attempt to secure help against the Turks, Stephen appeals to Poland and recognizes King Casimir IV as overlord.

1489 Poland fails its pledge by recognizing the Turkish capture of Chilia and Cetatea Albă. Stephen the Great is compelled to agree to the sultan's terms in a treaty (*ahdname*) that makes Moldova tributary again to the Sublime Porte. In exchange for an annual tribute of 3,000 gold pieces and the cession of the cities of Chilia and Cetatea Albă, the Ottoman Empire pledges not to interfere in the framework of church and state in the Principality of Moldova.

1497–1498 Moldova at war with Poland.

1504 Stephen the Great's death.

1527–1542 Macarius, bishop of Roman, writes *Letopiseț* (Chronicle) narrating Moldova's early history.

1529 Treaty of alliance between the Principalities of Moldova and Transylvania directed against the policies of the house of Habsburg. The Habsburg allies defeated, with Moldovan help, in the battle of Feldioara.

1534 Transylvanian pretender Aloysius Gritti, a favorite of the Turks, defeated and captured, with Moldovan help, at Mediaş, in Transylvania.

1538 Turkish campaign of reprisal. Sultan Suleiman I (a.k.a. Suleiman the Magnificent) crushes the Moldovan army and seizes Suceava.

1538 Moldova's southern hinterland between the mouths of the Nistru and Danube Rivers is seized in its entirety by the Ottoman Empire. Surrender of the fortress of Tighina on the Nistru, renamed Bender.

1552–1561 Reign of Alexandru Lăpuşneanu, who moves his court from Suceava to Iaşi in midland Moldova.

1572–1574 Moldova refuses to double the amount of the tribute paid to the sultan. Moldovans defeated by the Turks in the battle of Lake Cahul. Moldova ruler Ioan Vodă caught and executed.

1593 Increase of Moldova's tribute to the Ottoman Empire to 65,000 gold pieces per year, in exchange for preserving domestic autonomy.

1594 Secret anti-Ottoman agreement between Wallachian Prince Michael the Brave and Moldova's Prince Aron the Tyrant.

1595 Moldova's new ruler, Ieremia Movilă, recognizes the king of Poland as the principality's overlord.

May 1600 Following the conquest of Transylvania, Michael the Brave seizes Moldova. Prince Ieremia Movilă takes refuge in the fortress of Hotin, which Michael fails to capture. Michael proclaims himself prince of the three principalities (i.e., Wallachia, Transylvania, and Moldova). The short-lived personal union lasts until September, when Ieremia Movilă is returned to power by the army of the Polish king.

1620–1621 Poland at war with the Ottoman Empire. After the Polish-Moldovan defeat by the Turks in the battle of Țuțora, Moldova is compelled to reaccept the suzerainty of the Ottoman Empire. Enforcement of the rule that each aspirant to the Moldova throne has to buy the consent of the Sublime Porte.

1634–1653 Reign of Prince Vasile Lupu.

1637–1639 Vasile Lupu's aborted attempts to rule Wallachia are finally foiled in the wake of the Moldo-Wallachian battle of Ojogeni, where the Moldovans are defeated.

1643 Moldova Metropolitan Varlaam publishes *Cazania*, subtitled *Carte românească de învățătură dumenecele preste an si la praznice* (Romanian Book of Teachings for Sundays and Other Holidays), the first printed monument of the Romanian language.

1646 First Moldovan code of law printed in Iași: *Carte românească de învățătură de la pravilele împărătești și de la alte giudețe* (Romanian Book of Teachings from the Imperial Statutes and Other Judicial Pronouncements).

1652 Prince Lupu's alliance with Hetman Bogdan Khmielnitsky, leader of the trans-Nistrian Cossacks. The Hetman's son marries Princess Ruxandra, Vasile Lupu's daughter.

1653 Vasile Lupu's leadership over Moldova challenged by Wallachian Prince Matei Basarab and his allies. Defeated in the battle of Flinta, Vasile Lupu retreats across the Nistru and seeks help from the Cossacks.

1656 Lupu's successor, Gheorghe Stefan, concludes a secret agreement with Russia's Czar Aleksey Mikhailovich, pledging Russia's support for future Moldovan endeavors to regain from the Turks the principality's lost access to the Danube and the Black Sea.

1664 Romanian translation of the Old Testament by Moldovan scholar and polymath Nicolae Milescu (1636–1708).

1685 Writing of Miron Costin's *De Neamul Moldovenilor* (On the Origin of the Moldovan People), a historical work vindicating the Roman beginnings and Latin origin of the people of Moldova.

1685–1693 Reign of Prince Constantin Cantemir.

February 1690 Prince Cantemir's secret treaty with the Habsburg Empire signed in Sibiu, Transylvania, pledges Moldovan help in future anti-Ottoman actions undertaken by the Austrians.

1698   Debut of Constantin Cantemir's son Demetrius as a writer: *Divanul* (The Divan: Or the Quarrel of the Wise Man with the World), published in Iaşi.

1705   Demetrius Cantemir's satirical novel *Istoria Ieroglifică* (The Hieroglyphical History) is the first work of fiction in the Romanian language.

1710–1711   The short reign of Demetrius Cantemir marks a turning point in Moldova's history. Secret attempt to redirect the policies of the principality by decidedly staking its future on the rising power of Russia.

April 1711   Lutsk Treaty. Peter the Great guarantees Moldova's integrity and independence, provided it joins the anti-Ottoman struggle as an ally of the Russian Empire.

May 1711   In the wake of the Russo-Swedish War, the Russian army crosses the Nistru and enters Moldova. Peter the Great and Demetrius Cantemir meet in Iaşi on 24 June.

July 1711   Battle of Stănileşti, on the Prut River. The Russian troops and their Moldovan allies are defeated by the Turks. Prince Cantemir flees to Russia to become the czar's private counselor. In reprisal, the Ottoman Empire decrees that Moldova's rulers will be appointed directly by the Sublime Porte. Beginning of the Phanariote regime in Moldova.

1714–1716   Writing of Demetrius Cantemir's *Descriptio Moldaviae* (A Description of Moldavia), written in Latin at the invitation of the Berlin Academy.

1715–1716   Demetrius Cantemir composes in Latin his major work, *Incrementa atque Decrementa Aulae Othomanicae*. An English version—*The History of the Growth and Decay of the Othman Empire* (London, 1734–1735)—brings European celebrity to the author, whose work is also translated into French (Paris, 1743) and German (Hamburg, 1745).

1717   Writing of Demetrius Cantemir's *Historia Moldo-Vlachica*, assessing the Roman origin, unity, and continuity of the history of the Romanian-speaking people of Moldova and its neighboring countries of the same kin.

1735–1739   Russo-Turkish War. Russia voices an interest in extending its protection over Moldova. Treaty of Belgrade (1739) marks the beginning of Russia's naval supremacy in the Black Sea.

1766   Public education reform enacted by Prince Grigore Ghika III. A princely education foundation (Scoala Domnească) established in Chişinău. Other schools founded in Lăpuşna, Orhei, and Soroca.

1768   Outbreak of a new Russo-Turkish War. Russia emerges as winner in the battles of Larga and Cahul (1770) waged on the soil of Moldavia.

1774   Treaty of Kuchuk Kainarji. Russia establishes itself as a regional power, with a recognized right to intervene in favor of the Orthodox peoples living in the Ottoman Empire, including in the Principalities of Moldova and Wallachia.

May 1775   Dismemberment of northern Moldova. The Ottoman Empire surrenders to Austria a 10,441-square-kilometer area carved out from Moldova's northern lands, which becomes a military district of the Habsburg Empire under the name of Bucovina.

1787   Russia at war with the Ottoman Empire.

January 1792   Treaty of Iaşi. Moldova becomes a direct neighbor of Russia on the Nistru River.

1806   Russia declares war on the Ottoman Empire. The Russian armies cross the Nistru border into Moldova and occupy Iaşi.

May 1812   Russo-Turkish Treaty of Bucharest and partition of Moldova. The frontier between the Ottoman and the Russian Empires is moved westward inside the historical borders of the principality, back from the banks of the Nistru to the line of the Prut River, across the middle of the country's geographical heartland. Diminished by roughly one-half of its size and 482,630 of its inhabitants, the principality maintains its capital in Iaşi, with Prince Scarlat Callimachi as its ruler, under Turkish suzerainty. On the east bank of the Prut, the country's other half—renamed Bessarabia (ca. 46,000 square kilometers in area)—begins an existence of its own as an oblast, or province, of the Russian Empire.

1813   Russian ukase (a proclamation or edict) detaches Moldova's Orthodox Church in the new province from all its hierarchical links with its prior canonical authority across the Prut. Establishment of the new eparchy of Chişinău and Hotin, placed under the jurisdiction of the Russian Holy Synod in St. Petersburg. Beginning of the introduction of Russian as the language of church and liturgy.

1817   Beginnings of the Gagauz (Christian Turks) immigration in southern Bessarabia. Statistics mention 1,205 recent settlers having fled from the Ottoman-ruled territories south of the Danube Delta.

1818   Chişinău (renamed Kishinev) designated as capital of the oblast of Bessarabia. Promulgation of the statute of the province—"Aşezământul Obrazovaniei Oblastiei Basarabiei"—granting a certain degree of autonomy and the preservation of the local language, customs, laws, and traditions. Russian General Bakhmetiev is named governor of Bessarabia.

1826   Convention of Akkerman. Russia and Turkey agree on the reorganization of the Danubian Principalities under Russian control.

1828   The czar rescinds the initial statute of Bessarabia. Russian-held Moldova becomes subject to Russian civil and judicial institutions as part of "New Russia."

1829   Governor-General Mikhail Vorontsov's "Regulations" restrict several provisions inscribed in the previous statute. Article 63 forbids the use of the local language (called "Moldavian") in public documents and transactions. Russian becomes the language of government.

1836   Russian ukase gives the governor-general of the oblast of Bessarabia discretionary authority over all civil and military matters. Russian is decreed the official language of the province, to gradually replace Moldavian in all official acts over a seven-year period.

1853   Russian ultimatum to Turkey. Czar Nicholas I orders the occupation of the Danubian Principalities, the princes of which take refuge in Vienna. Beginning of the Crimean War.

1854   First issue of *Bessarbskie oblastnye vedemosti*, the official daily of the Russian administration of the province of Bessarabia. Called *Bessarbskie gubernskie vedemosti* after 1873, it would be published without interruption until 1917.

1856   Defeat of Russia and the Congress of Paris. Non-Russian Moldova regains three of its former districts—Bolgrad, Cahul, and Ismail—incorporated by Russia as part of Bessarabia in 1812. The retrieved land totals an area of roughly 9,000 square kilometers and a population of about 150,000. Russia maintains possession of the rest of the territories between the Prut and the Nistru Rivers but is removed from the Danube, no longer its southern border.

1857   On 1 March, Russia returns to Moldova the districts of Bolgrad, Cahul, and Ismail.

1858   Convention of Paris, signed by Great Britain, France, Australia, Prussia, Russia, Turkey, and the kingdom of Sardinia to set guidelines for the future status of the Danubian Principalities, Moldova, and Wallachia as twin political entities, under the name of the United Principalities, with a central legislative body and a common Court of Appeals, maintaining separate governments and separate ruling princes.

1859 Union of the Moldo-Wallachian Principalities under Moldovan Prince Alexandru Ioan Cuza.

1860 Latin alphabet introduced in the United Principalities (later to be named Romania). Inauguration of the first telegraph linking Chişinău to Russia's port city of Odessa on the Black Sea.

1861 Czar Alexander II promulgates a wide-ranging land reform in Russia. Serfdom abolished.

1864 Administrative reform of the Russian Empire, including Bessarabia. Creation of the *zemstvas* (governmental administrative bodies).

1867 Use of local vernacular language prohibited in Bessarabian schools. Russian-language teaching becomes compulsory and replaces "Moldavian" in all educational processes.

1871 Bessarabia's special status of oblast rescinded by Russia. The Moldovan province between the Prut and the Nistru becomes a *guberniia* (or regular administrative unit) of the Russian Empire.

1873 Decree of Russian archbishop of Chişinău, Pavel Lebedev, making the knowledge of Russian compulsory for all Bessarabian priests. Members of the clergy are obligated to teach their own children Russian at home.

1877 Czar Alexander II spends eight days in Chişinău, where he announces the beginning of Russia's war against Turkey (12 April). On 9 May, Romania proclaims its independence and goes to war as an ally of Russia. Turkish suzerainty—devolved on Romania as a successor state to the Principalities of Moldova and Wallachia—officially repudiated by Romania's Parliament. Russo-Romanian joint action on the battlefield leads to decisive victories south of the Danube. Turkish army crushed at Plevna.

1878 Congress of Berlin. Romania's independence internationally acknowledged. Russia seizes back the three districts of Bolgrad, Cahul, and Ismail, which it reincorporates into the *guberniia* of Bessarabia. Russia's southern border is back on the Danube.

1894–1917 Reign of Nicholas II. The crisis of the Russian imperial system reaches a first climax in 1905. In a manifesto prepared by liberal-minded Prime Minister S. Y. Witte, Czar Nicholas II (still retaining the title of autocrat, or *samoderzhets*) promises under pressure the inviolability of the rights of person and of freedom of thought, speech, and assembly, and he pledges that no law will be enacted without the consent of the newly created legislative body, the Duma. Pro-freedom Bessarabian intellectuals try to take advantage of the more liberal policies and publish the first Romanian-language magazine, *Basarabia* (May 1906). Under Peter Stolypin's government (1906–1911), national movements are stifled and crushed by Russian authorities. Romanian-language publications such as *Basarabia*, *Moldovanul*, and *Viaţa Basarabiei* are closed down.

1913 *Iuzhnyi krai* (after 1914 *Bessarabskii iuzhnyi krai*), a Russian-language daily, is published in Bender (Tighina). The Romanian-language literary and scientific monthly *Cuvânt moldovenesc* is published in Chişinău.

1914 Outbreak of World War I. Russia at war with the Central Powers. Over 200,000 of Russia's conscripts recruited from Bessarabia.

1916 Romania enters World War I against the Central Powers. Russian and Romanian armies fight together, forming the two wings of the Entente Eastern front. Russian troops' morale sapped by defeats and revolutionary propaganda. Romanians defeated on two fronts. Occupation of Bucharest by the Central Powers. Romania's capital moved to Iaşi.

March 1917 Abdication of Nicholas II.

April 1917 The Russian Revolution triggers chain reactions across the empire, undermining discipline in the army. Russia's military defeats bring the Austro-German forces right on Russia's frontiers. Bessarabia in turmoil. Administrative autonomy and the convocation of a national assembly to create legislation demanded by a congress of Bessarabian villages' representatives. Foundation of the Moldovan National Party (Partidul Naţional Moldovenesc) brings together leaders of the progressive intellectual elite and conservative personalities, with the common aim of taking action for an autonomous Romanian Bessarabia.

May 1917 Odessa congress of several thousand Moldovan soldiers and officers demanding political autonomy for Bessarabia. Announcement of the formation of special units, "Cohortele Moldoveneşti," to maintain public order against upheaval fomented in the army by Bolshevik revolutionaries. Chişinău congress of Moldovan teachers demands an end to the Russian system of education, a return to local language and traditions in the educational process, and the replacement of Cyrillic by Latin characters in writing and teaching the language.

June 1917   Ukraine proclaims its autonomy. Ukrainian nationalists claim Bessarabia's integration into Ukraine.

July 1917   Convocation of the General Assemby (Sfatul Țării) of the province to debate the national and territorial autonomy of Bessarabia.

September 1917   Russia proclaimed a republic.

November 1917   Victory of the Bolshevik Revolution in Petrograd. A general congress of Moldovan officers and soldiers convened in Chişinău proclaims the autonomy of Bessarabia, to be further submitted for ratification to Sfatul Țării. Election of delegates carried out through rural people's committees, local administrative units, and professional organizations representing all of the province's ethnic groups and its social and economic strata. Out of the 138 members of the newly elected body, 70 percent are Moldovan, and 30 percent represent the province's ethnic minorities—Ukrainians, Russians, Bulgarians, Germans, and Jews.

15 November 1917   Bolshevik Russia promulgates "The Declaration of Rights of the Peoples" of the former Russian Empire, including "the right of total separation."

December 1917   Sfatul Țării convenes in Chişinău under the chairmanship of Ion Inculeţ. On 2 December, the assembly solemnly proclaims the establishment of the Moldavian Democratic Federated Republic, a constituent of the Federation of Russian Republics.

January 1918   Occupation of Chişinău by Bolshevik revolutionaries. Sfatul Țării dispersed. Bessarabian appeal calls for urgent aid from Romania to restore order. From its Iaşi refuge, Romania's government sends in two infantry and two cavalry brigades across the Prut. Dispersion of Bolshevik troops. Sfatul Țării reconvenes in Chişinău.

24 January 1918   Sfatul Țării proclaims the independence of the Moldavian Democratic Republic and its separation from Russia.

27 March 1918   Confronted with threats of isolation or absorption by Ukraine, Sfatul Țării proclaims the conditioned union of the Moldavian Democratic Republic with Romania "in accordance with historical right and ethnic right, and the principle that peoples should determine their own fate." The vote is 86 in favor, 3 against, and 36 abstentions. Conditions for the union with Romania include the preservation of a certain degree of autonomy and Bessarabia's right to maintain its own provincial Diet. Constantin Stere elected president of Sfatul Țării.

October 1918   In the wake of the collapse of the Habsburg Empire, convocation of the Constituent Assembly in Cernăuţi composed of local members of the Austrian Parliament and of Bucovina's local Diet.

27 November 1918   In Cernăuţi, the Congress of Bucovina's Romanians, Germans, and Poles votes unanimously for the province's union with Romania. In Chişinău, in a final session held in the wake of the capitulation of the Central Powers, Sfatul Ţării abandons previous reservations and votes for Bessarabia's unconditional union with Romania.

September 1919   Treaty of St. Germain. Austria recognizes the union of Bucovina with Romania.

28 October 1920   Treaty of Versailles provisions regarding the status of Bessarabia signed in St. Germain by the Council of the Ambassadors, representing Great Britain, France, Italy, and Japan as signatory powers. The Nistru River recognized as the boundary between Romania and Russia's successor state, the Soviet Union, pending a bilateral settlement to be negotiated by the parties through future arbitration by the League of Nations. Great Britain ratifies the treaty in 1921, France in 1924, Italy in 1927.

1922   Beginning of the publication of the Russian-language daily *Bessarabskoe slovo*, in Chişinău.

April 1924   Recognition by Russia of Bessarabia's status discussed by Romanian and Soviet delegates in Vienna, under mediation of Austria's foreign minister. Talks end in deadlock over Moscow's claim for a plebiscite to be held in Bessarabia.

October 1924   Soviet Russia creates the Moldavian Autonomous Soviet Socialist Republic (MASSR), with Balta, later Tiraspol, as its capital. Foundation of the Moldavian Communist Party, a regional branch of the Communist Party of Ukraine.

1929   Romania adheres to the Moscow Protocol, proposed by the Union of Soviet Socialist Republics (USSR) as a means to expedite the provisions of the Kellogg-Briand Peace Pact.

1932   Latin alphabet introduced in the MASSR. Soviet-Romanian discussions on a bilateral treaty, held in Riga, end in deadlock over the Bessarabia issue. Negotiations resume in Geneva later in the year but founder on the Soviet Union's persistent claim for a plebiscite in Bessarabia.

1933   The USSR and Romania adhere to the London Convention for the definition of aggression in international relations, also subscribed to by Poland, Estonia, and Latvia, among other states.

1934   Romania and the USSR establish diplomatic relations.

1936   Opening of the Tighina railway bridge linking Romania and the USSR across the Nistru border.

1938   Soviet decree replaces Latin alphabet with Russian in the MASSR.

23 August 1939   Molotov-Ribbentrop Pact signed in Moscow. Secret Additional Protocol of the pact states Nazi Germany's endorsement of Soviet Russia's "interest" in Bessarabia.

26 June 1940   Soviet ultimatum to Romania demanding the cession of Bessarabia; additional demand claims Northern Bucovina.

28 June 1940   The Soviet army marches in and occupies Bessarabia and Northern Bucovina. Soviet-Communist power installed at all levels between the Prut and Nistru Rivers.

2 August 1940   Soviet administrative partition of Bessarabia. The central districts—forming the core of the new Moldavian Soviet Socialist Republic (MSSR) with Kishinev (Chişinău) as its capital—are attached to a narrow strip of the trans-Nistrian MASSR (3,400 square kilometers in surface), while the greater part (some 4,900 square kilometers) is returned to Soviet Ukraine. Bessarabia's northern districts, including Hotin, are attached to Soviet Ukraine, together with Northern Bucovina. Bessarabia's southern districts, down to the seashore, become a separate part of Ukraine. The new MSSR covers an area of 33,700 square kilometers.

15 August 1940   Soviet decree of nationalization.

1940–1941   Over 13,000 Soviet specialists and activists, including 500 teachers from Russia and 380 from Ukraine, assigned to instruct and teach in Moldavia.

January 1941   Promulgation of the Soviet Constitution of Moldavia, introducing the Communist form of government.

June 1941   Romania joins Germany in a concerted attack on the Soviet Union. Between 22 June and 26 July, Romanian and German troops reoccupy the entire territory ceded to the Soviet Union in June 1940. Bessarabia governed again as a Romanian territory, although without a formal decree of annexation (1941–1944).

August 1941   Tighina Convention. Germany puts the German-held military territory between the Nistru and Bug Rivers, dubbed Transnistria, under Romanian civil administration.

February 1942   Turning point of World War II on the Eastern front. Soviet victory at Stalingrad.

April 1944   Soviet troops reconquer Bessarabia and march past the Prut into Romania.

23 August 1944   Romania declares war on Germany and joins the Soviet offensive against the Axis powers. Armistice signed in Moscow on 12 September.

February 1947   First elections for the Supreme Soviet of the MSSR.

10 February 1947   Paris Peace Treaty restores Soviet territorial arrangements of 1940 regarding the statute of Bessarabia and Northern Bucovina.

May 1947   First session of the MSSR's Supreme Soviet held in Chişinău. The assembly includes 266 deputies, 178 of whom are Communist Bolshevik Party members or applicants for Communist Party membership.

February 1949   First postwar Congress of the Communist Party of the MSSR.

5–6 July 1949   Operation South ("Iug"). Forced deportation of 35,796 persons, mostly landowning farmers, to several distant places of the USSR, including Siberia.

1950–1952   Leonid Brezhnev's tenure in Chişinău as secretary-general of the Moldavian Communist Party's Central Committee. Stalinist policies of repression and collectivization of agriculture enforced across the board in the MSSR.

1 April 1951   Operation North ("Sever"). Soviet deportation of 2,617 persons, mostly Jehovah's Witnesses, to Siberia.

5 March 1953   Death of Soviet dictator Joseph Stalin.

February 1956   20th Congress of the Communist Party of the Soviet Union. Nikita Khrushchev's secret speech denouncing Stalin's crimes.

1956–1961   14,902 Moldovan families are allowed to return from their distant places of deportation back to their native places in the MSSR.

1961   Ivan Bodiul nominated secretary-general of the Moldavian Communist Party's Central Committee.

1962   Chişinău Orthodox Cathedral turned into an exhibition hall and its historic belfry demolished.

1964 Further dispersion of Moldovans through enforcement of policies assigning young graduates from Moldova's colleges and universities to compulsory workplaces scattered throughout the USSR, especially in Central Asia, the Urals, and the Far Eastern Territory. Increased transfer to Moldova of Russian white-collar workforce from other parts of the USSR.

October 1964 Brezhnev elected secretary-general of the Communist Party of the Soviet Union's Central Committee.

October–November 1967 Soviet Moldavia celebrates the 50th anniversary of the October 1917 Bolshevik Revolution.

1971–1974 "Moldavian experiment" in agriculture launched by Ivan Bodiul. Its guidelines call for a dramatic boost in Soviet Moldavia's agricultural production.

1974 On the occasion of the 50th anniversary of Soviet Moldavia (reckoned from the 1924 foundation of the MASSR), Brezhnev pays a solemn visit to Chişinău to celebrate the event as head of the Soviet Union's Communist Party.

1977 Brezhnev takes office as president of the USSR.

April 1978 Soviet Moldavia's Constitution adjusted to more closely resemble the October 1977 Constitution of the USSR.

1980 Inauguration of Friendship Hall, currently the Palace of the Republic, Chişinău's main center for performances, art, and culture.

November 1982 Upon Brezhnev's death, former KGB head Yuri Andropov elected Communist Party leader and president of the Soviet Union.

February 1984 Konstantin Chernenko succeeds Andropov as leader of the Soviet Union.

1985 Mikhail Gorbachev succeeds Chernenko as secretary-general of the Soviet Union's Communist Party.

1986 Hard-line leader Ivan Bodiul demoted on charges of having departed from the Communist Party's line.

1987 Gorbachev initiates perestroika and glasnost, programs of reform involving expanded freedoms and increased openness, in the Soviet republics, including the MSSR.

1988 The Alexie Mateevici Literary Musical Club founded in Chişinău against the backdrop of the glasnost policies.

March 1989 *Glasul*, the first periodical published in the Latin alphabet by Moldovan intellectuals, clandestinely printed in Latvia and smuggled into Soviet Moldavia.

31 August 1989 The Chişinău Supreme Soviet passes into law the establishment of the official language of the MSSR and the return to the Latin alphabet.

September 1989 Trans-Nistrian districts of the MSSR protest the establishment of Romanian written in Latin characters as the official language of the republic. Beginning of secessionist rebellion among Russian and Ukrainian speakers in Tiraspol and other trans-Nistrian districts where the Soviet 14th Army headquarters are located.

2 September 1990 Proclamation of the Moldavian Nistrian Soviet Socialist Republic, which secedes from Moldavia's central government.

March 1991 The MSSR refuses to take part in the referendum on preserving the USSR. Escalation of skirmishes between Moldovan loyalists and secessionist forces in the trans-Nistrian districts.

23 May 1991 Name of the Moldavian Soviet Socialist Republic changed to the Republic of Moldova.

27 August 1991 The Republic of Moldova is proclaimed an independent state with Mircea Snegur as president.

26 December 1991 The USSR is disbanded.

1 March 1992 In the breakaway trans-Nistrian republic, fighting erupts between Moldovan security forces and Slavic separatists—ethnic Russians and ethnic Ukrainians. Russian Cossacks, with logistic support from the 14th Army, start attacking the headquarters of local authorities loyal to the Chişinău government.

2 March 1992 The Republic of Moldova becomes a member of the United Nations.

May 1992 Russia's 14th Army, placed under General Aleksandr Lebed's command, intervenes from Tiraspol in support of the secessionist forces entangled in the trans-Nistrian conflict.

19 June 1992 Rebel troops mount attacks on the right bank of the Nistru River. Assault on the Tighina local police headquarters. Russia's 14th Army takes part in the action.

7 July 1992 Cease-fire agreement signed at Limanskoe. Russia and Moldova agree to send a joint peacekeeping force to the region. Beginning of disengagement between the warring factions.

27 February 1994 First multiparty parliamentary elections in Moldova.

6 March 1994 National referendum confirms the sovereignty of the Republic of Moldova.

29 July 1994 Chişinău Parliament passes the new Constitution of the Republic of Moldova. Article 11 stipulates that "the Republic of Moldova does not admit the stationing of foreign military units on its territory."

21 October 1994 Signing of a Moldo-Russian agreement regarding the future withdrawal, within three years, of Russia's 14th Army from the trans-Nistrian enclave.

16 April 1995 First multiparty elections held for local, self-governing bodies.

13 July 1995 Moldova admitted to the Council of Europe.

22 October 1996 Moldova ratifies the Council of Europe's Convention on the Protection of Ethnic Minorities.

13 November 1996 The State Duma in Moscow adopts a resolution asking the government of the Russian Federation to declare the Nistru east-bank region "a zone of special strategic interest for Russia."

1 December 1996 Presidential elections. Center-left candidate Petru Lucinschi, Speaker of the Chişinău Parliament, defeats incumbent Mircea Snegur and is elected president of Moldova with 53.14 percent of the vote. Two days later, in Lisbon, addressing a summit of the Organization for Security and Cooperation in Europe, outgoing President Snegur urges Moscow to withdraw its troops from eastern Moldova, in keeping with the October 1994 bilateral agreement.

3 December 1996 Moldova's Parliament ratifies the Friendship and Cooperation Treaty with Ukraine.

22 March 1998 National elections, validated by Moldova's Parliament on 9 April. The Party of Moldova's Communists wins 30.01 percent of the vote and 40 of the 101 seats in Moldova's Parliament. A majoritarian center-right coalition—the Alliance for Democracy and Reforms—counteracts in the aftermath of the vote by eventually holding 61 seats, shared by the Democratic Convention of Moldova (which had garnered 19.42 percent of the national vote), the pro-presidential Bloc for a Democratic and Prosperous Moldova (18.16 percent of the vote), and the Party of Democratic Forces (8.84 percent of the vote).

1999 Moldova's territory is reorganized in the traditional form of *judeţe*—namely, Bălţi, Cahul, Chişinău, Dubăsari, Edineţ, Lăpuşna, Orhei, Soroca, Taraclia, Tighina, Ungheni, and the autonomous territorial unit of Gagauzia.

Introduction

The Republic of Moldova showed up on the map of Eastern Europe in the wake of the demise of the Soviet Union, but its history as part and parcel of the old Continent dates back to more ancient times. One of the striking things about Moldova is that, in the group of the newly liberated nations, it appears to carry more singular traits than most of the other successor states of the Union of Soviet Socialist Republics (USSR), the huge Eurasian entity of which it became a part in 1940, at roughly the same time as the Baltic republics.

While still a part of the USSR—in the motley conglomerate of which it held a record low of less than 0.2 percent of the entire territory—this small republic, roughly the size of Belgium, ranked first in population density and sixth in terms of food production. It was also the only Soviet republic in which, strangely enough, the majority of the population spoke a Romance language. In terms of its cultural and historic profile, unlike most other geopolitical entities initially incorporated by Russia in the 19th century and integrated into the USSR during part of the 20th, Moldova claims a European lineage reaching back in time long before its 14th-century accession to statehood. In early times, the medieval Principality of Moldova asserted itself as one of the regional champions in the struggle against Ottoman Turkey. It waged a number of defensive wars, managed against all odds to avoid being conquered by Turkey, and—albeit an intermittent vassal after 1485—it maintained its autonomy and was never turned into a province of the Ottoman Empire.

Importantly, again, in the post-Soviet geopolitical context, Moldova carries the singularity of being the only successor state to have come into being as the end result of an earlier process of partition of what had previously been a unitary country, at some point in time split in two along its north-south axis, the Prut River—hence, the paradox of a now fully independent political body sharing the overwhelming part of its culture and traditions with a neighboring area, not necessarily the one that ruled it politically until it declared its independence in 1991.

Partly because of these singularities, against the variegated backdrop of the present-day Commonwealth of Independent States (CIS) that has succeeded the Soviet Union, Moldova's case also stands out today as one of the most misrepresented countries in the European segment of the former USSR. In many ways odd, Moldova's traditional characteristics have made it indeed an instance apart in the area of post-Soviet Eurasia and, for that reason, a particularly engaging subject to methodically explore and discover.

Given its past struggle with Turkey, it is no coincidence that it is in the Ottoman context that Moldova was first introduced to a wider Western audience in 1734, when a classic work on the Turkish Empire written by Moldova's Prince Demetrius Cantemir was published in London. Using the Latin form of the country's name, Cantemir's description of Moldova was terse and factual:

> Moldavia is divided into Upper and Lower. . . . To Lower Moldavia belonged formerly all Bessarabia, called by the Tartars Bujak. . . . The inhabitants of Upper Moldavia are noted for their riches, of Lower for their warlike bravery, and both—after all their losses—for their hospitality. But these things, if God grant me life and leisure, will be more largely explained in a separate Treatise.[1]

At the request of the Berlin Academy, of which he was a member, Cantemir wrote that treatise he titled *Descriptio Moldaviae,*[2] a classic monograph on historical Moldova, starting with its earliest beginnings, Dacia and the Roman Conquest.

How did such an old, Latinate, European country emerge in our day as a successor state to the Soviet Union? Why is it called Moldavia instead of Moldova? And why does the name of the country also apply today to a historic province of the same name lying next door, in neighboring Romania? Fraught with controversy, such issues as what the country's name should be—Moldavia, Moldova, Bessarabia—are part of a larger paradox that involves, in addition to issues of historic import and semantic denotation, such determining factors as the Russian and Soviet spheres of attraction and power, Moldova's cultural and linguistic heritage, and many other related topics that this dictionary endeavors to articulate in factual fashion.

LAND AND PEOPLE

Reborn as an independent republic in 1991, present-day Moldova covers an area of 33,700 square kilometers, occupying the zone from 47°00' north latitude to 29°00' east longitude, which overlaps with most of the northeastern lands of the historic Principality of Moldova. Stretching on a north-south geographical axis, its lay of land is comprised between the banks of the Nistru River, a tributary to the Black Sea, and the Danube's easternmost affluent, the Prut River, the lower 450-kilometer course of which separates Moldova from Romania, its neighbor to the west. North, east, and south, a 939-kilometer border—a small segment of it on the Nistru—separates Moldova from its eastern neighbor, Ukraine. The country's major rivers are the Nistru, Prut, Cogâlnic, Bâc, Botna, and Răut. There are less than half a dozen big cities, the main urban agglomerations being the capital, Chişinău, and the cities of Bălţi, Tighina, and Tiraspol.

Moldova has a temperate Continental climate with hot summers, warm, long autumns, and cold winters. The land is dominated by rolling hilly plains in the north, patches of forest in the center, and ravines in the south, extending into a fertile plain that descends toward the country's ancient seaboard lying between the estuary of the Nistru and the mouths of the Danube, now part of Ukraine. Moldova's highest elevation, Mount Bălăneşti, 430 meters high, is in the country's heartland, the Codri region.

Moldova is one of the most densely populated countries of Europe, ranking 15th among the nations of the old Continent, with an average density of 128 people per square kilometer. Out of a total population of over 4,237,000, 53 percent of Moldova's inhabitants live in the countryside, which makes it one of the few countries in Europe with a rural population majority. Over 60 percent of the urban population is concentrated in the capital city of Chişinău, which has 735,229 inhabitants (1994 est.).

Romanian-speaking Moldovans represent over 64 percent of Moldova's population. Ukrainians are Moldova's second largest ethnic group, making up 13.8 percent of the country's total population. About 29 percent of the Ukrainians currently living in Moldova are not natives of Moldova. Most of them came to the country in recent decades as migrants, under the Soviet policies of inner workforce migration and other forms of population resettlement. Moldova's third largest ethnic group is Russian. The Russian group constitutes 13 percent of the country's total population. Over 30 percent of the Russians currently living in Moldova are not natives of Moldova either. Just as a sizable segment of the Ukrainian ethnic group did, they became inhabitants of the republic after World War II, prompted by Soviet Russia's policies. The bulk of this Russian and Ukrainian input to the country's demographic profile settled in Moldova's cities, mostly as white-collar specialists, teachers, educators, administration personnel, and, in recent decades, retirees, which accounts for the fact that Moldova's urban clusters have shaped up increasingly as centers of powerful Russophone concentration.

In addition to the cities, massive proportions of Russian ethnics live in the Nistru east-bank districts, where a secession process broke out and an unrecognized pro-Russian Nistrian Republic was declared in Tiraspol in 1990. Russian and Ukrainian ethnics make up 59 percent of that region's mostly Russophone population of about 740,000. The trans-Nistrian secession continues to be Moldova's main unsolved problem, given the refusal of the Tiraspol leadership to accept the status of autonomy extended to the east-bank districts by the country's central government.

Another ethnic community is the Gagauz, a group of Christian Turks who settled in the country in the 19th century. They constitute about 3.5 percent of the republic's population, mostly concentrated in a patchwork of rural communities around the southern city of Comrat, the administrative center of the Gagauzia region, also called Gagauz Yeri, an autonomous territorial unit headed by an elected local governor, the *bashkan*.

Romanophone Moldovans also live outside the Republic of Moldova in other parts of the former USSR. They include over 380,000 people in neighboring Ukraine, most of them in the northern and southern areas contiguous to the border, in districts detached by the USSR from the Moldavian Soviet Socialist Republic (MSSR) and awarded by Joseph Stalin in the 1940s to Soviet Ukraine. Although there is no ethnic or linguistic divide between Moldovans living in the Republic of Moldova and those across the border in either of the contiguous areas, another 145,918 such people residing in Ukraine were registered in the last Soviet census of 1989 as Romanians rather than Moldovans. As a result of postwar inner workforce migration and Soviet deportation policies, Romanophone Moldovans are also to be found in more distant places of the former USSR, from Kazakhstan to the Russian Federation's Far East, including Siberia.

HISTORY

Central to Moldova's history has been a constant yearning for sovereignty, manifested as far back as the 14th century, at the time of the land's first accession to medieval statehood; then again, during the following centuries, as it sporadically fought Ottoman Turkey; and yet again, dramatically, in a modern resurgence, at the time of the disintegration and demise of the USSR.

The country's earliest archeological findings indicate that a portion of Moldova's southern territory—comprising about 5,500 square kilometers in area between the lower course of the Prut and the Nistru estuary—was organized as an extension of the Roman province of Moesia Inferior and served as an eastern outpost of Dacia, designed to secure the Roman Empire's strategic control over the mouths of the Danube and the western shores of the Black Sea. Fragments of ancient defense vestiges known to the locals as Valul lui Traian (Trajan's Wall), a *vallum* (bulwark) attributed by tradition to Roman Emperor Trajan, the conqueror of Dacia, testifies to this day to historic continuity in that area. The northern remnants of those defenses face east and northeast, while another segment cuts across the land from Leova, on the Prut, to Copanca, near the junction of the Botna and Nistru Rivers.

Free local populations continued to live there and elsewhere in the area after the eastern frontier of the Roman Empire crumbled. Archeological evidence dating back to the early centuries of the Christian Era, up to the 9th, 10th, and 11th centuries, reveals that the tracts between the lower Prut and the bend of the Danube, the hilly region of the Bâc valley, and the hinterland of the Nistru estuary were among the areas of present-day Moldova where clusters of sedentary local populations continued to live and produce, mingling with other incoming groups of free populations from across the Carpathian Mountains, as well as with successive waves of roving populations and warriors from the eastern steppes—Goths, Huns, Avars, Petchenegs, and others—including important movements of migrating Slavs.

The influx of Slavic peoples settling from the sixth to ninth centuries all across the former provinces of Romanized Dacia led to a process of assimilation by the local population, typically reflected in the formation of the Romanian language, which gradually emerged as the common instrument of communication for the new settlers in the melting pot of former Roman Dacia. A substantial number of early Slavic borrowings, including terms having to do with social organization (e.g., *voivode* for prince and *voivodate* for principality), were thus absorbed in the vocabulary, giving Romanian its specific profile in the family of the Romance languages. Linguistics and phonology specialists concur in the conclusion that the essential features of the Romanian language were established before the foundation—over most of former Dacia—of the Romanian-speaking states of Moldova and Wallachia, as well as the earlier organization of the *voivodates* of Transylvania, the latter turned into a possession of the Hungarian Crown after A.D. 1000. These included, among other political formations, the northern Wallachian *voivodate* of Maramureş, noteworthy, among other things, for having been the cradle of one of the oldest texts in the Romanian language, the 14th-century "Ieud Manuscript."

Even before Moldova's accession to statehood, under Bogdan I, who hailed from Maramureş, several historic places—such as the mining center of Baia in midland Moldova (mentioned as "civitas Moldaviae" in a Latin document dated 1334) and, much earlier, Maurocastron (later Cetatea Albă), on the Black Sea; and Chilia, on the Danube—were attested as active port cities on maps and in Byzantine books on sailing. Out of the 755 Moldovan villages mentioned in historical documents before the year 1449, 607 (i.e., 80.3 percent) had their boundaries marked before the year 1359, when Moldova became a principality.

Moldova's seaboard and the lowland areas north of the Danube Delta were initially under the authority of the Wallachian dynasty of the Basarabs, whose progenitor, Basarab I, founded in 1330 the Principality of Wallachia, south of Transylvania, about one century after the great Tatar invasion of 1241. Moldova acquired the "Land of the Basarabs" from Wallachia in the 1400s, which accounts for the fact that the southern tip of Moldova was traditionally known as Basarabia (Latinized form: Bessarabia, a name later extended to the entire area).

The medieval Principality of Moldova maintained a fragile independence for some time, defending itself against more inroads of the Tatar tribes of the Golden Horde, Moldova's primal neighbors to the east, and, later on, against Ottoman incursions from the Black Sea, the basin of which came under total Turkish control after the 1453 fall of Byzantium and the demise of the eastern Roman Empire.

In spite of Stephen the Great's (1457–1504) attempts to maintain independence, Moldova eventually had to surrender its seaboard and submit to the sultan's overlordship. Before the end of the 15th century, it became a vassal principality to the Ottoman Empire. In exchange for the tribute, the sultan pledged not to interfere in the framework of church and state in the principality. Due to that status (enshrined in the so-called capitulations), unlike other parts of Eastern and Central Europe, Moldova was never turned into a *pashalik*, or Turkish province. During the 16th and 17th centuries, it intermittently shook off Ottoman suzerainty by attempting to take advantage of Turkey's conflicts with the Habsburg and Russian Empires. However, being located along the direct invasion route to Turkey's provinces south of the Danube, Moldova, the same as neighboring Wallachia, soon became an area of warfare and military occupation for over a century of intermittent Russo-Turkish Wars.

With Russia progressively projecting its rising power west and southwest, Moldova first came under Russian military occupation, briefly, in 1739 and, later on, together with Wallachia, during the 1768–1774 Russo-

Turkish War, which ended with the Treaty of Kuchuk Kainarji. Russia's armies again occupied Moldova between 1787 and 1792, during a war that ended with the Treaty of Iaşi, which brought Russia's border to the Nistru. In 1782, in the interlude between those two wars, Russia's Empress Catherine the Great proposed to Austria's Emperor Joseph II what is called the "Greek Project," devised to establish a Russo-Austrian sphere of influence in Eastern and Central Europe and the Balkans. Catherine's plan included a reconstituted Dacia, based on the projected union of Moldova and Wallachia under the rule of an Orthodox sovereign, acceptable to both Russia and Austria. In terms of down-to-earth practicalities, such intent had already been epitomized, among other means, in the design and circulation of a Moldo-Wallachian currency ("Mold i Valak") issued by Russia between 1771 and 1774. These coins, minted at Sadagura for the use of the Russian army occupying Moldova and Wallachia during the 1768–1774 Russo-Turkish War, bore the seals of the two principalities—Moldova's bison and Wallachia's eagle—imprinted as twin shields in the kopeks, denghis, and paras issued in silver, bronze, and copper. The Greek Project did not materialize, and, alongside Wallachia, Moldova came again under Russian military occupation between 1806 and 1812, during the first Russo-Turkish War of the 19th century, when Russia's favorite church leader, Moldovan Bishop Gavril Bănulescu-Bodoni, was appointed to exert ecclesiastical jurisdiction over both principalities as Moldo-Wallachian exarch—"Ekzarkh Moldo-Vlachiiskii."

The 1812 Treaty of Bucharest, which ended the third occupation of the Principalities of Wallachia and Moldova by Russia, resulted in the partition of the latter, the eastern half of which was incorporated into Russia as Bessarabia, from then on the name of the entire stretch of land between the Nistru and Prut Rivers. The moment of the splitting of Moldova was a historic milestone in several ways, paving the way for a new course of social action, political change, and over 100 years of unprecedented acculturation. Russian rule over the eastern half of historic Moldova was interrupted over part of the annexed territory in the aftermath of the Crimean War, when the 1856 Congress of Paris returned three of Bessarabia's Danubian districts (most of historic Bessarabia proper) to the Principality of Moldova. That portion was a component of Moldova when the principality merged with Wallachia to form— under Moldova's Prince Alexandru Ioan Cuza (1859–1866)—the United Principalities, the core state of modern Romania (1862).

The status of southern Bessarabia changed again after the 1877 Russo-Romanian-Turkish War, when the 1878 Treaty of Berlin compelled Romania to cede to the czars' empire the three districts, thus restoring Russia's full authority over the lands between the Nistru and Prut Rivers and its riparian status on the Danube.

The period of Russian imperial rule over Bessarabia has been described by Soviet and Soviet Moldovan historians as beneficial to the province, resulting in social and economic progress, including urbanization. Moldovan independent historians argue to the contrary, indicating that Russia's czarist rule introduced imperial absolutism and the immigration of alien groups, encouraged by the czars to settle in their newly acquired province, in order to weaken the native Moldovan element in the population. Statistics show that the country's native Romanophone population dwindled from 86 percent in 1817 (the year of the first Russian census), to 66.4 percent in 1858, to 51.4 percent in 1862, whereas other ethnic groups started to make their appearance and grow, mostly in towns and cities. Moldovan historians also cite the fact that Bessarabia continued to be one of the most backward provinces of the Russian Empire, with a population that had one of the highest mortality rates in Europe, twice that of the Russian average. They point out that under Russia's autocratic rule, Bessarabia was treated as a colony; czarist censorship stifled public opinion; the native language of the majority of its population was banished from education and public life; and ethnic tensions gradually rose and flared up, culminating in the notorious 1903 Easter Massacre, which, among other things, gave the Russian word "pogrom" international circulation for the first time in history.

Russian absolutist administration of Bessarabia came to an end in the final stages of World War I, with the collapse of the Russian war effort on the Eastern front (which included, as a weakened ally, rump Romania) and the revolutions of February and October 1917. After the flight of the last Russian governor from the province's capital, Chişinău, and the formation of a provisional government in Petrograd, a Moldovan National Committee was organized in April 1917. It called for autonomy, land reform, and the return to the Romanian language in education, judicial, and public administration.

The overthrow of Russia's provisional government in October 1917 and the advent of Bolshevik power brought about the formation of a provisional form of self-government called Sfatul Ţării, Moldova's convocational assembly of soldiers, intellectuals, workers, and peasants, inspired by the country's traditional General Assembly, which dated back to the 15th century. Sfatul Ţării was dominated by a majority of native Moldovans rather than Bolsheviks. On 2 December 1917, it proclaimed the establishment of the Moldavian Democratic Federated Republic, a constituent of the Russian Federation. A month later, Bolshevik battalions occupied Chişinău and dispersed the fledgling republic's governing body, but the revolutionary troops were forced out and thrown back east of the Nistru with help from neighboring rump Romania, the government of which had been temporarily moved to Iaşi, the old capital of the former Principality of Moldova. With Bolshevik power out, Sfatul Țării reconvened in Chişinău, and on 24 January 1918, it declared the independence of the Moldavian Democratic Republic and its separation from Russia, then gradually engulfed in revolutionary turmoil.

Facing increased threats from the Bolshevik Revolution, which was gaining ground in neighboring Ukraine, Sfatul Țării voted for a conditioned union with Romania on 27 March 1918. On 27 November 1918, in the aftermath of the 11 November armistice that put an end to World War I, Sfatul Țării voted for Bessarabia's unconditional union with Romania, a move that prevented the former czarist province from coming under Communist rule, like all other components of the disintegrating Russian Empire (with the exception of the Baltics), including Moldova's next-door neighbor, Ukraine. The Bessarabia-Romania union was formally acknowledged by the Treaty of Versailles (28 October 1920) but was not recognized by Soviet Russia.

In 1924, under Stalin's instructions, the Supreme Soviet of the USSR established a largely artificial Moldavian Autonomous Soviet Socialist Republic (MASSR) on the east bank of the Nistru River. The extraneous entity, a pilot formation with a total population of 568,984 inhabitants (1926 est.), was carved out of southern Soviet Ukraine, in an area where a sparse rural population that had migrated from Moldova during the 18th and 19th centuries made up barely 30 percent of the population (versus a Ukrainian majority of 48.8 percent). With its capital in Balta and, later on, Tiraspol, the MASSR served as a bridgehead on the Nistru, designed to lay the groundwork for the planned expansion of Soviet power on the river's west bank, into Romanian-held Bessarabia. Stalin's push for an expanded Soviet Moldova materialized in 1940, when under the secret provisions of the 1939 Molotov-Ribbentrop Pact, Moscow annexed Bessarabia down to the Prut River, enfolding part of the east-bank MASSR in its borders, so as to make the new entity straddle both banks of the Nistru.

The incorporation into the Soviet Union of the Nistru west-bank lands (which also included Northern Bucovina) was carried out through military occupation, in the last days of June 1940, following a Soviet 48-hour ultimatum to Romania. Thirty-two Red Army divisions, including the USSR's 12th Army, the 10th, 38th, and 49th Tank Brigades, and the 5th Army's 34th Assault Division, took part in the operation that was completed on 3 July.

On 2 August 1940, the Supreme Soviet of the USSR passed into law the creation of the MSSR on most of Bessarabia's territory. Russian became the official language of communication, and Russian Cyrillics became mandatory in the writing of Romanian (dubbed "Moldavian" and described as separate from Romanian). On 15 August 1940, a Soviet decree passed into law the nationalization of all privately owned land, industries, businesses, and trading companies. Confiscation of private land began immediately, and the first kolkhozes (Soviet collective farms) were established in the countryside. By October 1940, 487 private enterprises had been taken over by the state in the MSSR's towns and cities. A Constitution based on the 1936 Soviet Constitution was promulgated on 10 February 1941, while the elimination of private property continued full scale.

In a dramatic turnabout, in June 1941, Germany attacked the Soviet Union, and a German-Romanian military coalition briefly recaptured Bessarabia between June 1941 and April 1944. In 1944, the Red Army reconquered Bessarabia, and the USSR reestablished Soviet power, which resumed the Russification process with increased vigor. The 1947 Paris Peace Treaty restored the Soviet territorial arrangements of 1940 regarding the status of Bessarabia and Northern Bucovina as parts of the USSR.

The post–World War II period in Moldova's history began with a return to the 1940 redrawing of its administrative borders within the USSR, which made it—as it is to this day—a landlocked territorial entity, cut off from the Danube Delta and the Black Sea. The MSSR was cut to include most of the midland of prewar Bessarabia, merged with an additional 3,400-square-kilometer strip of land from what had been the short-lived MASSR on the Nistru's east bank. Historic Moldova's seashore was attributed to Soviet Ukraine to form an appendage south of Odessa—much like an enclaved inlet between the mouth of the Nistru and the Danube Delta thalweg—attached to Ukraine's main body of land by several hundred meters of land passage, tangent to the northern tip of the Nistru estuary. Bessarabia's northern territories, together with Northern Bucovina, were also awarded to Ukraine and became a separate part of the neighboring Soviet republic, its sub-Carpathian region.

In May 1947, dominated by an overwhelming majority of Russophone Communist Party members, the first session of the MSSR's Supreme Soviet was held in Chişinău. Additionally, under strict directions from Moscow, a congress of Moldova's Communist Party was held in Chişinău on 5–6 February 1949, with the urgent task of bringing to completion the collectivization of agriculture. Between 1944 and 1948, in a follow-up to the operation begun immediately after the 1940 occupation, 578 kolkhozes had already been created. They included the properties of over 100,000 farming families but accounted for only 22 percent of the MSSR's private land. By 1 May 1949, the number of collectivized farms had risen to 925. During the night of 5–6 July 1949, under the code name "Iug" (Operation South), 35,796 persons, including 14,033 women and 11,889 children, were deported under military escort to distant wastelands of the USSR's eastern regions, their properties confiscated and turned overnight into kolkhozes. As a consequence, between July and August 1949, the number of state collective farms more than doubled. By deportations and other means of eradication of private property, the forced collectivization process was completed by the end of 1950. By then, 97.0 percent of the republic's private farmlands had been wiped out and merged into Soviet-style, state-controlled collective farms.

Sovietization and Russification of Moldova continued full scale in the 1950s under the direct supervision of the USSR's future head of state, Leonid Brezhnev, whom Stalin had appointed in 1950 to serve as secretary-general of the Moldavian Communist Party's Central Committee, with discretionary power over the new Soviet republic. During Brezhnev's tenure in Chişinău, under another code name, "Sever" (Operation North), more deportations were conducted in April 1951, while the USSR's policies of inner workforce migration brought in fresh waves of Russophone specialists to Moldova's urban centers. With Russian imposed as the first language of government, official communication, and education, Moldova was gradually transformed into a place where the majority of the native population became practically bilingual—speaking both Romanian and Russian. The language spoken by the Russian and Ukrainian political and administrative elites remained Russian.

Under Soviet rule, a moderate process of socialist industrialization was implemented, mostly in the Nistru east-bank strip of land where, from the outset, the Russophone population outnumbered native Moldovans. Steel mills and cement factories were built in Râbniţa, which became one of the MSSR's industrial centers. Energy-producing plants and other industrial units were built at Dubăsari, Râbniţa, and Cuciurgan, on the east bank, and the city of Tiraspol became the MSSR's second industrial center, after Chişinău. One of the consequences of this long-range policy is that, to this day, Moldova's industrial units, placed in the post–World War II years on the narrow strip of land on the east bank of the Nistru, account for about 90 percent of the country's energy production and 28 percent of its industrial enterprises.

Apart from this territorial distribution imbalance, Soviet planners' emphasis continued to be on the republic's agricultural potential. A "Moldavian experiment" in agriculture was launched in the early 1970s, calling for a dramatic increase in the republic's agricultural production, which soon brought Moldova the reputation of one of the USSR's breadbaskets and its main vineyard and orchard.

On the ideological and cultural front, a series of timid reactions against Russification began to take shape in the 1960s, in the context of the Sino-Soviet strife. Soviet rule over Moldova came under fire from the USSR's former ally, Communist China, which questioned Russia's past and current imperial ambitions. Karl Marx's unpublished notes dealing with Bessarabia were circulated clandestinely in the MSSR, where people were stunned to discover that, as far back as 1853, the revered author of the *Communist Manifesto* had written about Moldova's plight at the hands of the Russians, passing harsh judgment on the way in which the czarist empire conducted the 1812 annexation of Bessarabia. "Turkey had no right whatsoever to cede it," Marx wrote. "The Porte had recognized that such was the case at [the Peace of] Carlowitz, when being pressured by the Poles to surrender the Moldo-Wallachian Principalities, it responded that it had no right to cede such territories, since the capitulations granted it only the right of overlordship."[3] On the vexed issue of the language, Marx wrote: "The Romanian language is a kind of Oriental Italian. The indigenous population of Moldo-Wallachia call themselves Romanians; their neighbors call them Vlachs or Valachs."[4] Such bombshells started to shake the inculcated Communist dogma, according to which—no matter its historical forms—Moscow's sway over the land was connatural, beneficial, legitimate, and unchallengeable.

Against the backdrop of symptoms of gradual abrasion and attrition of the Communist system in general, the first signs of a national cultural awakening and reaction against the Soviet stranglehold became visible in the 1970s, later on encouraged by dramatic changes at the Kremlin helm, where—after Brezhnev's death in 1982 and the short-lived leaderships of Yuri Andropov and Konstantin Chernenko—Mikhail Gorbachev launched his glasnost and perestroika policies.

In the wake of these innovative programs of openness, a group of Chişinău intellectuals sent a memorandum to Andrei Gromyko, then president of the Supreme Soviet of the USSR, stating the desirability of a return to Moldova of the northern and southern territories attributed by the USSR to Soviet Ukraine in the years 1940–1944. Although the request was ignored, it marked a turning point in the burgeoning wave of demands for the restoration of historical truth about Moldova's land, its language, and its people. A literary debating society named after Moldovan poet and clergyman Alexie Mateevici (1888–1917)—the author of a celebrated ode to the Romanian language ("Limba noastră")—was founded in Chişinău in 1988. It played the part of a powerful intellectual ferment and launched a movement for national and cultural emancipation that eventually materialized in the form of Moldova's first independent political organization, the Popular Front of Moldova, which began to challenge the system of Soviet-imposed, one-party rule based on the monopoly of the Communist Party, subservient to Moscow. Furthermore, in March 1989, *Glasul* (The Voice), the first periodical published in the Roman alphabet, was clandestinely printed in Latvia. The entire edition was smuggled and distributed in the MSSR, where it had the effect of a watershed.

A sweeping current of public opinion triggered by these developments caused the Chişinău Supreme Soviet to pass into law the establishment of the native language of the majority as the official language of the MSSR and the return to the Latin alphabet (the Language Law of August 1989). In June 1990, a largely symbolic proclamation of sovereignty preceded Moldova's further moves toward independence. In March 1991, the MSSR refused to take part in the referendum on preserving the USSR. On 23 May that same year, the name of the Moldavian Soviet Socialist Republic was changed to the Republic of Moldova, the vernacular form—Moldova—superseding the long-standing use of Moldavia in foreign languages and in international documents. Moldova's independence was pronounced in an explosion of popular enthusiasm on 27 August 1991, in the immediate aftermath of the failed Communist putsch in Moscow. On that day, around 600,000 people from all parts of the country gathered in downtown Chişinău in front of the Communist-era executive power headquarters, in a show of solidarity that prompted the republic's legislative body to declare Moldova's independence and separation from the USSR.

On 26 December 1991, the USSR itself was disbanded, but in the Nistru east-bank districts with a Russophone majority—where, for decades, Sovietization had been more predominant than anywhere else in the country—pro-Russian nostalgia sparked separatist reactions, which soon culminated in an armed conflict. The trans-Nistrian strife took the initial form of an act of cultural and ideological secession, taking issue with Moldova's Language Law. As a reaction, a self-styled "Moldavian Nistrian Soviet Socialist Republic" was proclaimed in Tiraspol in 1990. The events took a violent turn with the outbreak of a short but bloody civil war in 1991–1992, in which Russian troops, under the command of General Aleksandr Lebed, took an active part. One of the consequences of that conflict is that the trans-Nistrian region—created by Stalin as an extraneous entity in 1924—

continues to host the Tiraspol headquarters of Russia's only military deployment outside Russia's borders in Europe, the Operational Group of Russian Forces, a downgraded version of Russia's 14th Army (formerly the Soviet Union's 14th Army). Tiraspol flies the Soviet-era flag and has preserved both Soviet state symbols and many of the tenets of Communist ideology. Currently renamed the Moldavian Nistrian Republic, the breakaway entity, which never gained international recognition, enjoys strong support in Russia's lower legislature, the Moscow State Duma, which passed in 1996 a resolution demanding that the Nistru east-bank region be declared "a zone of special strategic interest for Russia."

Moldova became a member of the United Nations in 1992 and was admitted to the Council of Europe in 1995. It has reaffirmed its right to enjoy full self-determination as defined by the United Nations Charter, the Helsinki Final Act, and the norms of international law. In 1997, Moldova ratified the European Charter of Local Self-Government.

The basic tenor of Moldova's progress across history was perhaps best expressed in one of the terse pronouncements of its 1991 Declaration of Independence, which states that the Republic of Moldova is a "sovereign, independent and democratic state, free to decide its present and future, without external interference, in keeping with the ideals and aspirations of its people, within the historical and ethnic area of its own national making."

POLITICAL DEVELOPMENT

Moldova's political development over time has been hindered by powerful factors with legacies that are identifiable to this day in the nation's search for structurally durable bearings. Moldova's early political structures were patterned after the medieval and Byzantine models. Its rulers were elected to the throne from among a number of indigenous princely families, many of them from the Muşat and Movilă dynasties, but Turkish suzerainty throughout the 16th and 17th centuries required the sultan's approval. After the ill-fated Moldo-Russian anti-Ottoman alliance of 1711, when Prince Demetrius Cantemir tried to regain the principality's independence but was defeated and fled to Russia under Peter the Great's protection, most of Moldova's subsequent rulers were handpicked by the Ottoman Porte from among a number of Greek Phanariote families living in the empire's capital, in what became known as the Phanariote era. During that period, which lasted until 1821, most of Moldova's princes ruled also, in alternate fashion, over Wallachia, enhancing the historic and political perception of the geminate status of two principalities that had always shared the same language, the same culture, and largely identical societal institutions. This twinlike condition of Moldova and Wallachia also came to be reflected in 18th-century political and diplomatic parlance, which routinely referred to them as the Moldo-Wallachian Principalities.

The same as before, the Greek Orthodox patriarch of Constantinople continued the tradition to solemnly anoint Moldova's political rulers after their nomination and confirmation by the sultan. Moldova's last ruler anointed in Constantinople by the patriarch of the Orthodox Church of the East was Prince Grigore Alexandru Ghika V (1849–1856). But by that time, most of the eastern half of historic Moldova had been incorporated into Russia and stripped of all autonomy and political authority of its own. In terms of 19th-century political development, Moldova (including southern Bessarabia) last enjoyed a governing structure of its own during the interval that immediately preceded its 1859 union with the Principality of Wallachia, under the rule of Moldova's Prince Alexandru Ioan Cuza.

During the first half of the 20th century, Bessarabia (i.e., the eastern half of historic Moldova) enjoyed a brief return to a distinct political identity in the wake of the downfall of the Russian Empire, described previously. On 15 November 1917, a week after the victory of the Bolshevik Revolution in Petrograd, Soviet Russia's government issued "The Declaration of Rights of the Peoples Kept Captive in the Czarist Empire"—which spelled out, among other things, their "right to total separation from Russia." On the heels of this declaration, the Moldavian Democratic Federated Republic was proclaimed in Chişinău on 2 December 1917, while the pressure of Bolshevik turmoil kept mounting throughout the provinces of the former empire. On 24 January 1918, reacting against the Leninist revolution's change of direction and Bolshevik attempts to take over, the republic declared its political separation from Russia and renamed itself the Moldavian Democratic Republic. As mentioned cursorily before, the tottering political identity of the Moldavian Democratic Republic, increasingly threatened by soaring Bolshevik tension in neighboring Ukraine, led in March to a conditioned union with Romania, declared "in accordance with historical right and ethnic right, and the principle that peoples should determine their own fate," a move inspired by President Woodrow Wilson's principles on self-determination. First spelled out before the U.S. Congress on 8 January 1918 in the famous Fourteen Points Speech, the Wilsonian doctrine was being embraced at that juncture by many of Central and Eastern Europe's provinces enfolded in the crumbling Habsburg, Russian, and Ottoman Empires. On 27 November, soon after the armistice and Romania's victory in World War I on the side of the Western Allies, the Chişinău General Assembly decided to join Romania without reservations, and the status of Moldova as an entity with a political identity of its own, one more time, came to an end.

Part of Romania from 1918 to 1940 and part of the USSR from both 1940 to 1941 and 1944 to 1990, Moldova returned to an individual political development only after decades of interruption, in 1991. Yet traces of past subjection are apparent in Moldova's current social and political fabric. One of the striking facts in this connection is the configuration of the postindependence political spectrum inside Moldova's society, which still reflects most of the ripple effects of the decades of Communist rule, during which left and far left came to be almost synonymous with totalitarian rule. Thus, today's political left in its broader sense appears to command the loyalty of most of Moldova's Russophone population (around 34 percent of the country's total population). The left declares itself less inclined to favor reform and entertains some veiled yearning for rejoining Russia. In a nutshell, its political incarnation is the breakaway Moldavian Nistrian Republic, which holds the largest territorial concentration of the Slavic population, an enclave where the left dominates the spectrum. The leftist Tiraspol leadership claims separate statehood and has expressed an interest in joining the Russia-Belarus union.

In contrast, the Romanophone majority of Moldova's political spectrum appears to command the loyalty of most of the right and center right (about 65 percent of the country's total population). It is by and large pro-reform and against reintegration with Russia or any further involvement in the structures of the CIS, established after the demise of the Soviet Union. A minority of Moldovans, mostly members of the literary intelligentsia and academic circles, seem favorable to some sort of future union with Romania, but most Moldovans appear to take pride in the internationally recognized status of their country's recently won independence and support its ongoing struggle for self-reliance.

The Republic of Moldova has been recognized by over 170 countries worldwide and is a member of the United Nations and the Council of Europe. The Constitution adopted in 1994 defines the Republic of Moldova as a sovereign, neutral, and democratic country. Moldova's head of state is the president, and the country's only legislative authority is the Parliament. The Constitutional Court is independent of any public authority and serves as an instrument in the exercise of the separation of powers within Moldova's new political institutions. Public administration by territorial units is carried out on the principles of local autonomy and democratic elections.

By the look of things, despite remarkable progress achieved lately, Moldova's fledgling democracy still suffers from the consequences, on the one hand, of the long interval of totalitarian rule and, on the other, of the lack of a consistently pursued independent political experience of its own in recent times.

ECONOMIC AND SOCIAL DEVELOPMENT

In its 1998 report *Nations in Transit* (published in 1999), the New York–based independent organization Freedom House considered Moldova in the category of countries with transitional polities and economies. Among a number of other relevant parameters, it assessed Moldova's political progress along the path of reform in correlation with the evolution of its gross domestic product. In 1998—on a scale in which a country's best performance was rated 3.62 and the worst 5.28—Moldova's rating of 4.08 was ahead of Romania's (4.18). In terms of trends in political reform—on a scale in which the best performance was rated 3.55 and the worst 4.80—Moldova's rating of 4.00 was ahead of the Russian Federation's (4.10) and Ukraine's (4.25). And concerning trends in economic reform—on a scale in which a country's best performance was rated 3.58 and the worst 5.00—Moldova, with 4.17, was rated ahead of Romania (4.50) and Ukraine (4.75).

Given the multiple social and political legacies of the decades of Soviet rule, Moldova has temporarily lagged behind in terms of overall human development. In 1998, the 1997 Human Development Index, an annual rating of the overall performance of the countries of the world, recorded Moldova's downward shift, from 81st place to 110th.

Moldova's active population is predominantly occupied in the production and processing of agricultural goods—agriculture being an area of the economy that typically accounts for about 42 percent of the total net material product of the country. If one includes the food-processing industry, the overall share of agriculture in the net material product is even higher. The country's agriculture relies chiefly on the region's rich soil and temperate climate. About 75 percent of Moldova's territory is covered by proverbially fertile and humus-rich black soil (*chernozem* in Russian). With practically no mountains and no significant mineral deposits, Moldova's topography has traditionally favored intensive agriculture. Its main products are vegetables, fruits, wine, grain, sugar beets, sunflower seeds, meat, milk, and tobacco. The main crop of the country is grapes, Moldova's vineyards being famous for producing good wine and a rich variety of alcoholic beverages. Grape production accounts for approximately 10 percent of the total value of Moldova's agricultural production.

As stated above, most of Moldova's industry was organized under Soviet rule as a component of the Communist-style command economy. Moldova thus also produces canned food, refined sugar, vegetable oil, consumer goods, furniture, carpets, refrigerators, bicycles, washing machines, spare parts for defense-related products, radios, television sets, electrical motors, and other electrical equipment. Although Moldova's industrial output accounts for about one-third of the gross domestic product, the striking fact is that most of its production sites are not currently under the control of the country's central government. Purposely placed by the Soviet Union on the east bank of the Nistru River, most of Moldova's industrial basis is currently on territory controlled by the separatist authorities in Tiraspol. The breakaway trans-Nistrian enclave holds about 16 percent of Moldova's territory and only 14 percent of its population, but it accounts for 21 percent of its industrial employment and over one-third of its total industrial output.

Moldova's energy sector relies almost entirely on imported coal, oil, and gas, with local resources accounting for less than 3 percent of the fuel and electric power needs of the country. The unsolved problem of Moldova's chronic dependency on foreign suppliers or transmitters of energy, chiefly Russia and Ukraine, is the Achilles' heel of the country's performance and proficiency at all levels of the economy.

Since most conduits supplying Moldova with energy come across the country's sore point, the Tiraspol secessionist enclave, the full dimension of the country's current predicament, both political and economic, cannot be grasped without an assessment of the roots and current status of the trans-Nistrian disjunction. In the years since it declared independence, most of the crucial drawbacks encountered by Moldova have been caused by the manifold malfunctions of its economy, an area where the direct and indirect impact of trans-Nistrian separatism is both a litmus test and the generator of a continuous series of snags. This peculiar set of circumstances appears to accentuate the consequences of the Soviet system of central planning, still at work full swing in the secessionist area. Importantly, it also perpetuates a new kind of dependence that plagues the industrial sector of the economy, first and foremost the energy sector, where, in the most concrete sense of the word, immunity from foreign exaction still remains to be achieved.

IDENTITY AND SELF-RELIANCE

Moldova's struggle for identity, to a large extent, is a reflection of the influences it has been exposed to and has been forced to assimilate throughout its history, especially over the latter half of the 20th century, when the combined processes of intensive Russification and Sovietization left their imprint, most glaringly, in the vital area of linguistic communication. At a couple of essential junctures in Moldova's history—under Russian rule as well as under Soviet domination—the language issue thus came to play the role of one of the most powerful catalysts for both political change and national assertion. The thrust and weight of the language debate, therefore, combined with the alphabet dispute, proved of defining importance in the assertion of Moldova's identity.

In parallel fashion, the other significant coordinate of Moldova's societal evolution has hinged on the evolving composition of its once unitary ethnic fabric, gradually changed over time, through policies of colonization conducted in various installments under two successive rules: Russian after 1812, Soviet after 1940 and 1944. A specific trait of Moldova's struggle for identity results from these policies and from the country's acculturation experience, first with czarist Russia and then with Soviet Russia, both of which worked methodically to transfigure Moldova's inherited culture in order to tone down its specific features and make it as akin to Russia's as possible.

Moldova's historic and cultural quandary can by and large be interpreted as a consequence of the fact that, in both its Russian and Soviet incarnations, the country became part of a larger empire, not as a rounded-out entity, but rather as part of a preexisting whole split into two, with twinlike vestigial elements left open-ended across the border in the old country. Here again, the historic paradox of one-half of a preexisting whole (the Principality of Moldova) integrated into an altogether different whole (the Eurasian empire of czarist Russia [1812–1918] and, later on, Soviet Russia [1940–1991]) is central to an explanation of modern Moldova's identity conundrum.

Since assimilation did not succeed across the board (except for a notable part of Moldova's urban culture), the resilience of the autochthonous culture, preserved mostly in the countryside, created a powerful reaction, particularly conspicuous in two of the 20th century's watershed junctures— 1917–1918 and 1990–1991—which shaped much of the country's response to historic alienation.

"A nation is a moral essence, not a geographical arrangement," wrote Edmund Burke. In this respect, the sinews of Moldova's identity and the chief distinctive features of its historic paradigm seem to lie in the already alluded to persistence of its set of ancient traditions as part of a nonexclusive whole, shared almost without exception with the western tract of a single land with which, up to the 19th-century cleavage, it had geminate patterns of development and a common cultural heritage.

Beginning with the folk myths relating to Roman Emperor Trajan and the memory of his *vallum*, or the widely popular Dochia legend, thought to evoke the name of Dacia, and continuing with such folklore creations as the "Miorița" epic, the oral and written traditions relating to the historic cradle of Moldova, and the long history of leading figures, heroes, and warriors, and ending with literary masterpieces—all of Moldova's major cultural landmarks are not Moldova's exclusively: they straddle the Prut and are shared with Moldova's next of kin across the border, where the same language is spoken. In the realm of high culture, this is obviously corroborated by Moldova's pantheon of classic writers, identical to Romania's, which includes literary and cultural personalities such as, to name but a few, humorist Ion Creangă; historian, playwright, and novelist Bogdan Petriceicu Hasdeu; cultural innovators Mihail Kogălniceanu and Alecu Russo; playwright and poet Vasile Alecsandri; and, last but not least, Moldova's national poet, Mihai Eminescu.

To sum up, the roots of modern-day Moldova's striking originality—the same as those of yesterday's Bessarabia—can at least in part be explained by the fact that, although historically grafted on a great Eurasian empire for over a century and a half, they have always maintained, in parallel fashion, a different polarization derived from their pristine and much older European roots, looking westward. This landmark condition contributed across time to the creation of beleaguered Moldova's unmistakable identity, a country ethnically and culturally located at a crossroads between East and West.

In the background of these polarizations looms also, of course, the larger issue of Moldova's general orientation in the post-Communist world: toward the Occident, like the three Baltic republics; or toward the new Eurasian model illustrated by the CIS. Moldova's dominant current appears to be the golden mean, acting as the nation's equipoise, which strongly favors independence and self-reliance, a view that seems, in the end, tantamount to the pro-Western option. It points, down the road, to the manifold integration of this small but pivotal country as an irrecusable member of Europe's greater family of nations.

NOTES

1. Demetrius Cantemir, *The History of the Growth and Decay of the Othman Empire* [originally written in Latin] (London: Printed for James, John, and Paul Knapton, at the Crown in Ludgate Street, 1734–1735), volume 1, chapter 3, subchapter 4, note 30, pp. 187–188.

2. The work enjoyed wide circulation in the German version, *Beschreibung der Moldau*, first published in 1769–1770 in *Magazin für die neue Historie und Geographie* and reprinted in book form in Frankfurt and Leipzig in 1771.

3. Karl Marx, *Insemnări despre români: manuscrise inedite* (Notes on the Romanians: as yet unpublished manuscripts), Andrei Oţetea and S. Schwann, eds. (Bucharest: Editura Academiei Republicii Populare Române, 1964), p. 67.

4. Ibid., p. 71.

The Dictionary

-A-

ABACLIA. Town in the newly reestablished *judeţ* of **Lăpuşna** on the **Cogâlnic River**, included, before 1999, in the former *raion,* or district, of **Basarabeasca**.

ACCULTURATION. A culture change that occurs in the wake of the interaction of two or more societies with different or diverging national and cultural traditions. The normal outcome of acculturation is deemed to be some form of cultural fusion or assimilation, with the culture superior in political power and technology usually serving as a melting pot for the weaker one. Other interpretations hold that new and creative mixtures often result in a two-way process generated by the intertwining and interaction of diverse cultural identities and national groups.

Moldova's pristine cultural traditions interacted with the political, linguistic, religious, and cultural ascendancy of the **Russian Empire** between 1812 and 1917 and with the political, linguistic, and ideological dominance of the **Union of Soviet Socialist Republics** during the 1940–1941 and 1944–1990 intervals of totalitarian rule. The specific type of acculturation that took place over those periods of time explains several distinctive traits and accentuated reactions that characterize modern Moldovan culture, including the stronger than ever emphasis on the Latin origin of the language and on the pre-Russian traditions of the land. Powerful symbols that epitomize this revival and the rebuttal of Russian acculturation include, among other things, the bronze monument titled "To Rome," featuring the Capitoline she-wolf suckling Romulus and Remus, a statue that dominates the entrance of the Chişinău Museum of History; the Roman eagle in Moldova's national emblem; and the Latin-language motto *Virtus Romana Rediviva* (Roman Virtue Reborn) on the great seal of the city of **Chişinău**. *See also* RUSSIFICATION.

ADRIANOPLE, TREATY OF. Russo-Turkish accord signed at Adrianople (Edirne, in present-day Turkey) on 16 September 1829, which put an end to the 1828–1829 war between the **Russian Empire** and the **Ottoman Empire**. In the aftermath of Ottoman Turkey's defeat, the accord expanded the territory of Russian-held **Bessarabia** southward so that it included all three arms of the **Danube** Delta, which put the Russian Empire in full control of the mouths of the river. The Treaty of Adrianople also put an end to the Turkish monopoly over the foreign trade of the **Danubian Principalities**, thus terminating one of the most important provisions that had bound them to Turkey for three centuries. Although remaining tributary to the Ottoman Empire, the Danubian Principalities became protectorates of Russia. *See also* RUSSO-TURKISH WARS.

AGRICULTURE. Moldova's economy is based primarily on agriculture, which, together with food production, accounts for about 50 percent of the country's gross domestic product. Moldova's agriculture is traditionally deployed on an overall surface of approximately 2.5 million hectares of farming land. Remarkably, while still a part of the Soviet Union—in the multinational conglomerate of which it held less than 0.2 percent of the entire territory—Moldova ranked sixth in terms of total food production, raising a record of about 2.3 percent of all Soviet agricultural production. Moldova's basis for agricultural production includes about 68 percent arable land, about 18 percent orchards and vineyards, and about 14 percent meadows and pastures. Moldova's yearly agricultural production (estimates based on 1994 figures) is 2.9 million tons of grain (chiefly winter wheat and corn), 800,000 tons of fruit and berries, 1 million tons of vegetables, 2.4 million tons of sugar beets, 210,000 tons of sunflower seeds, 410,000 tons of meat (live weight), 1.2 million tons of milk, and 55,000 tons of tobacco.

Traditionally, Moldova has been an important producer of grapes, with an annual yield of approximately 870,000 tons (1995 est.). The Moldovan wine industry produces over 100 brands of wines, brandies, and champagnes that have enjoyed a well-established international reputation. In 1997, wine production alone accounted for 27 percent of Moldova's total export earnings. The agriculture, beverages, and food industries employ about 36 percent of the country's available labor force. Food, wines, and animal products account for an average 65 percent of Moldova's exports. Approximately half of Moldova's agricultural and food production is traditionally exported to the former Soviet republics.

Since the late 1980s, due to Soviet-style **collectivization**, chronic lack of incentives, dysfunctions generated by the centralized system of agricultural production, and, in more recent years, adverse weather conditions, Moldova's agricultural production has been in decline, both in terms of overall production and in terms of per-hectare production of most crops. In 1993, overall agricultural production was down 15 percent from the previous year. The trend continued into 1994, when the agricultural output declined 58 percent from the 1993 level. The 1996 decline in the gross agricultural product was officially estimated at 13 percent less than the 1995 gross product. The 1997 estimates of specific outputs for 1996 compared to 1995 indicated a fall of about 47 percent in the production of vegetables, about 34 percent in cereals, about 12 percent in grapes, and about 13 percent in sugar beets. Moldova's agriculture sector remains by and large unprofitable and continues to receive budgetary support. About 490 large agricultural units, or 46 percent of the total, finished 1996 with losses.

In April 1997, only 8.6 percent of the total land subject to **privatization** had been transferred into so-called joint-venture companies, which de facto continue to be run by the same Soviet-era managers and administration. Recent developments show that most Moldovan farmers advocate withdrawing their land and properties from such companies in order to create their own individual farms. Privatization of land began in the early 1990s by converting collective and state farms into these joint-stock companies, with the land and property to be allocated later to their new owners. Whereas Moldova had about 500 small private farms in 1993, by 1995 this number had increased to almost 14,000. According to 1995 estimates, these held only 1.5 percent of Moldova's agricultural land, but their output had increased from 18 percent of the country's total agricultural output in 1990 to a significant 38 percent in 1994. By the end of 1996, there were 61,600 private farms in Moldova. In 1997, the **Chişinău** Parliament approved a law that, for the first time, made possible the sale of land. The **World Bank** approved a $5 million credit for a Rural Finance Project the following year, meant to develop and test a banking system that would provide financial services to small private farmers and rural entrepreneurs in Moldova. *See also* LAND LAW.

AKKERMAN. *See* CETATEA ALBA.

AKKERMAN, CONVENTION OF. Signed by the **Russian Empire** and the **Ottoman Empire** at Akkerman—the Turkish name for **Cetatea Albă**—on 7 October 1826, this accord confirmed the clauses of the 1812 Russo-Turkish **Treaty of Bucharest**, including the incorporation of **Bessarabia** into Russia, but it also reinstated the appointment of local rulers as princes of Moldova and **Wallachia**, nominated with the joint approval of Ottoman Turkey and Russia.

ALECSANDRI, VASILE (1818–1890). Writer, diplomat, and politician who took an active part in the 1848 revolution in Moldova, for which he wrote one of its main documents, "Protestul în numele Moldovei, a Omenirei, şi a lui Dumnezeu" (A Protest in the Name of Moldova, Mankind, and God). Alecsandri collected and published a number of old Moldovan folk ballads, including the epic ballad "Codreanu," culled at Cetăreni, near **Ungheni**, which evokes the legendary feats of the inhabitants of **Codru**, and the main variant of the national folk ballad **"Miorița."** Alecsandri is the author of the historical play *Despot-Vodă,* the main character of which is Moldova's 16th-century ruler **Despot Vodă**. A bronze statue of Vasile Alecsandri graces the entrance of Moldova's National Library in **Chişinău**.

ALEXANDER I (1777–1825). Czar of Russia from 1801 to 1825. He led some of the most important wars waged by the **Russian Empire** against the **Ottoman Empire** during the 19th century, attaining, among other things, the goal of bringing Russia's southern border to the mouths of the **Danube River**. Under the terms of the May 1812 **Treaty of Bucharest**, Danubian Moldova, including the whole eastern half of the principality, became part of the Russian Empire under the name of **Bessarabia**. Alexander I visited his newly acquired province of Bessarabia in April 1818. Other lands incorporated by Russia under the reign of Czar Alexander I included eastern Georgia (1801), Finland (1809), and Azerbaijan (1813). *See also* RUSSO-TURKISH WARS.

ALEXANDER II (1818–1881). Reigned as czar over the **Russian Empire** between 1855 and 1881. Under his rule, **Bessarabia,** which comprised most of present-day Moldova, underwent a number of economic and social transformations. His decree of emancipation of 19 February 1861 granted freedom to Bessarabia's 12,000 serfs, most of whom were Russian-owned serfs brought from other provinces of the empire after 1812. The imperial statute of 1868 promulgated an agrarian reform that changed Bessarabia's structure of landholding by giving property rights to individual families. Alexander II came to the throne at the end of the Crimean War, in which a defeated Russia was removed from the mouths of the **Danube River** and had to return southern Bessarabia to the **Principality of Moldova**. He again went to war in 1877 and, with help from

Romania, liberated Bulgaria. With the 1878 Treaty of Berlin, Alexander II regained southern Bessarabia, which in the meantime had become part of Romania, and thus made Russia again a riparian power on the Danube in 1878. Other lands attached to Russia under his reign included the Caucasus (1864) and Kazakhstan (1865). Alexander II visited **Chişinău** in April 1877, before the outbreak of the Russo-Romanian-Turkish War of 1877–1878 (*see* RUSSO-TURKISH WARS).

ALEXANDER III (1845–1894). Reigned as czar over the **Russian Empire** between 1881 and 1894. His policies were inspired by the Pan-Slavist determination to make his multinational empire as homogeneous as possible in language, religion, and administration. Such goals were pursued by imposing and promoting the three basic tenets of autocracy, nationality, and Eastern Orthodoxy. Alexander III completed Russia's conquest of Asia and started the construction of the trans-Siberian railway. The **Russification** of the **Orthodox Church** of **Bessarabia** was dramatically intensified under his reign.

ALEXANDER THE GOOD / ALEXANDRU CEL BUN (?–1432). Prince of Moldova between 1400 and 1432. He fortified the **Nistru River** checkpoints of **Hotin** and **Tighina** and successfully repelled the first Turkish raids aimed at gaining control over the river's estuary and the fortress of **Cetatea Albă**. During Alexander's reign, the head of Moldova's **Orthodox Church**, who had until then exerted ecclesiastical jurisdiction from Cetatea Albă, was confirmed by the Constantinople patriarchy as metropolitan and his see was moved to **Suceava**. Moldova's newly founded Alexandru Cel Bun Defense College is named for Alexander the Good.

ALEXANDRU IOAN I. *See* ALEXANDRU IOAN CUZA.

ALEXANDRU IOAN CUZA / ALEXANDRU IOAN I (1820–1873). Last reigning prince of Moldova, elected by the **Iaşi** Elective Assembly on 5 January 1859. Became prince of both Moldova and **Wallachia** as Alexandru Ioan I, on 24 January 1859, when the Bucharest Assembly elected him to rule over Wallachia too. Prince Cuza, popularly known as Cuza Vodă, established his capital in Bucharest (1862) and ruled both countries, first under the name of the **United Principalities**, then as **Romania**, until 1866, when he was forced to abdicate. Three districts of southern **Bessarabia**—**Bolgrad**, **Cahul**, and **Ismail**—annexed in 1812 by Russia, were part of Romania under Cuza's reign. Prince Cuza died in exile in Heidelberg, Germany, in 1873. Alexandru Ioan Cuza is also the name of a village in Moldova's southern *judeţ* of Cahul.

ALEXEI, NICOLAE (1948–). Major general in Moldova's police force and member of the country's Parliament between 1990 and 1994. A native of Recea, **Chişinău**, General Alexei holds degrees in mathematics and physics (1971) and law (1990) from the **State University of Moldova**. He served in Moldova's police force, both before and after the country's declaration of independence, chiefly in the former district of **Străşeni** (1989–1994). Between 1994 and 1997 he served as senior lecturer at Moldova's **Stefan Cel Mare** Academy of Police, and as head of the Department for Combating Organized Crime and Corruption (1997–1999). His repeated denunciation of alleged criminal activities in higher official circles got him temporarily in trouble between 1998 and 1999, and he had to leave his job at the Department for Combating Organized Crime and Corruption. In January 2000, the position was restored to him, and he was also named first deputy minister of internal affairs in the Moldovan government (V. N.).

ALEXIANU, GEORGE (1897–1946). Romanian politician and statesman, governor-general of the Romanian-held territory of **Transnistria** during World War II (30 August 1941–2 February 1944). Under his governorship, mass deportations and exterminations of **Jews** were perpetrated in the **Nistru** east-bank territory. He was tried by a Romanian war tribunal and executed by firing squad as a war criminal in June 1946. *See also* WAR DEPORTATIONS.

ALLIANCE FOR DEMOCRACY AND REFORMS / ALIANTA PENTRU DEMOCRATIE SI REFORME (ADR). Center-right parliamentary coalition formed in the wake of the 1998 elections by three of Moldova's main political forces: the **Democratic Convention of Moldova**, the **Bloc for a Democratic and Prosperous Moldova**, and the **Party of Democratic Forces**. Holding a total of 61 seats out of 101 in the **Chişinău** legislature, the ADR practically reversed the 1998 general elections results, which had given a 40-seat plurality to the Party of Moldova's Communists. *See also* COMMUNIST PARTY; POLITICAL BLOCS AND PARTIES.

ALPHABET ISSUE. The Moldovan alphabet issue ties in with the **language issue** and illustrates the unique situation of a Romance language using the **Cyrillic alphabet** rather than the Roman script. The first mention of the issue appears to have been made by **Demetrius Cantemir** in his 1714–1716 *Descriptio Moldaviae,* in which the chapter titled "De Litteris Moldavorum" describes such a situation as a linguistic anomaly and calls it a "barbarity" (Latin: *barbaries*).

Demonstrably, the remote root of this unexampled situation appears to lie in the early subordination of the Church of Moldova to the Slavic-rite **Orthodox Church**. As a consequence, **Romanian**, the local Romance language spoken to this day by the majority of Moldova's population, was written in Cyrillics from the early Middle Ages through the centuries-long East-West religious rift, up until 1917. In the other provinces with populations speaking Romanian—namely, **Wallachia**, **Transylvania,** and western Moldova, including between 1856 and 1878 the three Bessarabian districts of **Bolgrad**, **Cahul,** and **Ismail**—the Cyrillic script was discarded after 1860.

In Russian-held **Bessarabia**, the issue of Roman versus Slavonic script was publicly articulated at the time of the Bolshevik Revolution in May 1917, when a **Chişinău** congress of Bessarabian teachers demanded the return to the local language of the majority in the education process and the replacement of Cyrillic by Roman letters in the writing and teaching of the majority's mother tongue. The first Latin-characters printing house was inaugurated in Chişinău in September 1917, in the wake of these efforts.

The Roman script option was indicative of two determinations, one of which was historical and linguistic, aimed at eliminating the incongruity of Romanian, a non-Slavic language, dressed in Slavonic garb. The other had broader political overtones: it aimed to bring the eastern half of historical Moldova in step with the alphabet reform that, in the second half of the 19th century, had given the **United Principalities** of Moldova and Wallachia a cultural instrument for closing the gap that had separated them from what they considered to be sister nations, such as France and Italy, emulated as historic models throughout the 19th century.

The desiderata of the 1917 Chişinău congress of teachers were satisfied during the 1918–1940 interval, when former Russian Bessarabia became an ephemeral part of interwar **Romania**, and cultural unity came about naturally, without alphabetic differences in the writing of the language.

The alphabet issue emerged again periodically in the interwar years, after the creation by the **Union of Soviet Socialist Republics (USSR)** of a **Moldavian Autonomous Soviet Socialist Republic (MASSR)**, carved out of Ukraine in 1924 on the east bank of the **Nistru River**. Described by Soviet experts as different from the language spoken in Romania, and written again with Russian-Slavonic characters, the language spoken by the 30 percent Romanian-speaking minority in that region was officially called "Moldavian." In 1929, a *Moldavian Grammar* published in Russian Cyrillics by Leonid A. Madan in **Tiraspol** attempted to create a theoretical basis for the concept of Moldavian as separate from Romanian. However, in 1932, apparently for tactical reasons, the Roman script was introduced in the MASSR. The decision was interpreted as part of an effort to disseminate Communist propaganda books in the Romanian language across the border, and thus to facilitate the circulation of Marxist-Leninist literature printed in the USSR inside Romania.

In 1938, one year before the Soviet invasion of Poland, the Roman script was again proscribed in the MASSR, and the Cyrillic alphabet became, one more time, the official alphabet in the Nistru east-bank autonomous Soviet republic. After the 1940 Soviet annexation of Bessarabia, a Supreme Soviet decree passed on 16 May 1941 changed the Latin alphabet back to Russian-Cyrillic, which became compulsory in the newly founded **Moldavian Soviet Socialist Republic (MSSR)**.

Decades later, on 31 August 1989, the Supreme Soviet of the MSSR passed into law the establishment of the official language of the country and the return to the Roman script. In the trans-Nistrian districts, the alphabet issue fueled heated debates, became central to the secessionist movement, and was quick to develop into a "school war" waged by the Tiraspol separatists against schools that opted for Latin characters.

In 1996, Moldova appealed to the **Organization for Security and Cooperation in Europe** to use its influence and put an end to the closing down of schools in the trans-Nistrian breakaway region on grounds of their using the Latin alphabet in the education process. As of 1997, only seven schools (licensed as "private schools") were allowed to use the Roman script in the region controlled by the Tiraspol authorities. The other 81 Romanian-language schools in the breakaway region teach Romanian (dubbed "Moldavian") using the Russian-Slavonic alphabet. *See also* RUSSIFICATION.

AMFILOCHIE HOTINIUL (ca. 1730–1800). Bishop of **Hotin** at the end of the 18th century. His activity—concentrated in Hotin between 1767 and 1770—was mostly didactic and scholarly. A polyglot and a disseminator of knowledge, Amfilochie translated and adapted from the Italian Alessandro Conti's *Elementi aritmetici,* the first handbook of arithmetic printed in the **Romanian language**, as *Elementi aritmetice arătate firești* (Arithmetical Elements Naturally Propounded). His other important work is a treatise of world geography, *De obște gheografie* (General Geography), adapted from the French. Both works were published in **Iași** in 1795.

ANDRONIC, NICOLAE (1959–). Deputy prime minister for law and juridical issues in Moldova's governments of 1998 and 1999. A native of Cotiujenii Mari, **Şoldăneşti,** Andronic is by training a lawyer and a graduate of the Law School of the **State University of Moldova.** A member of the **Democratic Convention of Moldova,** Andronic served as prosecutor (1981–1986) and later held various functions in the Parliament of Moldova before first being appointed a member of the cabinet in the wake of the 1998 national elections (V. N.).

ANDRUS, ONOFRII (1908–1961). Pedagogue of pro-Russian training, Onofrii was born in **Balta,** the short-lived capital of the **Moldavian Autonomous Soviet Socialist Republic,** and was educated during the interwar period at the Tiraspol Pedagogical Institute (1926–1933), then at Soviet Ukraine's University of Kiev (1933–1936). He played an important role in preparing the **Russification** campaign through education launched by the Soviet authorities after the June 1940 incorporation of **Bessarabia** into the **Union of Soviet Socialist Republics.** Andrus followed the Soviet army in its 1941 retreat from Moldova, and immediately after the return of the Soviet rule to **Chişinău,** beginning in the summer of 1944, he served as chief instructor of the first echelon of 4,620 Soviet-trained teachers assigned to teach in the schools of the **Moldavian Soviet Socialist Republic** following World War II.

ANENII NOI. Chief town of the former *raion,* or district, of the same name, on the **Chişinău**-Odessa highway, 32 kilometers southeast of Chişinău. The former district was formed in 1961 and had a population of over 77,000 inhabitants (1993 est.). Anenii Noi is part of the newly established *judeţ* of Chişinău.

ANNEXATION. A term in international law denoting the act whereby a territory not previously held under the **sovereignty** of a state is acquired by another state. The **Russian Empire** expressed for the first time its intention to annex Moldova and neighboring **Wallachia** at the time of the **Russo-Turkish War** of 1806–1812, when Czar **Alexander I,** whose armies already occupied both **Danubian Principalities,** conferred with France's Napoleon I at Tilsit in July 1807. However, the May 1812 **Treaty of Bucharest,** which, shortly before Napoleon's armies invaded Russia, put an end to that war, stipulated the annexation of only the eastern half of Moldova, thereafter dubbed **Bessarabia.** The allegiance of the inhabitants of Bessarabia was then automatically assumed by Russia's sovereign, the czar, and although existing law and local government organization remained for a short time unchanged, they were soon modified by Russia, which turned Bessarabia into an **oblast** (later a *guberniia*) of its own empire. The annexation of Bessarabia by Russia must be distinguished from the prior status of that territory, which had been part of the autonomous **Principality of Moldova**, under the suzerainty of the **Ottoman Empire**. The Principality of Moldova was never annexed by Ottoman Turkey.

Conversely, according to pro-Russian interpretations, the territory of Bessarabia was subject to annexation in 1918, when, to avoid a Communist takeover, the short-lived Moldavian Democratic Republic (*see* MOLDAVIAN DEMOCRATIC FEDERATED REPUBLIC) joined neighboring **Romania**, which, after 1859, had comprised, alongside Wallachia, the western part of historic Moldova. Under international law, annexation can be validated only when consented to by the state whose territory is annexed (in whole or in part) or, in the case of territory not formerly held by another state, when consented to by the international community. In the case of Moldova, such consent was given in 1918 by **Sfatul Ţării**, the General Assembly of the Moldavian Democratic Republic, and by the international community through the diplomatic instruments of the **Versailles Conference**.

Historically a mechanism whereby the discovery of new land used to be credited to an expanding metropolitan state, annexation is currently one of the means by which major powers incorporate territories belonging to smaller powers. The 28 June 1940 annexation of Bessarabia by the **Union of Soviet Socialist Republics (USSR)** was carried out under the provisions of the **Molotov-Ribbentrop Pact** and was eventually consented to by both the predecessor state, Romania, and the international community, in the form of the 1947 **Paris Peace Treaty**. Its provisions—as embodied in the status of the **Moldavian Soviet Socialist Republic**, a part of the USSR after 1940—became null and void on 27 August 1991 by virtue of Moldova's **declaration of independence** as a sovereign state. *See also* NATION.

ANTI-BOLSHEVIK MILITARY INTERVENTION. The Romanian army intervened against the Bolshevik Revolution in **Bessarabia** in January 1918, at the request of the **Moldavian Democratic Federated Republic's** Sfatul Ţării (i.e., **General Assembly**). While most of **Romania** was under German occupation and the capital had moved from Bucharest to **Iaşi**, the government of rump Romania sent in two infantry and two cavalry brigades across the **Prut River**, where the Bolshevik

Revolution had dispersed the fledgling republic's legislature and proclaimed Soviet Communist power in **Chişinău**. The Romanian army entered Chişinău on 13 January and drove the Bolsheviks out of the city. With help from Moldova's improvised combat units, it subsequently restored order in **Hotin, Ismail, Tighina**, and **Cetatea Albă**. On 7 February, the last detachments of Communist revolutionaries were driven east of the **Nistru River** into what was later to become Soviet Ukraine. In the meantime, against the backdrop of Ukraine's own separation from Russia, Sfatul Ţării proclaimed the Moldavian Democratic Republic and broke all ties with Russia, which was increasingly plunging into revolutionary anarchy. Soon afterward, amid growing fears of forced absorption by Ukraine, which had proclaimed its own short-lived independence from Russia, Sfatul Ţării decided for a conditioned union with Romania (27 March), followed by a vote for unconditioned union with Romania (27 November), which in the meantime, alongside its Western allies, had emerged victorious against the Central Powers. The Romanian anti-Bolshevik intervention of January 1918 played a decisive part in foiling the establishment of Soviet Communist power in Bessarabia at the end of World War I. *See also* BOLSHEVIK POWER; MOLDOVAN COHORTS.

ANTONESCU, ION (1882–1946). Military leader and statesman, marshal of **Romania**. Ion Antonescu assumed supreme power in September 1940 and, soon after, concluded an alliance with Nazi Germany. On 22 June 1941, when Germany launched its all-out attack against the Soviet Union, following Antonescu's orders, the Romanian army crossed into **Bessarabia** and **Northern Bucovina** and reoccupied the territories Soviet Russia had detached from Romania in June 1940, under the secret provisions of the 1939 **Molotov-Ribbentrop Pact**. Antonescu's offensive did not stop at the line of the **Nistru River**, but continued with Hitler's armies into Soviet Ukraine, which fell under German-Romanian occupation in 1941. There, under German military authority, the Romanians were entrusted with the civilian governorship of **Transnistria**, where, between 1941 and 1942, notorious war atrocities were committed against **Jews**. Under Antonescu's command, Romania's army continued to fight as an ally of Germany, marching deeper into Soviet territory, as far east as Stalingrad and the Caucasus. During the crushing Soviet counterattack that eventually penetrated Romania in 1944, Marshal Antonescu was arrested in a military coup led by Romania's young King **Michael I**. In 1946, Ion

Antonescu was convicted on charges of war crimes in connection with the Transnistria exterminations and deportations and executed by firing squad at Fort Jilava, near Bucharest, in June 1946. *See also* WAR DEPORTATIONS.

ARAPU, ANATOLIE (1962–). Minister of finance in Moldova's governments of 1998 and 1999. A native of Văsieni, **Hânceşti**, Arapu is a graduate in economics from the **State University of Moldova**. He served as deputy minister of foreign economic relations (1992–1994), assistant in the Executive Directorate of the **World Bank** in Washington, D.C. (1994–1997), and ambassador of the Republic of Moldova to Belgium and the Netherlands (1997–1998) (V. N.).

ARBORE-RALLY, ZAMFIR (1848–1933). Publicist, historian, and leftwing activist, Arbore-Rally was a native of **Cernăuţi**. He took part in the Narodnik action, a 19th-century anticapitalist movement grown in the intellectual circles of the **Russian Empire** that propounded the decentralization of power, reform by virtue of charismatic force, and the redistribution of wealth without violent revolution. Arbore-Rally was deported to Siberia by the czarist authorities, but he escaped and emigrated to Switzerland (1871–1878) and, later on, to **Romania**, where, after 1878, he was active in the socialist movement. He published *Temniţă şi exil* (Prison and Exile) in 1894 and *In exil* (In Exile) in 1896, recounting his tribulations under the czarist autocratic regime. Arbore-Rally is also the author of a monograph devoted to **Bessarabia** in the 19th century, *Basarabia în secolul XIX* (1898), and of a geographic dictionary of Bessarabia, *Dicţionarul geografic al Basarabiei* (1904).

ARENA POLITICII. A monthly magazine of up-to-date information about developments in Moldovan society and the world published in **Chişinău** from 1996 to 1998. Its editorial board included a team of young political scientists, historians, and publicists—among them, Gheorghe Cojocaru (1963–), Ion Şişcanu (1951–), and Igor Munteanu (1965–). The *Arena Politicii* program aimed at disseminating knowledge of democratic thought and democratic institutions by making international information and relevant debate available to the general reader, political science students, political elites, and decision makers.

ARMED FORCES. Moldova's armed forces are part of the structural inheritance of the state system of the former **Union of Soviet Socialist**

Republics (USSR), of which it was a part until 1991. Under Moldova's old Soviet-style **Constitution**, defense was devolved to the Soviet armed forces, which the **Moldavian Soviet Socialist Republic** was supposed to equip, train, and provide with manpower. Under those circumstances, between 1980 and 1989, over 9,000 young Moldovans were drafted by the USSR to fight in Afghanistan.

This situation changed radically after the watershed of Moldova's **declaration of independence**. A 1997 draft for reforming Moldova's armed forces was initiated by President **Petru Lucinschi**, who called for a decisive change in defense policies and structures, including improving Moldova's fighting capability and upgrading military technology. Although faithful to the guidelines stemming from the 1994 Constitution, which proclaims the country's neutrality, such a reform is aimed at creating a reliable army, apt to ensure the country's security, independence, and territorial integrity. Moldova's military forces are trained at the Alexandru Cel Bun Defense College.

Taking into account the fact that Moldova is at a crossroads where the interests of several states intersect, a Moldovan modernized army should be more than a national guard, the Lucinschi guidelines stressed. A state commission directed to draw up the reform of Moldova's armed forces has based its concept on models offered by such neutral countries as Austria and Switzerland, smaller nations once abutting potentially dangerous neighbors. Slovenia and Slovakia have also been cited as potential models.

Moldova has some 9,000 servicemen, organized into three motor rifle brigades, one artillery brigade, and one reconnaissance assault division. According to official figures, Moldova's air force in 1994 consisted of one fighter regiment, one helicopter squadron, and one missile brigade. Moldova's main military airport is located at Mărculeşti, in the vicinity of **Bălţi**. At that time, Moldova's air force equipment included a fleet of 27 Soviet-made jet aircraft, including advanced MiG-29C jet fighters capable of carrying nuclear weapons and older MiG-29A and MiG-29B models. Other Soviet-made war equipment included 8 Mi-8 helicopters, 5 transport aircraft, and 25 SA-3/5 surface-to-air missiles. In 1997, the United States quietly bought 21 MiG jet aircraft from Moldova, including all but 6 of its high-performance model "C" MiG-29 jet fighters with nuclear capability, never previously observed in American inventory. The purchase was made under the Cooperative Threat Reduction program, meant to thwart acquisition of such equipment by third parties with terrorist connections interested in capturing high-technology war

material from the former Soviet republics. In 1998, Moldova was scheduled to cut its military forces by 1,000 men, including personnel from
among the border and security guards.

As head of state, Moldova's president is also the army's commander in
chief. Moldova joined the U.S. Partnership for Peace initiative, and in May
1997, the first ever Partnership for Peace exercise involving American and
Moldovan troops took place at Mărculeşti; this event also marked the very
first time that U.S. troops were present in the territory of a former Soviet republic. The following year, Moldova took part in various U.S. Partnership
for Peace exercises, including "Cooperative Key '98" in Turkey, "Cooperative Chance '98" in Slovakia, and "Cooperative Osprey '98" in the United
States. Apart from participation in this program, Moldova's military units
take part in bilateral military applications. Plans for 1999 included three exercises involving Moldova and U.S. troops—two in Moldova and one in the
United States. *See also* NORTH ATLANTIC TREATY ORGANIZATION,
RELATIONS WITH.

ARON VODA / ARON THE TYRANT (?–1595). The son of **Alexandru Lăpuşneanu**, Aron Vodă reigned twice over Moldova (1591–1592
and 1592–1595) at a troubled time, when an anti-Ottoman resistance involving Moldova, **Transylvania**, and **Wallachia** was trying to take
shape, with Wallachia's **Michael the Brave** attempting to rule for a short
time over the three principalities. Aron the Tyrant concluded anti-Ottoman agreements with both Transylvania's Sigismund Bathory and
Michael the Brave (1594). During the war that ensued, Moldova's army
briefly reconquered from the Turks the **Danube** stronghold of **Ismail**.
See also OTTOMAN EMPIRE.

ASACHI, GHEORGHE (1788–1869). Cultural trailblazer and writer
whose family hailed from **Hotin** and whose life spanned most of
Moldova's moments of change of status during the 19th century: the
1812 transfer of the eastern half of the principality to the **Russian Empire**, the 1821 end of the **Phanariote era**, and the 1859 union of
Moldova and **Wallachia** under Moldova's Prince **Alexandru Ioan
Cuza**, a move that Asachi personally opposed. His cultural initiatives included the publication of the first periodical in Moldova's history, *Albina
românească* (The Romanian Bee; 1829–1849), followed by other jour-
nals such as *Gazeta de Moldavia* (The Moldova Gazette; 1850–1858)
and *Spicuitorul moldo-român* (The Moldo-Romanian Gleaner; 1841),
the French editions of which were alternatively entitled *Le Glaneur*

Moldo-Valaque and *Le Glaneur Moldo-Roumain*. Having settled in **Iaşi**, Asachi was instrumental in the founding of the first higher-education college in the **Principality of Moldova**, Academia Mihăileană (1835), and in the inauguration of the Conservatory of Music and Drama (1836). Asachi's chief works published during his own lifetime are a collection of poems, *Culegere de poesii* (1836); *Dochia şi Traian* (Dochia and Trajan, 1840); *Nouvelles historiques de la Moldo-Roumanie* (1859); and the historical dramas *Elena, Dragoş* (1863) and *Turnul lui But* (The Tower of But, 1863). A bronze bust of Asachi graces the alley devoted to Moldova's classical writers in **Chişinău**'s Central Park.

ASEZAMANT. Traditional statutes of civil and judicial legislation in ancient Moldova. Such statutes codifying long-established local customs were promulgated in 1628, 1749, 1766, and 1805 by a succession of Moldova's ruling princes: **Miron Barnovschi-Movilă, Constantin Mavrocordat, Grigore Ghika III,** and **Alexandru Moruzi.** After the 1812 incorporation of the eastern half of the **Principality of Moldova** into the **Russian Empire**, Czar **Alexander I** promulgated for the last time such a statute, the 1818 act known as the "Aşezământul Obrazovaniei Oblastiei Basarabiei." It gave recognition to part of the former pieces of legislation enacted under the previous statutes, maintaining local language, customs, and traditions and a certain degree of administrative autonomy to the province, or **oblast**, of **Bessarabia**. To a certain extent, the Aşezământul Obrazovaniei Oblastiei Basarabiei was similar to the constitutions granted initially by Russia's czars to Poland and Finland. The Aşezământul was rescinded by Alexander's successor, **Nicholas I**, whose 1828 ukase attached Bessarabia to the general government of **New Russia** and made it subject to its civil, taxation, and judicial regulations. *See also* RUSSIFICATION.

ATAMANIUK, VLADIMIR (1943–). Parliamentarian and influential leader of the left-wing forces in the government of the self-proclaimed **Moldavian Nistrian Republic (MNR)**. Born in Hmelnitsky, Ukraine, Atamaniuk is by training an army officer. He graduated from the Iaroslav Military College (Russia) and the Kiev Military Academy (Ukraine) and was an officer on active duty in the Soviet army until 1991 before serving as deputy minister of defense in the government of the MNR until 1995. He was elected deputy in the **Tiraspol** legislative body in 1996, as well as its vice president. Atamaniuk took an active part in the **14th Army**'s intervention in the **trans-Nistrian conflict** of 1992 and became one of the close advisers of the president of the self-proclaimed east-bank republic, **Igor Smirnov**. Atamaniuk is credited with an influential role in articulating and defending the interests of the former Soviet military stationed in the separatist enclave on the east bank of the **Nistru River** (V. N.).

AUSTERITY BUDGET. In keeping with the recommendations of international financial institutions, Moldova adopted an austerity budget in 1998, which called for drastically cutting spending and tightening fiscal policies. It was passed into law despite opposition from Communist parliamentarians who left the chamber in protest. The 1998 budget cancelled all tax breaks and state guarantees that had previously drained the budget of Moldova of millions in revenues. *See also* ECONOMY, NATIONAL; INTERNATIONAL MONETARY FUND; WORLD BANK.

AUTONOMY. The issue of autonomy applies to two regions of the Republic of Moldova: **Gagauz Yeri** (Romanian: Gagauzia), which has officially been granted special autonomy status in the southern part of the country; and the **Nistru** east-bank districts, where the fragmentation conundrum has gone unresolved ever since the leaders of the Russia-aligned enclave proclaimed in September 1990 a breakaway Moldavian Nistrian Soviet Socialist Republic, later styled the **Moldavian Nistrian Republic**. Moldova's government offered the trans-Nistrian separatist districts autonomy within the framework of a single state, without infringement of the territorial integrity of the Republic of Moldova, a view turned down by **Tiraspol**, which objects to describing the Nistrian territorial entity as an integral part of Moldova. Although rejecting autonomy within the jurisdiction exerted from **Chişinău**, the Tiraspol leadership was later inclined to an eventual solution conducive in some way to **federalization**. In a departure from prior standpoints, Tiraspol indicated in 1998 its inclination to join the Russia-Belarus union. *See also* SEPARATISM.

-B-

BAC RIVER. Affluent of the **Nistru River,** 155 kilometers in length, it drains an area of 2,040 square kilometers and is Moldova's sixth longest river. Moldova's capital, **Chişinău**, is located on the Bâc River.

BAIA. First capital city of the **Principality of Moldova** after its foundation in the 14th century. First mentioned in 1334, it temporarily served as a residence for its first rulers, **Dragoş Vodă** and **Bogdan I**. A document dated May 1421, which reflects its initial status, carries Baia's traditional seal and a Latin inscription that reads: *x sigillum x capitalis x civitatis x Moldavie x terre x moldaviensis x* (the seal of the land of Moldavia, Moldavia's chief city).

BAKHMETIEV, ALEKSANDR (1744–1841). First Russian governor of **Bessarabia** after the province's incorporation into the **Russian Empire**, Bakhmetiev laid the foundations of the new **oblast**'s administration by the czarist authorities. The first general census of Bessarabia was conducted under his orders in 1817.

BALTA. Chief town of a district in the Odessa province of Ukraine, in a marshy region irrigated by the Kodima River, a tributary to the Bug. From its creation in 1924 to 1929, Balta ("pond" in Romanian) was the capital of the **Moldavian Autonomous Soviet Socialist Republic**. The religious movement of **Inochentism** started in Balta in 1909–1911.

BALTA LIMAN, CONVENTION OF. Russo-Turkish convention signed on 1 May 1849. It enforced the protectorate of the **Russian Empire** over the **Danubian Principalities** after the suppression of the 1848 revolutions. *See also* RUSSO-TURKISH WARS.

BALTI. Moldova's third largest city, at the confluence of the **Răut** and Răuţel Rivers on the Odessa-**Chişinău-Cernăuţi** highway. Bălţi (which means "ponds" in Romanian) was first mentioned as a place-name in a document in 1421. It was destroyed by the **Tatars** in the early 18th century and later rebuilt, initially as a prosperous settlement on the property of landowner Iordache Panait (1766). It developed rapidly during the last part of the 18th century. The St. Nicholas Cathedral, erected in 1785, is the city's most important landmark and its most ancient preserved building. Moldova's third largest industrial center, after Chişinău and **Tiraspol**, the city of Bălţi has a population of 159,420 inhabitants (1993 est.).

Bălţi is also the name of one of Moldova's new territorial units, established in keeping with the territorial reorganization of December 1998. The city of Bălţi is the administrative center of the new Bălţi *judeţ*, which also includes the former smaller territorial units of **Făleşti**, **Glodeni**, **Râşcani**, and **Sângerei**.

BANKING. Moldova's banking system includes two levels of financial institutions: the National Bank of Moldova / Banca Naţională a Moldovei (BNM), on the one hand, and 21 commercial banks, on the other. The

BNM is the central bank of Moldova. It regulates and supervises banking practices and defines monetary management and exchange policies. It sets interest and exchange rates and manages the hard currency reserves. As a separate legal entity, it is independent from the government and responsible to the **Chişinău** Parliament.

The second level of banking is represented by the commercial banks and three local agencies of foreign banks. Moldova's commercial banks are incorporated as joint-stock companies and licensed by the BNM. The most important banks using private and mixed capital are Fincombank, Petrolbank, Victoria Bank, Inc., Intreprinz-Banca, Inc., Gagauzcombank, Inc., and Mobiasbank.

All commercial banks have established correspondent relations with foreign financial institutions, including major Western banks and banks of member states in the **Commonwealth of Independent States**. Moldova-Agroindbank, Inc., Moldindconbank, Inc., Banca de Economii, Inc., Petrolbank, Universalbank, Inc., Gagauzcombank, Inc., and Fintorgbank, Inc., have joined the System of World Interbank Financial Telecommunications, allowing for immediate remittances of finances on behalf of clients and securing remittances from other countries in foreign currencies. Moldova's banking system is considered generally sound, but it is undercapitalized. As of mid-1997, the average interest rate on loans was about 37 percent.

BANULESCU-BODONI, GAVRIL (1746–1821). Bishop and theologian, first metropolitan of **Bessarabia** under Russian rule. Bănulescu-Bodoni was a native of Bistriţa, **Transylvania**, where he received part of his first religious education. In 1778, he taught Latin in **Iaşi**, where he also served as a preacher. He then moved to Russia and taught philosophy in Poltava (1782), was bishop of Akkerman under the Russian occupation of 1789, and was later metropolitan of Kiev (1799). Under the 1808 Russian occupation of the **Danubian Principalities**, the St. Petersburg Synod gave Bănulescu-Bodoni the title of "Ekzarkh Moldo-Vlachiiskii" (i.e., exarch of Moldo-Wallachia) and moved his residence to Bucharest. After the 1812 **Treaty of Bucharest** and the Russian annexation of Bessarabia, the links of the local **Orthodox Church** with its traditional metropolitanate in Iaşi were severed, and Bănulescu-Bodoni was entrusted by the Russians with the task of organizing a new Bessarabian diocese, created by Czar **Alexander I** and given the name of the eparchy of Chişinău and Hotin (1813). Gavril Bănulescu-Bodoni is buried at **Căpriana**.

BARNOVSCHI-MOVILA, MIRON (?–1633). Prince of Moldova between 1626 and 1629 and, for a few months, in 1633. Barnovschi-Movilă conducted a foreign policy favorable to Poland, secretly trying to move the principality away from the sway of the **Ottoman Empire**. In retaliation, Prince Barnovschi was summoned to Constantinople and executed (22 June 1633). His most important contribution to Moldova's history was the 1628 piece of legislation known as the "Aşezământul lui Barnovschi," enforcing fiscal, social, and administrative norms. *See also* MOLDOVA, PRINCIPALITY OF.

BASA-PRESS. Moldova's first private news agency, founded in 1992 in the aftermath of the country's **declaration of independence**. Under the leadership of its general manager, publicist Valeriu Reniţă, Basa-Press is credited with having pioneered the first breakthroughs toward unbiased, objective, Western-style news reporting in post-totalitarian Moldova. Basa-Press currently provides news bulletins in three languages— **Romanian**, **Russian**, and English—to a variety of **press** and media institutions, both in Moldova and abroad.

BASARAB. Wallachian dynasty founded by Basarab I (ca. 1310–1352). Among its most prominent members were Mircea the Old (1386–1418), Vlad Dracul (1436–1447) and Vlad the Impaler (1456–1462 and 1476–1477)—both of whom were the literary inspirations for the imaginary Dracula personage—**Michael the Brave** (1593–1601), and Matei Basarab (1632–1654). The Basarab dynasty became extinct with Constantin Şerban in 1658. In ancient times, Basarabia or **Bessarabia** was sometimes used as a synonym for **Wallachia**, dubbed "Land of Basarab" (Russian: Bassarabskaya Zemlya). A number of place-names inspired by the Basarab tradition (such as Basarabi, Basarabiţa, Basarabasa, **Basarabeasca**) are found throughout the territory where the **Romanian language** is spoken. An explanation of the name was attempted by **Bogdan Petriceicu Hasdeu** in his *Etymologicum Magnum Romaniae* (1886–1898).

BASARABEASCA. Chief town of the former Basarabeasca *raion* in southeastern Moldova, halfway between the **Nistru** and **Prut Rivers**. The former district had over 43,000 inhabitants (1993 est.). In 1998, the Basarabeasca local authorities requested a referendum on joining the **Gagauz Yeri** autonomous administrative unit. Moldova's central authorities ruled out the holding of a referendum in Basarabeasca as contrary to the provisions of the 1996 law on local administration. Basarabeasca is part of the reestablished *judeţ* of **Lăpuşna**.

BASARABIA. *See* BESSARABIA.

BASARABIA. Biweekly published in **Chişinău** by **Constantin Stere** from May 1906 to May 1907. *Basarabia* was the first publication in the **Romanian language** authorized under czarist rule. With the exception of the paper's banner, printed in large Latin characters, *Basarabia* was printed in Russian **Cyrillics**. *See also* ALPHABET ISSUE.

BASHKAN. Official name of the governor of **Gagauz Yeri**. The *bashkan* is ex officio a member of the Parliament of Moldova.

BATIUSHKOV, POMPEI (1811–1892). Russian historian of **Bessarabia** and the author of an informative monograph that encapsulates the history of the province prior to its 1812 **annexation** by the **Russian Empire**.

BENDER/BENDERY. *See* TIGHINA.

BERLIN, CONGRESS OF. Held in Berlin between 13 June and 13 July 1878 and concluded by the Treaty of Berlin, which put an end to the Russo-Romanian-Turkish War of 1877–1878 (*see* RUSSO-TURKISH WARS). The southern districts of **Bessarabia**—**Bolgrad**, **Cahul**, and **Ismail**—which had been returned to the **Principality of Moldova** by the Treaty of Paris of 1856, were reincorporated into the **Russian Empire**.

BERNARDAZZI, ALEKSANDR (1831–1907). Chief architect of **Chişinău** between 1856 and 1878. He played an important role in modernizing the city. His lasting achievements include the Greek Church and the St. Theodora Church, both in Chişinău. Bernardazzi also designed dozens of other public and private edifices in the capital and in other cities of Moldova.

BESLEAGA, VLADIMIR (1931–). Writer and activist for Moldova's cultural revival, Beşleagă made his literary debut in 1963 with the prose volume *La fântâna Leahului* (At the Leahu Fountain). One of his best-known works is *Sânge pe Zăpadă* (Blood on Snow), a historical trilogy devoted to 17th-century historian **Miron Costin**.

BESSARABIA. Name given by the **Russian Empire** to the 44,422-square-kilometer territory of the **Principality of Moldova** lying between the rivers **Prut**, **Nistru**, the **Chilia** arm of the **Danube** Delta, and the Black Sea at the time of its acquisition from the **Ottoman Empire**, in keeping with the provisions of the 1812 **Treaty of Bucharest**. Prior to that juncture, Bessarabia was a historical rather than a geographical name. It loosely denoted the coastal areas of Moldova between the Prut and the Black Sea, controlled for some time by the neighboring Principality of **Wallachia**, ruled by the house of **Basarab**, hence the name. The old toponym was extended by Russia to the entire province, in order to distinguish the newly acquired lands from the rest of the Principality of Moldova. The latter remained under Turkish suzerainty as a separate political entity until its union with the Principality of Wallachia in 1859.

Because of its Wallachian historical connotations, changing the name of the province became the object of some debate in 1865, when Prince Dmitrii A. Obolenski suggested to Czar **Alexander II** that the province be renamed either "Aleksandrovskaia" or "Aleksandroslavskaia" to link it, in collective memory, to the name of Russia's autocrat who annexed it in 1812, **Alexander I**. The name-change project never materialized. Part of Bessarabia—namely, the southern districts of **Bolgrad**, **Cahul**, and **Ismail**—was returned to the Principality of Moldova in 1856 and was part of **Romania** between 1862 and 1878.

In 1918, in the aftermath of the Bolshevik Revolution, Bessarabia as a whole joined Romania and was part of the sovereign state of Romania until 1940, when the latter surrendered it to the Soviet Union under the secret provisions of the **Molotov-Ribbentrop Pact**. In Russian practice, "Bessarabia" as a noun was officially pushed out of use after 1940, when the central part of its territory became a Soviet republic, under the name of the **Moldavian Soviet Socialist Republic**.

In recent years, Bessarabia has resurfaced in use as a synonym for Moldova, after the country's proclamation of independence. Bessarabian (vernacular Basarabean) is sometimes used as a synonym for Moldovan.

BEZVICONI, GHEORGHE (1910–1966). Author and historian who was born in Zhitomir, Ukraine, and died in Bucharest, **Romania**. Bezviconi wrote extensively on Moldova's past. He collected and published important documents regarding 19th-century Bessarabian personalities and the Russo-Romanian cultural relations. One of his important publications is a two-volume catalogue of **Bessarabia**'s nobility in 1821.

BIESU, MARIA (1934–). One of Moldova's most important opera singers, Bieşu has won an impressive reputation for herself as a chief vocalist of the Chişinău Opera and Ballet Theater ever since her debut in 1961. Her artistic excellence brought her international recognition and invitations to sing in other countries, including Italy, where she performed at the Milan Metropolitan Opera in 1965–1967.

BILHOROD DNISTROVSKY / BELGOROD-DNESTROVSKI. *See* CETATEA ALBA.

BLACK SEA ECONOMIC COOPERATION (BSEC). International body and regional process launched in 1992. In addition to Moldova, BSEC includes Bulgaria, Georgia, **Romania**, Russia, Turkey, and Ukraine, as well as a number of nonriparian states in the region, including Albania, Azerbaijan, and Greece. Historically, Moldova is a riparian state to the maritime **Danube** and both historically and geopolitically a part of the western basin of the Black Sea. One of the main objectives of the BSEC, as spelled out in its 1992 Founding Declaration, is to turn the Black Sea basin into an area of regional stability, flourishing trade, and good-neighborliness. *See also* BORDERS OF MOLDOVA; GIURGIULESTI.

BLOC FOR A DEMOCRATIC AND PROSPEROUS MOLDOVA / BLOCUL PENTRU O MOLDOVA DEMOCRATICA SI PROSPERA (BMDP). A centrist alliance of social democratic orientation, the BMDP was set up by the Movement for a Democratic and Prosperous Moldova / Pentru a Moldovă Democratică şi Prosperă, led by **Dumitru Diacov**; the Civic Party of Moldova / Partidul Civic din Moldova, led by **Vladimir Solonari**; the Popular Democratic Party / Partidul Popular Democratic, led by Serghei Scripnic; the New Force Movement / Mişcarea Noii Forţe, led by Valeriu Pleşca; the National League of Moldova's Youth / Liga Naţională a Tineretului din Moldova, led by Valeriu Streleţ; and other groups. In the March 1998 parliamentary elections, it received 18 percent of the vote and 24 seats in Moldova's 101-member legislature. *See also* POLITICAL BLOCS AND PARTIES.

BODIUL, IVAN (1918–). Politician and **Communist Party** leader in the **Moldavian Soviet Socialist Republic (MSSR)**, Bodiul entered the pro-Soviet propaganda movement in 1937 and, after the post–World War II Soviet incorporation of **Bessarabia** into the Soviet Union, held various executive positions in the Communist Party hierarchy of the MSSR. He eventually rose to the top position of secretary-general of the Central Committee of Soviet Moldavia's Communist Party, a position previously held by **Leonid Brezhnev**. Bodiul was demoted in 1986 on charges of having departed from the party line.

BOGDAN I (?–1365). Wallachian nobleman from Cuhea, **Maramureş**, and a vassal to Louis I of Anjou, king of Hungary. Also known as Bogdan Vodă—"Bogdan Wayvoda Olachorum de Maramorosio" in Latin court documents—he quarrelled with the king, relinquished his lands and other properties in Maramureş, and crossed the Carpathians into the Moldova settlement to become its first independent prince upon throwing off Hungarian suzerainty (ca. 1359–1365). Though controversial in terms of its exact origin in Turkish, "Bogdan" was a term used by the **Ottoman Empire** to denote Moldova. "Bogdan Serai," for example, was the name of the official Moldova House in Istanbul (cf. Demetrius Cantemir's *History of the Growth and Decay of the Othman Empire* [London, 1734–1735], vol. 1, chapter 3, p. 1, n. 17). As late as 1812, the Turkish version of the landmark **Treaty of Bucharest** referred to the **Principality of Moldova** as "Bogdan."

BOGDAN VODA. *See* BOGDAN I.

BOLGRAD/BOLHRAD. District of southern **Bessarabia** returned to the **Principality of Moldova** by the **Congress of Paris** after the defeat of the **Russian Empire** in the Crimean War (1853–1856). The Bolgrad district became part of **Romania** after Moldova's union with **Wallachia** in 1859. It was detached from Romania and returned to Russia along with the two other districts of southern Bessarabia, **Cahul** and **Ismail**, in the wake of the Russo-Romanian-Turkish War of 1877–1878 (*see* RUSSO-TURKISH WARS). Its territory joined Romania as part of the **Moldavian Democratic Federated Republic** in 1918. It was taken back by the Soviet Union in 1940 and awarded to Soviet Ukraine, together with southern Bessarabia after World War II. The city of Bolgrad (Ukrainian: Bolhrad), formerly the capital of the *judeţ*, or district, of the same name, lies approximately 70 kilometers north of the **Chilia** arm of the **Danube River**.

BOLSHEVIK POWER. Defined by V. I. Lenin as the dictatorship of the proletariat or the rule "won and maintained by the use of violence by the proletariat against the bourgeoisie, a rule that is unrestricted by any laws." It was proclaimed by revolutionary Russian soldiery in the province of **Bessarabia** after the November 1917 victory of the Communist revolution in Petrograd. It tried to impose its authority over **Sfatul Ţării** and vied for control of the province by occupying the railway station of **Chişinău** on 1 January 1918 and gaining control of the city on 5 January 1918. The Bolsheviks were driven out of Chişinău on

13 January by one of the brigades of the Romanian army sent in from across the **Prut River** by rump **Romania** at the urgent request of Sfatul Ţării to restore order throughout the province. The Bolshevik battalions were forced east of the **Nistru River**, and Sfatul Ţării reconvened in Chişinău. Encouraged by events in neighboring Ukraine, Sfatul Ţării proclaimed Bessarabia an independent republic and renounced all ties with Russia, where the Bolsheviks had taken over and dissolved the Moscow Constituent Assembly on 19 January 1918.

In southern Ukraine, Bolshevik power proved resilient, as military leader Evghenii M. Venediktov regrouped the Communist forces on the east bank of the Nistru, where he formed the **Tiraspol** detachment, which subsequently began its retreat toward the Don River. Venediktov was killed by the **Cossacks** in May 1918, but with military backing from Moscow, Bolshevik power was soon installed in Ukraine, which, unlike Bessarabia in the interwar period, became a full-fledged Soviet republic in 1922. Bolshevik power returned to Moldova under **Joseph Stalin** at the time of Bessarabia's annexation by the **Union of Soviet Socialist Republics** under the secret terms of the **Molotov-Ribbentrop Pact** of 23 August 1939. *See also* COMMUNIST PARTY.

BORDERS OF MOLDOVA. Moldova's area of 33,700 square kilometers is enclosed in a 1,389-kilometer-long land boundary, out of which 681 kilometers mark its western border with **Romania** along the **Prut** River. A small part of the over 900 kilometers that separate Moldova from its eastern neighbor, Ukraine, runs along the northern and southern banks of the **Nistru River**. Prior to the 1812 partition of the **Principality of Moldova**, the province's historical borders, as described in the 1711 Moldo-Russian **Lutsk Treaty,** enclosed an area that extended eastward from the Carpathians all the way to the Nistru and southward all the way to the mouths of the **Danube River** and the Black Sea. The halved eastern lands annexed by the **Russian Empire** in 1812, called **Bessarabia**, constituted the territory of the short-lived **Moldavian Democratic Federated Republic**, established in 1917, which joined Romania in 1918.

It was that territory that was incorporated into the **Union of Soviet Socialist Republics (USSR)** in 1940 and the borders of which were subsequently altered by the Soviet Union in two ways: by slightly expanding their lines across the Nistru, into part of what had been, beginning in 1924, the **Moldavian Autonomous Soviet Socialist Republic**, and by shrinking them north and south so as to exclude **Hotin** and the lowland districts of Akkerman and **Ismail**, awarded by **Joseph Stalin** to

Soviet Ukraine. The surface resulting from these administrative amputations (roughly speaking, the surface area of the Republic of Moldova today) was 62.3 percent of Bessarabia's territory enfolded into the USSR in June 1940. In 1946, Nikolai Kovaly, chairman of the Soviet of Ministers of the **Moldavian Soviet Socialist Republic**, and N. Salagor, secretary of the Central Committee of the republic's **Communist Party**, sent Stalin a petition supported by a map, asking for the return of the southern districts with the Danube port cities of **Reni**, Ismail, and **Vâlcov** and of the Hotin district in the north. Their request was ignored in Moscow.

The administrative border between Soviet Moldova and Soviet Ukraine was drawn by Stalinist Russia with a number of flaws, one of which was the erratic meandering of the borderline in the **Bugeac** region cutting across the Odessa-**Bolgrad** railway, made to enter and exit Moldova and Ukraine at several junctions. For example, north of the estuary of the Nistru, the Palanca railway station was cut into two, with the boundary running along the middle of the preexisting railway, half of the rails belonging to Moldova and half to Ukraine. As of 1998, negotiations with Ukraine for correcting such aberrations were under way. An important correction was meant to include a several-hundred-meters rectification of Moldova's border with Ukraine south of **Giurgiuleşti**, expected to restore the country's access to the maritime Danube.

BOTNA RIVER. A tributary to the **Nistru River** in southeast Moldova, 152 kilometers in length.

BOTNARU, TUDOR (1935–). Minister of national security in the Moldovan governments of 1998 and 1999. A native of Lipceni, **Rezina**, Botnaru is a graduate of the Philological Institute of the **State University of Moldova**. Between 1963 and 1991, he served in different positions in the Committee on National Security of the **Union of Soviet Socialist Republics** and the **Moldavian Soviet Socialist Republic**. From 1990 to 1991, he was minister of national security of the Republic of Moldova and from March to December 1994, first deputy minister of foreign affairs. Botnaru also served for a short time as Moldova's ambassador to the United Kingdom, Belgium, Luxemburg, and the Netherlands (V. N.).

BRAGHIS, DUMITRU (1957–). Prime minister of Moldova's government formed in December 1999, Braghiş is a native of Grăţieşti, a suburb of **Chişinău**. He graduated from Chişinău Technical University in 1980, where he earned a degree in civil engineering. He held various functions in Moldova's Communist Youth Union beginning in 1981, and served as that organization's first secretary between 1988 and 1990. In 1989 he was elected member of the **Soviet Union**'s Supreme Soviet and, from 1990 until the 1991 downfall of the USSR, also served as secretary general of the Central Committee of the Soviet Union's Youth Union. After independence he held various positions in Moldova's Ministry of Economy and Reform, serving as director of the Department of External Economic Relations and deputy minister and first deputy minister of economy and reform in the **Ciubuc** and **Sturza** governments (V. N.).

BREZHNEV, LEONID (1906–1982). Soviet political leader and statesman. He was secretary-general of the Moldavian **Communist Party**'s Central Committee (1950–1952) at the height of the Stalinist campaign of **Russification**, when post–World War II **deportations** of Moldova's native population to other parts of the **Union of Soviet Socialist Republics (USSR)** continued. After wielding supreme political authority in **Chişinău**, Brezhnev was assigned a similar job over Soviet Kazakhstan (1955). Following his appointment as secretary-general of the Central Committee of the Soviet Union's Communist Party in 1966, Brezhnev's political ascent reached its climax in 1977, when he became head of state of the USSR, as president of the Supreme Soviet Presidium, a position he held until his death in 1982.

BRICENI. Chief city of the former *raion,* or district, of the same name, located 230 kilometers northwest of **Chişinău** on the Chişinău-**Cernăuţi** highway. The first documented mention of Briceni dates back to 1616. The city has a population of over 83,000 inhabitants (1993 est.). Briceni is part of the newly established *judeţ* of **Edineţ**.

BRUCHIS, MICHAEL (1919–). Historian, philologist, and expert in Moldova's **language issue**. A former member of the Moldavian Soviet Academy of Sciences and of the Communist Party History Institute in **Chişinău**, Bruchis is currently a senior researcher at Tel Aviv University in Israel, where he settled in 1974.

BUCHAREST, TREATY OF. The treaty that ended the 1806–1812 **Russo-Turkish War**, signed in Bucharest, the capital of **Wallachia**, on 28 May 1812. The defeated **Ottoman Empire** ceded half of the territory of the **Principality of Moldova**, then under its suzerainty, to the **Russian Empire**, which renamed it **Bessarabia**. It comprised the lands stretching east of the **Prut River** down to the principality's border on the **Nistru River**. According to some interpretations of international law, Ottoman Turkey lacked the right to cede a land it had never annexed or possessed and over which it had merely exerted suzerainty without ownership. Another province ceded to Russia by Ottoman Turkey under the terms of the Treaty of Bucharest of 1812 was western Georgia in the Caucasus. *See also* ANNEXATION; SOVEREIGNTY.

BUCOV, EMILIAN (1909–1984). Writer and left-wing political activist, Bucov made his literary debut in 1936 with *Clocotul muncii* (In the Heat of Labor), a volume of poems dedicated to workers. He asserted himself as a public personality mostly after 1944, when he became a strong advocate of Moldova's appurtenance to the Soviet Union. *Primăvara pe Nistru* (Spring on the Nistru, 1944) and *Țara mea* (My Homeland, 1947) express gratitude to Soviet Russia and praise the advent of communism. Beginning in 1966, he served as chief editor of the literary monthly *Nistru*.

BUCOVINA. Name given by the **Habsburg Empire** to the 10,441-square-kilometer territory detached from historical Moldova in the 18th century and forming the northeastern segment of the Moldo-Transylvanian Carpathians with the adjoining plain. Bucovina had no separate history of its own until the **Ottoman Empire** ceded it to Austria by the Act of Palmuta (7 May 1775). The new rulers transformed it into a Habsburg military district, first as a part of Galicia and later as a separate Austrian Crown land with Czernowitz (the Germanized form of **Cernăuți**) as its capital, which was to become the seat of its provincial Diet. A strategic link between **Transylvania** and Galicia, Austrian-held Bucovina joined **Romania** on 25 November 1918, when a congress of local Romanians, Germans, and Poles voted for the union of the whole province with Romania, in the wake of the collapse of the Austro-Hungarian Empire. A Ukrainian national committee representing Bucovina's Ukrainian minority had previously failed to implement the incorporation of the northern districts of the province into the short-lived West Ukrainian Democratic Republic, soon to be engulfed by Soviet Russia's Red Army, in January 1919.

On 28 June 1940, in addition to **Bessarabia**—stretching the terms of the Secret Additional Protocol of the **Molotov-Ribbentrop Pact** of 23 August 1939—the **Union of Soviet Socialist Republics** occupied all of

Northern Bucovina (5,489 square kilometers), incorporating a population of about half a million inhabitants, including 71 percent of the total Ukrainian ethnic minority living in the province before its **annexation**.

The region is the historic cradle of the **Principality of Moldova** and was the seat of its ancient chief city, **Suceava**, until the 16th century. Southern Bucovina, now a part of Romania, is the repository of some of the finest artifacts of Moldovan church architecture, including the Moldovița, Sucevița, Voroneț, Putna, and Dragormirna Monasteries erected by **Stephen the Great.**

BUGEAC/BUDJIAK. The name denotes historic Moldova's seaboard lying along the Black Sea, between the mouth of the northern **Nistru River** and the **Chilia** arm of the southern **Danube River**. The name "Bugeac" is of **Tatar** origin, meaning "nook" or "corner." It was applied to the coastal area of Moldova during its occupation by the roaming tribes of the Golden Horde, which controlled the area for part of its medieval history. The region was initially ruled by the **Basarab** dynasty of **Wallachia**, which accounts for its earliest name, Basarabia or **Bessarabia**, later extended by Russia to the whole of Moldova's eastern half at the time of its first incorporation into the **Russian Empire**.

The region's strategic and economic importance has played a part in the history of the Black Sea trade ever since antiquity, when its seashore was controlled by Greek merchants and seamen, who founded the port city of **Tyras** overlooking the mouth of the Nistru. Tyras and the surrounding area were later taken over by the Roman Empire, which established there the rough line of its northern boundary by building the earthworks that stretch to this day across the region parallel to the coastline, the southernmost segment of what is known as **Trajan's Wall**. The place was revived in the early Middle Ages by Genovese tradesmen and seamen, who renamed the old port city Moncastro (Maurocastron on Greek Byzantine maps). Later called **Cetatea Albă** (Romanian for the "white citadel" or "white city"), it was the see of Moldova's first metropolitan bishopric (1401). Cetatea Albă was renamed Akkerman by the Turks, who conquered the whole of Moldova's seashore in the 16th century. Bugeac's twin strongholds, Cetatea Albă and Chilia, were then turned into *sandjaks* (military districts) of the **Ottoman Empire**.

Bugeac became part of the Russian province of Bessarabia in 1812, and aggressive policies of **colonization** were performed by czarist authorities in the area. The Danubian districts of Bugeac were returned to the **Principality of Moldova** in 1859, then taken back by Russia in 1878. As part of Bessarabia, Bugeac joined **Romania** in 1918, only to be taken back yet again, this time by the **Union of Soviet Socialist Republics (USSR)** in 1940, together with the rest of the former czarist province lying between the **Prut River** and the Nistru. After World War II, the Bugeac districts were detached from Soviet Moldavia and attributed by the USSR to Soviet Ukraine.

In present-day Moldova, Bugeac is also the name of a small town in **Gagauz Yeri**. *See also* COLONIZATION/MIGRATION.

BUKOVINA. *See* BUCOVINA.

BULGARI, VALERIU (1956–). Deputy prime minister in the government of Moldova formed in 1997 and minister of agriculture and food processing in the governments formed in 1998 and 1999. A native of Larga, **Briceni**, Bulgari was chairman of the Direction of the Briceni Committee of the Communist Party of the **Moldavian Soviet Socialist Republic** from 1987 to 1988. From 1988 to 1994, he served as chairman of the Executive Committee of the Briceni district. In 1994, he was elected deputy in the Parliament of Moldova on the ticket of the **Democratic Agrarian Party of Moldova** and then served as deputy prime minister in **Andrei Sangheli**'s cabinet (V. N.).

BUSUIOC, AURELIU (1928–). Poet, novelist, and playwright, Busuioc was also the former editor in chief of *Tinerimea Moldovei,* a publication for Moldova's youth. His most recent book is the allegorical novel *Lătrând la Lună* (Barking at the Moon), published in 1997.

BUZDUGAN, ION (1887–1967). Writer, translator, and folklorist, Buzdugan is the author of several books of poems, including *Miresme de stepă* (Scents of the Steppe, 1922) and *Ţara mea* (My Country, 1928). He translated works by **Alexander Pushkin**, Mikhail Lermontov, Sergey Esenin, Anna Akhmatova, and other Russian authors, and he published a two-volume anthology of Bessarabian folk songs, *Cântece din Basarabia* (1921–1928).

BUZILA, SERAFIM (1931–). A composer and musician, Buzilă is the author of several symphonies and symphonic cantatas, including *Scrisorile* (The Letters), inspired by one of the masterpieces of **Mihai Eminescu**, and *Pământ natal* (Native Land).

-C-

CAHUL. Chief town and administrative center of the newly reestablished Cahul *judeţ* in southwestern Moldova, on the right bank of the **Prut River**, 174 kilometers south of **Chişinău**. The former *raion* of Cahul (Russian: Kagul) had a population of over 44,000 inhabitants (1993 est.). The town of Cahul was erected from scratch in 1838 by the Russian governor of **Bessarabia**, Pavel Feodorov, on the site of the neighboring village of Frumoasa. The name of the town was borrowed from Lake Cahul (90 square kilometers in surface area), lying south of the city, north of the **Chilia** arm of the **Danube** Delta. Greater Cahul, then bordering on the Danube, was one of the three districts of Bessarabia returned to the **Principality of Moldova** by the 1856 **Congress of Paris**. It joined **Romania** as a whole, as part of Moldova, at the time of the union of the **Danubian Principalities**. It was taken back by the **Russian Empire** after the Russo-Romanian-Turkish War of 1877–1878 (*see* RUSSO-TURKISH WARS) and returned to Romania during the 1918–1940 interwar period. The newly reestablished *judeţ* of Cahul includes the territorial unit of **Cantemir**.

CAINARI. Chief town of the former *raion,* or district, of the same name, in southern Moldova, first mentioned as a village in the 16th century. The former district of Căinari had a population of over 42,000 inhabitants (1993 est.). It is part of the reestablished *judeţ* of **Tighina**.

CALARASI. Chief town of the former Călăraşi *raion,* or district, located on the **Ungheni-Chişinău** railway, 49 kilometers northwest of Moldova's capital. The former district had over 84,000 inhabitants (1993 est.). After 1999, Călăraşi became part of the newly established *judeţ* of Ungheni.

CALLIMACHI. Family of local Moldovan noblemen (originally named Călmaşu) who ruled over the **Principality of Moldova** during the last stages of the **Phanariote era**. Ioan Theodor Callimachi ruled between 1758 and 1761. He passed on the throne to his son Grigore Callimachi, who reigned twice, 1761–1764 and 1767–1769, at a time of dramatic escalation of the **Russo-Turkish Wars**. His other son, Alexandru Callimachi, ruled the Principality of Moldova—by then a direct neighbor to the **Russian Empire**—between 1795 and 1799. The last ruler of the Callimachi dynasty was Scarlat Callimachi, who reigned briefly in 1806, at the outbreak of the 1806–1812 Russo-Turkish War; nominally between 1807 and 1810, under Russian occupation; and yet again between 1812 and 1819, after the Russian **annexation** of the eastern half of the principality under the terms of the **Treaty of Bucharest** of 1812. Scarlat Callimachi was the last ruling prince of Moldova in its traditional historic borders, with the principality straddling both banks of the **Prut River**. One of the accomplishments of Scarlat Callimachi's reign was the publication of Moldova's first civil code of laws ("Codul Callimachi"), inspired in great part by Austrian civil law.

CAMENCA. Chief town of the *raion,* or district, of the same name, 160 kilometers north of **Chişinău** and 35 kilometers northwest of **Râbniţa,** located on the east bank of the **Nistru River**. The town of Camenca is currently under the authority of the self-proclaimed **Moldavian Nistrian Republic**. The Camenca district, now straddling both banks of the river, was initially established by the **Union of Soviet Socialist Republics** as part of the **Moldavian Autonomous Soviet Socialist Republic,** carved out of Soviet Ukraine, east of the Nistru, in 1924. The Camenca district has a population of over 59,000 inhabitants (1993 est.).

CAN, ALEXANDRA (1952–). Minister of industry and commerce in Moldova's government of 1999, Can was the first woman to serve in independent Moldova as a cabinet member. Between 1990 and 1992, she served as chief accountant in Moldova's Ministry of Economy.

CANTACUZINO, IOAN (1757–1828). Diplomat, soldier, and writer, Cantacuzino was a member of the Mavrocordat family that ruled over Moldova during the **Phanariote era**. He was knighted by Russia's Empress **Catherine II** in recognition of his merits in the **Russo-Turkish War** of 1787–1792 and given land and property in Ukraine, where he founded the village of Cantacuzinca (or Kantakuzinka), on the right bank of the Bug River. Cantacuzino's chief contribution to the cultural history of Moldova is a book titled *Poezii Noo* (New Poems), published some time between 1792 and 1796, probably in **Dubăsari**. It contains Cantacuzino's own poems and a selection of poems in translation from the works of such important European poets as Alexander Pope, Jean de La Fontaine, Pietro Metastasio, Jean-François Marmontel, and Thomas Gray. *Poezii Noo* is credited as the first published book containing original poetry and poetry in translation in the **Romanian language**.

CANTAREAN, VLADIMIR (1952–). Orthodox archbishop of **Chişinău** and metropolitan of Moldova, Cantarean is a graduate of the Moscow Orthodox Theological Academy. He took the holy orders in 1974 and served as a deacon and priest in Smolensk, Russia, and in Chernovtsy. The Russian patriarchy then elevated Cantarean to the office of archbishop of Chişinău (1989) and metropolitan of "all Moldova" (1992). A native of Ukraine (born at Kolinkovtsy, formerly Colincăuţi), Cantarean is the head of Moldova's **Orthodox Church** that is canonically subject to the jurisdiction of Russia's patriarchy in Moscow. In 1992, a part of Moldova's Orthodox clergy—headed by pro-Romanian prelate **Petru Păduraru**, at that time bishop of **Bălţi**—challenged Cantarean's subordination to the Russian Orthodox Church and consequently put him and his subordinate clergy under the canonical jurisdiction of the Romanian Orthodox patriarch in Bucharest. Metropolitan Cantarean decried the move and warned against the danger of a war among Orthodox Christians and even a schism in the Orthodox Church of Moldova on the basis of generating a split between Romanian-speaking and Russian-speaking Orthodox believers, likely to lead to further divisions along ethnic and linguistic lines in the Republic of Moldova (V. N.).

CANTEMIR. Chief town of the former *raion*, or district, of the same name on the **Prut River**, north of **Cahul** in southern Moldova. The former district had a population of over 61,000 inhabitants (1993 est.) and used to be part of the former **Fălciu** *judeţ* that straddled both banks of the Prut before 1812. In keeping with the December 1998 law on the reorganization of Moldova's territory, Cantemir became a part of the reestablished *judeţ* of Cahul.

CANTEMIR, ANTIOCH (1708–1744). Son of **Demetrius Cantemir**, Prince Antioch Cantemir served as Russia's ambassador to London (1731) and Paris (1736). Antioch Cantemir is the first personality of Moldovan descent entirely educated in the Russian culture. He was a poet and the first author of satires in Russian literature.

CANTEMIR, CONSTANTIN (?–1693). Prince of Moldova between 1685 and 1693, Constantin Cantemir was born into a small landowning family of the ancient **Fălciu** *judeţ*. One of the boldest actions undertaken by Prince Constantin Cantemir—nominally a vassal of the **Ottoman Empire**—was the signing of the 15 February 1690 secret agreement with the **Habsburg Empire**, a move designed to free Moldova from Turkish suzerainty and bring it into the European sphere of influence. Concluded in Sibiu, a city in **Transylvania**, the treaty stipulated Cantemir's pledge to provide assistance to Emperor Leopold I at the time when the Habsburg armies would be ready to carry out their planned offensive against the Turks, east of the Carpathians. The secret alliance was supposed to go into effect as soon as the Austrian armies would reach either Brăila on the **Danube River** or the banks of the **Siret** River. The secret treaty of Sibiu was never enforced. A biography of Prince Constantin Cantemir—*Vita Constantini Cantemyrii, cognomento Senis, Moldaviae Principis* (1714–1716), was written by his son and successor to the throne, **Demetrius Cantemir**.

CANTEMIR, DEMETRIUS (1673–1723). During a very short reign (1710–1711), Prince Demetrius Cantemir's rule marked a watershed in the history of the **Principality of Moldova**. A scholar, historian, and politician, Cantemir attempted to turn his country's political allegiances away from the **Ottoman Empire** and, in a bold, albeit unsuccessful, move, orient it toward the rising power of Russia under **Peter the Great**, whose just-begun Europeanization process seemed rife with the promise of enlightenment and freedom. The son of Prince **Constantin Cantemir,** Demetrius Cantemir was born in **Iaşi** and educated in the cosmopolitan environment of Constantinople (1688–1691), where he assimilated a solid cultural foundation in Oriental, Turkish, and European studies. As a young courtier and soldier, he took part in the battle of Zenta (1697) and witnessed Ottoman Turkey's defeat by the Austrians, a prelude to what was soon to be the final decline of the Ottoman Empire.

The most important political action of his short reign was the **Lutsk Treaty**, a secret alliance with Russia's Peter the Great concluded in the city of the same name in April 1711. In exchange for Russia's pledge to guarantee the principality's old borders, down to the estuary of the **Nistru**, the **Danube River**'s northern mouth, and the Black Sea, and its independence under a Cantemir hereditary monarchy, Demetrius Cantemir agreed to side with Russia's czar against the Turkish sultan. After their personal meeting in Iaşi (June 1711), Peter the Great and Demetrius Cantemir joined forces against the Turks, but the Russian and Moldovan armies were severely defeated at the battle of Stănileşti on the **Prut River**. Cantemir fled to Russia with his family and servants, where Peter the Great gratified him with land and a title of nobility. Until his death, Prince Cantemir was the czar's private adviser, dedicating himself to scholarship and writing and asserting himself as one of the most learned men of his century.

In 1714, Cantemir was elected a member of the Berlin Academy. His best-known work is his *History of the Growth and Decay of the Othman Empire* (published in London, 1734–1735), written originally in Latin, as was his *Descriptio Moldaviae* (1714–1716), the first geographical, ethnographical, and economic description of his native land, composed at the request of the Berlin Academy, and his *Historia Moldo-Vlachica* (1717). Cantemir's roman à clef, *Istoria Ieroglifică* (A Hieroglyphic Story), written in Constantinople (1703–1705), is the first novel composed in the **Romanian language**. His *Divanul* (a bilingual work, in Romanian and Greek), published in Iaşi in 1698, is the first piece of philosophical disputation in the history of Moldo-Romanian culture.

The mortal remains of Demetrius Cantemir were returned by Soviet Russia's government to **Romania** in 1935. They were reinterred in the prince's native city and former capital, Iaşi, in the Three Hierarchs Church. A bronze statue of Prince Demetrius Cantemir graces the alley devoted to Moldova's classic writers in **Chişinău**'s Central Park.

CAPCELEA, ARCADIE (1956–). Minister of the environment, a new ministry in Moldova's governmental structure, established in the wake of the 1998 elections. A native of Izvoare, **Floreşti**, Capcelea is a member of the **Democratic Convention of Moldova**. He holds a Ph.D. in geography from the Moscow Lomonosov State University and is the author of several scientific works, including a monograph in which he describes Moldova's natural environment and its interaction with the economy (V. N.).

CAPRIANA MONASTERY. One of medieval Moldova's oldest monasteries, founded around 1429 by **Alexander the Good** and restored by **Petru Rareş** in 1547. One of its abbots, Eftimie, who died at Căpriana in 1558, authored a chronicle of Moldova's history between 1541 and 1554 that covers part of the events of the reign of **Alexandru Lăpuşneanu**. The monastery was restored again in 1820 by Bishop **Gavril Bănulescu-Bodoni**. The Căpriana complex, which includes three historic churches, currently houses a newly established theology school and a seminary. *See also* ORTHODOX CHURCH.

CARAMAN, ALEKSANDR (1956–). Vice president of the self-proclaimed **Moldavian Nistrian Republic (MNR)** and one of the leaders of the **Tiraspol** government. Born in **Slobozia**, he graduated from the Chişinău Medical Institute and practiced medicine in Moldova's capital and in Tiraspol between 1980 and 1982. His political career began in

1990, when he was elected in the district of Slobozia and, soon after, in the Supreme Soviet of the breakaway political entity. He is considered one of the chief theoreticians promoting the idea of the MNR as a separate state and the ideologist of the **federalization** of the Republic of Moldova (V. N.).

CAROL I (1839–1914). Between 1866 and 1881, *domnitor,* or reigning prince, of **Romania**, proclaimed king in 1881. In the opening years of his reign, southern **Bessarabia** was part of Romania. Carol I gained huge popularity during the Russo-Romanian-Turkish War of 1877–1878 (*see* RUSSO-TURKISH WARS), when the Romanian and Russian troops under his command crushed the enemy's resistance at the key battle of Plevna in August 1877. After the defeat of the **Ottoman Empire**, Carol I secured international recognition for Romania's complete independence, which the Parliament of the country had single-handedly proclaimed on 9 May 1877. However, under the provisions of the 1878 Treaty of Berlin, southern Bessarabia, comprising the districts of **Bolgrad, Cahul,** and **Ismail**, was reincorporated by the **Russian Empire**, which restored the provisions of the 1812 **Treaty of Bucharest** that had made it part of Russia until 1856, alongside the rest of Bessarabia. Carol I strongly opposed the reannexation of southern Bessarabia, which he considered an infringement on Russia's promise to respect Romania's territorial integrity, as the two nations went together to war against the Ottoman Empire as allies in 1877.

CAROL II (1893–1953). King of **Romania** from 1930 to 1940. Under his reign, an administrative reform restored **Bessarabia**'s territorial units in a way similar to the traditional pre-1812 configuration, in the form of four *ţinuturi* stretching longitudinally from the Carpathians to the **Nistru River**. These territorial units comprised smaller districts, or *judeţe,* straddling both banks of the Prut River. Except for the northernmost territorial division, named **Suceava** after Moldova's former capital, the administrative units created by Carol II bore the names of Moldova's traditional waterways, namely **Prut**, Nistru, and Lower **Danube** ("Dunărea de Jos" in Romanian).

Under pressure from Nazi Germany, Carol II bowed to the Soviet ultimatum of midnight, 26 June 1940, and two days later, after a dramatic session of the Crown Council, Romania surrendered Bessarabia and **Northern Bucovina** to the **Union of Soviet Socialist Republics**, a renunciation that heavily damaged Carol's prestige and precipitated his loss of authority and his subsequent forced abdication on 6 September 1940, when the supreme powers of the state were taken over, under military rule, by General (later Marshal) **Ion Antonescu**.

CASIAN, ION (1950–). Minister of telecommunications and informatics in Moldova's government formed in 1997, Casian is a graduate of the Chişinău Polytechnic Institute and a doctor of technical sciences. His professional career includes various managerial positions in Moldova's technical industries. From 1988 to 1992, he served as director of the Chişinău Computers Factory. He was first appointed minister of telecommunications in 1992 (V. N.).

CASSO, LEV (1865–1914). Bessarabian jurist and politician, Lev Aristidovici Casso served as Russia's minister of education between 1910 and 1914. A native of **Soroca**, he received his education in France and Germany. Casso authored a number of books, including a study on Byzantine law and its relevance to the legal traditions of the province of **Bessarabia**, published in 1907, and an account of Russia's advances toward the **Danube River**, highlighting the specific identity of Bessarabia within the czars' empire, published in 1913.

CATANA, VICTOR (1949–). Minister of internal affairs in the Moldovan governments of 1998 and 1999. A native of Druţa, **Răşcani**, General Catană is a graduate of the Kiev Superior School of Internal Affairs in Ukraine. Between 1992 and 1997, he served as assistant deputy minister in Moldova's Ministry of Internal Affairs and as a member of the Unified Control Commission, established to oversee the cease-fire in the wake of the 1992 **trans-Nistrian conflict**. Prior to his nomination as minister of internal affairs, General Catană served as deputy minister of justice in the previous cabinet (V. N.).

CATHERINE II / CATHERINE THE GREAT (1729–1796). Empress of Russia from 1762 to 1796. Her foreign policy was aimed at the expansion of the **Russian Empire**, the armies of which waged two successful wars against the **Ottoman Empire** in 1768–1774 and 1787–1792. The **Treaty of Iaşi** brought her empire's border to the **Nistru River** and made the **Principality of Moldova** for the first time a neighbor of Russia. Catherine the Great's anti-Ottoman **Greek Project**, which she proposed to the **Habsburg Empire** in 1782, included the design of a reconstituted **Dacia**, with Moldova and **Wallachia** forming a unified buffer state from the Nistru and the Carpathians down to the **Danube River**. A restored Greek Empire was to serve as a buffer against Turkey south of the Danube.

CAUSENI. Chief town of the newly reestablished **Tighina** *judeţ* on the **Botna River**, 88 kilometers southeast of **Chişinău**. Căuşeni fell under Turkish occupation in 1538. In 1806, it was conquered by the Russians, who used it as an outpost of Tighina (or Bender), on the **Nistru River**. The Soviet-era district had a population of over 73,000 inhabitants (1993 est.). Căuşeni is the birthplace of one of Moldova's national poets, **Alexie Mateevici**. A point of touristic attraction in Căuşeni is the Dormition of the Virgin Church, erected in the 17th century.

CEBOTARI, MARIA (1910–1949). Moldova's most famous and internationally recognized opera singer, born in **Chişinău** and educated at the Conservatory of her native city and at Berlin's Superior School of Music (1924–1929). Her naturally golden voice developed a quality that won highest acclaim in opera performances in the musical capitals of Europe: Dresden, Berlin, Vienna, London, Bruxelles, Milan, and Paris. She excelled as the main soloist in several operas by Verdi, Mozart, and Gounod. Having settled in Germany after her debut in 1931, she was vilified as a nonperson during the Soviet era for her operatic appearances during the Nazi era, although her profile as a soprano was entirely nonpolitical. Cebotari died in Vienna in 1949. A street in downtown Chişinău is named for her.

CEIBAS, VICTOR (1950–). Minister of transport and communication in Moldova's government of 1999. A native of Satu Nou, **Reni** (Ukraine), Ceibas is a graduate of the Chişinău Polytechnic Institute. He studied at the Cybernetics Institute of Kiev (1979–1984) and served as director of the **Chişinău** joint-stock company Informinstrument Center (1992–1999).

CERNAUTI. A city lying on the right bank of the **Prut River**, first mentioned in 1408, under the reign of **Alexander the Good**, as a customs checkpoint on Moldova's northern border. It became part of the **Habsburg Empire** in 1775, when northern Moldova was incorporated into Austria's possessions under the name of **Bucovina**. Renamed Czernowitz, the town developed rapidly into a flourishing city and an outpost of German culture in the eastern reaches of the Habsburg Empire. Its university, opened in 1875, played an important role in turning the city into a regional center of learning, with lasting impact on building a German, Romanian, Ukrainian, and Jewish cultural melting pot and a pole of attraction to many of Moldova's intellectuals. Cernăuţi became part of **Romania** after World War I, when Bucovina joined the other Romanian provinces in 1918. As a part of **Northern Bucovina**, together with **Bessarabia**, it was incorporated into the **Union of Soviet Socialist Republics (USSR)** in 1940. It was recaptured during World War II by Romania, then taken back by the USSR in 1944, which made it a part of Soviet Ukraine, and renamed Chernovtsy. Moldova's national poet, **Mihai Eminescu**, spent some of his early years in Cernăuţi, where his intellectual formation first took shape and where he made his literary debut (1866). Cernăuţi is also the birthplace of the well-known German-Jewish poet Paul Celan (1920–1970).

CERNOMAZ, NICOLAE (1949–). Minister of state in the governments formed in 1997, 1998, and 1999. A native of Ţiganca, **Cantemir**, Cernomaz is a graduate of the **State University of Moldova** and Moscow's Lomonosov State University. From 1973 to 1976, he served as instructor in the Youth Organization of the **Moldavian Soviet Socialist Republic (MSSR)**. Between 1979 and 1982, he was senior professor at the State University of Moldova and served as adviser to the Soviet of Ministers of the MSSR. Cernomaz also served as faculty chairman at the Ion Creangă Pedagogical Institute in **Chişinău** from 1982 to 1990. From 1990 to the time of his appointment to Moldova's government, he headed Moldova's national tourism company, Moldova Tour (V. N.).

CETATEA ALBA. Historic seaport of medieval Moldova, on the right bank of the **Nistru** estuary, about 19 kilometers from the Black Sea. First mentioned in antiquity as **Tyras** and later in the early medieval epoch as Maurocastron, it was surrendered by Moldova to the **Ottoman Empire** in 1484 and thereafter renamed Akkerman by the Turks. The Russians conquered it several times during the 18th century while preserving its Turkish name. In the 14th century, Cetatea Albă was the see of Bishop Iosif I, first metropolitan of Moldova (1391). **Stephen the Great** rebuilt its citadel, which, after the fall of Byzantium, played a strategic role in defending Moldova against 15th-century Ottoman fleet inroads. In 1770, 1774, and 1806, the armies of the **Russian Empire** captured it but each time returned it to the Turks. It became Russian in 1812, when the czarist empire annexed **Bessarabia**, and was incorporated in **Romania** in 1918. It was then incorporated into the Soviet Union in 1940 and has been part of Ukraine ever since. The current Ukrainian name of the city—Bilhorod Dnistrovsky—reflects the historical name of Cetatea Albă (Romanian for "white city").

CHERNOVTSY. *See* CERNAUTI.

CHILIA. Port city and trade center on the left bank of the **Danube River** in historical **Bessarabia**, Moldova's southern seaboard. A Byzantine foundation, Chilia's first known attestation dates back to the beginning of the 14th century. In 1479, **Stephen the Great** built a fortress to defend it against the Turks, who eventually conquered it in 1484. Initially named Chilia Nouă (New Chilia), in order to distinguish it from an older port of the same name on the right bank of the river (Chilia Veche), it came under Russian control with the 1812 **annexation** of Bessarabia, but it was returned to the **Principality of Moldova** in 1856 as part of the district of **Ismail**, in the aftermath of the defeat of the **Russian Empire** in the Crimean War. It became part of the **United Principalities**, later **Romania**, between 1859 and 1878 and was ceded again to Russia in the wake of the 1877–1878 Russo-Romanian-Turkish War. Chilia was returned to Romania after World War I, it was annexed by the **Union of Soviet Socialist Republics** at the outbreak of Word War II, and it finally became part of Soviet Ukraine, which renamed it Kilija.

Chilia is also the historic name of the northern arm of the Danube Delta.

CHINN, JEFF (1946–). American specialist in post-Soviet and Moldovan studies, political science professor at the University of Missouri, Columbia. Chinn is a graduate of the University of Wisconsin, where he took his Ph.D. in 1975. He is also the author of the studies *Russians As the New Minority: Ethnicity and Nationalism in the Soviet Successor States* (1996) and "Ethnic Mobilization and Reactive Nationalism: The Case of Moldova" (1995), both of them relevant analyses of ethnicity and nationalism in the post-Soviet context.

CHIRTOACA, NICOLAE (1953–). Director of Moldova's Euro-Atlantic Center and of the **Invisible College of Moldova**. A native of **Glodeni, Bălţi**, Nicolae Chirtoacă is a graduate of the Moscow Military Institute (1977–1980) and the NATO Fellowship Democratic Institution (1994–1980). From 1980 to 1990 he served in the Soviet military, where he rose to the rank of lieutenant colonel. After Moldova's **declaration of independence**, he served as general director of the government's Department for Military Affairs (1990–1992) and chief state counselor to Moldova's president (1992–1994) (V. N.).

CHISINAU (CITY). Capital of the Republic of Moldova, located on the banks of the **Bâc River** and the surrounding hills, about 85 meters above the river. Chişinău was first mentioned as a small village in a court document dated 17 July 1436. Together with its surrounding lands, it became the property of the St. Vineri Monastery of **Iaşi** in 1641. Again mentioned as a small town in 1666, Chişinău had 7,000 inhabitants in 1812, at the time of the first Russian **annexation** of **Bessarabia**. It grew rapidly after 1818, when Czar **Alexander I** designated it to become, under the Russified name of Kishinev, the capital of the newly established **oblast**, or province, of Bessarabia. The city's older architecture owes part of its distinct touch to **Aleksandr Bernardazzi**, Chişinău's chief architect between 1856 and 1878. A notable **pogrom**, the **Easter Massacre** was perpetrated against the city's **Jews** in 1903.

It was in Chişinău that, in the wake of the collapse of the **Russian Empire**—within the framework of the Russian Soviet Federated Socialist Republic—the **Moldavian Democratic Federated Republic** was proclaimed in December 1917; and it was in Chişinău too that **Sfatul Ţării** proclaimed the republic's independence in February 1918, its conditioned union with **Romania** in March 1918, and its unconditioned union with Greater Romania in November 1918. In August 1940, in the aftermath of the Soviet annexation of Bessarabia, the Supreme Soviet of the **Union of Soviet Socialist Republics (USSR)** passed the law on the formation of the **Moldavian Soviet Socialist Republic**, with Chişinău (renamed once again Kishinev) as its capital. Following the demise of the USSR, the Republic of Moldova was proclaimed a sovereign state in Chişinău, on 27 August 1991.

Chişinău is divided into five administrative boroughs—Centru, Botanica, Buiucani, Râşcani, and Ciocana—with a total population of over 700,000 inhabitants. Chişinău is Moldova's chief center of **industry**, business, and **trade**.

Over a dozen nations, including China, Romania, the **Russian Federation**, Turkey, and the United States, have embassies in Chişinău. Great Britain's and Spain's ambassadors to Chişinău reside in Bucharest.

CHISINAU (DISTRICT). Separate from the city of **Chişinău**, which has the status of an administrative district of its own, this reestablished *judeţ* comprises 154 towns and villages, belonging to the former smaller districts of **Anenii Noi**, **Criuleni**, **Ialoveni**, and **Strășeni**, with Ialoveni as its administrative center.

CHITAN, VALERIU (1955–). Minister of finance in Moldova's governments of 1994 and 1997, Chițan is a graduate of the Chișinău Polytechnic Institute. From 1976 to 1987, he worked with the Executive Council of the former district of **Dondușeni**. Between 1987 and 1994, he held various executive positions in Moldova's Ministry of Finance.

CHITCANI MONASTERY. Monastery on the west bank of the **Nistru River**, southeast of **Tighina**, near the confluence with the **Botna River**. Built in 1864 on land donated in perpetuity to the Neamț Monastery by Prince **Alexander the Good** in 1429, it is also known as the Monastery of Noul Neamț (New Neamț). The initial Noul Neamț–Chițcani donation was renewed and extended by **Stephen the Great** in 1463 and 1500, by **Petru Rareș** in 1546, and by **Aron Vodă** in 1581. The four churches of the complex were built between 1865 and 1905 while the place was under Russian czarist rule. Under Soviet rule, the Chițcani Monastery was converted into a museum dedicated to Soviet military glory. The monastery's 55-meter-high tower, which overlooks the Nistru, is one of its chief attractions. As a monastic establishment belonging to the metropolitanate of Moldova, Chițcani is ultimately subject to the Russian Orthodox Church and suffers its strong cultural influence. The Chițcani–Noul Neamț complex also includes a theological seminary. *See also* ORTHODOX CHURCH.

CHRISTIAN DEMOCRAT POPULAR FRONT / FRONTUL POPULAR CRESTIN DEMOCRAT (FPCD). One of Moldova's main political movements, it grew out of the broad-based **Popular Front of Moldova / Frontul Popular din Moldova (FPM)**, established in 1989 while the country was still a part of the Soviet Union. The FPM contributed decisively to the move toward independence in the wake of the policies of **glasnost**. It started to break up in 1990 and renamed itself the Christian Democrat Popular Front in February 1992, when it became a right-wing separate and independent political formation, in the same league with Western Europe's Christian Democrat parties. Moldova's FPCD is a member of the European Christian Democrat Union. Its policies advocate European integration, gradual disentanglement from the **Commonwealth of Independent States**, and the shedding of ties binding Moldova's economic future to that of the **Russian Federation**. The FPCD asserted itself as the main force in the bloc of the **Democratic**

Convention of Moldova, from which it withdrew in 1999 over disagreements about the representation of its members in the formation of the government headed by Prime Minister **Ion Sturza**.

CIADAR-LUNGA. Chief town of the territorial unit of the same name, 130 kilometers south of **Chişinău**, on the Lunga River, in the autonomous territorial unit of **Gagauz Yeri** (Romanian: Gagauzia). Ciadâr-Lunga was founded by **Gagauz** settlers from Bulgaria invited by czarist Russia in the newly acquired province of **Bessarabia** after the **Treaty of Bucharest** of 1812, when eastern Moldova escaped Turkish suzerainty and became part of the **Russian Empire**. The district of Ciadâr-Lunga has a population of over 68,000 (1993 est.), mostly ethnic Gagauzi.

CIMISLIA. Chief town of the former *raion*, or district, of the same name, 75 kilometers south of **Chişinău**, first mentioned as a village in the 17th century. The former Cimişlia district, with a population of over 61,000 inhabitants (1993 est.), was formed in 1940 as part of the Soviet reorganization of the territory of the then newly established **Moldavian Soviet Socialist Republic**. Cimişlia is part of the new *judeţ* of **Lăpuşna**.

CIMPOI, MIHAI (1942–). A writer and literary critic, Cimpoi is a member of Moldova's Academy of Sciences and the president of the Moldovan Writers Union. He took an active part in reasserting the cultural and linguistic rights of the people of Moldova, a movement begun in the late 1980s that has continued in full swing since then. Cimpoi is the author of one of the most comprehensive surveys of Moldova's literature, both ancient and modern: *O istorie deschisă a literaturii române din Basarabia* (An Open History of Romanian Literature in Bessarabia), published in 1997.

CIOBANU, CESLAV (1952–). Politician and diplomat, former minister of privatization and state property administration in Moldova's government (1994–1997). He was credited for the successful **privatization** of 2,225 state enterprises during that interval. Ceslav Ciobanu's aggressive views on accelerating privatization clashed with the more conservative stand of the then ruling **Democratic Agrarian Party of Moldova**. Between 1992 and 1994, he served as deputy director of the Office of the President of Moldova. After 1997, he was appointed deputy minister of foreign affairs in Moldova's government. A graduate of Moscow's Lomonosov State University's Institute of Economics and of the University of Cairo (Egypt), Ciobanu held teaching positions at the Chişinău State University (1978–1986) and, from 1980 to 1986, at the Central Committee of the Communist Party of the **Moldavian Soviet Socialist Republic**. Earlier in his career, from 1987 to 1991, Ciobanu was a member of the Department of International Relations of the Communist Party of the **Union of the Soviet Socialist Republics**. Between 1991 and 1992, he served as senior professor at the Moscow Academy of Oil and Gas. In 1999, Ciobanu became Moldova's ambassador to Washington, D.C. (V. N.).

CIOBANU, GHENADIE (1957–). Minister of culture in Moldova's governments formed in 1997, 1998, and 1999. A native of Brătuşeni, **Edineţ**, Ciobanu is by training a composer, pianist, and musicologist. He studied music and composition at the Chişinău Eugen Coca Music College and the Moscow Music Institute. A graduate of the Gavril Musicescu Conservatory in **Chişinău** and of the European Academy of Musical Theater in Germany, Ciobanu is also the chairman of Moldova's Composers Union (V. N.).

CIS. *See* COMMONWEALTH OF INDEPENDENT STATES.

CIUBUC, ION (1943–). Former prime minister of the 1997 and 1998 governments of Moldova. A native of Hădărăuţi, **Ocniţa**, in northern Moldova, Ciubuc holds a Ph.D. in economics from the Odessa Agricultural Institute. From 1984 to 1986, while Moldova was still part of the **Union of Soviet Socialist Republics (USSR)**, he served as deputy chairman of the State Planning Committee of the **Moldavian Soviet Socialist Republic**. From 1990 to 1991, he was assistant deputy minister in Moldova's Ministry of Economy and, from March 1991 to September 1992, deputy prime minister of independent Moldova's first government. Until the dissolution of the USSR, he also served as Moldova's permanent representative to the Council of Ministers of the Soviet Union. Ciubuc was then appointed assistant deputy minister of Moldova's Ministry of Foreign Affairs (1992–1994), and from December 1994 until the time he became prime minister in 1997, he chaired Moldova's Court of Accounts (V. N.).

COCA, EUGEN (1893–1954). Composer and violinist, Coca wrote two symphonies and two symphonic poems. One of his masterpieces is the opera *Pasărea Măiastră,* based on the folk legend of Măiastra, the central character of which is a magic bird. The Măiastra motif has become known worldwide thanks to Romanian sculptor Constantin Brancusi, who gave it expression in bronze and marble. The Chişinău Music College is named after Eugen Coca.

CODRU. Traditional toponym (plural: Codri) denoting a woodland, as well as the name of an ancient district in central Moldova stretching around the basin of the **Bâc River**, which rises from the country's topmost elevation, Mount Bălăneşti (430 meters). The region was also named Codrul Bâcului because of its landscape dominated by thick forests (Romanian *codru* means "forest"). The Codru inhabitants (*Codreni*) were renowned for their warlike qualities and formed the core of the elite units of Moldova's army during the times of the **Tatar** and Ottoman invasions.

In present-day Moldova, Codru is the name of a small town south of **Chişinău**, and Codri is the name of a natural region northwest of the capital, about 500,000 hectares in area. A small remnant patch of the old forest, it stretches across a picturesque region halfway between the **Prut River** and the Bâc. Some 2,700 hectares of the region have the status of a national park and form one of Moldova's main tourist attractions.

COGALNIC/KOGALNIC RIVER. This 183-kilometer-long river, of which 125 kilometers are contained inside Moldova, rises from the hills of the **Codri** region west of **Chişinău** and flows through **Hânceşti**, **Cimişlia**, and **Basarabeasca**, before crossing into the **Bugeac** lowlands, where it flows sluggishly through southern Ukraine into the Sasâk lagoon, near **Tatarbunar**.

COLLECTIVIZATION. A Soviet policy applied to Moldova's farmers and landowners who were forcibly expropriated by the authorities of the **Union of Soviet Socialist Republics** in order to create what was being advocated as the Leninist basis of socialist **agriculture**. Coupled with **deportations** of resisting landowners, kolkhozes, or collective farms, were first organized in November–December 1940, in the immediate aftermath of the Soviet **annexation** of **Bessarabia**. The process was interrupted during World War II and resumed full swing after 1946. In Soviet Moldova, as in all other Soviet republics, the kolkhoz was by law the joint property of its owners, each of them being nominally entitled to a share of its profits. However, the collective owners of each kolkhoz did not have the right to sell it or to trade their produce to anyone other than the Soviet state, which determined the conditions of sale unilaterally. Most of today's woes in Moldova's agriculture sector appear to stem from the former Soviet Union's policies of forced collectivization.

COLONIZATION/MIGRATION. A component of the **Russification** process, begun soon after the 1812 incorporation of **Bessarabia** into the **Russian Empire**. At its earliest stage, czarist colonization included a motley influx of foreign-born populations invited to settle mostly in the areas of southern Bessarabia, or the **Bugeac** region, where the retreat of the Turkish military occupation had temporarily left wide stretches of uninhabited land. In addition to the **Gagauz**, thousands of Bulgarian, German, and Swiss colonists were settled and given privileges by Russia in rural areas in Bessarabia's southern lowlands, where a multiethnic quilt gradually took shape during the 19th century, between 1814 (when the first German colonists established the village of Tarutino) and 1861 (when one of the last groups of Bulgarians settled at Calceva and Caraclia).

On the other hand, by order of Czar **Nicholas I** beginning in 1826, over 20,000 Russian and Ukrainian peasants were moved from inner Russia's districts of Chernigov, Poltava, Oriol, Kursk, Kaluga, Tula, and Riazan to various other areas of rural Bessarabia. Russian policies also attracted massive groups of Russian, Ukrainian, and Jewish immigrants to Bessarabia's towns and cities, a process that dramatically changed the demographic balance of the province. Whereas in 1817 local natives accounted for over 86 percent of the total population of Bessarabia, the 1862 Russian census recorded only 51.4 percent of the population in the province as local "Moldavians."

Resumed on a larger and more complex scale after Bessarabia's 1940 **annexation** by the **Union of Soviet Socialist Republics**, colonization assumed the administrative form of internal migration. The process included fresh waves of incoming white-collar Russians and Ukrainians, coupled with successive removals of tens of thousands of the local population, sent to settle and work in the Astrakhan and Rostov regions of Russia, Kazakhstan, Uzbekistan, and other distant places, including the Urals and Soviet Russia's Far East.

Post–World War II movements of population, as shown by Soviet census figures, indicate that of the migrants having settled in Moldova's cities between 1959 and 1979, 46 percent came from the Russian Soviet Federated Socialist Republic and 36 percent from Soviet Ukraine.

Demographic figures that include the natural growth factor indicate that Moldova's Ukrainian group (currently 13.8 percent of Moldova's population, out of which about 67 percent are natives of Moldova) grew from 421,000 in 1959, to over 561,000 in 1979, and to approximately 600,000 in 1989, whereas the Russian group (currently 13 percent of Moldova's population, out of which about 64 percent are natives of Moldova) grew from 292,900 in 1959, to 414,400 in 1970, to 505,700 in 1979, and to over 560,000 in 1989, with highest concentrations for both groups typically present in Moldova's cities. Subtracting the natural growth factor, census figures for the 1959–1969 decade show that during that period alone, about 165,000 Russians and Ukrainians settled in Moldova. In terms of urban population growth boosted by in-migration, the Russian population of **Chişinău** grew from 69,600 to 149,700 between 1959 and 1979, and that of **Tiraspol**, Moldova's second largest city, from 26,900 to over 60,000 in the same period of time. *See also* DEPORTATIONS; RUSSIAN ETHNICS; UKRAINIAN ETHNICS.

COMMONWEALTH OF INDEPENDENT STATES (CIS). A loose confederation of former Soviet republics, also known as the Newly Independent States, in which a number of coordinating bodies oversee common interests of its members in the areas of the economy, foreign policy, and defense. Russian foreign policy pronouncements about the role of Moscow in the CIS have tended to present the **Russian Federation** as being the first among equals, with a determination to protect the rights of **Russian ethnics** in the CIS. In 1998, this was described by CIS Executive Secretary Boris Berezovski as a "Big Brother mentality." The founding act of the CIS was the 8 December 1991 Minsk Agreement, signed by Belarus, Russia, and Ukraine. On 21 December 1991—with the exception of Georgia and the Baltic states—the successor states of the **Union of Soviet Socialist Republics (USSR)** signed the Alma Ata Declaration, virtually extending CIS membership status to all republics that had formerly been part of the USSR. Four former Soviet republics— Russia, Belarus, Kazakhstan, and Kyrgyzstan—form the CIS Inter-State Council. The Republic of Moldova declined to join the political and military structures of the CIS but adhered to its commercial and economic structures. Moldova signed the CIS charter on economic union in 1994. According to an index based on the CIS countries' gross domestic product, the economies of all 12 member countries declined from 1989 to 1996. At a CIS heads-of-state meeting held in **Chişinău** in 1997, Russia was harshly criticized by Moldova for its approach to the unresolved conflict with the **Tiraspol** separatists. In 1999, Moldova threatened to leave the CIS Interparliamentary Assembly because of Russia's Duma stance on holding a debate on recognizing the separatist region on the

east bank of the **Nistru River** as an independent state. *See also* MOL-
DAVIAN NISTRIAN REPUBLIC; SEPARATISM.

COMMUNIST ATHEISM. Official doctrine of the Soviet regime, also
called "scientific atheism." It was aggressively applied to Moldova
throughout the decades of Soviet regime, more especially in the 1960s
and after, in keeping with directives given from Moscow. In **Chişinău**,
most churches were either pulled down or turned into facilities designed to serve secular or even profane purposes. The St. Theodora
Church in downtown Chişinău was turned into the city's Museum of
Scientific Atheism, the St. Pantelimon Church was turned into a facility for wine-tasting and liquor-tasting events, the St. Nicholas Church
was turned into the Cultural Hall of the Medical University, the St.
Haralambie Church was used as a theater hall, the Mother of God
Church was used as the headquarters of Soviet Moldova's addresses
center, and the Transfiguration Cathedral (previously dedicated to St.
Constantine and Helena) housed the city's planetarium. Indeed, only
four churches in Chişinău were allowed to function during the last
decades of the Soviet era. Out of about 900 churches existing across
Moldova in 1944, almost 200 were closed down or turned into work-
ers' clubs or movie theaters, while the Communist authorities took aggressive steps to eradicate religion, in keeping with the Marxist-
Leninist tenet, "Religion is the opiate of the masses." *See also*
RELIGIOUS DENOMINATIONS.

COMMUNIST PARTY. The history of Moldova's Communists as an or-
ganization began in 1924, when the Communist Bolshevik Party of the
Union of Soviet Socialist Republics (USSR) established its first action
unit, the Moldavia Regional Organization of the Ukraine Communist
Party, a small offshoot of Ukraine's Communist Bolshevik Party, with
the mission to run the policies of the then newly founded **Moldavian
Autonomous Soviet Socialist Republic**, on the east bank of the **Nistru
River**. Until the 1940 Soviet **annexation** of **Bessarabia**, the Moldavian
Communist Party had the subordinate status of a regional organization
within the structure of the Ukrainian Communist Bolshevik Party.

Its status was changed from that of a "regional organization" into a
full-fledged political party on 14 August 1940, when the Communist
Party of the Bolsheviks of Moldavia was formally established by a decree of the Central Committee of the Communist Bolshevik Party of the
Soviet Union, in the wake of the Soviet annexation and the founding by
the USSR of the **Moldavian Soviet Socialist Republic (MSSR)**.

The Communist Party of the Bolsheviks of Moldavia held its first congress the following year, in February 1941. In the summer of the same year, after the outbreak of World War II and the withdrawal of the Red Army from Bessarabia, it began to function clandestinely behind the lines and led sabotage actions against Romanian and German forces engaged in the war against the USSR. In 1944, it welcomed the return of the Soviet armies and Soviet power and thereafter acted as the sole leading political force in the MSSR, in its capacity as an integral component of the Communist Bolshevik Party of the USSR. Its most conspicuous leader in the first years of Soviet rule was **Leonid Brezhnev**.

The Moldavian Communist Party was banned in 1991 in the wake of the Moscow putsch against **Mikhail Gorbachev**. In 1993, the Communists were granted the right to reorganize, and a Party of Moldova's Communists was legalized in 1994. Two Communist formations eventually emerged as a result of the legalization process: the Party of Moldova's Communists / Partidul Comuniștilor din Moldova (PCDM), whose candidate, **Vladimir Voronin**, won some 10 percent of the vote in the 1996 presidential elections, and the Union of Moldova's Communists / Uniunea Comuniștilor din Moldova, a breakaway group of hardliners led by Florin Hristev, which split from the PCDM in 1997 and entered an electoral body initially called the Bloc of Popular Patriotic Forces, based on an alliance with the **Unity-Edinstvo Movement** and the Socialist Party of Moldova / Partidul Socialist din Moldova (PSM). It was renamed the bloc of **Socialist Unity / Unitatea Socialistă (US)**. Voronin's PCDM came in first in the 1998 parliamentary elections, in which over 480,000 voters cast their ballots for its candidates, who, albeit short of an absolute majority, won 40 out of Moldova's 101 parliamentary seats. In the aftermath of the elections, the PCDM called for the unification of the leftist political forces in order to defeat what it called the "threat" posed by national radicals and **unionist** forces in the new center-right majoritarian coalition, the **Alliance for Democracy and Reforms**. The PCDM's political allies are the former governing **Democratic Agrarian Party of Moldova**, the US, and the PSM, none of which gained representation in Moldova's Parliament in the 1998 national elections. *See also* POLITICAL BLOCS AND PARTIES.

COMRAT. Chief town of the **Gagauz Yeri** autonomous administrative region. The town of Comrat is located on the right bank of the **Ialpug River**, about 100 kilometers south of **Chișinău**. Comrat was first mentioned as a village in 1443, but archeological evidence indicates that the place has been inhabited since antiquity. Its main tourist attraction, the Comrat Archeological Monument, holds several layers of artifacts, including early Christian Era Roman vestiges. The former Comrat district had over 71,000 inhabitants (1993 est.), most of them belonging to the Gagauz ethnic minority, whose **autonomy** status was granted in the wake of a March 1995 local referendum that led to the recognition of Gagauz Yeri (Romanian: Gagauzia) as an autonomous entity within the borders of the Republic of Moldova.

COMUNISTUL. The official press organ of the Party of Moldova's Communists (*see* COMMUNIST PARTY), published in **Chişinău,** in Romanian and in Russian. *See also* PRESS.

CONACHI, COSTACHE (1778–1849). Author, translator, and politician, Conachi played an important role in the writing of Moldova's code of laws promulgated by Prince Scarlat Callimachi (*see* CALLIMACHI). Later in his career, he was one of the countercandidates in the election of one of Moldova's last ruling princes, **Mihail Sturdza**. A distinguished man of letters and a polyglot, Conachi translated Alexander Pope's philosophical poem *Essay on Man* (*Cercare de voroavă asupra Omului*) and wrote a pioneering treatise of Romanian versification titled *Meşterşugul stihurilor româneşti* (The Wordsmith of Romanian Verse).

CONSTITUTION. Moldova had two Soviet-style Constitutions before its accession of independence in 1991. The initial one, a local replica of the 1936 Constitution of the **Union of Soviet Socialist Republics (USSR)**, was promulgated six months after the Soviet **annexation** of 1940, on 21 January 1941. Its use was interrupted in June 1941, with the advent of World War II and the return of Romanian authorities to **Bessarabia**. The 1941 Constitution was restored after 1944, when the Soviet authorities reinhabited the land. Moldova being still a part of the USSR, it was replaced, on 15 April 1978, by an updated local version of the Soviet Constitution of October 1977.

Independent Moldova's Constitution was adopted on 29 July 1994 and took effect on 27 August of the same year, the anniversary of the country's **declaration of independence**. It defines Moldova as a sovereign, neutral, and democratic country; it mandates a free market economy based on the protection of private property rights; and it guarantees the personal rights of all citizens of the country regardless of ethnic or social origin, language, or religious and political affiliation. Moldova's Constitution guarantees the rights of political parties and of other public organizations as well.

Public administration is carried out on the principles of local **autonomy** and democratic elections. Under the Constitution, the president is the head of state but not of the executive authorities. He has the power only to nominate the prime minister and needs the Parliament's confirmation for the nomination of the cabinet. In order to change the Constitution, the president must initiate a referendum, but the draft bill outlining any given change has to be previously approved by the **Constitutional Court**, after which the approval of two-thirds of the Parliament is required. A referendum on changing Moldova's semipresidential system of government, as stipulated by the 1994 Constitution, was held in May 1999. Under the proposed change, the president would become responsible for the appointment of the prime minister, currently the responsibility of the Parliament.

CONSTITUTIONAL COURT. Created by virtue of Moldova's 29 July 1994 **Constitution**, the role of this judicial body is to serve as a legal instrument in the exercise of the separation of powers within Moldova's new political institutions. The Constitutional Court is Moldova's state entity endowed with full constitutional jurisdiction, independent of any public authority. It exercises sole jurisdiction over constitutional disputes and has overturned several actions of both Parliament and the president.

COSARCIUC, VALERIU (1955–). Deputy prime minister in Moldova's government formed in December 1999. A native of Clocuşna, **Edineţ**, Cosarciuc graduated from the Chişinău Polytechnic Institute and later earned a degree in mechanical engineering from the Moscow National Academy of Economics. Between 1995 and 1999 he served as executive director of the **Bălţi** agricultural equipment factory, Moldagrotechnica (V. N.).

COSERIU, EUGENIO (1921–). Professor of linguistics at the University of Tübingen (Germany) and an international authority on Romance philology, Coseriu was born at Mihăileni, near **Bălţi**, and has written extensively on the unity of the **Romanian language** and its relation to other Romance languages. In *Language and Folklore of Bessarabia, Bessarabian Linguistic Materials,* and *A Geography of Linguistics,* he approached, among other things, the relationship between Romanian and kindred languages of Latin descent spoken in Europe and other parts of the world, such as Spanish and

Portuguese in the Western Hemisphere. In 1997, in recognition of his outstanding scholarly contributions to the revival of Moldova's cultural and linguistic legacy, Moldova's president, **Petru Lucinschi**, awarded Professor Coseriu the Medal of the Order of the Republic.

COSNITA. Village in the neighborhood of **Dubăsari** on the east bank of the **Nistru River**, where some of the heaviest fighting took place during the 1992 war triggered by the separatist claims of the self-proclaimed **Moldavian Nistrian Republic**. The Coşniţa plateau is located in one of the most convoluted meanders of the Nistru and is vulnerable to attacks from both banks. It constitutes one of the several small enclaves controlled by the **Chişinău** central authorities on the east bank of the Nistru. *See also* TRANS-NISTRIAN CONFLICT.

COSSACKS. A warrior caste of horsemen that evolved on the largely uninhabited steppes between the **Nistru** and the Don Rivers from a mixing of Ukrainians, Russians, **Tatars**, Turks, and various migrants and fugitives. The Cossacks were first mentioned in Russian history in 1441. They concluded a pact to serve as Russian czars' mercenaries in 1614. They fought as periodic allies of Moldova's ruling princes, such as **Ion Vodă Cel Cumplit** and **Vasile Lupu**.

In 1917, the Cossacks declared their own short-lived independent republic amid the strife and unrest created by the Bolshevik Revolution. Between 1918 and 1921, they were split into two factions—the Red Cossacks and the White, or anti-Soviet, Cossacks—who fought on both sides of Russia's civil war, with the final defeat of the White Cossacks, who suffered persecution and deportation in the aftermath of the victory of the Bolshevik Revolution.

In the breakaway **Moldavian Nistrian Republic (MNR)**, prosecession Cossack detachments were active in Moldova's civil war of 1992, and they maintain a visible military presence in the districts of the east bank. By 1994, there were approximately 1,000 Cossack fighters in the trans-Nistrian districts of Moldova, serving as volunteers of Russia's **14th Army**. The All-Russian Cossack Union convened a congress in **Tiraspol** in 1998, calling on the **Russian Federation** and Belarus to help the MNR join their union as an associate member and to maintain Russia's military presence in the region.

COSTESTI. A hydroelectric plant on the Stânca-Costeşti accumulation lake, on Moldova's border with **Romania** along the upper course of the

Prut River. The Costeşti plant produces about 2 percent of Moldova's consumption of electric power. *See also* ENERGY.

COSTIN, MIRON (1633–1691). Historian, diplomat, and politician whose life spanned the reign of 12 Moldova rulers, from Prince **Vasile Lupu** to Prince **Constantin Cantemir**. Costin's chief work (written in 1677) is *De neamul Moldovenilor, din ce ţară au ieşit strămoşii lor* (On the Descent of the People of Moldova and the Land of Their Original Lineage), in which he describes the Latin origin of his nation, providing linguistic, ethnographic, and historical evidence to support the conclusion that Moldovans are the descendants of the Romanized population of **Dacia**. Costin was chief magistrate of **Hotin** between 1660 and 1664.

COSTIN, NICOLAE (1660–1712). Chronicler and diplomat, Nicolae Costin is the author of a chronicle of Moldova from its earliest beginnings, *Letopiseţul Ţării Moldovei de la zidirea lumii* (A Chronicle of the Land of Moldova from the Creation of the World), which he finished the year of his death. The son of **Miron Costin**, Nicolae was also the author of the earliest translation from a Spanish author into the **Romanian language**: Antonio de Guevara's didactic novel *El Reloj de Principes,* translated (from a Latin version) under the title *Ceasornicul Domnilor* (The Clock of Princes).

COUNCIL OF EUROPE. Moldova became a member of the Council of Europe in 1995. In June 1997, the Council of Europe opened an information center in **Chişinău**, with the secretary-general of the council, Daniel Tarschiz, attending the opening meeting. By 1998, the Republic of Moldova had ratified over 20 Council of Europe documents. *See also* EUROPEAN UNION, RELATIONS WITH.

CREANGA, ION (1839–1889). Prose writer and humorist born in Humuleşti, **Romania**. He is considered one of the main personalities of Moldova's literary realm, although he spent all of his life and published all of his works in his native country, where, the same as in Moldova, he is revered as one of the greatest literary classical authors.

Creangă made his debut in 1875 in **Iaşi**'s literary journal *Convorbiri literare* (Literary Conversations), in which he also published one of his best-known masterpieces, *Amintiri din copilărie* (Memories of My Boyhood) in 1881. Prior to his literary debut, as a teacher of **Romanian**, Creangă published two elementary school textbooks: *Metodă nouă de scriere şi cetire* (A New Method for Writing and Reading) in 1867 and *Povăţuitorul de cetire şi scriere după sistema fonetică* (A Guidebook for

Reading and Writing According to the Phonetic Alphabet) in 1871, both widely used as handbooks during the last decades of the 19th century.

A bronze statue of Creangă graces the alley devoted to Moldova's famous writers in **Chişinău**'s Central Park, and the State Pedagogical University of Moldova is named after him. As in the case of many other writers, Creangă's classic reputation spanning two bodies of literature using the same language epitomizes the difficulties of a cultural separation between the Moldovan and the Romanian literary traditions.

CRIULENI. Chief town of the former *raion*, or district, of the same name, 43 kilometers northeast of **Chişinău** on the west bank of the **Nistru River**. Criuleni was first mentioned in an official document at the beginning of the 17th century. The former district had a population of over 91,000 inhabitants (1993 est.). After the 1999 reorganization of Moldova's territory, Criuleni became a part of the newly established *judeţ* of Chişinău.

CROWTHER, WILLIAM (?–). Author of several studies on ethnic groups in post-totalitarian Moldova, Romania, and other countries of the former Communist bloc. Dr. Crowther received his Ph.D. from the University of North Carolina in 1986, and taught at the University of California, Duke University, and the University of North Carolina. He is the author of *The Politics of Ethnic Confrontation in Moldova* (1993), published by the National Council for Soviet and East European Research.

CRUSEVAN, PAVEL (1860–1909). Politician and publicist, Cruşevan is the author of the monograph *Bessarabia,* written in Russian and published in Moscow in 1903. Cruşevan was also the editor of two Russian-language dailies published in **Chişinău**, *Basarabets* (1897–1905) and *Drug* [The Friend] (1905–1909), which expressed pro-Russian views. *See also* RUSSIFICATION.

CUCIURGAN. Moldova's largest thermal power plant; also the name of an accumulation lake on the east bank of the **Nistru River** in the district of **Slobozia** in the self-proclaimed secessionist **Moldavian Nistrian Republic**. In 1998, the **Chişinău** authorities and the breakaway leadership in **Tiraspol** agreed in principle to cooperate in a controversial project aimed at continuing the modernization of a coal-fired power plant at Cuciurgan. The project, which reportedly included adding six more power-producing blocks, was prompted by pressure from Russia's energy company, **Gazprom**, which repeatedly threatened to cut gas supplies to Moldova because of its huge unpaid debts. In November 1998, by order of the Tiraspol authorities, the Cuciurgan power plant ceased to provide energy to westbank Moldova, which prompted Chişinău to request **Romania** to start furnishing energy from the Romanian grid. *See also* ENERGY.

CUVANT MOLDOVENESC. A literary, cultural, and scientific periodical and newspaper published by **Pan Halippa** in the years that preceded **Bessarabia**'s separation from Russia in 1917. *Cuvânt moldovenesc* (Moldova's Word) began as a monthly in 1913 and was later published three times a week. During World War I, when its circulation reached 10,000 copies, it played an important role in establishing a communication link between Bessarabian intellectuals and the province's readership at large, including Bessarabian soldiers in the Russian army and Transylvanian soldiers in the Austro-Hungarian army stationed in the province as allies of Russia. In March 1917, Moldova's pro-independence Moldovan National Party was established by members of the circle of intellectuals who wrote for *Cuvânt moldovenesc*.

CUZA VODA. *See* ALEXANDRU IOAN CUZA.

CYRILLIC ALPHABET. Also called Slavonic, the Cyrillic alphabet was created by St. Cyril (827–869), a missionary to the Slavs, among whom he and his brother, St. Methodius (825–884), preached in a series of missions. Cyril based the new script on the Greek alphabet of the Byzantine period, with several additional symbols devised to express the sounds of Slavonic for which no corresponding symbols were to be found in the Greek alphabet. Most Slavonic languages were fixed in writing in Cyrillics at the time of the Slavs' conversion to Christianity. After the 1054 rift, which separated the Eastern Church from the Western Church, the alphabet barrier accentuated the cultural and communication impasse between the Orthodox East and the Catholic West.

In the case of Moldova, whose local population had inherited earlier forms of Christianity, long before the conversion of the Slavs and the invention of the Cyrillic alphabet, the Latin script appears to have been used in parallel for some time after the rift, as shown in the example of Moldovan coins minted between 1400 and 1500, some of which bear Roman-alphabet incriptions with the names of the principality's rulers, from **Alexander the Good** and his successors, such as Iliaş Vodă and **Petru Aron**, down to **Stephen the Great**.

In the Moldovan context, the issue of the Latin versus Cyrillic or Slavonic script also epitomizes a cultural facet of the debate triggered later on by the Russophile claim that **Moldavian** is a separate language from **Romanian**.

In Soviet use, the Cyrillic alphabet was intended to make the language spoken by native Moldovans, though identical with Romanian, look sharply different in writing. Historically, Romanian is the only Romance language that—due to the region's ecclesiastical allegiance to the Slavonic rite of the **Orthodox Church**—was traditionally written in the Cyrillic alphabet from the early Middle Ages until the 19th century. The **United Principalities** discarded the Cyrillic alphabet in 1862. The eastern half of historical Moldova, or **Bessarabia**, preserved the Slavonic script until 1917.

After the 1940 incorporation of Bessarabia into the **Union of Soviet Socialist Republics (USSR)**, Russian Cyrillic was reimposed as the official alphabet of the newly founded **Moldavian Soviet Socialist Republic**. While still a Soviet republic, on 31 August 1989, Moldavia's Supreme Soviet passed into law the use of the Latin alphabet in writing the language spoken by the majority of the citizens' republic.

The Cyrillic alphabet is currently used in the writing of the Slavic languages spoken in the **Russian Federation**, Ukraine, Belarus, other parts of the former USSR, Bulgaria, Serbia, and selected parts of former Yugoslavia. In the writing of Romanian, Russian Cyrillics are currently used in the self-proclaimed **Moldavian Nistrian Republic**. *See also* ALPHABET ISSUE; LANGUAGE ISSUE.

CZERNOWITZ. *See* CERNAUTI.

-D-

DABIJA, EUSTRATIE (?–1665). Ruling prince of Moldova between 1661 and 1665. Known also as Dabija Vodă, Eustratie Dabija was the last ruler of Moldova to mint coins imprinted with his own portrait in effigy, thus reasserting the principality's right of coinage, in spite of the **Ottoman Empire**'s suzerainty over the land. *See also* SOVEREIGNTY.

DABIJA, NICOLAE (1948–). Author, publicist, and cultural animator; after 1986, editor-in-chief of Moldova's most important cultural weekly, *Literatura şi Arta*. Under Dabija's leadership, *Literatura şi Arta* became one of the most significant cultural instruments of Moldova's reawakening to national consciousness in the context of the 1980s policies of **glasnost**. Dabija's most recent work, *Libertatea are chipul lui Dumnezeu*

(Freedom Is in the Likeness of God), was published in 1997. He won Germany's Stettin International Poetry Award in 1998 and the Rome Columna Award of the Accademia di Romania in 1994. Nicolae Dabija is a member of Moldova's Parliament and one of the vice presidents of the **Party of Democratic Forces**.

DACIA. An ancient territory in Central-Eastern Europe bounded to the north by the Carpathian Mountains, to the south by the **Danube River**, and to the east by **Tyras**. A kingdom of Dacia was in existence from as early as the beginning of the second century B.C. to the time of the gradual conquest of most of its territory by Roman Emperor Trajan (A.D. 101–107). The series of vestiges known as **Trajan's Wall** indicate collective memory preservation of the Roman Conquest, also kept alive across time in the language and in local folklore. The idea of Dacia was revived in 1782, when Russia's Empress **Catherine the Great** proposed to Austria's Emperor Joseph II the re-creation of a new kingdom of Dacia encompassing the **Principalities of Moldova** and **Wallachia**. According to the project, Dacia was to be ruled as a single state by an Orthodox sovereign acceptable to both the **Russian Empire** and the **Habsburg Empire**. *See also* GREEK PROJECT.

DACIA LITERARA. A Moldovan literary publication that played a seminal role in determining the spirit and direction of modern literature written in the **Romanian language** in the 19th century. Published in **Iaşi** in January 1840 in the form of a three-in-one issue, it featured landmark contributions from writers who are now considered classics of Moldova's as well as **Romania**'s literary history: **Vasile Alecsandri**, **Gheorghe Asachi**, **Alexandru Donici**, **Constantin Negruzzi**, **Constantin Stamati**, and **Alecu Russo,** among others. *Dacia literară*'s inspirer and editor was **Mihail Kogălniceanu**.

DANUBE RIVER. Europe's most important river, 2,857 kilometers in length. It is inferior only to the Volga in terms of length and drainage area, but it comes in first as regards the volume of its outflow. Moldova was riparian to the Danube since ancient times and throughout most of its history, a status that was rescinded by the **Union of Soviet Socialist Republics (USSR)** after the 1940 **annexation** of **Bessarabia** and the creation of the **Moldavian Soviet Socialist Republic (MSSR)**. On 4 November 1940, a decree of the Supreme Soviet of the USSR incorporated into Soviet Ukraine the newly founded MSSR's seaboard, lying amid the Danube, the Black Sea, and the estuary of the **Nistru River**. The MSSR attempted to recover its riparian status to the maritime Danube in 1946, when the **Chişinău** leadership addressed a petition to Soviet dictator Joseph **Stalin,** arguing, among other things, that Moldavians were more numerous than Ukrainians in the region and that taking away the southern districts was going to damage Soviet Moldavia's trade and economic development by depriving it of the Danube ports of **Chilia, Ismail, Reni,** and **Vâlcov**. The USSR ignored the request. *See also* BORDERS OF MOLDOVA; GIURGIULESTI.

DANUBIAN PRINCIPALITIES. In 19th-century political parlance, the **Principalities of Moldova** and **Wallachia**, as riparian countries to the **Danube River**. *See also* UNITED PRINCIPALITIES.

DECLARATION OF INDEPENDENCE. Moldova's Declaration of Independence was proclaimed in **Chişinău** on 27 August 1991. It reaffirmed the right of the people of Moldova to enjoy full self-determination, as defined by the United Nations Charter, the Helsinki Final Act, and the norms of international law. Its tenor was expressed in the powerful statement that "the Republic of Moldova is a sovereign, independent, and democratic state, free to decide its present and future, without any external interference, in keeping with the sacred ideals and aspirations of its people within the historical and ethnic area of its own national making." *See also* SOVEREIGNTY.

DELETANT, DENNIS (1946–). Senior lecturer in Romanian studies at the School of Slavonic and East European Studies at the University of London. Professor Deletant's special interest in the area of Moldovan history was stimulated by his work and research in the field of Romanian studies. His work addressing aspects of Moldova's culture and history include such studies as "Slavonic Letters in Moldavia, Wallachia, and Transylvania from the 10th to the 17th Centuries" (1991), "A Shuttlecock of History: Bessarabia" (1991), and "Language Policy and Linguistic Trends in the Republic of Moldavia, 1924–1992" (1996).

DELOVAYA GAZETA. A popular business and economic newspaper published in the **Russian language** in **Chişinău**.

DEMOCRATIC AGRARIAN PARTY OF MOLDOVA / PARTIDUL DEMOCRAT AGRAR DIN MOLDOVA (PDAM). A leftist political formation made up mostly of former Communists and moderate supporters of maintaining economic contacts with the **Russian Federation**. The PDAM dominated Moldova's political scene for five years in the wake of the 1994 elections, when it won 43.18 percent of the vote. Its appeal diminished dramatically in the meantime, as its performance during the interval when it was Moldova's governing party did not meet the expectations of the electorate. In the 1998 elections, the PDAM garnered only 3.63 percent of the vote and did not gain parliamentary representation. In the aftermath of its defeat, negotiations were under way for a merger of the PDAM with the Party of Moldova's Communists and other leftist formations. *See also* POLITICAL BLOCS AND PARTIES.

DEMOCRATIC CONVENTION OF MOLDOVA / CONVENTIA DE-MOCRATA DIN MOLDOVA (CDM). A right-wing political bloc, Convenţia Democrată din Moldova was formed in 1997 by **Iurie Roşca's Christian Democrat Popular Front / Frontul Popular Creştin Democrat (FPCD)**, **Mircea Snegur's** Moldovan Party of Revival and Accord / Partidul Renaşterii şi Concilierii din Moldova, the Ecological Party of Moldova / Partidul Ecologist din Moldova, and other smaller political groups, in what was a successful attempt to unite Moldova's center and right-wing **political spectrum** in view of the 1998 parliamentary elections, where it came in second, winning 19.42 percent of the national vote. In 1999, in the wake of a government crisis triggered by the resignation of Ion **Ciubuc's** cabinet, the FPCD withdrew from the CDM. *See also* POLITICAL BLOCS AND PARTIES.

DEMOCRATIC PARTY FOR REBIRTH AND PROSPERITY / PAR-TIDUL DEMOCRAT PENTRU RENASTERE SI PROSPERITATE (PDRP). A party formed in late 1990, its constituency is based primarily on young Romanian-speaking intellectuals interested in promoting a less intense nationalistic agenda. It has been active chiefly in **Chişinău**. In the 1998 parliamentary elections, it acted as a component of the **Bloc for a Democratic and Prosperous Moldova**. *See also* POLITICAL BLOCS AND PARTIES.

DEPORTATIONS. There were several waves of deportations of Moldova's native population carried out under Soviet rule: the first one just months before the outbreak of World War II; the second in the war's immediate aftermath; and a third in the mid-1950s. The first wave of mass deportations linked with atrocities was executed by the **NKVD** over a period of 12 months, between 1940 and 1941. In the first months of 1941, 3,470 families, with a total of 22,648 persons labelled as "anti-Soviet elements"—mostly landowners, merchants, priests, and members of the urban bourgeoisie—were deported to Kuzbas, Karaganda, Kazakhstan, and other faraway parts of the **Union of Soviet Socialist Republics (USSR)**, amid reports of atrocities and exterminations. In **Chişinău** alone, evidence indicates that over 400 people slated for deportation were summarily executed in July 1940 and buried on the grounds of the Metropolitan Palace, the Chişinău Theological Institute, and the backyard of the Italian consulate building, where the NKVD had established its headquarters. In **Bălţi**, according to eyewitnesses, almost half of the city's population of about 55,000 was deported to the interior of the USSR between 14 and 22 June 1941.

A second wave of deportations was carried out beginning with the Soviet reoccupation of **Bessarabia** of August 1944. It was executed in short and brutal installments over a period of several years by the NKVD and its successor agency, the MVD. The 1949 deportations from the **Moldavian Soviet Socialist Republic (MSSR)** were carried out under the code name "Iug" (Operation South), which enforced the confidential Executive Decision No. 390-138 issued by the Soviet Union's Council of Ministers on 29 January 1949. Moscow's decision was aimed, among other things, at expediting the forced **collectivization** of Moldova's **agriculture** by getting rid of all of those suspected of resistance to the suppression of private property. On 17 February 1949, an action memo signed by Soviet General I. L. Mordovetz, who headed the Chişinău Ministry of Security, indicated that 40,854 persons, most of them kulaks, or small landowners, had been earmarked for deportation from the MSSR. Enforcing secret Decree No. 509 of 28 June 1949 issued by the Soviet authorities in Chişinău, on the night of 5–6 July 1949, 35,786 persons—9,864 men, 14,033 women, and 11,889 children—were deported under military escort to several faraway regions of the USSR. On the night of 5 July that same year, some 25,000 Moldovans were deported from **Bolgrad, Ismail,** and **Akkerman** and sent to Siberia or Kazakhstan.

The immediate effects of these deportations in terms of eradicating resistance to surrendering private property to the Soviet state can be gauged by the fact that in only two months—July and August 1949—the number of Moldovan properties turned into Soviet kolkhozes more than doubled, growing from 32.2 percent at the end of June 1949 to 72.3 percent at the end of August 1949. By deportations as well as other means, the dramatic process leading to the eradication of private property in Moldova's countryside was completed by the end of 1950, when 97 percent of the Soviet republic's private farmlands had been wiped out and merged into state-controlled collective farms.

The last stroke of that second wave of deportations enforced secret Decree No. 00193 of the Soviet Union's State Security Ministry, issued in Moscow on 5 March 1951. It was carried out between 4:00 A.M. and 8:00 P.M. on 1 April 1951, when, under the code name "Sever" (Operation North), 2,617 persons—808 men, 967 women, and 842 children making up 723 families of Jehovah's Witnesses—were deported under military escort to Siberia.

Under the less brutal policies of "planned transfer of labor," a third wave of deportations began in 1955, with emphasis on the transfer of thousands of Moldova peasants to the trans-Ural regions of the USSR's **Russian Federation**, where they were lured to move by offers of lesser taxation and other forms of material assistance. Moldovan settlements bearing such names as Teiul, Zâmbreni, Bălcineşti, Logăneşti, and Basarabia Nouă are to be found, for instance, north of Vladivostok in the Ussury valley. Other Moldovan settlements can be found in the region of Tomsk, in the vicinity of Irkutsk, and in the Arkhangelsk region.

Definitive figures are hard to assess, but the number of Moldovan deportees throughout the years of Soviet rule is considered to range anywhere between 200,000 and 500,000. According to the 1958 edition of the *British Encyclopedia* (vol. 15, p. 662), it was estimated that by mid-1955, the Soviet authorities had deported about half a million people from the MSSR. Corroborating this is the fact that in 1979, according to Soviet statistics, there were 415,371 Moldovans living in Ukraine, over 100,000 in various parts of the USSR's Russian Federation, including Siberia and Russia's Far East, and over 33,000 in Soviet Central Asia and other distant places of the USSR. *See also* COLONIZATION; RUSSIFICATION; WAR DEPORTATIONS.

DESPOT VODA (?–1563). Prince of Moldova between 1561 and 1563, also known by the name of Jacob Basilus Heraclides. During his brief and violent tenure, he unsuccessfully tried to introduce Protestantism among the Orthodox population of the land and reasserted the principality's right of coinage by minting silver and gold coins in various denominations, an act of defiance vis-à-vis the suzerain power of the **Ottoman Empire**. His tragic end is the subject of the historical play *Despot-Vodă* by **Vasile Alecsandri**.

DIACOV, DUMITRU (1952–). Speaker of Moldova's Parliament, Diacov headed the electoral **Bloc for a Democratic and Prosperous Moldova**, which won over 18 percent of the vote in the March 1998 parliamentary elections. A journalist by training, Diacov was born in Soviet Kazakhstan, where his family had been deported in 1949. He graduated from the Minsk (Belarus) Institute of Journalism in 1974 and worked as a reporter for Moldova's State Television (1974–1979) and for Moscow's *Komsomolskaya Pravda* (1984–1986). Between 1989 and 1993, he was ITAR TASS bureau chief in Bucharest; and from 1993 to 1994, he was political counselor at the Moldovan embassy in Moscow. He was a member and a parliamentarian deputy of the **Democratic Agrarian Party of Moldova** from 1994 until his exclusion in 1997, when he formed the centrist Movement for a Democratic and Prosperous Moldova, which later became a party of the same name before the 1998 elections (V. N.). *See also* POLITICAL BLOCS AND PARTIES.

DNESTROVSKAYA PRAVDA. Official newspaper of the **Tiraspol** soviet, it expresses the policies of the breakaway **Moldavian Nistrian Republic**.

DNIESTER/DNESTR RIVER. *See* NISTRU RIVER.

DOCHIA. Legendary female character whose name in Moldovan folktales has been interpreted as an etymological deformation of the ancient name of **Dacia**. According to legend, Dochia (a.k.a. Baba Dochia) was a local shepherdess who tried to resist the unwanted advances of Trajan (in other versions, Mars). Dochia fled to the mountains, shaking the snow off her sheepskin coats and gradually undressing, until she froze to death and was turned into a stone block, on top of the Ceahlău (a mountain in the Romanian Carpathians). From time immemorial, the capricious snowfalls of early March are considered to be "Dochia's Days" in Moldovan folklore. **Gheorghe Asachi**'s *Dochia şi Traian* (Dochia and Trajan), published in 1840, is the most famous literary evocation of the Dochia motif.

DOLGANIUC, VALENTIN (1957–). Deputy prime minister for industrial policies in Moldova's government formed in 1998, Dolganiuc was active earlier in his career as a parliamentarian and the leader of the **Sfântul Gheorghe** independent farmers association, a cartel affiliated with the **Christian Democrat Popular Front**, a wing of the **Democratic Convention of Moldova**. Dolganiuc studied at the Agricultural University of Moldova in **Chişinău**. Before the country's ascension to independence, he worked as an agricultural engineer on collective farms in his native district of **Edineţ** in northern Moldova (V. N.).

DOMN/DOMNITOR. The Latin-origin name of the rulers of Moldova and **Wallachia** until the 19th century. Comparable with the Portuguese "Dom" (similarly applied to kings), the title was last used by **Alexandru Ioan Cuza**. *Domn* was loosely used throughout Moldova's history as a synonym for the Slavic *vodă* or *voivode*.

DONDUSENI. Chief town of the former *raion*, or district, of Donduşeni on the railway linking **Bălţi** and **Ocniţa**, 197 kilometers north of **Chişinău**. It was founded as an extension of the old Donduşeni village, first mentioned in an official document in the 16th century. The former Donduşeni district on the west bank of the **Nistru River** had over 66,400 inhabitants (1993 est.). After 1999, Donduşeni became part of the newly established *judeţ* of **Edineţ**.

DONICI, ALEXANDRU (1806–1866). Author, fabulist, and translator, Alexandru (or Alecu) Donici was born in Stânca, **Orhei**. He studied at the St. Petersburg Military Academy and became a junior lieutenant in the Russian army. After 1828, Donici assumed the duties of a civil servant in **Chişinău**, but later on he chose to resign and in 1835 settled in **Iaşi**, where most of his literary career unfolded, as he became a frequent contributor to the local periodicals *Albina românească*, *Dacia literară*, *Zimbrul*, and *România literară*. His chief work, a two-volume book of fables titled *Fabule*, was published in Iaşi in 1840. A bust of Donici graces the alley dedicated to the classic writers of Moldova's literature in Chişinău's Central Park.

DOSOFTEI, METROPOLITAN (1624–1693). By his lay name Dimitrie Bărilă, Dosoftei was a cleric of learning, a writer, a polyglot, and one of the most important church figures in the history of Moldova. Having entered the clergy at a young age, Dosoftei was appointed metropolitan of Moldova in 1671. Two years later, he published his major masterpiece, a verse rendition of the Psalms in Romanian (first edition: Uniew, Poland, in 1673; second edition: **Iaşi**, in 1679). Dosoftei's *Psaltirea Svântului Prooroc David* played an important part in establishing the norm of premodern poetry in the **Romanian language**. Dosoftei prefaced all editions of his Psalter with a prologue, *Stihurile la luminatul herb a Ţării Moldovei* (Verses to the Enlightened Emblem of the Land of Moldova), an introduction considered to be one of his finest poetic achievements. *See also* NATIONAL EMBLEM.

DRAGOS VODA (?–ca. 1353). Fourteenth-century Wallachian nobleman, a vassal to Louis I, king of Hungary, in the northern Transylvanian *voivodate* of **Maramureş**, and legendary founder of Moldova. According to Hungarian and Moldovan chroniclers, Dragoş was assigned the defense of **Transylvania**'s eastern borders against **Tatar** inroads and sent to establish to that effect an advanced outpost east of the Carpathians, a land he called Moldova (Latin: Moldavia). Traditional interpretation has it that Dragoş discovered the new country by chance, during a black bison hunt down the slopes of the Carpathians, along a river. According to that medieval legend, Dragoş named the river and the new land Moldova after his hound, Molda, and gave it its coat of arms from the head of the slain bison, his trophy. The legend of the foundation of Moldova by Dragoş was analyzed by Mircea Eliade in *De Zamolxis à Gengis Khan* (Paris: Payot, 1970), in which chapter 4, titled "Voivode Dragoş and the Ritual Hunt," discusses the relation between myth and history in the 14th-century beginnings of the **Principality of Moldova**. Dragoş is considered to have ruled the newly settled frontier land in the name of Louis I for about two years (ca. 1352–1353). *See also* MOLDOVA, ETYMOLOGY.

DROCHIA. Chief town of the former Drochia *raion,* or district, on the **Bălţi-Ocniţa** railway, 167 kilometers northwest of **Chişinău**. The town was founded in the 19th century, at the time of the building of the railway. The former Drochia district, which had over 80,800 inhabitants (1993 est.), is part of the reestablished *judeţ* of **Soroca**.

DRUC, MIRCEA (1941–). Politician and former prime minister of Moldova, Druc holds doctoral degrees from the Universities of Moscow (1970) and Bucharest (1994). He clandestinely acted against **Russification** starting in the early 1960s. Because of his anti-Soviet views, he was marginalized in the early 1970s, but he returned to the limelight in the mid-1980s, in the wake of the policies of **glasnost**, then beginning to reach Soviet Moldova. After serving as prime minister between 1990 and 1991, Druc started to increasingly advocate **unionist** views and moved to **Romania**, where he became a presidential candidate in the neighboring country's election of 1992. Druc is the leader of a small unionist party, the Party of Unification–The Daco-Latin Option / Partidul Unificării–Opţiunea Daco-Latină (V. N.).

DRUTA, ION (1928–). Author of literary works depicting rural life in Moldova, written in both **Romanian** and **Russian**. His best-known prose works include the novels *Frunze de dor* (Leaves of Desire), published in 1957, and *Povara bunătăţii noastre* (The Burden of Our Kindness), published from 1961 to 1967. Druţă moved to Moscow in 1969. His left-leaning political stand was expressed with renewed emphasis in a 1997 article titled "Moldova şi Moldovenii" (Moldova and the Moldovans), harshly criticized by his right-wing opponents. *See also* POLITICAL SPECTRUM.

DUBASARI. Chief town of the district of the same name, 47 kilometers east of **Chişinău** on the east bank of the **Nistru River**, currently under the authority of the self-proclaimed **Moldavian Nistrian Republic (MNR)**. The town has a population of over 24,000 inhabitants (1993 est.). The Dubăsari *raion*, with over 53,000 inhabitants (1993 est.), was established under Soviet rule to straddle both banks of the Nistru. A power plant along the Nistru at Dubăsari is one of Moldova's important generators of electricity.

A smaller, pre–World War II *raion* of Dubăsari (Russian: Dubossary) was established in 1924 by the **Union of Soviet Socialist Republics** on the east bank of the Nistru, as part of the **Moldavian Autonomous Soviet Socialist Republic**. Dubăsarii Vechi (Old Dubăsari), first mentioned as a settlement in 1702, is a village on the west bank of the Nistru, in the ancient **Criuleni** district. The more recent east-bank settlement of Dubăsari came under Russian control in 1792, when the Nistru River became for the first time the state boundary between the **Russian Empire** and the **Principality of Moldova**, at that time still a vassal to the **Ottoman Empire**.

A virtual Dubăsari *judeţ* is supposed to include, in the future, Moldova's territorial units lying on the east bank of the Nistru, once the **trans-Nistrian conflict** is resolved. It would virtually overlap with the surface currently controlled by the authorities of the breakaway MNR and would include 10 cities and a total of 137 towns and villages.

DUBASARI LAKE. An artificial barrier lake along the middle course of the **Nistru River**, 128 kilometers in length and 6,750 hectares in surface area. It has an average width of 0.53 kilometers, a maximum width of 2 kilometers, and an average depth of 7.5 meters.

DUBOSSARY. *See* DUBASARI.

DUCA, GHEORGHE (?–1684). Also known as Duca Vodă, he ruled over Moldova three times (1665–1666, 1668–1672, and 1678–1683), as well as over **Wallachia** (1673–1678). From 1681 to 1683, Duca Vodă also exerted authority over the east bank of the **Nistru River** as hetman of Ukraine, appointed to that position by the **Ottoman Empire**, at that time Moldova's suzerain power. Gheorghe Duca's rule was marked by unpopular policies of heavy taxation and exactions.

DVOICHENKO DE MARKOV, DEMETRIUS (1921–). Scholar and expert on Moldovan history and literature; professor emeritus of history, geography, and Russian at Monmouth University. Dvoichenko de Markov is the author of a number of notable discoveries on historic Moldova and its relationship with Russia, including studies on Lomonosov and the 1739 Russian capture of **Hotin**, the diplomatic contacts between Moldova's Prince **Stephen the Great** and Ivan III, the relations between Prince **Gheorghe Duca** and 17th-century Ukraine, the earliest mentions of the Vlachs in Russian chronicles, and Russia and the first accredited diplomat in the **Danubian Principalities** between 1779 and 1808.

DVOICHENKO-MARKOV, EUFROSINA (1901–1980). Literary historian and the author of studies on the relationships and cultural confluences among Moldovan, Romanian, and Russian literary trends and artistic personalities. Her studies include monographic essays on **Constantin Stamati** (1933) and **Bogdan Petriceicu Hasdeu** (1936) and a book on *Pushkin in Moldova and Wallachia,* published in Moscow (1979).

DVORENIME. The name of Moldova's upper class under Russian rule. It is derived from the title of *dvornic,* a traditional nobility title. "Cartea Dvorenimii" was the title of the official catalogue of **Bessarabia**'s nobility under the czars' rule. *See also VORNIC.*

DYER, DONALD (1958–). Associate professor of Russian linguistics at the University of Mississippi, a specialist in Balkan and Slavic linguistics, and the author of a series of papers on linguistics and sociolinguistics of the **language issue** in Moldova. Professor Dyer is the author of *Moldavian Linguistic Realities,* a study of the Soviet policies vis-à-vis the language of the majority of Moldova's population; it was published in the 1994 collective volume *Non-Slavic Languages of the USSR: Papers from the Fourth Conference* (Slavica Publishers).

-E-

EAST-EAST PROGRAM FOR MOLDOVA. A cross-cultural program created in 1997, conceived as a tool to encourage the exchange of ideas and open dialogue among institutions and persons in Central and Eastern Europe. It focusses on sharing and learning from each other's experiences in the post-Communist transformation and developing skills to address the common problems of post-Communist societies. It is aimed at easing Moldova's transition to democracy and market economy by encouraging comparison in a variety of fields with other areas of post-totalitarian Eastern Europe. *See also* SOROS FOUNDATION MOLDOVA.

EASTER MASSACRE. The first major rapine and mass slaughter of a Jewish population in the 20th century, the Kishinev Easter Massacre took place in **Chişinău** on Easter Sunday, 1903, the last day of Passover. It gave for the first time international circulation to the Russian word "**pogrom**," the original meaning of which was "storm." The Chişinău Easter pogrom drew a remarkable amount of world attention to Russia's treatment of its Jewish minority. The pogrom lasted two days, leaving 51 people dead and over 500 injured, with one out of every three buildings in the city destroyed. Hundreds of people were left homeless and jobless. It is significant for the fact that it strengthened the feeling that the establishment of a Jewish homeland was absolutely necessary, and it thus provided one of the earliest impetuses to the Zionist movement. *See also* JEWS.

ECONOMY, CRIMINAL. According to a 1997 report issued by the Market Problems Research Center of Moldova's Academy of Sciences to assess the overall gross domestic product of Moldova, criminal economy is part of the country's **shadow economy**, which may contribute to the growth, not the shrinking, of Moldova's economy as a whole, albeit not reflected as such in official statistics. This particular sector encompasses criminal activities and underground economic activities conducted in such areas as drug trafficking, prostitution, illegal import-export transactions, bribery, extortion, and smuggling. *See also* ECONOMY, FICTITIOUS; ECONOMY, INFORMAL; ECONOMY, UNOFFICIAL.

ECONOMY, FICTITIOUS. The fictitious economy is a part of Moldova's **shadow economy**, the size and growth of which accounts for the possible conclusion that, in spite of official figures, Moldova's gross domestic product may have grown, not shrunk, since 1991. According to a 1997 report issued by the Market Problems Research Center of Moldova's Academy of Sciences, Moldova's fictitious economy encompasses off-book transactions conducted by state officials who take advantage of their positions to manipulate expenses and income to reduce tax liabilities. *See also* ECONOMY, CRIMINAL; ECONOMY, INFORMAL; ECONOMY, UNOFFICIAL.

ECONOMY, INFORMAL. According to a 1997 study released by the Market Problems Research Center of Moldova's Academy of Sciences, Moldova's informal economy represents transactions among economic factors based on personal contacts and relationships that substitute for, or replace, officially documented transactions and whose beneficiaries thus routinely avoid taxation. *See also* ECONOMY, CRIMINAL; ECONOMY, FICTITIOUS; ECONOMY, SHADOW; ECONOMY, UNOFFICIAL.

ECONOMY, NATIONAL. Moldova's national economy is agro-industrial, with **agriculture** accounting for over 44 percent of the net material product. Its major products are vegetables, fruits, wine and liquors, tobacco, grain, sugar beets, and sunflower seeds. Moldova is Europe's ninth largest producer of grapes and its seventh largest producer of tobacco. About 46 percent of Moldova's industrial sector is based on food processing, which operates in close interaction with agriculture. Electric **energy** production accounts for 17.7 percent, engineering and metal processing for about 10.8 percent, and light industry for about 6 percent of Moldova's total industrial output. The country's labor force is estimated at over 2 million. While the official unemployment rate was only about 2.5 in 1999, the numbers on unpaid leave and people working part-time were estimated to be about five times the number of the unemployed.

Moldova's economy relies heavily on an agricultural sector vulnerable to weather. It is also chronically affected by dysfunctions generated by the unresolved **trans-Nistrian conflict**, as most of Moldova's industry and energy-producing units are located on the east bank of the **Nistru River**. Moldova's industrial sector accounts for approximately 32 percent, construction for approximately 10 percent, and transport and communications for approximately 8 percent of the net material product. In 1998, Moldova's economy remained at around one-third of its preindependence size. In terms of industrial output, the 1998 figures indicated an overall decline of 42.2 percent as compared to the 1990 benchmark.

Since its accession of independence, despite a number of specific difficulties, Moldova has more consistently pursued policies of economic reform than most successor republics in the **Commonwealth of Independent States (CIS)**. A 1998 report drafted by the New York–based independent organization Freedom House placed Moldova among the countries with economies in transition. The year before, the same Freedom House report gave Moldova the third highest ranking on economic reform in the CIS.

Before the 1998 financial crisis in Russia, Moldova's economic reforms had resulted in relatively low inflation and relatively stable currency. The inflation rate decreased after 1992. It dropped from an all-time high of 2,700 percent in 1993 to 104.5 percent in 1994, 23.8 percent in 1995, and 15.1 percent in 1996. In December 1998, Moldova's inflation rate was estimated by the National Bank of Moldova at about 10 percent, with a 1999 forecast of about 15 percent. Whereas consumer prices fell by 2 percent from January through August 1998, they rose by almost 9 percent in November alone and increased by about 10 percent for the year. Exchange rates were also seriously affected by Russia's financial crisis. In January 1999, Moldova's **monetary unit**, the leu, stood at 8.5 for U.S.$1. In the aftermath of Russia's financial crisis, Moldova's hard currency reserves were halved in 1998, from $300 million before the crisis began to about $150 million in January 1999.

Agriculture has traditionally accounted for about 50 percent of Moldova's gross domestic product (GDP), **industry** for about 26 percent, and services for about 24 percent. In 1995, Moldova's GDP was estimated at $10.4 billion and the per capita GDP at $2,310. Fiscal deficits have been low by CIS standards, with the consolidated budget showing deficits of 5.9 percent of GDP in both 1994 and 1995. In 1996, the GDP fell by 7.8 percent, making for a cumulative decline of 64 percent from 1991 to 1996. GDP grew by 1.3 percent in 1997. Although the government initially forecast GDP growth of about 6 percent in 1998 (revised to 3 percent in June of that year), it announced in December that the 1998 decline would actually be 10 percent. Officials predicted a 1 percent growth in Moldova's GDP for 1999.

There are indications that official data fail to capture a substantial portion of the country's economic activity, with some estimates maintaining that nearly half of the country's overall economic activities are unofficial. Financial experts maintain that the recorded GDP curves may be an effect of the inadequate record of exports to other successor states within the CIS, which either transit through or originate from the breakaway Nistru east-bank region, currently controlled by the **Tiraspol** separatist authorities.

The 1998 budget provided for a deficit of 3.5 percent of the GDP, in line with **International Monetary Fund (IMF)** and **World Bank** recommendations. The IMF was pleased with the passage of Moldova's 1999 austerity budget. The country's $1.3 billion foreign debt amounted to 60 percent of the GDP in 1998.

In 1998, foreign **investments** amounted to over $51 million, marking an 18 percent increase from 1997. Most foreign investments are in Moldova's energy industry, water supplies administration, and food-processing sector. According to a 1998 Moody's rating, Moldova's investment climate is similar to that of the Baltic states, more favorable to foreign investments than that existing at the end of 1998 in **Romania**, Turkey, and Jordan. In 1999, in order to create better conditions for investments in the crucial sector of energy, the **Chişinău** government froze the $152 million debt owed by **Moldenergo** to the state budget, to make that company more attractive to prospective investors. Overall figures indicate that foreign direct investment amounted to only $265 million cumulatively since the year of Moldova's ascension to independence to 1997.

Moldova's principal exports are food and beverage products (58.2 percent), livestock and animal products (7.1 percent), and machinery and textiles (6.4 percent). Estimates from 1998 show that the main destinations of Moldova's exports are the **Russian Federation** (with 44.8 percent of the total), **Romania** (with 5.2 percent), Ukraine (with 4.6 percent), and Germany (with 3.7 percent). CIS export destinations are estimated to make up an average of 68 percent of the grand total.

Mostly due to the consequences of Russia's financial crisis of 1998, total exports were 22.5 percent lower in January–November 1998 than they were over the same period for 1997, with big declines in the exports of food, beverages, and tobacco. In 1997, Moldova's principal imports were mineral products and fuel (35.3 percent), machinery and equipment (12.8 percent), and chemicals (9.6 percent). Moldova's imports from Russia accounted for 19.9 percent of the total, from Ukraine, 15.7 percent, from Romania, 7.1 percent, and from Belarus, 6.2 percent (1998 est.). Imports from CIS countries are estimated to constitute an average of 60 percent of the grand total. *See also* ECONOMY, CRIMINAL; ECONOMY, FICTITIOUS; ECONOMY, INFORMAL; ECONOMY, SHADOW; ECONOMY, UNOFFICIAL; PRIVATIZATION; TRADE.

ECONOMY, SHADOW. According to Moldova's state-level Bureau for Statistics, the shadow economy represented 15 percent of Moldova's total gross domestic product (GDP) in 1996. However, a 1997 report prepared by the Market Problems Research Center of Moldova's Academy of Sciences reached the conclusion that the shadow economy (namely, that part of Moldova's total economy not documented by official reports) encompasses not one, but four, distinct economies: the unofficial, the informal, the fictitious, and the criminal, the activities of which may have grown to as much as 40 percent or more of the official GDP. According to that 1996 analysis, the shadow economy thereby accounts for a much larger and growing share of Moldova's economy, and recent official figures regarding the decline in Moldova's GDP may be misleading by overstating the case. According to official statistics, Moldova's GDP fell by 8 percent in 1996, making for a cumulative decline of 64 percent from 1991 to 1996. However, if the shadow economy really increased to almost half of the official GDP—as tentatively indicated by the report prepared by the Market Problems Research Center—it could be possible that the total economy of Moldova did not shrink in 1996 and that, all in all, it may have even grown.

ECONOMY, UNOFFICIAL. A 1996 study of the Market Problems Research Center of Moldova's Academy of Sciences, based on a variety of methodologies, defines the unofficial economy as encompassing business entities and private persons engaged in both legal and illegal economic activities, who thus avoid taxation. As part of Moldova's **shadow economy**, the unofficial economy is said to account for a sizable share of Moldova's gross domestic product, which would point to growth instead of shrinkage of the country's overall economy. *See also* ECONOMY, CRIMINAL; ECONOMY, FICTITIOUS; ECONOMY, INFORMAL.

EDINET. Chief town of the reestablished Edineţ *judeţ* on the highway linking **Chişinău** and **Cernăuţi**, 202 kilometers northwest of Chişinău. The town was founded in the 19th century. The former Edineţ *raion* had over 90,000 inhabitants (1993 est.). The *judeţ* of Edineţ includes the former districts of **Briceni**, **Donduşeni**, and **Ocniţa**.

EDUCATION. Moldova inherited the Soviet education system, marred by decades of ideological indoctrination and governed by the requirements of socialist central planning. Beginning in 1995, the Parliament adopted a new set of regulations to reform and modernize education and make it adequate to prepare Moldova's future workforce and decision makers in keeping with the challenges and demands of the civil society and market economy. The country's educational system consists of 1,880 kindergartens, 1,698 primary and secondary schools, and 53 public schools and lyceums. Additionally, there are 54 colleges and higher-education institutions, including the **State University of Moldova**, the Technical University of Moldova (formerly the Polytechnic Institute of Moldova), the Ion Creangă State Pedagogical University, the **Free International University of Moldova**, the Nicolae Testemiţeanu State Medical and Pharmaceutical University, the Agriculture State University of Moldova, the Alecu Russo State University of Bălţi, the Academy of Economic Studies of Moldova, Tiraspol State University, Comrat State University, the Arts Institute of Moldova, the Gavril Musicescu Music Academy, the Humanities University of Moldova, the Cooperative-Commercial University of Moldova, the Academy of Public Administration, and the Stefan Cel Mare Police Academy.

Moldova's governmental efforts in reforming the educational system are being supported by the **World Bank**, which in 1997 approved a $16.8 million loan to finance the General Education Project, designed to enhance the quality of primary and lower-secondary education (grades 1–9) through improved curricula, new textbooks, teacher training, and the introduction of a modern system of proficiency assessment. The General Education Project consists of four components to be implemented over a period of five years, under the supervision of Moldova's Ministry of Education.

EFROS, GHEORGHE (1955–). Economist and specialist in industrial management and management of resources, currently executive director of Moldova's **World Bank**–sponsored Agency for Industrial Restructuring and Assistance. Efros has performed several functions in Moldova's government, including deputy prime minister (1991–1992), deputy minister of economy (1992–1994), and deputy minister of industry (1994–1995). A graduate of the Technical University of Moldova (1984) and of the Bucharest Academy of Economic Studies (1990), he also took training courses in Cambridge (England), Cologne (Germany), and at the MIT Center for Industrial Competitiveness (V. N.).

ELECTORAL LAW. Moldova's Electoral Law was passed by the **Chişinău** Parliament in November 1997. On promulgating it in December 1997, President **Petru Lucinschi** expressed misgivings about parts of it, criticizing, among other things, the system of nationwide proportional representation in a single constituency as being undemocratic. Changes advocated for Moldova's Electoral Law include a majoritarian system based on single-member districts, designed to better serve the need for accountability. Fifteen political parties and blocs and 68 independent candidates registered for the 22 March 1998 parliamentary elections. *See also* POLITICAL BLOCS AND PARTIES.

EMINESCU, MIHAI (1850–1889). Regarded as the national poet of both Moldova and **Romania**, Eminescu was born in Ipoteşti, on the west bank of the **Prut River**, and died in Bucharest. Although he journeyed extensively in other parts of the territories where his native language was spoken—including **Transylvania** and **Bucovina**—there are no records of Eminescu having ever travelled east of the Prut, in what was, during his lifetime, Russian-held **Bessarabia**.

Eminescu made his literary debut in 1866 in **Cernăuţi**, which, as part of the **Habsburg Empire**, had become one of the region's main cultural centers. Later on, in a series of articles published in 1878 in the Bucharest daily *Timpul,* Eminescu sharply contested the Russian czars' historical rights over Bessarabia. His argument was triggered by the reattribution of the southern part of Bessarabia to the **Russian Empire** by the Treaty of Berlin. Eminescu's writings on 19th-century Moldova and Moldova's historical past were collected by Ion Creţu and published in 1941 under the title *Bucovina şi Basarabia: Studiu istorico-politic* (Bucovina and Bessarabia: A Historical-Political Study). Moldova's National Theater in **Chişinău** is named for Eminescu. There are several Eminescu statues in the country's capital, including a bronze bust of the poet gracing the alley devoted to Moldova's classic writers in Chişinău's Central Park. As in the case of **Ion Creangă** and many others, it is difficult, if not impossible, to draw a dividing line between Moldova's and Romania's pantheon of writers.

ENERGY. Moldova's energy sector relies mainly on imported coal, oil, and natural gas, with local sources accounting for a very small share of the fuel and electrical power needs of the country. Its energy sources consist of a system of small hydroelectric plants on the west bank of the **Nistru River** and on the east bank of the **Prut River**, at **Costeşti**-Stânca. Local thermal power plants are providers of electricity in **Bălţi, Chişinău**, and **Râbniţa**. There have been plans to expand and renovate Moldova's largest thermal power-producing plant at **Cuciurgan** on the east bank of the Nistru, which produced 33 percent of Moldova's consumption of energy in 1998. Cuciurgan, however, is located on the sliver of land over which Moldova's central authorities lost control after 1992 and where—under the direction of the separatist authorities of the **Moldavian Nistrian Republic**—the other main national producers of energy, **Dubăsari** and Râbniţa, are also located.

Toward the end of 1998, Moldova started to import energy from **Romania**, which is reportedly able to provide about 12 percent of Moldova's electricity needs through the existing links across the Prut. As of 1998, Russia and Ukraine supplied over 90 percent of Moldova's total imports of energy. According to earlier figures (1994), Moldova's annual imports of fuel from Russia alone included 88,000 tons of diesel oil, 65,000 tons of gasoline, 365,000 tons of fuel oil, and 2.8 billion cubic meters of natural gas.

In the future, reducing the degree of dependency on Russian and Ukrainian supplies of energy may hinge in part on the opening of a controversial oil terminal at **Giurgiuleşti** on the **Danube River** and on the controversial project of Moldova's planned participation in the construction of a second reactor at Romania's nuclear energy–producing complex of Cernavoda. However, for the foreseeable future, such a participation, requiring an investment of about $500 million, seems to make it a nonviable venture from an economic point of view.

To find ways of expediting a solution to Moldova's chronic shortage of energy, the U.S.-owned company Redeco received a concession to explore and exploit gas and oil deposits throughout Moldova. Redeco experts have begun to test seismic lines in the southern region of the country, to see if any deeper reserves of oil and gas are to be found in the lowland areas where, by 1998, it had performed a number of successful drills that resulted in a small domestic production of gas. On the other hand, Redeco has been exploring the possibility of putting together a consortium to include **Moldovagas** (Moldova's main gas company), the Russian company **Gazprom** (Moldova's main energy supplier), and the Romanian company Romgaz in order to build a 120-kilometer-long pipeline linking **Drochia** to **Ungheni** on the Prut and farther west, across the Prut, to **Iaşi**. The materialization of such a project, considered a possibility for 1999, would allow Moldova to import gas from the Romanian grid. A Romanian proposal of cooperation with Moldova in the area of energy grids was introduced to the Chişinău authorities in the summer of 1998. Another project would involve Moldova gaining access to the future trans-Caspian pipeline, which Romania is very interested in, and the possibility of building an oil pipeline across Romania and Moldova.

The difficulties encountered because of Moldova's dependency on foreign suppliers of energy resurfaced dramatically in 1998, when Ukraine—from where Moldova currently imports one-third of its electricity—temporarily suspended exports after one of its nuclear reactors at Chernobyl was shut down. The shortage of hard currency has also impacted negatively on the other energy-supplying arrangements of the Republic of Moldova. The state-owned company **Moldenergo**, which administers the unified energy sector of Moldova, has been struggling hard to find solutions to the predicament. In 1998, Gazprom bought 50 percent of Moldovagas, the assets of which amount to about $285 million. Moldova owed Gazprom over $600 million, and the transfer was meant to cover part of that debt.

An aggressive concept for the **privatization** of Moldova's energy sector was approved by Moldova's Parliament in 1998. It stipulated the sale to foreign investors of a majority share of 51 percent in three power and heating plants and the sale of 100 percent shares in five regional energy-distribution networks. In 1998, Moldova's energy sector was in urgent need of **investments** amounting to some $700 million.

ENVIRONMENT. Extensive use of chemicals in **agriculture** and intensive livestock development during the Soviet era have exerted a negative impact on Moldova's environment. Centralized planning during the Communist period, including excessive utilization of water and land resources, led to a severe imbalance between unexploited natural reserves and systems turned to account for various industrial branches. Currently, Moldova's unexploited geosystems reserves amount to 1.25 percent of the total of the country's resources, 86 percent being involved in pollution-generating economic circuits.

One of the chief factors in Moldova's environmental degradation was the extensive process of livestock industrialization before 1989. Livestock development, primarily swine and cattle, led to a massive concentration of offal, much larger than the bulk of animal production. By the end of the 1980s, Moldova's swine-breeding complexes had an average capacity of 54,000 head and an annual meat production of 6,300 tons, generating an offal of over 464,000 tons. The impact of this imbalance on the environment translated into ammoniacal, bacteriological, and nitrates pollution, as well as soil and underground pollution that affected underground waters.

To counter these developments, Moldova's government took action as early as 1990, when it issued a state decision on "Urgent Actions for Ecological Situation Amelioration." Specific laws on environmental protection, water resources, and the protection of the underground were adopted in June 1993. Article 37 of Moldova's **Constitution** specifically refers to environmental protection in four paragraphs. In 1999, the **World Bank** contributed $125,000 to Moldova's program for protecting and preserving the biodiversity of its environment. *See also* WATER RESOURCES.

EUGENE IONESCO THEATER. The avant-garde theater of **Chişinău** founded in 1991, with the approval of the Romanian-born member of the French Academy, the world-renowned playwright Eugene Ionesco (1909–1994). The Eugene Ionesco Theater epitomizes some of the aspirations of Moldova's culture to be recognized as a part of Western Europe's heritage. The company won applause in recent years at international festivals in Avignon, Cairo, Moscow, and Bucharest.

EUROPEAN UNION, RELATIONS WITH. One of Moldova's main foreign policy objectives is the country's intensified cooperation with and eventual integration into the European Union (EU). In 1998, the EU rejected as untimely Moldova's request to join the so-called European Conference, a forum that brings together 15 countries that have expressed their interest in being admitted to the EU. Moldova hopes to become an associate member of the EU. The foreign policy program adopted by the **Chişinău** government in 1998 hinged on the central concept of fully opening Moldova to the West through a number of specific initiatives, including the creation of an interministerial Committee for European Integration, headed by the prime minister, and of a Department of European Integration to coordinate domestic initiatives designed to ensure the compatibility of Moldova's legislation with the norms of the EU.

The EU has repeatedly expressed concern about the continued military presence of the **Russian Federation** in the trans-Nistrian region of the Republic of Moldova, where an unverified number of Russian troops comprise Moscow's only deployment of armed forces outside Russia's borders in Europe. *See also* FOURTEENTH (14th) ARMY.

-F-

FALCIU. District, or *judeţ,* of the historic **Principality of Moldova**, which used to straddle both banks of the **Prut River** before 1812. One of the earliest descriptions of the Fălciu district ("Ager Falcziensis") is found in **Demetrius Cantemir**'s *Descriptio Moldaviae* (written 1714–1716). The defeat of **Peter the Great** by the Turks in 1711 took place near the Fălciu village of Stănileşti, on the west bank of the Prut. The battle of Stănileşti removed the rising power of the **Russian Empire** from direct involvement in the affairs of Moldova for almost a century.

FALESTI. Chief town of the former *raion,* or district, of the same name, 125 kilometers northwest of **Chişinău**. The former Făleşti district had a population of over 95,000 inhabitants (1993 est.). Făleşti is part of the reestablished *judeţ* of **Bălţi**.

FEDERALIZATION. Controversial political blueprint initially advocated by separatist leaders in **Tiraspol** who called for the reorganization of the Republic of Moldova into a federation in which the self-proclaimed **Moldavian Nistrian Republic** would have a separate legislature, government, anthem, and state symbols, while at the same time forming a loose political unity with the Republic of Moldova. A Moscow agreement signed by experts of the two sides of the **trans-Nistrian conflict** on 9 October 1997 was interpreted as providing for a de facto federalization of Moldova, a view contradicted by the central authorities in **Chişinău**, according to whom the agreement would ensure that the Chişinău government will have "sole competence over Moldovan citizenship, foreign policy, customs and frontiers." *See also* AUTONOMY; SEPARATISM.

FERDINAND I (1865–1927). King of **Romania** from 1914 to 1927. Under his reign, **Bessarabia** joined Romania in two successive steps: first, under the provisions of the **Sfatul Ţării** decision of 27 March 1918, which proclaimed a conditioned union of the former czarist province with rump Romania, then at war with the Central Powers, the armies of which had occupied most of the country's territory; and second, after the 11 November 1918 armistice, when the same Sfatul Ţării voted for Bessarabia's unconditioned union with the sovereign kingdom of Romania (27 November 1918). *See also* MOLDAVIAN DEMOCRATIC FEDERATED REPUBLIC.

FILAT, VLADIMIR (1969–). State minister in Moldova's government of 1999, Filat is a native of **Hânceşti**, **Lăpuşna**. A graduate of Alexandru Ioan Cuza University in **Iaşi**, he served as general director of the trading company Romold (1994–1997) and as chairman of the board of the joint-stock company Dosoftei (1997-1998), also in Iaşi. Furthermore, he served as executive director of privatization and state property affairs in Moldova's Ministry of Economy and Reforms (1998–1999).

FLORESTI. Chief town of the former *raion,* or district, of the same name, 131 kilometers north of **Chişinău** on the **Răut River** and the **Bălţi-Soroca** highway. Floreşti and its surrounding lands were the property of the family of **Miron Costin,** one of Moldova's statesmen in the 17th century and a reputed chronicler and historian. In 1993, the Floreşti district had an estimated population of 76,987 inhabitants. After the 1999 reorganization of the country's territory, Floreşti became part of the reestablished *judeţ* of Soroca.

FLUX. An influential press group running one of **Chişinău**'s main independent news agencies. Flux also publishes Moldova's only daily, *GPF Flux,* and the popular weekly *Flux Magazin Săptămânal.* GPF (Grupul de Presă Flux) is run by publicist Val Butnaru.

FOUNDING OF MOLDOVA. According to ancient chronicles, Moldova was founded in approximately 1352 by **Dragoş Vodă,** a Wallachian nobleman from **Maramureş** who took possession of the province in the name of Hungary's king, to whom he was a vassal. Moldova's history of statehood begins in 1359, when another Wallachian nobleman from Maramureş, **Bogdan I,** proclaimed himself independent of the Hungarian Crown. But Moldova had borne its name and had been inhabited by its own local population before Dragoş and his successors organized it as a principality. As far back as 1334, a Latin document already mentioned **Baia** as "civitas Moldaviae." Out of the 755 villages mentioned in official documents before the year 1449, 607 (i.e., 80.3 percent) had their boundaries established before Moldova became a principality under Bogdan I.

FOURTEENTH (14th) ARMY. The former 14th Army of the **Union of Soviet Socialist Republics** stationed in the **Nistru** east-bank districts of the Republic of Moldova as Russia's 14th Army after 1992. Downgraded to the status of an operational group and reportedly downsized from around 10,000 men to less than 5,000, it remains a sizable regional force and the only Russian military presence on foreign territory outside the **Russian Federation** in Europe.

Moscow was accused of ignoring repeated requests to allow **Organization for Security and Cooperation in Europe (OSCE)** monitors to check the real levels of troops, equipment, and arms still deployed on the

Nistru east-bank districts. In 1998, the **European Union** delegate to the OSCE said that there is in fact no real information on how many Russian troops are still there.

The Russian army's headquarters are in **Tiraspol**. Despite attempts to blur the distinction between the Russian troops and the local Republican Guard (mostly achieved through demobilizing army troops and transferring them to the Guard), such a military presence in the self-styled separatist **Moldavian Nistrian Republic** remains a cause of concern to the **Chişinău** authorities, who have continued to demand its withdrawal.

Although officially neutral, Russia's 14th Army played a crucial part in the 1992 conflict between the government of Moldova and the secessionist forces in the Nistru east-bank districts. During that conflict, weapons were transferred from the 14th Army stockpiles to the trans-Nistrian militia. The army also accepted the services of **Cossack** armed volunteers, who entered the region as the conflict erupted. Strong indications suggest that detachments of the 14th Army actively intervened on the side of the Tiraspol separatists, using heavy weapons to influence the outcome of the fighting whenever necessary. Under its new name of the **Operational Group of Russian Forces** in Moldova, this military body is said to perform a peacekeeping mission in the troubled area, pursuant to the 1992 cease-fire agreement. An agreement on its withdrawal from Moldova within three years was signed in October 1994 by Moldova's and Russia's prime ministers but was not ratified by Russia's State Duma, which stated that the **North Atlantic Treaty Organization**'s expansion eastward makes the presence of Russian troops in the region one that meets the strategic interests of Russia.

In 1998, the army's equipment consisted of 119 battle tanks, 7 assault helicopters, 180 armored combat vehicles, 101 armored personnel carriers, and 129 artillery pieces, including multiple rocket launchers and mortars. It comprised one motor rifle division, one tank battalion, one artillery regiment, and one antiaircraft brigade. The Operational Group of Russian Forces benefits from the Transnistrian region's weapon-producing capacity, which provides Tiraspol with sizable arsenals. There are about 45,000 tons of ammunition in the breakaway region, where the Colbasna depot in the **Râbniţa** district alone is said to be huge enough to cause concern in case of explosion to areas in the Nistru west-bank districts of Moldova as well as in Ukraine. To maintain the state of military readiness of Russia's Operational Group, only about 6,000 tons of that stockpile is said to be necessary. This would leave an estimated 13,000 tons of ammunition available for Russian use outside the area, provided removal is possible, and another 20,000 tons of ammunition proposed for sale.

There have been reports that stocks from the Colbasna depot are being stolen and sold outside Moldova. According to 1998 figures, the Colbasna depot contained 2,830 carloads of live ammunition and a stockpile of over 49,500 light arms. The continued presence of Russian troops in the east-bank districts is allegedly linked to the guardianship of these huge weapons and ammunition dumps, some of them in unstable condition. In November 1997, Russia declared that all of the military arsenal stationed in the area was Russian property but that, in a gesture of goodwill, it was ready to share with Chişinău and Tiraspol the profits from selling part of that arsenal to interested parties.

The daily link between the Russian Federation and the Russian enclaved command in Tiraspol is an air corridor used for Russian military transport over Ukraine. Given the cost for the use of such a corridor, commercial flights have been considered by Moscow as an alternative. *See also* RUSSIAN FEDERATION, RELATIONS WITH; TRANSNISTRIAN CONFLICT.

FRANCOPHONY INTERNATIONAL ORGANIZATION. Moldova is one of the 52 member states of the Francophony International Organization, which promotes French as a language of international communication among countries speaking Romance languages. In the area of trade and finance, Moldova took part in a 1999 Francophone countries' world conference on investments and trade, held in Monaco. As part of its policy of asserting the Romance identity of its language, Moldova became a participant in the programs of the Francophone Universities agency, which includes 400 colleges and universities worldwide. In 1998, Alliance Française's office in **Chişinău** launched the "100,000 Books for Moldova" program, an initiative designed to help Moldova's schools and colleges develop Francophone curricula. *See also* LANGUAGE ISSUE; ROMANIAN LANGUAGE.

FREE INTERNATIONAL UNIVERSITY OF MOLDOVA. An independent university established in 1992. It includes six departments—law, modern languages, medicine, economics, natural science, and ecology—as well as the Department of Preacademic Studies. Courses are taught in **Romanian**, **Russian**, English, and French. In addition to students from Moldova, it includes students from **Romania**, Ukraine, Russia, France,

China, Pakistan, Syria, Venezuela, and several other countries. *See also* EDUCATION.

-G-

GAGAUZ. Turkic ethnic group of Christian religion that settled in the southern part of present-day Moldova, or **Bessarabia**, at the beginning of the 19th century. An early group of 1,205 Gagauz refugees from Ottoman-held Bulgaria, where they were subject to religious repression, is mentioned in Russian documents in 1817. The Gagauz preserved their language and Orthodox religion and kept growing under the Russian policies of **colonization** during the first half of the 19th century. The group grew more substantially in the wake of the Russo-Romanian-Turkish War of 1877–1878 (*see* RUSSO-TURKISH WARS), during which Bulgaria was under Russian military occupation for three years, allowing ethnic Turks of Orthodox religion to migrate more freely. At the end of the 19th century, Russian statistics recorded the presence of about 57,000 Gagauz settlers in Bessarabia. The last Romanian census before the Soviet incorporation of the province in 1940 recorded 98,172 Gagauz in historic Bessarabia.

Soviet Moldavia's last census (1989) indicated a total Gagauz population of 153,458, which is roughly the figure today. According to Moldova's official surveys, the Gagauz ethnic group represents less than 4 percent of the country's total population.

The Gagauz language is a dialect of Turkish written in a **Cyrillic**-based alphabet, adopted under Soviet rule in 1957. Until 1990, only 33 books had been published in Cyrillized Gagauz, most of the cultural life of the Gagauz minority being practically featured in Russian. After Moldova's proclamation of independence, the Gagauz Section of the Moldovan Academy of Sciences developed a Latin alphabet for the writing of the Gagauz language. Gagauz-language sections function in the Ion Creangă Pedagogical University in **Chişinău**, and the Gagauz University functions in **Comrat**.

GAGAUZ HALKI. A minority political group representing the common interests of the Gagauz Turkophone population in parts of southern Moldova. Gagauz Halki (translation: Gagauz People) controls local government in **Gagauz Yeri**, the five southern districts of Moldova where the group's constituency is sparsely concentrated. *See also* GAGAUZ SEPARATISM.

GAGAUZ SEPARATISM. In the context of the Soviet Union's breakdown, a separatist movement with strong pro-Communist overtones developed within the **Gagauz** ethnic group. In 1990, a short-lived Gagauz Soviet Socialist Republic was proclaimed in **Comrat**. Through negotiations with Moldova's central authorities in **Chişinău**, a compromise was eventually reached, and the Gagauz ethnic group dropped its secessionist claims. In March 1995, the results of a local referendum secured the autonomy of **Gagauz Yeri** (Romanian: Gagauzia) within the unitary state of Moldova. By virtue of its special status, Moldovan Gagauz elect their own executive and legislative officials and their governor, the *bashkan*. Gagauz Yeri recognizes three official languages: Gagauz, **Russian**, and **Romanian** ("**Moldavian**").

In 1997, leftist opposition forces tried to muster support to change the name and status of the autonomous region to make it a republic and part of a "renewed **Union of Soviet Socialist Republics**."

Moldova's policy toward its Turkophone Christian minority was praised by Suleyman Demirel, Turkey's president, who visited Moldova twice, in 1996 and 1998. The Turkish leader welcomed the status of the Gagauz ethnic group in the Republic of Moldova as one of the best solutions to the explosive issue of national minorities after the collapse of the Soviet empire.

GAGAUZ YERI / GAGAUZIA. An autonomous national-territorial unit (formally named Unitatea Teritorială Autonomă Gagauzia) enjoying special status in the south of the Republic of Moldova. Gagauz Yeri comprises 3 towns—**Comrat** (its administrative center), **Ciadâr-Lunga**, and **Vulcăneşti**—23 villages, and 3 suburban townships. The head of Gagauz Yeri is the *bashkan* (Romanian: *guvernator*), elected by the region's legislative assembly and, by law, a member of Moldova's Parliament. Although Moldova's **Gagauz** ethnic group makes up less than 4 percent of the country's total population, Gagauz Yeri itself is a multiethnic quilt that includes 5.5 percent Bulgarians, 5.1 percent Russians, and about 4 percent Ukrainians, most of them living in rural communities, interspersed with Romanian-speaking Moldovan villages. In this complex patchwork, the ethnic Gagauz population forms an absolute majority in only two subterritorial units, Comrat and Ciadâr-Lunga. According to the last Soviet-era census (conducted in 1989), over 70 percent of Gagauz ethnics named **Russian** as their second language. *See also* AUTONOMY.

GAGAUZIA. Romanian form of **Gagauz Yeri**.

GALAICU-PAUN, EMILIAN (1964–). One of the members of Moldova's new generation of poets, Galaicu-Păun is considered one of the leading personalities of present-day literature written in the **Romanian language** in both Moldova and **Romania**. Galaicu-Păun won two awards of the Moldovan Writers Union and the special Award of the Romanian Writers Union. A recently published anthology of four centuries of Romanian-language poetry, beginning with the work of **Metropolitan Dosoftei**, closes with a selection from the poems of Galaicu-Păun.

GAMURARI, BORIS (1946–). Minister of defense in Moldova's government formed in December 1999. He served in the same capacity beginning in May 1999 while a member of the **Sturza** cabinet. A native of Văscăuţi, **Soroca**, Gamurari holds a Ph.D. in history from the **State University of Moldova**. Earlier in his career he held a number of positions within the **Communist Party** of Moldova. After Moldova's **independence** Gamurari served as deputy minister in Moldova's Ministry of Security, from 1991 to 1994 (V. N.).

GAZPROM. Russian natural gas monopoly and main provider of Moldova's energy firms **Moldenergo** and **Moldovagas**. As of 1997, Gazprom supplied Moldova with an average 3 billion cubic meters of gas per year at a preferential price of $58 per 1,000 cubic meters. However, most of the natural gas supplied by Gazprom goes to state-controlled firms in the breakaway self-proclaimed **Moldavian Nistrian Republic**, and payments have been chronically lagging behind. Gazprom has threatened several times to cut supplies to Moldova unless it pays off its debt. In 1999, Moldova's debt to Gazprom was over $600 million, out of which **Chişinău** owed about $210 million and the **Tiraspol** breakaway entity over $400 million. Chişinău threatened to cut off gas supplies to Tiraspol, since the trans-Nistrian region is responsible for most of the arrears. For its part, the Tiraspol authorities threatened to halt the transmission of electricity to west-bank Moldova. Most of Moldova's electricity is generated on the **Nistru** east bank, whereas Russian gas deliveries to Moldova are managed by the country's central authority in Chişinău. In 1998, Gazprom bought 50 percent of Moldovagas, becoming the largest shareholder of the company. *See also* ENERGY.

GERMAN-ROMANIAN MILITARY OCCUPATION. Between 22 June and 25 July 1941, Germany's 11th Army and **Romania**'s 3rd and 4th Armies recaptured the entire territory between the **Prut** and **Nistru**

Rivers, or **Bessarabia**, which the **Union of Soviet Socialist Republics (USSR)** had detached from Romania a year before, establishing over most of its territory the **Moldavian Soviet Socialist Republic (MSSR)**, a part of the USSR. The short-lived wartime occupation of Bessarabia by the German and Romanian armies ended in June 1944, when the Red Army reinstated Soviet power, establishing one more time the MSSR as a component of the USSR. *See also* ANNEXATION; MOLOTOV-RIBBENTROP PACT; SOVEREIGNTY.

GHIKA, GHEORGHE (?–1664). Prince of Moldova for one year (1658–1659) and in Wallachia from 1659 to 1660. He was a member of a family of Albanian origin that had become thoroughly assimilated in Moldova. The Ghikas were to form a local dynasty and play an important role in the history of both Moldova and **Wallachia**. Many of Gheorghe Ghika's successors were later assigned by the **Ottoman Empire** as ruling princes of the **Danubian Principalities** during the **Phanariote era** and its immediate aftermath.

GHIKA, GRIGORE II (?–1752). Prince of Moldova at the time of the **Russo-Turkish Wars**. He reigned three times in Moldova (1726–1733; 1735–1741; 1747–1748) and twice in **Wallachia** (1733–1735 and 1748–1752).

GHIKA, GRIGORE III (?–1777). Prince of Moldova in 1764–1767 and 1774–1777, at a time when the tensions between the **Russian Empire** and the **Ottoman Empire** intensified. He also reigned in **Wallachia** for one year (1768–1769). In Moldova, he reformed the education college of **Iaşi**, which he renamed the Academy for Learning and the Advancement of Knowledge. Grigore Ghika III was decapitated by order of the sultan on 12 October 1777 for having clandestinely opposed Turkey's policies vis-à-vis Moldova, especially the 1775 cession of its northern districts, renamed **Bucovina**, to the **Habsburg Empire**. A landmark play titled *Occisio Gregorii in Moldavia Tragice Expressa* (The Murder of Gregorius in Moldavia Tragically Expressed), attributed to Transylvanian cleric Samuil Vulcan and written between 1778 and 1780, was inspired by Prince Grigore Ghika's tragic assassination.

GHIKA, GRIGORE V / GRIGORE ALEXANDRU GHIKA (1807–1857). Prince of Moldova from 1849 to 1856. His reign was interrupted by the Russian occupation of October 1853–September

1854. He was the last reigning prince of Moldova before the reorganization of the principality under the terms of the 1856 **Congress of Paris** and the 1858 **Convention of Paris**. He was also the last prince of Moldova to be anointed by the ecumenical patriarch of Constantinople in the ancient Byzantine ritual, a tradition followed by most of his predecessors.

GHIKA, MATEI (?–1756). Prince of Moldova between 1753 and 1756. He also reigned in **Wallachia** for one year before occupying Moldova's throne (1752–1753).

GHIKA, SCARLAT (?–1766). Prince of Moldova from 1757 to 1758. He also ruled twice over **Wallachia, in** 1758–1761 and 1765–1766.

GHIMPU, GHEORGHE (1937–). Political leader and national activist. A native of Colonița, **Lăpușna**, Ghimpu was the founder and chairman of the Democratic Party of Moldova (1990–1994), a political formation that merged with the **Party of Democratic Forces** in 1994. He later founded a small right-wing party, the Party for Reform. Ghimpu is the president of Moldova's Association of the Victims of the Communist Regime (V. N.). *See also* POLITICAL BLOCS AND PARTIES.

GIURGIULESTI. Southernmost point of Moldova, 200 meters away from the northern bank of the maritime **Danube River**, near its confluence with the **Prut River**. Giurgiulești is located about 7 kilometers upstream from the Danube port city of **Reni**, in neighboring Ukraine. A 1999 border agreement with Ukraine created a several-hundred-meter exit on the bank of the Danube, south of the village of Giurgiulești, that restored Moldova's riparian status on the Danube. In 1994, Moldova's Parliament approved a concession agreement on the construction of an oil terminal at Giurgiulești by the Moldovan-Greek joint-stock company Terminal, with technical assistance from Dutch and Russian companies. Giurgiulești was said to have the potential of delivering a minimum of 365,000 tons of fuel in the first year of the terminal's functioning and over 2 million tons a year thereafter, but in 1999 a more conservative estimate questioned these figures and concluded that the Giurgiulești project should be reexamined.

Located upstream of the Danube Delta, where Europe's largest river is accessible to seagoing tankers, the Giurgiulești opening is expected to break Moldova's landlocked position and contribute to strengthening its economic independence from energy suppliers located across its north-eastern borders. Moldovan ecologist groups and some **nongovernmental organizations** have strongly opposed the construction of the Giurgiuleşti terminal, arguing that it will pose a threat of industrial pollution and will damage the **environment** of the Danube Delta and its eco-habitat. *See also* BORDERS OF MOLDOVA.

GLADUN, EUGENIU (1936–). Minister of public health in Moldova's governments of 1998 and 1999. A native of Nesfoaia, Noua Suliţă, **Northern Bucovina**, Dr. Gladun is a member of the Moldovan Academy of Sciences. He has headed Moldova's Institute for Mother and Child Health Care and Scientific Research since 1987 (V. N.).

GLASNOST. Political concept launched in 1986 by **Mikhail Gorbachev** to promote more openness in the debate of policies and more freedom of the media. The glasnost policies triggered an explosion of open discussions that ended in challenging the Soviet Communist Party's policies not only in the **Union of Soviet Socialist Republics (USSR)**, but also, with the exception of Albania and **Romania**, in all of Eastern Europe's Communist-dominated countries. The glasnost climate exerted a tremendous impact in Soviet-held Moldova, where it provoked an open debate about the country's **language issue** and **alphabet issue**, the cultural and political underpinnings of which gave the first impulse to Moldova's struggle for independence and emancipation from the USSR. *See also* PERESTROIKA.

GLASUL. The first periodical published in the Latin alphabet by Moldovan intellectuals while the country was still a Soviet republic. The groundbreaking issue was printed illegally in March 1989 by members of the Dacia Society, a group of Moldovans living outside Moldova in what was then the Latvian Soviet Socialist Republic. Though not a Romance language, Latvian was allowed by the Soviets to be written in Latin characters throughout all the years of Moscow's rule over the Baltic republic. Unavailable in Moldova under Moscow's policies of **Russification**, Latin characters were nevertheless available in Latvia, where the alphabet issue had no direct political relevance to Soviet Russia's policies, as was the case in Moldova. Carried clandestinely into what was then Soviet Moldavia, the approximately 60,000 copies of the March 1989 edition of *Glasul* had a huge cultural impact in the context of the country's pro-independence movement. *See also* ALPHABET ISSUE.

GLODENI. Chief town of the former *raion,* or district, of the same name, 164 kilometers northwest of **Chişinău**. The first recorded mention of the village of Glodeni dates back to the 17th century. The former Glodeni district had over 65,700 inhabitants (1993 est.). Glodeni is part of the reestablished *judeţ* of **Bălţi**.

GOLEA, ANTON (1965–). Director of the press service of the presidency of Moldova. A graduate of the Journalism Department of the **State University of Moldova**, Golea worked for several years with the government news agency Moldova-Press. After 1992, he served as **Chişinău** correspondent of the Russian news agency Interfax and was one of the cofounders of the Russian independent news agency **Infotag** in 1993.

GORBACHEV, MIKHAIL (1931–). Russian statesman and politician, secretary-general of the Communist Party of the Soviet Union between 1985 and 1991, and last leader of the **Union of Soviet Socialist Republics (USSR)** before its dissolution. Gorbachev initiated a program of reforms including a democratization of the political process through the policies of **glasnost** and **perestroika** and a wide array of measures calling for economic, political, and social change that eventually backfired, ending in the disbanding of the Soviet Communist Party and of the Soviet Union itself in 1991. Gorbachev's policies exerted a liberating influence on the independence movements of the Soviet republics, including Moldova, which proclaimed its own independence in August 1991, while Gorbachev was still in charge as leader of the USSR. Gorbachev is widely considered responsible for the end of the Cold War. He was awarded the Nobel Peace Prize in 1990.

GORE, PAUL (1875–1927). Writer, historian, and specialist in heraldry, Gore founded in 1905 the Moldovan Cultural Society, which fought for the recognition of the Moldovan people's cultural rights by czarist Russia. In 1917, he was elected president of the Moldovan National Party and adopted a **unionist** stance. His writings in **Russian** (published in *Bessarabskie oblastnye vedemosti*) include essays on Moldovan writers **Alexandru Donici** and **Vasile Alecsandri**. Gore was a member of the Heraldic Council of France and of other international societies devoted to the study of blazonry.

GREEK PROJECT. A plan devised by Russia's Empress **Catherine the Great** and proposed to Austria's Emperor Joseph II in 1782. The design was meant to establish an Austro-Russian sphere of influence against the **Ottoman Empire** in East-Central Europe and the Balkans. The Greek Project included the creation of two buffer states: a reconstituted **Dacia** encompassing Moldova and **Wallachia**, to be ruled by an Orthodox sovereign acceptable to both the **Russian Empire** and the **Habsburg Empire**, and a restored Greek Empire south of the **Danube River**, to be ruled by Catherine the Great's grandson Konstantin.

GRIGORIOPOL. Chief town of the Grigoriopol *raion*, or district, on the east bank of the **Nistru River**, currently under the authority of the self-proclaimed **Moldavian Nistrian Republic**. The town was founded in the wake of the Russian conquest of the new lands stretching between the Bug and the Nistru Rivers and the establishment of the frontier of the **Russian Empire** on the Nistru in 1792. Most of its first settlers were Armenian refugees from Moldova's Turkish-held territory, chiefly from the towns of **Ismail, Chilia**, and **Căuşeni**. The Grigoriopol district had an estimated population of over 52,000 inhabitants in 1993.

GRIMALSCHI, ANATOL (1951–). Minister of education and science in Moldova's governmental cabinets of 1998 and 1999. A native of Chiperceni, **Orhei**, Grimalschi is a graduate of Chişinău Polytechnic Institute and a member of the **Party of Democratic Forces**. He served as assistant deputy minister of education and science in Moldova's government between 1992 and 1993. Grimalschi is also the author of over 100 specialized studies and the creator of 22 patented technical and scientific inventions (V. N.).

GROSU, GURIE (1877–1943). Metropolitan of **Bessarabia** between 1928 and 1936. A native of **Lăpuşna**, Grosu was educated in **Chişinău** and Kiev, Ukraine. In 1902, he became a monk at the **Chiţcani Monastery** and began taking an active part in the attempts to shed the cultural consequences of **Russification**, but he was forced to leave Bessarabia under pressure and persecution. Between 1909 and 1917, he lived in Smolensk and other monasteries of Russia. He returned to his native land in 1917 at the time of the Bolshevik Revolution and became the key religious figure in Bessarabia's struggle for independence and, later on, union with **Romania**. He was the author of *Abecedarul Moldovenesc* (1917), the first Moldovan primer, or handbook, published in Bessarabia in the Roman alphabet in the 20th century. *See also* ORTHODOX CHURCH.

GROSUL, IACHIM (1912–1976). Historian and pro-Soviet cultural activist and a member of the **Communist Party** since 1939, Grosul was one of the chief figures of Soviet Moldavia's intelligentsia. He authored a book on the economic development of **Bessarabia** under Russian rule in the 19th century and coordinated an eight-volume pro-Russian encyclopedia of the **Moldavian Soviet Socialist Republic** (*Enciclopedia Republicii Sovietice Socialiste Moldoveneşti*), published between 1964 and 1981 by Soviet Moldavia's Academy of Sciences.

GROSSU, SEMION (1934–). Secretary-general of the **Communist Party** of the **Moldavian Soviet Socialist Republic**, appointed in 1980 by **Leonid Brezhnev** to replace **Ivan Bodiul**. He was the last Moscow-appointed hard-line leader before Moldova's **declaration of independence**. **Mikhail Gorbachev** replaced Grossu with **Petru Lucinschi** as first secretary of the party in the fall of 1989. *See also* GLASNOST; PERESTROIKA.

GUAM. An informal grouping of former Soviet republics—namely, Georgia, Ukraine, Azerbaijan, and Moldova—sharing specific economic and trade interests within the broader economic structures of the **Commonwealth of Independent States**.

GUARANTEE ADMINISTRATION UNIT (GAU). State-owned company operating in Moldova as a separate legal entity on an independent and commercial basis. With the support of the **World Bank**, the mission of the GAU is to help develop and stimulate foreign commercial sources of financing to fund Moldovan enterprises through the issuance of special **Political Risks Guarantees** to foreign sources of credit. *See also* BANKING.

GUBERNIIA. Between 1874 and 1917, most of present-day Moldova, which was incorporated into the **Russian Empire** as **Bessarabia** under the terms of the 1812 **Treaty of Bucharest**, was governed as a *guberniia*, or administrative-territorial unit, strictly dependent on Russia's central government. Russia's division into *gubernii* dates back to 1708. The *gubernii* system was replaced by a Soviet-style centralized form of administration in 1923.

GURITENCO, VLADIMIR (1954–). Minister of labor, social protection, and the family in Moldova's governments formed in 1998 and 1999. A native of Molovata, **Orhei**, Guritenco is a member of the **Dem-**

ocratic Convention of Moldova. His career includes various appointments in the public administration of the city of **Chișinău** (V. N.).

GUTU, ION (1943–). Economist and politician, former minister of economy and reform, and deputy prime minister in Moldova's government of 1997, Guțu has a doctorate in economics. He is the author of a book on the country's economic situation titled *The Republic of Moldova: An Economy in Transition,* published in 1998. Between 1967 and 1980, he held leading positions in the Youth Organization of the **Moldavian Soviet Socialist Republic**. From 1980 to 1982, he headed an organization of the **Communist Party** in **Chișinău**; from 1982 to 1987, he served as chairman of the Industry Direction of the Central Committee of the Communist Party; and from 1990 to 1991, he was general director of the Industrial Union of Moldova (V. N.).

GUTU, LIDIA (1954–). Deputy prime minister in Moldova's government formed in December 1999. A native of Verejeni, **Edineț**, Guțu is a graduate of the Polytechnic Institute of Moldova. Since 1998 she has worked as executive manager of the Credit and Financial Protection Department of Unibank, and was a chief economist in the Ministries of Health and Finance between 1975 and 1995. From 1996 to 1998 she served as vice president of Moldova's General Federation of Trade Unions (V. N.).

-H-

HABSBURG EMPIRE. Political entity that evolved across time from the earlier Ostmark established in A.D. 976, which came under the rule of the Habsburg family in 1273. It gradually accumulated territories in Central and Eastern Europe and asserted itself as a European power of first magnitude in the 16th and 17th centuries. Among other imperial pursuits, it eventually came to clash with the **Ottoman Empire** over Hungary and the Principality of **Transylvania**, Moldova's western neighbor. In 1689, the Diet of Poszony (Bratislava) proclaimed Hungary a hereditary kingdom under the authority of the Habsburg Crown. Under the terms of the 1699 Peace of Carlovitz, Transylvania, at that time under Turkish suzerainty, came under the Habsburg rule, whose continuous expansion led to several alliances with the **Russian Empire**, one of which ended up in the 1772 partition of Poland among Austria, Russia, and Prussia.

To make the new territorial gains contiguous with their recently acquired possessions, the Habsburgs incorporated the northern territories of historic Moldova, ceded by Ottoman Turkey to Austria in 1775, and dubbed them **Bucovina**. Between 1867 and 1918, the Habsburg Empire was ruled as a dual entity as Austria-Hungary.

At the end of World War I, in keeping with the **Wilsonian principles** of self-determination, the territories that had constituted the Habsburg Empire were divided between Austria (proclaimed an independent republic on 12 November 1918) and Hungary (proclaimed an independent republic on 16 November 1918), while other Habsburg possessions either declared themselves independent states (Czechoslovakia, Poland, and Yugoslavia) or merged with the countries to which they were ethnically and historically akin (Venetia with Italy, Bucovina and Transylvania with **Romania**). Bucovina proclaimed its union with Romania on 27 November 1918 in **Cernăuți**, and Transylvania proclaimed its union with Romania on 1 December 1918 in Alba Iulia. *See also* NATIONAL UNIFICATION.

HADARCA, ION (1949–). Writer and cultural-political activist, Hadârcă played an important role in his country's cultural and national revival of 1989 and its **declaration of independence** in 1991. As one of the leaders of the **Popular Front of Moldova**, he served as the first vice president of independent Moldova's initial legislature. His most recent book, *Ambasadorul Atlantidei* (The Ambassador of Atlantis), published in 1997, is a multifaceted political satire crafted in modernist verse.

HAJDEU, ALEXANDRU (1811–1872). Scholar and author, Hâjdeu is one of the representative personalities of the first generation of local writers raised in **Bessarabia** under Russian rule. He was educated in **Chișinău** and Harkov, Ukraine, and travelled widely across various parts of the **Russian Empire**, Poland, and Ukraine. He owned property and land at Cristinești, in the region of **Hotin**, and was active in the cities of Hotin and Chișinău as a lawyer and a local school inspector. Writing mostly in **Russian**, Hâjdeu published poems and other short writings in *Vestnik Evropi* (1830), *Teleskop* (1833), and *Molva* (1835). Two of Hâjdeu's end-of-school-year speeches—"Cuvânt cătră elevii școalei ținutului Hotinului, ruși și moldoveni" (An Address to the Students of the Hotin District, Russians and Moldovans) and "Suvenire de cele trecute" (Memories of Things Past)—were published in *Curierul românesc* (1839) and *Dacia literară*. His essay on Bessarabian writers published in the Russian journal *Teleskop* in 1835 is a survey of the men of letters Hâjdeu knew, among them **Alexandru Donici** and **Constantin Stamati**. Hâjdeu's son, Bogdan—who changed his family name to Hasdeu (*see* BOGDAN PETRICEICU HASDEU)—followed in his father's footsteps and became a 19th-century scholar. Alexandru Hâjdeu's bust graces the alley dedicated to Moldova's classic writers in Chişinău's Central Park.

HALIPPA, PAN (1883–1979). Political, cultural, and military leader born in Cubolta, **Soroca**, Pan (short for Pantelimon) Halippa was the founder and editor of *Cuvânt moldovenesc*, a periodical that played the part of a linchpin in unifying **Bessarabia**'s movement for separation from Russia in the final stages of World War I amid the upheaval created by the Bolshevik Revolution. In March 1917, Halippa was elected secretary-general of the Moldovan National Party and soon after became the organizer of the first 16 Moldovan battalions that maintained order in Bessarabia in the aftermath of the disintegration of czarist authority over the province at the outbreak of the Russian Revolution. He was elected vice chairman of **Sfatul Ţării**, which proclaimed the independence of the **Moldavian Democratic Federated Republic** and, later on, its union with **Romania**, in the government of which he was twice a minister (1927 and 1930). His lifelong experiences are mirrored in his political testament: *Testament pentru urmaşi* (Chişinău, 1991). After World War II, Halippa was arrested by the Soviet authorities and sentenced to forced labor. He was freed before completing his 25-year sentence and died in Romania at the age of 96.

HANCESTI. Chief town of the newly reestablished *judeţ* of **Lăpuşna** and one of the important agricultural centers of Moldova, located 36 kilometers southwest of **Chişinău** along the valley of the **Cogâlnic River**. Hânceşti is the administrative center of an integral dairy products, cattle-breeding, and grape-growing economic area. Currently boasting a population of over 118,000 inhabitants, Hânceşti was first mentioned as a village in an official document of 1522. Under the post–World War II policies of **Russification**, Hânceşti was renamed Kotovsk.

HASDEU, BOGDAN PETRICEICU (1838–1907). The son of **Alexandru Hâjdeu**, Hasdeu was born at Cristineşti, **Hotin**. He was educated in **Chişinău**, at various schools in Poland, and at the University of Harkov, Ukraine, which he eventually left to serve for some time in the army of the **Russian Empire**. He left Russia in 1857 and settled in the **Princi-**

pality of Moldova, where he served for a short time as a judge in **Cahul**, then embarked on an impetuous cultural career, asserting himself as a historian, philologist, and literary author. In 1859, Hasdeu edited the first history journal in the **Romanian language**, *Foaia de storiă română* (A Paper of Romanian History), followed in 1862–1863 by *Din Moldova* (From Moldova) and numerous other scholarly, philological, and literary publications. Hasdeu's major works pertaining to the history of the language are *Cuvente den betrani* (Words from Yore), published between 1877 and 1881, and the unfinished *Etymologicum Magnum Romaniae* (Romania's Great Etymological Dictionary), published between 1886 and 1898. Hasdeu died at Câmpina, **Romania**. His bronze statue is one of the monuments that grace the pantheon of Moldova's writers in Chişinău's Central Park.

HEALTH. Moldova has over 300 hospitals with a total of over 50,000 beds, to produce a ratio of 124.7 hospital beds per 10,000 people. The largest number of medical institutions operate in **Chişinău**, including the National Clinical Hospital, an oncology research, cancer treatment, and cardiology center. In Chişinău and throughout the country, outpatient medical care is provided by about 560 medical centers. Moldova's medical staff consists of over 17,000 doctors and about 48,000 nurses and other medical professionals. Moldova's pharmaceutical supplies rely mostly on imports. The government is currently implementing the Project for Pharmaceutical Industry Development, designed to build new factories based on foreign **investments**.

HOSPODAR. A Slavic term used to denote the office of the prince of Moldova while under the suzerainty of the **Ottoman Empire**, more especially during the **Phanariote era**. Alongside *voivode, hospodar* was used as a Slavic synonym for the older vernacular *domn* or *domnitor,* derived from the Latin *dominus,* traditionally denoting the prince of the land.

HOTIN. A city on the west bank of the **Nistru River**, north of **Chişinău** (now part of Ukraine, under the name of Khotin). Its fortress was erected by Moldova's Prince **Alexander the Good** as a military outpost and border checkpoint on what used to be a much-frequented crossing of the Nistru. During the war waged by **Wallachia**'s Prince **Michael the Brave** against Moldova's Prince **Ieremia Movilă**, Hotin became the temporary residence of the latter's court (1600). A peace between Poland and the **Ottoman Empire** was signed in Hotin in 1621. It became an advanced military outpost of Turkey (*raya*) in 1723 and went to Russia at the time of the 1812 **annexation** of the eastern half of historical Moldova, or **Bessarabia**, by the **Russian Empire**. The Hotin citadel was dismantled as a military facility in 1855.

The first mathematics handbook in the **Romanian language** was published in Hotin in 1795 by Bishop **Amfilochie Hotiniul**. The city of Hotin was part of **Romania** during the interwar period. In the wake of the 1940 incorporation of Bessarabia into the **Union of Soviet Socialist Republics**, it was detached from the rest of the then newly established **Moldavian Soviet Socialist Republic** and awarded to Soviet Ukraine.

HUMAN RIGHTS. Moldova ratified the European Convention on Human Rights on 24 July 1997 but declared that for the time being, it considers itself unable to ensure the convention's implementation in the breakaway trans-Nistrian districts. U.S. State Department reports have acknowledged that human rights are generally respected by Moldova's government but are being abused in the trans-Nistrian region. In 1998, the **Tiraspol** State Committee for Information shut down the newspaper *Novaya Gazeta,* allegedly for not being compliant with the ideological demands of the leftist leadership of the breakaway region. The paper's editorial policies tried to steer away from political extremism. Human rights violations in the Tiraspol region have been cited by Amnesty International, the International Human Rights Law Group, and the Romanian Helsinki Committee, with special emphasis on the case of the **Ilaşcu Group**, detained by the authorities of the self-proclaimed **Moldavian Nistrian Republic**.

-I-

IALOVENI. Chief town of the former *raion,* or district, of the same name, 12 kilometers southwest of **Chişinău**. Ialoveni was first mentioned in an official document in 1502, under the reign of **Stephen the Great**. At the time of the establishment of the Ialoveni district by the Soviet administration (1977), Ialoveni was renamed Kutozov, after the name of Russian Marshal Mikhail Kutuzov (1745–1813). Ialoveni regained its original name after Moldova's independence. The former district of Ialoveni had a population of over 87,000 inhabitants (1993 est.). The law on the reorganization of Moldova's territory, promulgated in 1999, included Ialoveni in the newly established *judeţ* of Chişinău.

IALPUG RIVER. Located in southeastern Moldova, tributary to a large lake of the same name that stretches north of the **Danube** Delta in Ukraine. The total length of the river is 142 kilometers, out of which 135 kilometers lie in the territory of the Republic of Moldova.

IASI/JASSY. A city in **Romania**, formerly the capital of the **Principality of Moldova**. In 1565, Prince **Alexandru Lăpuşneanu** moved Moldova's court from **Suceava** to Iaşi. The ancient Iaşi district, which used to straddle both banks of the **Prut River**, was cut into two at the time of the Russian **annexation** of the river's east-bank territories in 1812. The **Russian Empire** preserved the Iaşi district under its original name as a territorial unit of **Bessarabia** until 1887. In west-bank Moldova, the district of Iaşi is in existence to this day, but the city of Iaşi ceased to be an administrative capital soon after the principality's union with **Wallachia**. A number of religious and historical monuments founded by Moldova's rulers across time have given Iaşi a distinct profile that illustrates the city's past—among them, the St. Nicholas Church, erected under the reign of **Stephen the Great**; the Dancu Monastery, founded in 1541 by **Petru Rareş**; the Barnovschi Church, founded in 1627 by **Miron Barnovschi-Movilă**; the Three Hierarchs and Golia Churches, erected in 1639 and 1640 by **Vasile Lupu**; and the St. Spiridon Foundation, built in 1727 by **Grigore Ghika II**. It was in Iaşi that Moldova's **Demetrius Cantemir** met with Russia's **Peter the Great** ahead of the 1711 Russo-Moldo-Turkish battle of Stănileşti. The **Treaty of Iaşi** brought Russia's border to the **Nistru River** and made Russia a direct neighbor of Moldova in 1792. During World War I, Iaşi was temporarily the capital of rump Romania (1916–1918).

IASI, TREATY OF. Signed in the capital of the **Principality of Moldova** on 9 January 1792 (Eastern calendar date: 29 December 1791). Under the terms of the Iaşi Treaty, the **Ottoman Empire** ceded the entire territory lying between the Bug River and the **Nistru River** to the **Russian Empire**, a move that made Moldova, for the first time in its history, a direct neighbor of Russia. *See also* RUSSO-TURKISH WARS.

ILASCU, ILIE (1952–). Activist against the Russophone separatist movement in the **Moldavian Nistrian Republic**. A native of Taxobeni, **Făleşti**, Ilaşcu was arrested by the **Tiraspol** authorities in June 1992 for what was described as an alleged involvement with five others in the killing of two trans-Nistrian separatists in the spring of 1992. After a dubious trial in Tiraspol, in which Ilaşcu pleaded not guilty, he was sentenced to death. The sentence has never been carried out, and two of those convicted were released. Foreign observers of the Ilaşcu trial think it was characterized by many procedural errors and **human rights** violations. Whereas most **Nistru** west-bank Moldovans consider Ilaşcu a freedom fighter, most Nistru east-bank separatists consider him a convicted killer. Regardless of such diverging viewpoints, Ilaşcu has emerged as one of the most visible persons brought to the forefront by the 1992 **trans-Nistrian conflict**. In Moldova's 1998 parliamentary elections, though behind bars, Ilaşcu was elected deputy on the ticket of the **Party of Democratic Forces**. In that capacity, in March 1999, he cast his ballot by mail in the decisive vote that led, by one voice, to the confirmation of the **Ion Sturza** cabinet. Ilaşcu's vote was challenged as illegal by the Party of Moldova's Communists.

Ilaşcu's case (described as that of "the only European parliamentarian serving his mandate in jail") was brought to the attention of the Council of Europe. In 1998, a deputy chairperson of the Parliamentary Assembly of the Council of Europe was allowed to visit Ilaşcu. However, the visit did not take place in the prison where he is usually detained, but in a different place, described by the Tiraspol authorities as a "hotel." A 1998 Amnesty International report called one more time for a review of the Ilie Ilaşcu case. *See also* ILASCU GROUP.

ILASCU GROUP. The notion of the Ilaşcu Group appeared in the wake of the arrest and prosecution by the **Tiraspol** authorities of six men, allegedly conspirators and accomplices in the killing of two trans-Nistrian separatists in 1992. In 1993, **Ilie Ilaşcu** was tried in Tiraspol as the leader of a group that included Andrei Ivanţoc, Alexandru Leşco, Tudor Petrov-Popa, Petru Godiac, and Valeriu Garbuz. Some Moldovans believe that the Ilaşcu Group was framed by the Russophone authorities in Tiraspol to provoke anti-**Chişinău** exacerbation among the **Nistru** east-bank Moldovans. A 1998 Amnesty International report said that their trial apparently failed to meet international standards of fairness and that the men had allegedly been prosecuted for political reasons, due to their membership in the **Christian Democrat Popular Front**, a party in favor of Moldova's eventual reunification with **Romania**. *See also* SEPARATISM.

IMPERIALISM. A notion frequently used by advocates of Moldova's independence to denote the country's underprivileged status while a part of the Russian imperial system between 1812 and 1917 and of the Stalinist Soviet

Union after World War II. Historically, the term denotes the extension of power of a state through the acquisition—usually by military conquest—of a territory, the subjection of its native population to alien rule imposed by force, and the exploitation of the new land's natural and economical resources. Imperialism is characteristically based on maintaining a sharp distinction between the ruling nation, described as preeminent, and the subordinate population, usually also subject to **colonization**. This discrimination was typically applied in Moldova's case by means of language and cultural policies, as well as by the totalitarian use of law and coercive power. *See also* ANNEXATION; RUSSIAN EMPIRE; SOVEREIGNTY.

INCULET, ION (1885–1940). Politician and scientist, Inculeț studied medicine and physics in czarist Russia, where he was active as a professor at the University of St. Petersburg. He was an acute observer of the Russian Revolution, which he vividly described in his memoirs, *O revoluție trăită* (Living through a Revolution), republished posthumously in **Chişinău** in 1994. In 1917, he was elected chairman of **Sfatul Țării** and president of the **Moldavian Democratic Federated Republic**. After the latter's 1918 union with **Romania**, he moved to Bucharest, became a member of the Romanian Academy, and served as minister in several governments.

INDEPENDENCE. *See* DECLARATION OF INDEPENDENCE; SOVEREIGNTY.

INDUSTRY. Moldova's industrial sector accounted for about 23 percent of the net material product of the **national economy** in 1998, down from 38.9 percent in 1993. The industrial sector accounts for less than one-third of the gross domestic product. It comprises about 600 major and midsized enterprises and provides over 250,000 jobs. In 1997, Moldova's industrial output was down 2.2 percent from 1996, with 54 percent of the enterprises reporting a fall in production.

About 46 percent of the industrial sector is based on food processing, which operates in close interaction with **agriculture**. Electric **energy** production accounts for 17.7 percent of Moldova's total industrial output; engineering and metal processing, which includes agricultural machinery and foundry equipment, for about 10.8 percent; and light industry, which includes refrigerators and freezers, washing machines, hosiery, textiles, and shoes, for about 6 percent.

Most of Moldova's industry was created during the Soviet era and is located on the east bank of the **Nistru River**, on territory currently controlled by the separatist authorities of **Tiraspol**. That sliver of land, not controlled by the Moldovan government, holds only about 16 percent of the country's territory and 14 percent of its population, but it accounts for 28 percent of the country's industrial enterprises, 21 percent of its industrial employment, and over 33 percent of its total industrial output, which includes textiles, power transformers, cement, and steel. In 1995, via Ukraine, it exported $6 million worth of steel to the United States—that is, 80 percent of Moldova's total trade with the United States during that year.

Moldova's food-processing industry, which is less affected by the consequences of the east-bank separatist conditions, includes over 200 enterprises producing wines, canned fruit and vegetables, meat and dairy products, sunflower seed oil, sugar, perfumes, and cosmetics. The average potential capacity per season includes the processing of 1.4 million tons of grapes, 1.6 decaliters of brandy, over 10 million bottles of sparkling wines, 500,000 tons of sugar, and 50,000 tons of tobacco.

The virtual lack of a supportive network for industrial small- and medium-sized enterprises is an acute problem in Moldova, with its traditional small market economy and its agricultural and agro-processing specialization. Industrial restructuring is being implemented with assistance from the **World Bank**, which by 1997 had helped to successfully complete the radical restructuring of over 15 industrial enterprises. An additional 40 industrial enterprises were slated for restructuring in 1997–1998.

In 1998, a number of important industrial units were acquired by foreign investors, among them Farmaco, Moldova's main pharmaceutical producer, with 84 percent of its shares bought by the Anglo-Romanian firm Eurofarm; the **Rezina** cement plant Ciment, with over 50 percent of its shares bought by the French firm Lafarge; Agropetrol, with 80 percent of its shares bought by the American company Transoil, Ltd.; and the textile plant Floare Carpet, with 58 percent of its shares bought by the German company Kulikoni.

Moldova's industrial sector was affected by Russia's financial crisis in 1998, which triggered a diminution of the country's exports to the **Russian Federation** and other **Commonwealth of Independent States** foreign trade partners. Official statistics indicated that before the end of 1998, the machine-building industrial sector output was down 89 percent as compared to 1997. Comparing 1998 with 1997, the timber industry output was down over 76 percent, the light industry output was down over 85 percent, the wine and liquor industry output was down over 64 percent, the canned food-processing industry was down over 72 percent, and the sugar-processing industry was down over 87 percent. The 1998 overall figures of Moldova's industrial output indicate a decline of 42.2 percent as compared to 1990.

INFOTAG. One of Moldova's leading private news agencies, based in **Chişinău**. It distributes a daily news report, a weekly business bulletin, and a bimonthly banking and financial news bulletin to approximately 1,500 subscribers.

INOCHENTISM. A millenarian religious movement initiated between 1909 and 1911 in the monastery of **Balta** by the Moldovan monk Inochentie (by his lay name, Ion Levizor), who preached that the end of the world was near and that the age of the Antichrist had arrived. Inochentie's ideas were fast to spread from the east bank of the **Nistru River** all over the rural areas of **Bessarabia**, where his sermons in the local language and his charitable assistance to the poor and the sick stirred up fervor and popular upheaval, with strong adverse reactions from the hierarchy of the Russian-speaking **Orthodox Church**, which had him deported. When Inochentie died in 1917, the movement had fizzled out, but the sense of his appeal helped articulate the growing estrangement of Bessarabia's faithful from the Russian-speaking church that had officially dominated Bessarabia's religious life for over a century.

INTERFRONT. Political movement formed in July 1989 by delegates representing Moldova's ethnic minorities in an effort to counter the initiatives of the **Popular Front of Moldova**, which was trying to establish the local language of the republic's majority as the official language of Moldova and to acknowledge the common cultural roots shared by Moldovans and Romanians. Interfront fought back by emphasizing the existence of a distinct Moldovan identity, separate from that of neighboring **Romania**. It pleaded vigorously in favor of maintaining **Russian** as the common language of communication of the country and for naming the language of the majority "**Moldavian**" rather than **Romanian**. In December 1991, Interfront changed its name and reestablished itself as the **Unity-Edinstvo Movement**.

INTERNATIONAL MONETARY FUND (IMF). The International Monetary Fund provided a $71 million loan to Moldova in 1994, a $65 million loan in 1995, and a $41 million loan in 1996. A three-year $185 million standby loan was approved in 1996, but only part of it had been disbursed by 1998, due to what the IMF considered to be the country's unsatisfactory economic performance. The credit was suspended in 1997 after Moldova's Parliament blocked proposed reforms in **agriculture** and **industry**. Its first three tranches released before the 1998 general elections totalled about $52 million. In 1998, the IMF praised Moldova's efforts toward reform in the **energy** and agricultural sectors, but it described as worrisome the growing external debt, which amounted to $1.3 billion, as well as the government's increasing difficulties in tightening spending and reining in borrowing.

In 1999, the IMF commended Moldova for having adopted strict financial policies and a budget of austerity. Under the circumstances, in January 1999, the IMF considered resuming lending to Moldova. Payments of IMF loans to Moldova were expected to amount to approximately $100 million for 1999, pending evaluations of the country's overall performance and political stability. *See also* ECONOMY, NATIONAL.

INTERNATIONAL ORGANIZATIONS. The Republic of Moldova is a member of several international organizations, which include, in addition to the United Nations, the Council of Europe, the **Organization for Security and Cooperation in Europe**, the North Atlantic Cooperation Council, the **Black Sea Economic Cooperation**, the Community of Riparian Countries of the Black Sea, the United Nations Development Program, the United Nations Industrial Development Organization, the **International Monetary Fund**, the **World Bank**, the European Bank for Reconstruction and Development, the International Labour Organisation, the World Intellectual Property Organization, and the World Health Organization. Moldova has observer status at the World Trade Organization. It is also a member of the **Commonwealth of Independent States**.

INTERNATIONAL REPRESENTATIONS. International bodies represented in the capital of Moldova include the **Organization for Security and Cooperation in Europe**, the **International Monetary Fund**, the **World Bank**, the United Nations Development Program, the United Nations Children's Fund, the United Nations Educational, Scientific, and Cultural Organization, the Central and East European Law Initiative, the Technical Assistance to Commonwealth of Independent States Coordination Unit, the U.S. Peace Corps, **Soros Foundation Moldova**, Alliance Française, and the American Council for Cooperation in Education and Language Studies.

INVESTMENT. Moldova's investment policies are governed by the Act on Foreign Investments of April 1992, subsequently amended in July 1994. There are few formal barriers on foreign investment, and foreign investors enjoy a number of customs remissions and exemptions from taxes and duties. They have the right to transfer abroad foreign currencies earned as investment profits after appropriate payments have been made. Foreign investors may set up joint ventures and enterprises with 100 percent foreign capital by participating in the **privatization** of state-owned properties. Foreigners, legal entities as well as individuals, can participate in these privatizations on an equal footing with citizens of Moldova. Generally speaking, foreign direct investment has been comparatively low, with a cumulative total of $161 million by the end of 1996, a mere $37 per capita. Moreover, most of this investment is dominated not by private firms, but by the European Bank for Reconstruction and Development. Figures for 1998 indicate that by mid-1997, foreign portfolio investment in Moldova had increased steadily to a total of $234 million ($54 million in 1996).

Moldova has accepted the obligations of the **International Monetary Fund**'s contract, Article VIII, Sections 2–3, which require the government to refrain from imposing restrictions on payments and transfers for international transactions or from engaging in discriminatory currency arrangements. The Bilateral Investment Treaty has been approved by the U.S. Senate and ratified by the Moldovan Parliament. *See also* BANKING.

INVISIBLE COLLEGE OF MOLDOVA. A **Soros Foundation Moldova** program started in 1996 in partnership with the Open Society Institute and three universities in **Chişinău**, with the goal of serving as an international higher-education pilot program under the title "Development of Social Sciences in the Higher Education of Moldova." It is oriented toward the amplification of the teaching and research processes in the field of social sciences, by focussing on four main disciplines: political science, sociology, psychology, and philosophy. The goal of the program is to contribute to the preparation of a core group of academics in social sciences and a new generation of leaders in Moldova's fledgling democracy.

ION VODA CEL CUMPLIT (?–1574). Prince of Moldova (1572–1574), Ion Vodă, surnamed "the Terrible" (Cel Cumplit), refused to pay the tribute to the **Ottoman Empire** and tried to shed the sultan's vassalage over the **Principality of Moldova**. In a series of fierce battles waged on the

Nistru and **Danube Rivers**, he unsuccessfully attempted to recapture the strongholds of **Tighina** and **Cetatea Albă,** occupied by the Turks. Crossing into neighboring **Wallachia**, he attacked Brăila, another Turkish-held port city, southwest of the Danube Delta. Eventually, in the battle of Lake Cahul, Moldova's army was crushed by the Ottoman forces. Taken prisoner, Ion Vodă was slain by the Turks (11 June 1574). A historical study devoted to Moldova under his brief reign, titled *Ion Vodă Cel Cumplit,* was published by **Bogdan Petriceicu Hasdeu** in 1865.

IOVV, VASILE (1942–). Former minister of transportation and road construction in Moldova's government of 1997, Iovv is a graduate of the Institute of Food Industry of Kiev (Ukraine). His political career has included various functions after 1980 in the **Communist Party** of the **Moldavian Soviet Socialist Republic**. In the 1998 parliamentary elections, he ran and campaigned on the ticket of the Party of Moldova's Communists. Between 1993 and 1994, he served as economic counselor for the embassy of Moldova to Moscow. He also served as Moldova's minister of transportation and road construction in 1992.

IPSILANTI, ALEXANDRU (1726–1807). Phanariote ruler of Moldova between 1786 and 1788. Ipsilanti also reigned twice in **Wallachia**, in 1774–1782 and 1796–1797.

IPSILANTI, CONSTANTIN (1760–1816). Son of **Alexandru Ipsilanti**, he occupied the throne of Moldova between 1799 and 1801, at the time of heightened tensions between the **Ottoman Empire** and the **Russian Empire**. Like his father, he also reigned over **Wallachia** between 1802 and 1806 and again in 1807.

ISMAIL. Port city of ancient Moldova on the left bank of the **Chilia** branch of the **Danube River** (now Izmail in Ukraine). It was controlled by the **Basarab** princes of **Wallachia** in the 15th century, when the town was known as Smil. Under Moldova's rule, it became the chief town of a historical district mentioned by **Demetrius Cantemir** in his 1714–1716 *Descriptio Moldaviae*. Occupied by the **Ottoman Empire** in the 16th century, it was incorporated into the **Russian Empire** in 1812, as a component of **Bessarabia**. Ismail was returned to Moldova, together with **Bolgrad** and **Cahul**, in the aftermath of Russia's defeat in the Crimean War (1853–1856), and it became part of the **United Principalities**, later **Romania**, until 1878.

The Treaty of Berlin returned it to Russia in the wake of the Russo-Romanian-Turkish War of 1877–1878 (*see* RUSSO–TURKISH WARS). Ismail was returned to Romania when the **Moldavian Democratic Federated Republic** joined the kingdom of Romania in 1918. It was incorporated into the **Union of Soviet Socialist Republics (USSR)** in June 1940 and was attributed by the USSR to Soviet Ukraine, together with the whole of historic Bessarabia's seaboard. After the collapse of the USSR, Ismail remained a part of the Republic of Ukraine.

The **Trilateral Agreement** on transborder cooperation among Moldova, Romania, and Ukraine was signed in Ismail in 1997. It stipulates the creation of a Euro-Region to comprise the areas of the **Lower Danube** and **Upper Prut** and a free trade zone including Galaţi in Romania, **Reni** in Ukraine, and **Giurgiuleşti** in Moldova.

ISTRU, BOGDAN (1914–1993). Author and political activist under Soviet rule, Istru was one of the most vocal proponents of Communist ideology in Moldova's literary life. Between 1947 and 1951, he served as deputy chairman of the Soviet of Ministers of the **Moldavian Soviet Socialist Republic** and was one of Soviet Moldova's representatives in the Supreme Soviet of the **Union of Soviet Socialist Republics**. His collected literary works were published in 1971 and 1991.

-J-

JASSY. *See* IASI.

JEWS. According to 1990 estimates, Moldova's Jews constitute 1.5 percent of the country's population, a sharp decrease from all available historical figures. At the time of the first Russian **annexation** of **Bessarabia**, there were 19,130 Jews in the newly acquired province, making up roughly 4.2 percent of the total population, according to the czarist census of 1817. Through internal migration, especially from Galicia and other provinces of the **Russian Empire**, the Jewish population increased steadily during the 19th century, most of the new settlers establishing themselves in towns and cities, where they were granted privileges, beginning with the 26 September 1830 decree issued by Czar **Nicholas I**. In 1856, Bessarabia's Jews totalled 8 percent of the population, and 11.8 percent in 1897. By 1912, Bessarabia's Jews had become a majority in the cities, accounting for 37.2

percent of the total urban population, with the Russians coming in second with 24.4 percent and the Ukrainians third, with 15.8 percent.

Antagonism against this massive influx occurred, notoriously, in the form of the **Easter Massacre**, a **pogrom** perpetrated in **Chişinău** for two consecutive days at Passover in 1903. Before the end of the century, sporadic anti-Jewish riots had also taken place in smaller cities, **Ismail** and **Cahul** among them.

After Bessarabia's union with **Romania**, anti-Semitic sentiment was fueled by the rhetoric of Romania's extremist nationalist circles and by the perception that some of Bessarabia's Jews were sympathizers of the Soviet Union or activists of the **Communist Party**. This perception was fed in part by the presence of Jewish activists in the underground Communist movement of Bessarabia. In the 1920s and 1930s, that movement entertained ties with Moscow-subordinated Communist Party organizations from across the **Nistru River**, in the then newly established **Moldavian Autonomous Soviet Socialist Republic (MASSR)**. Although numerically small, Romania's interwar Communist movement had some of its strongest constituencies in the Jewish circles of Bessarabia's towns and cities (overall figures for Romania in the Comintern files indicate that in 1933—out of a total of some 1,200 Communist Party members—375 were Romanians, the rest being Jews [300], Russians and Ukrainians [170], Bulgarians [140], and "Moldavians" [70] from the Nistru eastbank MASSR). In its early stages, Communist action in interwar Romania included such Bessarabian activists and operatives as Russian-educated Iosif Chişinevschi and Leonte Răutu, who contributed to the propagation of Communist ideas and later became leading members in the first echelon of the pro-Soviet governing power installed in Bucharest after World War II.

Between the two world wars, the overall demographic figures regarding Bessarabia's Jews remained, roughly speaking, unchanged. Statistics indicate a stable presence of high percentages of Jewish populations in all of Bessarabia's towns and cities. The Romanian 1930 census recorded 205,958 Jews in Bessarabia, making up 7.2 percent of the total population of the province, almost all of them urban dwellers.

The 1940–1941 events in the history of Bessarabia brought about dramatic changes in that configuration. Upon the June 1940 incorporation of Bessarabia into the **Union of Soviet Socialist Republics (USSR)** and the establishment of the **Moldavian Soviet Socialist Republic (MSSR)**, a part of the Jewish population, more especially in Chişinău, **Tighina**, **Bălţi**, and other cities, welcomed the advent of the Soviet rule.

One year later, as the USSR withdrew, almost half of Soviet Moldavia's Jews—81,000 according to Jewish statistics—retreated with the Red Army. Many died on their way, others were deported to Siberia. Upon the return of the Romanian troops in 1941, the remaining 125,000 or so Bessarabian Jews were subject to dire penalties, including atrocities, summary executions, and deportations. According to Jewish statistics, between 1941 and 1942, following orders from Marshal **Ion Antonescu**, the Romanian authorities deported 56,089 Jews from Bessarabia to **Transnistria**. Many of them died or were exterminated during the occupation of that territory by the German and Romanian armies, at war with the Soviet Union.

In the wake of World War II, the Jewish population of the reestablished MSSR amounted to less than 100,000, with a sharp tendency to decline, chiefly through emigration to Israel. Demographic statistics indicate that Jews constituted 3.3 percent of the MSSR population in 1959, 2.7 percent in 1970, and 2.0 percent in 1979. In present-day Moldova, the Jewish community, which includes some 60,000 people, is not discriminated against. However, in the self-proclaimed **Moldavian Nistrian Republic**, which is currently home to almost one-fourth of Moldova's Jews, some authorities' anti-Semitic attitudes prompted many of them to envisage emigration. A periodical in Yiddish and **Russian**—*Undzer Kol* and *Nash Golos,* respectively—is published in Chişinău, and Hebrew and Yiddish programs are transmitted on Moldova's State Television one and one-half hours per month; Yiddish-language programs are aired by Moldova's State Radio one hour per month. *See also* WAR DEPORTATIONS.

JOSU, VICTOR (1953–). Politician and publicist, Josu was one of the founders and leaders of Moldova's Social Democratic Party (1990–1994). Since 1996, he has served as director of the Department of Political Analysis of the Moldovan Party of Revival and Accord, headed by Moldova's former president **Mircea Snegur** (V. N.). *See also* POLITICAL BLOCS AND PARTIES.

JUDET. Traditional territorial and administrative unit of Moldova (plural: *judeţe*), dismantled under Russian and Soviet rule and reestablished in 1999, after Moldova's Parliament voted into law the country's territorial reform, calling for the reorganization of the territory into *judeţe*: **Bălţi, Cahul, Chişinău, Dubăsari, Edineţ, Lăpuşna, Orhei, Soroca, Tighina**, and **Ungheni**, plus the autonomous territorial unit of **Gagauz Yeri** and, later on, **Taraclia**. Prior to the 1940 creation of the **Moldavian**

Soviet Socialist Republic, most of the territory covered by present-day Moldova was similarly divided into a roughly equivalent number of *judeţe,* namely, Bălţi, Cahul, **Cetatea Albă**, **Hotin**, **Ismail**, Lăpuşna, Orhei, Soroca, and Tighina.

In terms of historical usage, the noun *judeţ*—equally in administrative use in **Romania**—is derived from *jude,* a traditional title meaning "judge" and, by extension, a local lord in charge of justice. *See also RAION; TINUT.*

JUS VALLACHICUM. Moldova's oldest system of law based on traditional norms and customs, enforced in the principality ever since its inception in the 14th century. Jus Vallachicum, or the Wallachian Law in English, was part of Moldova's legal system until late in the 19th century. Also known as *obiceiul pământului* (Romanian for "custom of the land"), it was absorbed in part in the *Carte Românească de Învăţătură* (Romanian Book of Instructions), the written code promulgated in 1646 by Prince **Vasile Lupu**. The area of application of Jus Vallachicum covered **Wallachia** and most regions with ethnic Wallachian populations, in and around the Carpathian basin. The treatise *Jus Vallachicum in Polonia,* by the jurist Dumitru D. Mototolescu-Vădeni (1916), explains the uses and connotations of the "custom of the land" in an alien (viz. Polish) context.

-K-

KAGUL. *See* CAHUL.

KARAMZIN, NIKOLAI (1766–1826). Russian historian and the author of a 12-volume work on the history of the **Russian Empire** published between 1816 and 1829. This work deals with, among other subjects, **Bessarabia** and contains important information on historic Moldova, at that time one of the most recent acquisitions of the Russian Empire.

KGB. Soviet Russia's political police, in full an acronym for Komitet Gosudarstvennoy Bezopastnost (Committee for State Security). The KGB was originally established in December 1917 as CHEKA (Russian acronym for the All-Russian Extraordinary Commission for Repression of the Counterrevolution and Sabotage), which functioned as the coercive instrument of the dictatorship of the **Communist Party** over Russia and all Soviet republics. It successively bore the names of GPU (an acronym for the State Political Administration) and **NKVD** (an acronym for the People's Commissariat of Internal Affairs). In Soviet Moldova, the KGB's record (like that of its predecessor organizations) was that of a pivotal instrument of political control and repression, with its key positions entrusted, as a rule, to Russian or Ukrainian officers. After the breakup of the **Union of Soviet Socialist Republics**, the assets and part of the personnel of the KGB in the **Moldavian Soviet Socialist Republic** were transferred to Moldova's Ministry of National Security. According to 1997 official reports, only some 30 percent of the personnel currently working in Moldova's Ministry of National Security were hired before 1990 as KGB officers.

The KGB was officially disbanded by Soviet leader **Mikhail Gorbachev** in October 1991. *See also* NATIONAL SECURITY.

KHOTIN. *See* HOTIN.

KING, CHARLES (1967–). American specialist in Moldovan studies and professor at Georgetown University, where he holds the Ion Raţiu Chair in Romanian Studies. His doctoral thesis, *The Politics of Language in Moldova,* received the Bagehot Prize for outstanding doctoral dissertation in comparative politics in the United Kingdom in 1995. Professor King is the author of the monograph *The Politics of Language: Nationalism and Ethnic Identity in Moldova* and other studies on Moldovan culture and history, including "Moldovan Identity and the Politics of Pan-Romanianism," *Post-Soviet Moldova: A Borderland in Transition,* and the 1999 book *The Moldovans: Romania, Russia and the Politics of Culture.* He is a member of the Executive Committee of the Georgetown University Center for Eurasian, Russian, and East European Studies.

KISHINEV. *See* CHISINAU.

KISHINYOVSKYE NOVOSTI. In English *The Chişinău News, Kishinyovskye Novosti* is one of the largest newspapers in terms of circulation published in the **Russian language** in **Chişinău**.

KOGALNICEANU, MIHAIL (1817–1891). Author, politician, and diplomat, Kogălniceanu was prime minister of the **Principality of Moldova** between 1860 and 1861 and of the **United Principalities** between 1863 and 1865. He published the studies *Moldau und Wallachei, Romanische oder Wallachische Sprache und Literatur,* and *Histoire de la Valachie, de la Moldavie et des Valaques trans-danubiens* while still a student (1837), and he soon after became the inspirer and editor of the influential magazine *Dacia literară*. In the aftermath of the 1848 revolution, while in exile in **Cernăuţi**, Kogălniceanu also authored a draft of a Moldovan Constitution.

KOMMERSANT MOLDOVY. In English *Moldovan Tradesman, Kommersant Moldovy* is one of the popular business newspapers published in **Chişinău** in the **Russian language**.

KOMSOMOL. Acronym for Kommunisticheskii Soyuz Molodezhi, or Communist League of Youth, founded in 1924 to serve as a nursery for the Soviet **Communist Party**. Its Moldavian branch was formed in **Balta**, in the **Moldavian Autonomous Soviet Socialist Republic** on 6–7 January 1925, where it was active until 1940, expanding thereafter in the **Moldavian Soviet Socialist Republic**. Most high-ranking officials in present-day Moldova were at some time leading members in the republic's Komsomol.

KOTOVSK. *See* HANCESTI.

KOTOVSKII, GRIGORII (1881–1925). Communist military leader at the time of the Bolshevik Revolution. A native of **Hânceşti**, he rebelled several times against the region's landowners and was sentenced to various terms of prison under czarist rule. A deserter from the czar's army, a convict in a labor camp, and a fugitive sentenced to death (1916), Kotovskii was sent to the Romanian front during the last stages of World War I. In 1918, he joined the Soviets in **Tiraspol**, where he took the leadership of a revolutionary battalion and helped the Soviets gain control of Ukraine. In 1924, he took an aggressive part in the foundation of the **Moldavian Autonomous Soviet Socialist Republic** on the east bank of the **Nistru River**. He was murdered in 1925 near Odessa. While Moldova was part of the **Union of Soviet Socialist Republics**, Kotovskii's name was given to his place of birth, Hânceşti—renamed Kotovsk by the Soviets.

KOVALY, NIKOLAI (1904–1970). Secretary-general of the Central Committee of the Moldavian **Communist Party** (1946–1950), deputy to the Supreme Soviet of the **Union of Soviet Socialist Republics** at the 1946 and 1950 congresses, and chairman of Soviet Moldavia's State Planning Commission (1960). Kovaly took an active part in starting the process of post–World War II Sovietization of Moldova and in the brutal policies of the Communist Party that led to the elimination of most forms of private property from Moldova's economy.

KRUPENSKI, ALEKSANDR (1861–1939). Bessarabian statesman under the czarist rule, Aleksandr Krupenski served as marshal (1914–1917) of **Bessarabia**'s nobility, or **dvorenime**. In the wake of the Bolshevik Revolution and of Bessarabia's union with **Romania** in 1918, he retreated from all public positions and fled the country. At the **Versailles Conference**, he protested against the Treaty of St. Germain, which gave recognition to Bessarabia's status as part of Romania at the end of World War I. *See also* ANNEXATION.

KRUPENSKI, MATEI (1775–1855). Descendant of a family of rich Moldovan noblemen attested since the 17th century, Matei Krupenski served as vice governor of **Bessarabia** at the beginning of Russian rule over the province (1816–1823). He achieved recognition as a cultural leader and became famous for theatrical events and performances hosted in his mansion, as well as for having befriended the Russian poet **Alexander Pushkin**, exiled to **Chişinău** between 1820 and 1823.

KUCHUK KAINARJI, TREATY OF. Signed on 21 July 1774 to end the 1768–1774 **Russo-Turkish War**, which had led to the military occupation by Russia of Moldova and **Wallachia**. The **Russian Empire** withdrew its armies and restored the two principalities to Turkish suzerainty, but the czar was accorded a virtual protectorate, with the right to intervene in favor of Christian Orthodox believers living under the rule of the **Ottoman Empire**. Other provisions gave Russia the right to free navigation in the Black Sea and across the Bosphorus Strait.

KUTUZOV. *See* IALOVENI.

-L-

LAND LAW. A law on standard pricing, registration, purchase, and sale of land adopted by the Parliament of Moldova in July 1997. In keeping with its provisions, all citizens of Moldova, as well as Moldovan legal entities, without foreign participation, are able to purchase agricultural land. Foreigners cannot purchase Moldovan land for agricultural use. Resale of land lots is allowed only five years after the purchase. Land is to be sold at free market prices. The left-wing **Unity-Edinstvo Movement**

and the Communist faction in Moldova's Parliament attempted to counter the passage of Moldova's Land Law by proposing a referendum. Communist leader **Vladimir Voronin** accused the legislature of betraying "the interests of the people" by passing the 1997 law. *See also* AGRICULTURE.

LANGUAGE ISSUE. Moldovans speak **Romanian**, a Romance language that is the language of communication of the majority of Moldova's native population and the mother tongue of about 65 percent of the country's residents. Russia in the 19th century and the Soviet Union in the 20th century called the Romanian language spoken in Moldova "**Moldavian**." The roots of the issue are political, and they date back to the beginnings of the process of **Russification**, started after the incorporation of the eastern half of historic Moldova by czarist Russia in 1812. As far back as 1829, under Article 63 of Governor **Mikhail Vorontsov**'s "Regulations" for the **oblast** of **Bessarabia**, the use of the local language was banned in administration and public documents and replaced by the **Russian language**.

The last two handbooks in the province's local language, Ioan Doncev's *Curs primitiv de limba rumână* (An Elementary Course in the Romanian Language) and *Abeceda rumână* (A Romanian Primer), were published in 1865. Increasingly referred to as "Moldavian," the local language came to be banned from all schools in 1871 while, up until the collapse of the **Russian Empire** in 1917, Russification steadily continued its course in public administration, church, and **education**. After the 1918–1940 interwar period, the return of Moscow's rule over the land at the outbreak of World War II brought back Russian as the language of the newly founded **Moldavian Soviet Socialist Republic**, with the local language fallaciously dubbed "Moldavian" one more time.

Currently, Moldova's language issue involves two interconnected questions. The first one stems from the dispute involving Moldavian versus Russian as the first common language of communication. In Moldova's secessionist trans-Nistrian districts, where Russian is spoken as a first language by the majority of the population, the issue became a powerful bone of contention in 1989, when it was used as a political means of sharpening ethnic divisions before the proclamation of the **Moldavian Nistrian Republic**, where Russian continues to be the self-proclaimed republic's language for education, business, the courts, and general communication.

The second question boils down to whether the local language spoken by the country's majority should be called "Moldavian" or "Romanian." Some Russophile views hold that, in the family of the Romance languages, the language spoken by the majority of Moldova's population is a distinct one, to be viewed as a separate language in its own right, and thus justifiably entitled to a different name. Linguistic authority and common sense concur, however, in the conclusion that there is no such thing as a "Moldavian" language. The language recognized in 1989 as the official language of the Republic of Moldova is Romanian, with a regional touch and accent, just as—in spite of its specific southern drawl—English, not "Georgian," is spoken in the U.S. state of Georgia. The semantic fallacy of Moldavian as a separate language is exemplified by the impossibility of ever compiling a Moldovan-Romanian dictionary. *See also* ALPHABET ISSUE.

LAPUSNA. Name of the reestablished *judeţ* enfolding part of the historic Lăpuşna region, which used to stretch across the core of present-day Moldova from the **Prut** to the **Nistru River**. A village by the name of Lăpuşna was first recorded in an official document in 1454. Sparse remnants of age-old forests that used to cover most of the Lăpuşna territory are still to be found around the region. **Chişinău** used to be the capital of the ancient Lăpuşna district, as described in 1716 by **Demetrius Cantemir** in *Descriptio Moldaviae*. In keeping with the December 1998 territorial reform, **Hânceşti** has become the chief city of the Lăpuşna *judeţ*, which includes the former Soviet-era districts of **Basarabeasca**, **Cimişlia**, and **Leova**.

Religious monuments in the Lăpuşna region include the historic **Vărzăreşti**, **Căpriana**, and **Suruceni Monasteries** and the convents of Hâncu (1678) and Condriţa (1783).

Lăpuşna is also the name of a river rising from Mount Bălăneşti in the Codri region (*see* CODRU).

LAPUSNEANU, ALEXANDRU (?–1568). Prince of Moldova, who, under his given name Petru Alexandru, took the name of Lăpuşneanu from **Lăpuşna**, his birthplace. He reigned twice—1552–1561 and 1564–1568. Alexandru Lăpuşneanu is also the title and main character of a literary masterpiece by **Constantin Negruzzi** published in 1857.

LARI, LEONIDA (1949–). Poet and civic activist who made her literary debut in 1974 and published several books of poetry until 1989, when she started to play an important role in Moldova's pro-independence movement. She led the publication of the premier issue of *Glasul*, the first Moldovan periodical clandestinely printed in the Latin alphabet in Riga, the capital of what was then Soviet Latvia. Lari was also one of the founding members of the right-wing **Popular Front of Moldova** and the leader of the Moldovan Women's Christian Democratic League (1990–1992). In 1992, she was elected to **Romania**'s Parliament on the list of the National Peasant Christian Democratic Party, a party from which she later resigned to join the right-wing nationalist party România Mare (V. N.).

LASCOV, VASILE (1861–1932). Writer and critic, the author of several books in which he broached such philosophical issues as the meaning of life (*What Is Life*, 1888). In Moldova's political life, Lașcov took an anti-czarist stand and was one of the members of **Sfatul Țării**, which proclaimed Moldova an independent republic in 1917.

LATCO VODA (?–1375). Son of **Bogdan I** and his successor as ruler of Moldova (ca. 1365–1375). Lațco embraced the Catholic faith in an attempt to bolster protection from the two suzerain powers neighboring Moldova—Hungary and Poland—and supported the founding of a Roman-Catholic bishopric in the city of **Siret**, one of the early capitals of the newly founded principality. After Lațco, Moldova's religious allegiance definitively switched to the **Orthodox Church**. This entailed several important cultural consequences, including the historic dominance of Slavonic literacy. *See also* ALPHABET ISSUE.

LAZAREV, ARTEM (1914–). Historian and pro-Soviet politician, member of the Central Committee of Moldova's **Communist Party**, and minister of education (1949–1952) and minister of culture (1954) in the **Moldavian Soviet Socialist Republic**. Lazarev is considered to be one of the chief theoreticians of Moldova's history as intrinsically linked to Russia's and of the role of the **Union of Soviet Socialist Republics** as particularly beneficial to Moldova. His Marxist-Leninist analysis of Moldova under Soviet rule, published in 1974, generated strong controversies and rebuttals. *See also* RUSSIFICATION.

LAZO, SERGHEI (1894–1920). One of Moldova's Communist leaders at the time of the Bolshevik Revolution, Lazo was born in the village of Piatra, **Orhei**. A cadet of the czarist military academy in 1917, he joined the Leninist forces and was entrusted with several revolutionary missions in Siberia and Russia's Far East, including the port city of Vladivostok, where he was captured by Japanese troops and burned to death in the firebox of a steam engine in 1920. While Moldova was part of the Soviet Union, the name Lazovsk, in honor of Lazo, was given to the city and district of **Sângerei**.

LAZOVSK. *See* SANGEREI.

LEANCA, IURIE (1963–). Deputy minister of foreign affairs in Moldova's governments of 1998 and 1999, Iurie Leancă holds a Ph.D. in international relations from the Moscow Institute of International Relations (1986) and is a graduate of the University of Leeds Diplomats Course, organized by Britain's Foreign Office (1992). Between May and October 1989, he served as second secretary at the Soviet embassy in Bucharest, **Romania**, first secretary in the Political Department of the Foreign Ministry of Moldova (1989–1990), and counselor of Moldova's Ministry of Foreign Affairs specializing in European affairs (1990–1992). From 1993 to 1996, Leancă was minister counselor and deputy chief of mission at the Moldovan embassy in Washington, D.C. (V. N.).

LEANCA, TUDOR (1951–). Former minister of transportation and communications in Moldova's 1998 government. A native of Lesnaia, Russia, Tudor Leancă is politically affiliated with the **Party of Democratic Forces**. He is a graduate of the Chişinău Polytechnic Institute and a specialist in construction engineering (V. N.).

LEBED, ALEKSANDR (1950–). Former commander of Russia's **14th Army** in the breakaway **Moldavian Nistrian Republic** between 1992 and 1995. Before leading Russia's military in **Tiraspol**, Lebed's military career included two years of field assignments as battalion commander in Afghanistan (1981–1982). Later on, under his command, Soviet troops quelled the ethnic strife between the Soviet republics of Georgia and Azerbaijan (1989–1990). As a negotiator, he signed the cease-fire agreement that ended the armed conflict between the Tiraspol separatists and Moldova's central authority (July 1992) and Russia's agreements with the separatist leaders of Chechnya (August 1996), which brought to a temporary end 20 months of fighting in the breakaway Chechen Republic. General Lebed finished third in Russia's presidential race of June 1996. He was elected governor of the Siberian region of Krasnoyarsk in

1998. General Lebed's views on post-Soviet Russia and its mission were spelled out in his 1997 book, *My Life and My Country*, in which he articulated the notion of Russia's greatness as residing in its Orthodox faith and its military grandeur.

LEOVA. Chief town and administrative center of the former Leova *raion*, or district, on the east bank of the **Prut River**. The former district had over 51,900 inhabitants (1993 est.). The town of Leova (population 12,000) is situated on a small elevation above the Prut, overlooking the river's west-bank plain, on the Romanian side. The vestiges of the earthworks of **Trajan's Wall** start stretching eastward north of Leova. The town is located 96 kilometers southwest of **Chişinău** on the road linking the capital with the southern city of **Cahul**. Leova is part of the newly reestablished *judeţ* of **Lăpuşna**.

LESANU, ION (1945–). Minister of industry and energy in Moldova's government formed in December 1999. A native of Ciuculeni, **Bălţi**, Leşanu holds degrees from the Polytechnic Institute of Moldova and the Moscow Academy of Social Sciences. He served in various positions in Moldova's **Communist Party** before the country's **independence**. Between 1989 and 1994 he held a number of executive positions in government, and from 1994 to 1998 served as Moldova's ambassador to Belarus. From 1998 to 1999 he was special adviser to Moldova's president in the ongoing negotiations with the **Tiraspol** separatist authorities on the issue of the **Nistru** east-bank districts (V. N.).

LIBRARIES. Moldova's national library system includes its National Library and other specialized academic and technical libraries in **Chişinău**, **Bălţi**, and **Tiraspol**, as well as a network of public libraries across the country. There are over 1,700 public libraries in Moldova (1993 est.), but a major part of their collections consists of books in the **Russian language**, circulated throughout Moldova during the Soviet era as part of the process of **Russification**.

LIMAN. Navigable estuary of the **Nistru River**. It covers a surface of 360 square kilometers and has a total length of 40 kilometers from the mouth of the river down to the Black Sea, with which it communicates through a small gap of about 300 meters. Its average width is from 4 to 12 kilometers. The estuary was part of historic Moldova until the 1940 **annexation** of **Bessarabia** by the **Union of Soviet Socialist Republics**, which cut off the newly founded **Moldavian Soviet Socialist Republic**'s access to the region's traditional seaboard, which it attributed to Soviet Ukraine. The railway station of Palanca in Moldova's district of **Ştefan Vodă** overlooks the estuary, from which it is currently separated by a patch of land several hundred meters in size. *See also* BORDERS OF MOLDOVA.

LITERATURA SI ARTA. Weekly publication of the Moldovan Writers Union, emphatically subtitled "A Publication in the Romanian Language." At the time of its foundation in 1954, in what was then Soviet Moldavia, *Literatura şi arta* was published in Russian Cyrillics. After 1986, it played an important role in the cultural reawakening of Moldova in the context of the **glasnost** and **perestroika** policies, when its circulation attained a record of over 200,000. *Literatura şi arta* is run by writer and publicist **Nicolae Dabija**. *See also* ALPHABET ISSUE; LANGUAGE ISSUE.

LOTEANU, EMIL (1936–). Film director and writer, Loteanu is one of Moldova's best-known cultural personalities. His movies include *The Red Glades* (1966) and *The Fiddlers* (1972), the latter of which won the grand prize at the San Sebastian International Film Festival in 1973. Loteanu is also the author of several volumes of poetry and fiction.

LOWER DANUBE. A Euro-Region for transborder economic cooperation that includes Moldova's *judeţ* of **Cahul**, **Romania**'s *judeţe* of Brăila, Galaţi, and Tulcea, and southern Ukraine's Odessa region. *See also* TRILATERAL AGREEMENT.

LUCINSCHI, PETRU (1940–). President of Moldova, elected in December 1996. He ran as an independent candidate and garnered over 53 percent of the vote, defeating his main rival, incumbent president **Mircea Snegur**. Lucinschi had the electoral backing of center-left and leftist forces, including the then ruling **Democratic Agrarian Party of Moldova**, the **Unity-Edinstvo Movement**, and Communist political formations. Prior to becoming Moldova's chief of state, Lucinschi was the speaker of the Parliament of the Republic of Moldova (1993–1996). Before 1991, he was the highest-ranking ethnic Moldovan in the hierarchy of the Communist Party of the **Union of Soviet Socialist Republics (USSR)**, for which he was Central Committee secretary. Between 1986 and 1989, he served as second secretary of the Tajik Communist Party's Central Committee, in Dushanbe. He led the team of Soviet officials who prepared the liquidation of the Soviet Communist Party. After Moldova's

accession of independence (*see* DECLARATION OF INDEPEN-
DENCE), he served as his country's ambassador to Moscow. Lucinschi
held several activist positions earlier in his career, when he worked as instructor and leader of several of Moldova's youth organizations. Lucinschi's manifold experiences over the years are reflected in his book *Ultimele zile ale URSS* (The Last Days of the USSR), published in 1999.

LUNGU, GHEORGHE (1949–). Former minister of agriculture in the
government of Moldova formed in 1997, Lungu is a graduate of the
Chişinău Agricultural Institute. Between 1971 and 1989, his professional
career included various functions in Moldova's collective farms; he then
served as general manager of an agricultural farm from 1989 to 1994.
Lungu was elected deputy in the Parliament of Moldova in 1994 on the
Democratic Agrarian Party's list and was chairman of the Parliament's
Committee on Foreign Policy from 1995 to 1997.

LUPAN, ANDREI (1912–). A political activist and writer, Andrei Lupan became a member of the **Communist Party** in 1936 and held various positions in Moldova's political hierarchy after its post–World War II incorporation into the Soviet Union. Between 1963 and 1967, he served as
chairman of the Supreme Soviet of the **Moldavian Soviet Socialist Republic**.

LUPAN, NICOLAE (1921–). Writer, broadcaster, and publicist born at
Cepeleuţi, **Hotin**, in the northern part of **Bessarabia** that the **Union of
Soviet Socialist Republics (USSR)** incorporated into Ukraine after
World War II. Nicolae Lupan studied in **Cernăuţi**, where he took degrees
in Romanian and Slavic studies in 1961. After moving to the **Moldavian
Soviet Socialist Republic**, he worked as an editor with Moldova's State
Radio and State Television in **Chişinău**. The Soviet authorities fired him
for pro-nationalist and pro-Romanian propaganda, and he was eventually
expelled from the USSR in February 1974, the same week in which
Alexander Solzhenitsyn was deported. He settled in Belgium, where he
contributed articles to the press in an effort to make Moldova's condition
better known in the West.

LUPU, VASILE (?–1653). Prince of Moldova from 1634 to 1653. His long
reign was marked by a number of cultural achievements, including the
building of the sculptured Three Hierarchs Church in **Iaşi** in 1639, the inauguration of the first printing press in Moldova in 1642, and, in the same

year, the convocation of the Synod of Iaşi, which adopted the "Confession of the Orthodox Faith," written by Metropolitan **Petru Movilă**. Landmarks of Moldovan culture during Prince Vasile Lupu's reign include the 1643 publication of a book of homilies and other religious texts by **Metropolitan Varlaam**, *Carte românească de învăţătură* (Romanian Book of Teachings for Sundays and Other Holidays), which played a unifying role in the fixation of the **Romanian language**, and the 1650 publication of the first Romanian-language code of laws, *Carte românească de învăţătură de la pravilele împărăteşti şi de la alte giudeţe* (Romanian Book of Teachings from the Imperial Statutes and Other Judicial Pronouncements). With the exception of a **Tatar** invasion in 1650 and of two brief wars that set Moldova at odds with Matei **Basarab**, prince of **Wallachia**, Lupu's reign was generally peaceful. Lupu briefly occupied Bucharest in 1639 and titled himself "Prince of Moldova and Wallachia," but, with help from the **Ottoman Empire**, Prince Basarab regained control of his capital, and the Moldovan army retreated. Matei Basarab defeated the Moldovans one more time at Finta, in the year of Prince Vasile Lupu's death (1653). A bronze statue of Lupu erected in 1936 graces the entrance of the St. Demetrius Cathedral in the city of **Orhei**.

LUTSK TREATY. A treaty of alliance between the **Principality of Moldova** and the **Russian Empire** signed in Lutsk on 13 April 1711. The document was signed by Count Gavriil Golovkin, for Russia's **Peter the Great**, and by Captains Procopie and Stefan Luca, for Moldova's Prince **Demetrius Cantemir**. The Lutsk Treaty guaranteed the integrity, **sovereignty**, and independence of the Principality of Moldova as an ally of Russia in the common struggle against the **Ottoman Empire**. Article 11 of the treaty recognized the right of Prince Cantemir and of his successors to reign over Moldova within the principality's old **borders**, stretching from the Carpathians to the **Nistru River** and the Black Sea, including the **Bugeac** in the south and the northern arm of the mouths of the **Danube**. Article 16 stated Russia's determination to respect "these articles to the letter, strengthen them and keep them for ever."

-M-

MAGDEI, MIHAI (1945–). Former minister of health in Moldova's government formed in 1997. Dr. Magdei is a graduate of the Chişinău Medical Institute and a specialist in epidemiology. Between 1969 and 1994, he worked as a medical doctor and served as chief health officer of Moldova (V. N.).

MANOLI, MIHAI (1954–). Minister of finance in Moldova's government formed in December 1999. A native of Valea Mare, **Ungheni**, Manoli is a graduate of the Chişinău Polytechnic Institute. He specialized in economics and taught in the accounting department of the **State University of Moldova** between 1978 and 1991. Manoli served as deputy minister of finance in each of Moldova's governments after 1995 (V. N.).

MARAMURES. Historic region of northern **Transylvania** first mentioned as a hunting domain of the Hungarian Crown in 1199. Maramureş noblemen **Dragoş Vodă** and **Bogdan I** played an important part in the 14th-century **founding of Moldova**, first as a mark or military outpost subject to the king of Hungary, then, after 1359, as an expanding independent principality in its own right. Toponymical comparisons appear to corroborate the conclusion that some of Moldova's early settlements came from the north of Transylvania and Maramureş, where old placenames like **Orhei** (Orheiul Bistriţei), **Nistru**, **Lăpuşna**, Lăpuş, and Târgu-Lăpuş—not to be found in other neighboring provinces—provide evidence of ancient human settlements bearing identical or very similar names, both east and west of the Carpathians, both in Maramureş and in Moldova. However, the northern Transylvanian immigration did not find an empty land east of the Carpathians. Findings indicate that out of Moldova's 755 villages registered before 1449, 607 (80.3 percent) had had their boundaries marked before the founding of the principality. Maramureş is the cradle of one of the oldest texts in the **Romanian language**, the "Ieud Manuscript," composed around 1391–1392 near Cuhea, the native land of Moldova's first independent ruler, Bogdan I.

MATCOVSCHI, DUMITRU (1939–). Poet, novelist, playwright, and cultural activist, Matcovschi won Moldova's highest national award for literature (the "Premiul de Stat") in 1990. He played an important part in the **language-** and **alphabet-issue** campaigns of the late 1980s and early 1990s. In a 1988 article titled "Anti-Teze" (Anti-Theses), published in *Literatura şi arta,* he argued convincingly against the objections raised by the leadership of the **Communist Party** in **Chişinău** concerning the language issue.

MATEEVICI, ALEXIE (1888–1917). Poet and clergyman, born in **Căuşeni**. He made his literary debut in 1906 in the newspaper *Basara-*

bia and died as a military priest after having taken part in the battles of World War I. In the context of Moldova's cultural reawakening preceding its **declaration of independence**, Mateevici became a household word, notably in the dispute revolving around the **language** and **alphabet issues**. The Alexie Mateevici Literary Musical Club, created in **Chişinău** in 1988 against the backdrop of the policies of **glasnost**, gave a major impetus to the movement in favor of writing the language in the Latin alphabet. Mateevici's name is chiefly associated with "Limba noastră" (Our Language), a poem of praise to the **Romanian language**. Set to music, "Limba noastră" is the text of Moldova's new national anthem, passed into law in 1998.

MATEI, VALERIU (1959–). Political leader, president of Moldova's center-right **Party of Democratic Forces**, and deputy speaker of Moldova's Parliament. A native of Cazangic, **Leova**, Matei was one of the writers of Moldova's 1991 **Declaration of Independence**. He is a respected cultural personality and the author of a number of acclaimed books, including a monograph devoted to the 17th-century Moldovan scholar and polymath **Nicolae Milescu**, coauthored with **Serafim Saka**. Matei ran for president in 1996 and came in third, winning 8.9 percent of the vote. In the wake of the 1998 parliamentary elections, Matei's party, which garnered 8.84 percent of the vote, joined the **Alliance for Democracy and Reforms** and became an important part of Moldova's governing coalition. *See also* POLITICAL BLOCS AND PARTIES.

MAVROCORDAT, CONSTANTIN (?–1769). Member of the Mavrocordat dynasty that reigned several times over the **Danubian Principalities** in the 18th century. The son of **Nicolae Mavrocordat**, Constantin was appointed by the **Ottoman Empire** to reign over Moldova at four different times (1733–1735; 1741–1743; 1748–1749; 1769) and over **Wallachia** at six different times (1730; 1731–1733; 1735–1741; 1744–1748; 1756–1758; 1761–1763). Constantin's alternate reigns over the two principalities enhanced a political practice initiated by his father, which became a current pattern throughout the **Phanariote era**. He also introduced new tax legislations favorable to Moldova's landowners, high clergy, and monasteries.

MAVROCORDAT, NICOLAE (1680–1730). First **Phanariote** ruler of Moldova, he succeeded Prince **Demetrius Cantemir** after the latter's flight to Russia in the aftermath of the Moldo-Russian defeat by the armies of **Ottoman** Turkey at Stănileşti in 1711. After a short reign over Moldova (1711–1715), Nicolae Mavrocordat ruled over **Wallachia** twice (1715–1716 and 1719–1730), thus initiating a practice of alternate rule that was to be followed by his son and successor, **Constantin Mavrocordat**, and by other Phanariote rulers as well.

MAZAREANU, VARTOLOMEI (ca. 1720–ca. 1790). Clergyman and scholar, Măzăreanu studied at the Putna Monastery, becoming its abbot in 1757, and at the Kiev Theology College. He headed a delegation of Moldovan clergymen who travelled to St. Petersburg in 1769 to ask for support from Russia's **Orthodox Church**. His vivid account of that trip was first published in 1841 by **Mihail Kogălniceanu**.

MEDIA. The media in the Republic of Moldova include the state company Teleradio Moldova, which runs the three television stations that broadcast throughout Moldova. Private Catalan TV debuted in 1995, but its transmissions are limited to **Chişinău** and 40 kilometers around the city. The state also owns and operates several major radio stations. There is one independent radio station in Moldova's capital, the Chişinău-based Unda Liberă, broadcasting from the campus of the **State University of Moldova**. Unda Liberă is an affiliate of the Voice of America. The same as the Catalan TV station, its transmissions are limited to the capital and about 40 kilometers around the city.

Moldova's national TV broadcasts daily in **Romanian** and **Russian**. As of June 1995, 89.3 percent of Moldova's households had television sets, which means one TV set for 3.7 persons. Over 15 percent of Moldova's households receive cable television. Cable receivers have access to approximately 18 hours of daily broadcasting aired by the Russian-language television-radio company Ostankino. In addition to its programs in the Romanian language, Moldova's national TV carries five hours per day of Russian-language programs, three hours per month of Ukrainian, **Gagauz**, and Bulgarian, and one and one-half hours per month of Hebrew- and Yiddish-language programs. **Romania**'s private television company ProTV launched a channel in Moldova in 1998, operating with financial assistance from the U.S.–Central European Media Enterprises, which owns a majority of the shares in ProTV.

Moldova's State Radio broadcasts two programs on AM and FM, which carry a total of 37 hours of airtime per day. In 1995, there were over 782,000 radio receivers in Moldova. In addition to its daily programs in the Romanian language, Moldova's national radio carries five hours per day of Russian-language broadcasts and one hour per month of Gagauz-, Bulgarian-, and Yiddish-language programs. Beginning in 1992, Moldova's State Radio started a seven-hour per day shortwave program called *Radio Moldova International,* in English, French, and Spanish, which targets listeners worldwide. It also carries special programs in Romanian and Russian, custom tailored to listeners in neighboring Romania and the **Russian Federation**. By 1999, over 90 private TV and FM radio stations with low transmitter power had obtained licenses to broadcast in the Republic of Moldova. Their operations are regulated by Moldova's Telecommunications Law, passed in December 1995. According to that law, the radio frequency spectrum constitutes a national patrimony that is administered by the State Committee on Radio Frequencies, which is subordinate to the government. *See also* PRESS.

MESAGERUL. A **Romanian-language** weekly published by the **Party of Democratic Forces**. It has over 19,000 subscribers in **Chişinău**.

MICHAEL I (1921–). King of **Romania** under a royal regency between 1927 and 1930 and under the military dictatorship of General (later Marshal) **Ion Antonescu** between 1940 and 1944, then chief of state between 1944 and 1947. During his first reign, **Bessarabia** was part of the kingdom of Romania. Romania surrendered Bessarabia to the **Union of Soviet Socialist Republics** in 1940, shortly before Michael's second and mostly ceremonious ascension to the throne. During the last phase of World War II, in a bold coup d'état, young King Michael overthrew Marshal Antonescu on 23 August 1944, when he proclaimed the end of Romania's alliance with Nazi Germany and ordered the Romanian army to change sides and fight the Nazis, whose armies were still occupying the country. As a result of that sudden shift of alliances, Nazi Germany's positions in Romania were completely annihilated in a matter of days, and before the end of October 1944, the entire Eastern front moved 600 miles westward. In the wake of King Michael's action, over half a million Romanian troops participated alongside the Red Army in the defeat of Nazi Germany on Romanian territory, and further on, almost a quarter of a million contributed to the success of the Soviet campaigns in Hungary and Czechoslovakia (1944–1945). In 1947, for exceptionally meritorious conduct in performance of outstanding services, President Harry S. Truman awarded King Michael I the U.S. Legion of Merit. King Michael opposed the anti-Western Communist grab of power, but ultimately he was forced to abdicate in a Communist-staged coup d'état on 30 December 1947, when Romania was proclaimed a people's republic.

MICHAEL THE BRAVE (ca. 1558–1601). A member of the dynasty of the **Basarabs** and ruler of Moldova (1600) and of **Wallachia** (1593–1601), Michael the Brave (Romanian: Mihai Viteazul or Mihai Bravu) tried to organize an anti-Ottoman coalition and fought several wars in order to shed Turkish suzerainty over the Principality of Wallachia. With sporadic help from neighboring Moldova and **Transylvania**, he defeated the Turks at Călugăreni in 1595 and, later on, managed to briefly control—in addition to Wallachia—Moldova (May–September 1600) and Transylvania (November 1599–August 1601).

MILESCU, NICOLAE (1636–1708). Scholar, theologian, and polymath, better known by his nobility title as Spatarul Milescu. He was the author of the first work by a native of Moldova to be published in France, a Latin treatise on the Eucharist, *Enchiridion sive Stella Orientalis Occidentali splendens* (Enchiridion or Eastern Star Shining to the West), printed in Paris in 1669. The book's title page carries a brief description of the author's title and credentials: *"Nicolao Spadario Moldavolaccone barone ac olim generali Wallachiae"* (Moldo-Wallachian Spatharius and Baron, former Wallachia General). Spatharius—or sword-bearer—was a local nobility title in the Byzantine tradition. Milescu's two most important works are a translation of the Old Testament into **Romanian** (finished around 1667 and incorporated into the Bucharest Bible of 1688) and a description of his own expedition to China (1675–1676), written in **Russian** at the behest of Czar Aleksey Mikhailovich. Initially a confidential state document, Milescu's diary is one of the earliest European travelogues carrying firsthand information about Russia's Far East and 17th-century imperial China. The first Russian edition, *Putesestvie tsarstva Sibirskogo ot goroda Tobolska i do samogo rubeja Kitaiskogo,* was published by J. N. Arseniev in 1882. It aroused great interest and was followed by E. Picot's *Notice biographique et bibliographique sur Nicolas Spathar Milescu,* published in Paris in 1883, and by G. Sion's Romanian translation *De la Tobolsk până în China* (From Tobolsk to China) in 1888. Milescu's career at Russia's imperial court started in 1671, when he began to contribute his polyglot expertise as chief translator for the czar and, later on, as his special envoy and diplomat.

"MIORITA." A pastoral ballad of wide circulation, central to Moldova's and other neighboring regions' traditional folklore. Anthropomorphic in vision, its main character, Miorița, giving the poem its name, is a speaking and clairvoyant ewe who warns her master that two of his fellow shepherds are plotting to kill him. The young shepherd makes no attempt to resist, and fate unfolds as foretold. He accepts death with serenity, as a cosmic wedding, envisioning his own burial in a pantheistic vision in which death assumes the aspect of a nuptial mystery, with stars, the moon, and the sun as high priests. Eight variants of "Miorița" have been identified in Moldova's oral folklore and dozens more in other regions sharing the same tradition, from **Romania** to the Balkan regions inhabited by Romanian-speaking pastoral populations. The ballad, which probably dates back to the 17th or 18th century, was first collected in western Moldova and published in **Cernăuți** in the newspaper *Bucovina* in 1850. Appropriately, Moldova's paper currency carries the first verses of the poem inscribed in the design of its banknotes.

MOHYLA/MOGHILA. *See* MOVILA, PETRU.

MOLDAVIA. The Latin form for the vernacular Moldova. It was used in diplomatic correspondence and political documents since the early Middle Ages. It gained widespread European acceptance in the 18th century, after Prince **Demetrius Cantemir** made the country better known through his Latin works and their versions in other languages. *See also* MOLDOVA, ETYMOLOGY; MOLDOVA, HISTORICAL SPHERE; MOLDOVA, TOPOGRAPHIC SPHERE.

MOLDAVIAN. Name given by Russian authorities after 1812 to the **Romanian language** spoken in Moldova to distinguish it from the Romanian language spoken in **Wallachia**. Moldova's 1994 **Constitution** gives the language the same name, although linguists agree that there is no difference between what is called "Romanian" and what is called "Moldavian," which is nothing more than Romanian with a regional accent. As far back as 1643, Moldova's **Metropolitan Varlaam** subtitled his groundbreaking book *Cazania* as *Carte românească de învățătură,* further describing his own work as *"un dar limbii românești"* (a gift to the Romanian language).

In the first stages of Russia's rule over Moldova—in an attempt to avoid the use of the name Romanian—the language spoken by the province's natives was called "Wallacho-Moldavian," which was given academic circulation when czarist Russia established a chair of Romanian at the University of St. Petersburg soon after the 1812 **annexation** of **Bessarabia**. "Wallacho-Moldavian" was the name used to denote the Romanian language in textbooks written by 19th-century Bessarabian linguist Iacov Hânculov, who taught at the University of St. Petersburg from 1839 onward, first as a lecturer and later as the head of studies devoted to the language spoken in Bessarabia. *See also* ALPHABET ISSUE; LANGUAGE ISSUE.

MOLDAVIAN AUTONOMOUS SOVIET SOCIALIST REPUBLIC (MASSR). Autonomous political entity established by the **Union of Soviet Socialist Republics** (USSR) as part of the Ukrainian Soviet Socialist Republic, on 12 October 1924, with **Balta** as its first administrative center and capital. Its 8,300-square-kilometer territory was carved out of Ukraine along the east bank of the **Nistru River**, at that time the USSR-Romania border. The MASSR's first Constitution of 23 April 1925, which was copied from that of other Soviet republics, indicated the **Prut River**, not the Nistru, as its western frontier. The MASSR had a population of 568,984 inhabitants (1926 Soviet est.), mostly Ukrainians, Russians, and Jews, and a 30.3 percent Moldavian minority. In 1929, the MASSR's capital was moved to **Tiraspol**.

In 1940, in the aftermath of the Soviet **annexation** of **Bessarabia**, a narrow strip of the MASSR territory (3,400 square kilometers) became part of the then newly founded **Moldavian Soviet Socialist Republic (MSSR)**, while the bulk of its territory was returned to Soviet Ukraine. Sharply distinct from the rest of the republic in terms of ethnic composition and cultural and linguistic traditions, the left-bank MASSR served as a pilot political construct for the shaping of the MSSR. In present-day Moldova, the Nistru east-bank districts continue to play a distinct role, particularly visible in the Tiraspol authorities' strife for secession and the proclamation of the self-styled **Moldavian Nistrian Republic**. *See also* AUTONOMY.

MOLDAVIAN DEMOCRATIC REPUBLIC. *See* MOLDAVIAN DEMOCRATIC FEDERATED REPUBLIC.

MOLDAVIAN DEMOCRATIC FEDERATED REPUBLIC. Proclaimed on 2 December 1917 as a constituent of the moot Federation of Russian Republics, in the aftermath of the departure from **Chişinău** of the czar's last governor of **Bessarabia**, Mikhail M. Voronovich, after the victory of Russia's Bolshevik Revolution in Petrograd and Moscow. After a brief occupation of Chişinău by the Bolshevik revolutionary army, which dispersed **Sfatul Ţării**, it proclaimed its independence on 24 January 1918 under the name of the Moldavian Democratic Republic, renouncing all ties with the new authorities of Soviet Russia. Confronted with threats of isolation or absorption into Ukraine, on 27 March 1918, the newly founded republic proclaimed its conditioned union with **Romania** "in accordance with historical right and ethnic right and the principle that peoples should determine their own fate." On 27 November 1918, Sfatul Ţării renounced all previous reservations and voted for the country's unconditional union with Romania. *See also* ANNEXATION; SOVEREIGNTY; WILSONIAN PRINCIPLES.

MOLDAVIAN NISTRIAN REPUBLIC (MNR). Internationally unrecognized entity proclaimed in **Tiraspol** on 2 September 1990, initially styled the Moldavian Nistrian Soviet Socialist Republic. Currently known as the Moldavian Nistrian Republic (or sometimes the Moldavian Transdnestr Republic; Russian name: Pridnestrovskaya Moldavskaya Respublika), the breakaway entity consists of a narrow strip of land (180 km by 32 km) buttressing the east bank of the **Nistru River** on a small part of what used to be, between 1924 and 1940, the **Moldavian Autonomous Soviet Socialist Republic**. The separatist authorities in Tiraspol exert their rule over five Soviet-style districts—**Camenca**, **Dubăsari**, **Grigoriopol**, **Râbniţa**, and **Slobozia**—comprising a total population of about 740,000. Except for two small enclaves bordering the river (Coşniţa, northeast of Moldova's capital, and a small area between Dubăsari and Molovata), the area controlled by the MNR includes all of Moldova's land on the east bank of the Nistru. On the river's west bank, the self-proclaimed MNR controls the city of **Tighina**.

The MNR, which declared itself a "customs control zone," uses the ruble (dubbed "Suvorov") as the local currency, preserves the Soviet-era state symbols, and maintains a strategic importance due to the deployment of Russian troops there and the industries and power plants concentrated on its soil throughout the years that preceded the disbanding of the **Union of Soviet Socialist Republics (USSR)**. About 30 percent of Moldova's industries and over 90 percent of its energy production are located on territory controlled by the Tiraspol authorities, whose policies have made evident that the conflict with the government in **Chişinău** is not essentially about ethnic and linguistic issues, but mostly about political systems.

The Tiraspol leadership is leftist, antireform, and conservative. In a diminutive form, this last bastion of Soviet communism in Eastern Europe is generally regarded as evocative of the former USSR. In 1999, Gheorghi Maracuţă, chairman of the MNR's Supreme Soviet, acknowledged that the Republic of Moldova and the MNR were developing along diametrically opposed lines: Moldova "in the direction of Europe" and the MNR toward "a union of the Slavic states." The MNR's future should be built "in cooperation not with the West, but with the Commonwealth of Independent States," the Tiraspol leader has said.

Tiraspol broke away from Chişinău in protest over the 1989 laws regarding the return to the Latin script, the establishment of **Moldavian** rather than **Russian** as the official language of the country, and the change of the republic's Soviet-style flag to a new one, almost identical with **Romania**'s tricolor flag. Romanian-speaking Moldovans make up about 40 percent of the breakaway entity's population, but their language is taught in only 88 schools, out of which only seven are allowed to use the Latin alphabet. Russophone Ukrainians and Russians make up about 59 percent of the MNR's population. Secession triggered by ethnic Russians and Ukrainians resulted in a powerful backlash that, in 1992, took the form of an armed conflict in which Russia's **14th Army** was able to keep the fractious government proclaimed in Tiraspol in power.

In the wake of a cease-fire agreement signed at Limanskoe on 7 July 1992 under the mediating authority of the commander of Russia's 14th Army, **Aleksandr Lebed**, negotiations have been going on between Moldova's authorities and the self-appointed Tiraspol authorities in a series of attempts to settle the conflict by reaching an agreement on granting expanded autonomy to the Nistru east-bank districts, as Moldova's "Trans-Nistrian Self-Administered Territories." The arrangement would provide the region with the right to exert jurisdiction over taxation, police forces, budget decisions, and other issues. However, the Tiraspol leadership has constantly turned down Chişinău's offers to grant the east-bank districts such a status, sticking to its claim to statehood.

A key factor in the stalemate is the continuing presence of Russia's military base in Tiraspol, where Moscow keeps its only permanent deployment of armed forces outside Russia's borders in Europe. The Tiraspol enclave is considered to be a strategic stronghold in the proximity of the volatile Balkans region and a turntable in terms of arms trafficking between this internationally unrecognized entity and other unstable regions, including Kosovo and the Caucasus.

In December 1998, Russian extremist leader Vladimir Zhirinovsky visited Tiraspol, where he declared that the Nistrian enclave is "part of Russia" and that his own Liberal Democratic Party of Russia "will be happy if it officially becomes one of Russia's provinces." In 1997, the MNR applied for membership in the Parliamentary Assembly of the **Commonwealth of Independent States (CIS)** and, later on, for full-scale integration into the CIS political and military structures. That same year, the Tiraspol Supreme Soviet chairman declared that the Nistrian republic will demand that Moldova accepts full integration into the CIS and that it joins the **Russian Federation**–Belarus union, viewed as a possible future model for the MNR's status vis-à-vis the Republic of Moldova. A nonbinding referendum on joining the Russia-Belarus union was held between April and June 1998, with over 66 percent of the ballots supporting the union. However, like the province of Kaliningrad on the Baltic Sea (isolated from Russia by independent Lithuania and Poland), the east-bank separatist region has no common borders with either Belarus or the Russian Federation. *See also* FEDERALIZATION; SEPARATISM; TRANS-NISTRIAN CONFLICT.

MOLDAVIAN SOVIET SOCIALIST REPUBLIC (MSSR). Created by a law of the Supreme Soviet of the **Union of Soviet Socialist Republics (USSR)** on 2 August 1940, in the wake of the June 1940 **annexation** of **Bessarabia**, which enforced the Secret Additional Protocol of the **Molotov-Ribbentrop Pact**. Based on the principles and provisions of the 1936 Stalinist Constitution of the USSR, the MSSR's first **Constitution** was promulgated on 10 February 1941. Its application was disrupted by the outbreak of World War II, when Soviet troops were repelled beyond the **Nistru River**. Throughout the postwar decades, the MSSR's fundamental law adapted itself to the changes in its master model—the Soviet Constitution. On 15 April 1978, a new Constitution of the MSSR was put forth, reflecting the stipulations of the Soviet Constitution of 1977. The MSSR proclaimed its **sovereignty** on 23 June 1990. On 23 May 1991, the **Chişinău** legislative body changed the name of the MSSR to the Republic of Moldova, which proclaimed itself an independent state on 27 August 1991. *See also* ANNEXATION; SOVEREIGNTY.

MOLDENERGO. State-owned company for the production, transport, distribution, and sale of electric and thermal **energy**. Moldenergo administers the unified energy sector of Moldova.

MOLDOVA, ETYMOLOGY. Vernacular form for **Moldavia**. In his *Descriptio Moldaviae*, written in Latin in the 18th century at the request of the Berlin Academy, **Demetrius Cantemir** was the first to discuss the origin of the toponym in a chapter titled "De antiquis et hodiernis Moldaviae nominibus." Subsequent research has given Moldova (German: Moldau; Hungarian: Moldva; Polish: Multany) different explanations. Ancient Romanian forms such as Mulduha and Mulduva, attested in early manuscripts, for example, indicate a process of successive phonetic mutations, which went through older variants like Moldua and Molduva, down to the finally accepted norm, Moldova. Evidence indicates that at the time of the region's first conquest and settlement by northern Transylvanian emigrants from **Maramureş** that included Wallachians, Saxons, and others, the name was first applied to a river, the Moldova, a tributary to the **Siret**. Later on, the name came to be applied to the lands stretching down the river's stream and, by extension, to the whole new country, down to its natural frontier in the east, the **Nistru River**. As far back as 1421, an early German document calls **Baia**—for a short time Moldova's first capital—"Stadt Molde." Phonological evidence expounded in the 19th century by **Bogdan Petriceicu Hasdeu** and corroborated in the 20th century by Alexandru Rosetti points to the conclusion that the origin of the toponym Moldova is most probably akin to a Saxon-channel borrowing derived from the Old High German noun *Molta* (Gothic: *Molda*), whose sphere of denotation ("loose earth," "mold") indicates, in its adjectival form, the brownish color of a muddy water swirling downstream, usually fraught with slime. A parallel explanation applies, according to linguists, to the etymon of the Moldau River (or Vltava) in the Czech Republic.

Significantly, the root word "Moldova" can be found in over half a dozen place-names throughout **Romania**'s provinces, such as Moldova-Nouă and Moldova-Veche in western Romania; Slănic-Moldova, Moldova Suliţa, and Moldoviţa at the foot of the northeastern Carpathians; Moldoveneşti in central **Transylvania**; and Moldoveni, south of Bucharest in the **Danube** plain. Moldoveanu (English: the Moldovan) is Romania's highest mountain peak, rising to a record 2,544 meters over the Făgăraş ridge, in the southern Carpathian Mountains, which separate **Wallachia** from Transylvania.

Toponymical explanations advanced in the past attempted to prove the derivation of Moldova from the name of an Alpine conifer, the common European spruce, Molid or Molidv in Romanian. Linguistic authorities now agree that, given the phonetic laws having governed the evolution of the Romanian language over the past centuries, a phonological glide from Molidv to Moldova appears improbable.

MOLDOVA, HISTORICAL SPHERE. As a historical division, Moldova (Medieval Latin and English: Moldavia; French: Moldavie) is the name of a principality (Romanian: Ţara Moldovei) that, until the 1812 **Treaty of Bucharest**, included **Bessarabia**, a name applied from then on by Russia to its eastern half, lying between the **Prut** and **Nistru Rivers** and the Black Sea. That part of Moldova was attached to the **Russian Empire** between 1812 and 1918, became independent for a short time in the wake of the Bolshevik Revolution of 1917, joined **Romania** between the two world wars, and was taken back in 1940 by the **Union of Soviet Socialist Republics (USSR)**, which downsized it in its northern and southern extremities, cut it off from the seashore, renamed it the **Moldavian Soviet Socialist Republic**, and attached its landlocked middle part to a 3,400-square-kilometer section of the **Moldavian Autonomous Soviet Socialist Republic**, an entity previously carved out of southern Ukraine by the USSR in 1924 along the left bank of the Nistru.

Within those **borders**, Soviet Moldavia became independent from the USSR in 1991 under the name of the Republic of Moldova. From a linguistic point of view, the name switch—from Moldavia to Moldova—illustrates a case of vernacular versus transnational designation (like choosing to call Italy "Italia"). The deeper overtone of this option asserts the political will to stress the newly reborn state's identity as distinct from its previous incarnations. Moldova was last a political entity of its own in 1859, when its western half was united with **Wallachia** to form the **United Principalities.** Its eastern half (most of today's Republic of Moldova) was already at that time a province of the Russian Empire.

MOLDOVA, PRINCIPALITY OF. Political entity first established as an independent country in 1359, when Wallachian ruler **Bogdan I**, who hailed from the Transylvanian land of **Maramureş**, rejected the vassalage of the Hungarian Crown and proclaimed himself prince over the country lying east of the Carpathian Mountains, which his predecessor, **Dragoş Vodă**, had ruled after 1352 as a boundary province on behalf of Hungary's King Louis I of Anjou. Initially a defensive eastern outpost against incursions by **Tatar** invaders from the steppes across the northern and middle course of the **Nistru River**, the Principality of Moldova soon expanded its borders southward, reaching down to the **Chilia** arm of the **Danube River** and the Black Sea. By 1392, Moldova had secured the region's seaboard, between the mouths of the Nistru and Danube, the lowlands of which had been routinely used by migrating tribes as a shortcut passage toward the Balkans. The port city of **Cetatea Albă**, with its harbor on the estuary of the Nistru, became the residence of the principality's chief bishopric, and in 1401, Bishop Iosif of Cetatea Albă was confirmed by the Constantinople patriarchy as metropolitan of Moldova and his see moved to the principality's new capital, **Suceava**.

The 1453 fall of Constantinople and the dramatic advent of the **Ottoman Empire** as the dominant power in the Black Sea basin marked a turning point in the history of the Principality of Moldova. After several attempts by the Ottomans to conquer Moldova from the sea and the imposition of Ottoman suzerainty over neighboring **Wallachia** (1432), Moldova's Prince **Petru Aron** was forced to pay tribute in exchange for peace, and the Principality of Moldova, while preserving—the same as Wallachia—domestic autonomy, became a vassal to Ottoman Turkey (1456). Aron's successor, **Stephen the Great**, rejected Ottoman suzerainty, and a series of fierce wars ensued.

Launching its campaigns from bases in Wallachia, the Ottoman army crossed into Moldova but was defeated at Vaslui (1475). Later on, with Tatar help from across the Nistru, the invaders emerged victorious at the battle of Valea Albă (1476). After further battles, Stephen the Great had to surrender the stronghold port cities of Cetatea Albă and Chilia. Faced with the crushing superiority of its foe, Moldova reaccepted Ottoman suzerainty in 1489. The sultan pledged not to interfere from then on in Moldova's framework of church and state in exchange for a series of conditions, including a heavy tribute in gold. In 1538, the entire southern hinterland of Moldova, or **Bugeac**, became a Turkish possession, the Ottoman Empire also taking control of several other strategic points on the Nistru, including the upstream fortress of **Tighina,** renamed Bender by the Turks. Other conditions included Moldova's pledge to help Ottoman Turkey as an ally in war and peace and a strict monopoly over its foreign trade, the principality being obliged to sell all crops and livestock to the suzerain power at marginal and noncompetitive prices. In exchange, Ottoman Turkey pledged that no other lands or estates of the Principality of Moldova would be alienated and that the sultan's subjects or institutions would claim no right to ever own property, open mosques, and interfere with the country's customs, language, and traditional ways.

The status of the Principality of Moldova was similar to that of its neighbors Wallachia and **Transylvania**, which were never annexed and turned into *pashaliks,* or Turkish provinces, as were Serbia, Bulgaria, and Hungary. However, after 1621, stricter rules of suzerainty were enforced, the sultan demanding that each aspirant to the throne of Moldova buy beforehand the consent of the Sublime Porte. Throughout the 17th century, Moldova's ruling princes made several attempts to shed Ottoman vassalage, turning secretly for help to several neighboring rising powers, notably, the **Habsburg** and **Russian Empires**.

A second major turning point in the history of the principality occurred in 1711, when a formal anti-Ottoman alliance was secretly signed at Lutsk by delegates of Moldova's Prince **Demetrius Cantemir** and Russia's Czar **Peter the Great**. The **Lutsk Treaty** guaranteed the territorial integrity, sovereignty, and independence of the Principality of Moldova as an ally of Russia in the common struggle against the Ottoman Empire. Russia recognized the right of Demetrius Cantemir and of his successors to reign over Moldova within the principality's old borders, stretching from the Carpathians to the Nistru, including the Bugeac in the south and the northern arm of the Danube. The 1711 Moldo-Russo-Turkish battle of Stănileşti on the **Prut River**, which ended in a resounding Ottoman victory, removed the rising power of Russia from direct involvement in the affairs of Moldova for almost 100 years. Prince Cantemir went into exile in Russia, and the Ottoman Empire took reprisal measures, among them, putting an end to the election of local nationals as reigning princes of Moldova. Thus, between 1711 and 1821, the sultan exclusively designated Moldova's rulers, handpicked from the Greek high class of the Phanar quarter in the capital of the Ottoman Empire. Moldova had 36 such rulers, over a period of time known as the **Phanariote era**.

As Russia was increasingly asserting itself as a regional power, 18th-century Moldova became the battleground of several **Russo-Turkish Wars**. In 1775, the Ottoman Empire broke its pledge not to alienate land from the Principality of Moldova and ceded a chunk of its northern territories to the Habsburg Empire, which Austria renamed **Bucovina**.

After a series of gradual territorial conquests along the northern shores of the Black Sea and Crimea, Russia established its border on the east bank of the Nistru River, and the Principality of Moldova became the Russian Empire's direct neighbor in 1792. In the aftermath of the 1806–1812 Russo-Turkish War, the Turkish Empire one more time broke its pledge not to alienate land from Moldova and ceded the principality's eastern half to Russia, which turned it into a province of its empire, renamed **Bessarabia**. The 1829 Russo-Turkish **Treaty of Adrianople** eased the conditions of Moldova's status of subjection to the Ottoman Empire but brought about a Russian military occupation of the principality that lasted until 1834. The Principality of Moldova was occupied again by the czar's armies during part of the Crimean War (1853–1854), in which Russia was eventually defeated. As a result of the **Congress of**

Paris of 1856, Russia returned to the Principality of Moldova part of the lands it had annexed in 1812—namely, southern Bessarabia, including the Danubian districts of **Bolgrad**, **Cahul**, and **Ismail**. Pending a resolution on its future status, the Principality of Moldova was put, together with Wallachia, under the joint protection of France, Great Britain, Austria, Prussia, the Italian kingdom of Sardinia, Ottoman Turkey, and Russia, all acting as international guarantors.

On 24 January 1859, Moldova's **Alexandru Ioan Cuza** was elected prince of Wallachia, and the principality merged with Wallachia to form the **United Principalities**, a dual political entity renamed **Romania** after 1862. See also NATIONAL UNIFICATION.

MOLDOVA, TOPOGRAPHIC SPHERE. Moldova traditionally denotes the unitary territorial entity belonging to the Carpathian basin, lying east of the Transylvanian plateau and north of the Wallachian plain, abutting the outer edge of the Carpathian arc and stretching east down to the banks of the **Nistru River**. The region is drained southward by a system of headstreams descending mainly from the Carpathians. Apart from the Nistru—a tributary to the Black Sea—all rivers feed the **Danube**, joined a little above its delta by two major rivers, the **Siret** and the **Prut**, both of which run southward, roughly across the territory's geographical middle. Similar to the topographical pair California/Baja California, or to the two Kashmirs, the term "Moldova/Moldavia" is loosely applied to two entities sprung from what used to be a single territorial unit. Thus, depending on cultural and conversational context, Moldova applies either to the republic of the same name, east of the Prut River, or to the province of the same name, lying west of the Prut border in **Romania**.

MOLDOVA SOCIALISTA. Chief daily newspaper of Soviet Moldova and principal instrument of the **Communist Party** and state-run propaganda. Its publication started in 1924 under the initial name of *Plugarul roşu* (The Red Ploughman), edited by the Moldavia Regional Organization of the Ukrainian Communist Party and the Odessa district section for "political enlightenment." *Plugarul roşu* assumed the name of *Moldova socialistă* in December 1930. From June 1940 to June 1941, it was published in **Chişinău**; from December 1942 to August 1944, in Moscow; and from 1944 until the collapse of Soviet rule, once again in Chişinău.

MOLDOVA SUVERANA. Newspaper of the government of Moldova published in **Romanian** and in **Russian** (Russian version: *Nezavisimaya*

Moldova). It carries the official viewpoints of the **Chişinău** government. Circulation is estimated at over 10,000 copies.

MOLDOVAGAS. Gas company of Moldova privatized in 1998, in conjunction with the Russian company **Gazprom**, which took 50 percent of the company's assets, the total value of which was then $285 million. Of the remaining portfolio, Moldova's government was to own 35 percent, the separatist **Tiraspol** authorities 14 percent, and a small number of private entrepreneurs 1 percent. In 1997, Moldovagas bought over 2,000 cubic meters of gas valued at $166 million. *See also* ENERGY.

MOLDOVAN COHORTS / COHORTELE MOLDOVENESTI. Military units formed in Moldova in April 1917 to maintain order against domestic anarchy, as Russia's army was disintegrating and plunging into revolutionary turmoil during the final stages of World War I. The name Cohortele Moldoveneşti (from the Latin *cohorta*) was inspired by the ancient title given to the Roman army's divisions. A first gathering of several thousand Moldovan soldiers and officers, which took place in Odessa on 18 April 1917, called for a separation into distinct detachments or "cohorts" of the more than 200,000 Moldovan servicemen enrolled in Russia's armies on various fronts, where discipline was breaking down. In the spring of 1917, faced with the growing mutiny of the Russians under his command on the Romanian front, General D. G. Sherbatchev, commander of Russia's army in **Iaşi**, authorized the formation of the first 16 Moldovan Cohorts, two for each district of **Bessarabia**, while in Odessa, the Russian army headquarters recognized Russia's 40th Regiment stationed in that city as an all-Moldovan military unit.

A gathering of 989 Moldovan officers and soldiers held in **Chişinău** on 2–9 November 1917 demanded the formation of more units to counter the increasing debacle and rebellion among Russia's soldiery, as the number of deserters grew and the Bolshevik Revolution was gaining ground on all fronts and throughout the former **Russian Empire**. In addition to its organizing role, the Chişinău General Assembly (**Sfatul Ţării)** played a key part in articulating Bessarabia's demand for **autonomy** and the first convocation of the province's Sfatul Ţării. On Christmas Day in 1917, a military parade and the solemn blessing of the detachments' flags took place in downtown Chişinău.

Organized in haste, under pressure, and amid social turmoil, Moldova's military detachments were unable to resist the Bolshevik armed units that occupied Chişinău in the first days of January 1918, thus prompting Sfatul Ţării's urgent request for assistance from the Romanian army, which crossed into Bessarabia and helped restore order as of 13 January, when the Bolshevik revolutionaries were driven out of the capital. In a combined effort, the last Communist battalions were driven east of the **Nistru River** on 7 February 1918. *See also* ANTI-BOLSHEVIK MILITARY INTERVENTION.

MOLDOVANUL. A weekly published in **Chişinău** by cultural leader Gheorghe V. Madan between January 1907 and October 1908. *Moldovanul* argued for the right of Bessarabian Moldovans to have schools that employed their native language. It exerted a seminal influence on the national and cultural reawakening process that gradually laid the groundwork for **Bessarabia**'s 1917 separation from Russia in the context of the Bolshevik Revolution. *See also* RUSSIFICATION.

MOLDTELECOM. Moldova's state-owned telecommunications company, the **privatization** of which—for both policy and fiscal reasons—was considered to carry great importance in the government's strategy of reform. In December 1998, Moldova's government approved a plan to sell a 51 percent share of Moldtelecom to a strategic investor. Moldtelecom has been the largest state-owned enterprise up for privatization in Moldova, and its sale has reportedly created the basis for an over $60 million yield in budgetary revenues.

MOLOTOV-RIBBENTROP PACT. A 10-year nonaggression pact between Hitler's Germany and **Stalin**'s **Union of Soviet Socialist Republics (USSR)**, signed in Moscow on 23 August 1939 by Viacheslav Molotov, people's commissar of foreign affairs, on behalf of the USSR, and Joachim von Ribbentrop, Germany's foreign minister, on behalf of Nazi Germany. Although the pact became null in June 1941 when Nazi Germany went to war against the USSR, the provisions of its Secret Additional Protocol shaped much of Eastern Europe's history—including Moldova's—in the post–World War II years.

Article 1 of the Secret Additional Protocol apportioned the Soviet and Nazi spheres of influence in the Baltic states, Estonia, Latvia, and Lithuania (annexed by the USSR on 17–21 June 1940). Article 2 described the future partition of Poland, with the border between the USSR and the Nazi Reich running across the middle of Poland, "approximately delimited by the lines of the rivers Narev, Vistula and San" (this provision was enforced by both signatories through military occupation on

1–17 September 1939). Article 3 referred explicitly to **Bessarabia**. It stated the USSR's interest in annexing Bessarabia from **Romania** and Nazi Germany's consent to that **annexation**. The incorporation of Bessarabia into the USSR was carried out through military occupation in the last days of June 1940. A Soviet law of 2 August 1940 officially established the **Moldavian Soviet Socialist Republic** on most of Bessarabia's territory and made it a component of the USSR.

Today's eastern border of Poland and Moldova's status (now a country in its own right for the first time since 1859) are among the indirect, lingering consequences of the 1939 Molotov-Ribbentrop Pact. The republics of Estonia, Latvia, and Lithuania regained their full pre-1940 status in 1990–1991. *See also* ANNEXATION; SOVEREIGNTY.

MONETARY UNITS. The official monetary unit of the Republic of Moldova is the leu (plural: lei). One leu equals 100 bani. It was introduced in November 1993 to replace the Soviet-era ruble and the Moldovan "coupons" created after Moldova's **declaration of independence**. In 1999, the exchange rate was fluctuating around 875 lei for U.S.$100. In 1998, there was a sudden drop in the exchange rate toward the end of the year as the National Bank of Moldova stopped its intervention in the currency market while not renouncing the bank's right to resort to its own currency reserves. The move was designed to defend the leu and to let commercial banks set their own exchange rates so that market forces could start establishing the value of the country's monetary unit. Ever since Moldova proclaimed its independence, the separatist self-proclaimed **Moldavian Nistrian Republic** has refused to accept the leu as legal tender and has used the old Russian ruble instead, later renamed "Suvorov" (after Russian Marshal Alexander Suvorov, whose effigy is imprinted over the notes). The new Russian ruble is also in circulation in the trans-Nistrian districts.

MORUZI, ALEXANDRU (?–ca. 1810). Son of **Phanariote** ruler **Constantin Moruzi**. He reigned over both Moldova and **Wallachia** twice: 1792–1793, 1802-1806 and 1793–1796, 1799–1801, respectively.

MORUZI, CONSTANTIN (?–ca. 1790). Ruler of the **Principality of Moldova** between 1777 and 1782. His intrigues in the high circles of the **Ottoman Empire** and the sultan's court, as well as his ambition to grab the throne of Moldova, seem to have led to the political assassination of his immediate predecessor, Prince **Grigore Ghika III**.

MORUZI, DUMITRACHE (?–1812). Brother of Moldova's **Phanariote** ruler **Alexandru Moruzi**. Dumitrache Moruzi was one of the **Ottoman Empire**'s envoys assigned to negotiate with the envoys of the **Russian Empire** the 1812 **Treaty of Bucharest**, which led to the partition of the **Principality of Moldova** and the **annexation** of its eastern half by Russia under the name of **Bessarabia**. Upon his return to Constantinople, Moruzi was decapitated for high treason by order of the sultan. There were reports that Moruzi had played a role in hastening the conclusion of the treaty ahead of the invasion of Russia by Napoleon, an impending act of war that he and others had been secretly apprised of while in Bucharest. Procrastinating in the bargaining would probably have caught Russia in a weakened position, and its territorial demands from Turkey would have been lowered or dropped altogether. Indeed, 26 days after the signing of the Russo-Turkish Treaty of Bucharest, Napoleon's army invaded Russia and caught the czar's army by surprise, causing it to withdraw in an initial state of disarray.

MOSANU, ALEXANDRU (1932–). Politician and historian, elected speaker of the Parliament of Moldova in 1992, a function he later resigned. Professor Moşanu is the author of over 100 works on the history of Moldova and of other countries. His most important contribution as an author is a study on Romanian historiography between the second half of the 19th century and the beginning of the 20th century, published in Moscow in 1988. He taught in the history department of the **State University of Moldova** in Chişinău. One of the writers of Moldova's 1991 **Declaration of Independence**, Moşanu is furthermore one of the leading personalities of Moldova's **Party of Democratic Forces** and the vice president of the **Alliance for Democracy and Reforms**.

MOTPAN, DUMITRU (1940–). Political activist; founder and first chairman of the **Democratic Agrarian Party of Moldova (PDAM)**. A native of Selişte, **Nisporeni**, Moţpan is a graduate of the Soroca Technical College (1966) and of the Odessa Communist Party Superior School (1977). After Moldova's accession of independence, he pleaded for the country's integration in the **Commonwealth of Independent States** and advocated a left-leaning political stand. Between 1994 and 1996, Moţpan served as deputy speaker of Moldova's Parliament, in which the PDAM detained a majority. In the wake of that party's poor performance in the May 1998 elections, Dumitru Moţpan resigned his position and was replaced by Anatol Popuşoi (V. N.).

MOVILA, IEREMIA (?–1606). Prince of Moldova between 1595 and 1606. His reign was briefly interrupted by the conquest of Moldova by **Wallachia**'s Prince **Michael the Brave**, from May to September 1600, during which time he took refuge in the northern fortress of **Hotin** on the **Nistru River**.

Other members of the Movilă family briefly reigned over Moldova for short periods after 1606: Simion Movilă (1606–1607), who had also reigned over Wallachia (1600–1602); Mihai Movilă (for a few months in 1607); Constantin Movilă (1607–1611); and Alexandru Movilă (1615–1616). **Miron Barnovschi-Movilă** reigned between 1626 and 1629 and, for a short time, in 1633. The last reigning prince of the Movilă dynasty was Moise Movilă, who ruled from 1630 to 1631 and from 1633 to 1634. One of the illustrious members of the Movilă reigning family was Metropolitan **Petru Movilă**.

MOVILA, PETRU (1596–1646). The nephew, son, and brother of three Movilă princes of Moldova: **Ieremia Movilă** (1595–1606); Simion Movilă (1606–1607), who between 1600 and 1602 had also reigned over **Wallachia**; and Moise Movilă (1630–1631, 1633–1634). Born in **Suceava**, Petru Movilă received his theological and humanistic education at the Catholic University of Lwów in Poland. He became an Orthodox monk in 1625, was anointed metropolitan of Kiev in 1633, and soon asserted himself (under the Ukrainianized name of Petro Mohyla) as one of the most important spiritual leaders of the Kiev church. Metropolitan Movilă wrote in Latin his most famous theological work, an Orthodox definition and confession of faith (*Orthodoxa Confessio Fidei Catholica et Apostolica Ecclesiae Orientalis*), instrumental in the refutation by the **Orthodox Church** of Calvinist influences. It was approved by the Synod of **Iași** in 1642 and accepted by the patriarchs of Constantinople, Jerusalem, Alexandria, and Antioch (1642–1643) and by the Synod of Jerusalem in 1672. A Greek version was published in 1667. The first of the 18 widely circulated **Romanian-language** editions of the work (*Mărturisire ortodoxă*) was published in Buzău, **Wallachia**, in 1691. The canonization of Petru Movilă by the Orthodox Church of Ukraine has been under consideration for some years.

MÜNNICH, BURKHARD CHRISTOPH (1683–1767). Military leader and statesman of German origin who became field marshal in the army of the **Russian Empire** in 1732 and president of the czar's Council of War. In 1736, he started a series of Russian campaigns against the **Ot-**

toman Empire, advancing down from Crimea along the shores of the Black Sea. He captured **Hotin**, crossed the **Nistru River** into Moldova, and made a triumphant entry into **Iaşi** in 1739, accompanied by the grandson of Prince **Demetrius Cantemir**, Constantin, who had been brought up in Russia. Prince **Grigore Ghika II** fled the capital, and Münnich put the principality under the czar's protection, proclaiming what was to be a short-lived semblance of **autonomy** of Moldova under his own governorship (September–October 1739). Münnich withdrew from Moldova under the conditions of the Treaty of Belgrade. *See also* RUSSO-TURKISH WARS.

MURAVSCHI, ALEXANDRU (1950–). Deputy prime minister in Moldova's government of 1999, Muravschi is a native of **Chişinău**. He holds a Ph.D. in economics from the **State University of Moldova** (1977) and studied at the London Higher School of Economics and Political Studies (1983–1984). He served as head of the Department of Market Economy at Moldova's Institute of Agro-Industrial Economics (1990–1992). He was elected to the Parliament of Moldova on the tickets of the **Democratic Agrarian Party** (1994) and the **Bloc for a Democratic and Prosperous Moldova** (1998).

MURAVSCHI, VALERIU (1949–). Politician and economist; currently the president of the Association of Moldova's Banks. Muravschi was born in **Orhei** and is a graduate of the economics department of the Chişinău Polytechnic Institute of Moldova (1971). Between 1990 and 1991, he served as minister of finance and between 1991 and 1992, as prime minister of the government of Moldova. He played an important role in Moldova's bid for independence and free market reforms (V. N.).

MUSEUMS. Moldova has 83 museums, the collections of which contain over 600,000 artifacts and items of historical, cultural, and documentary value—all preserved and put on display. The country's most important museums are located in **Chişinău**, including the National Museum of History, the National Fine Arts Museum, the National Museum of Archeology, and Moldova's oldest museum, the National Museum of Local Ethnography and Natural History, founded in 1889.

MUSICESCU, GAVRIL (1847–1903). Composer and musician, Musicescu (Muzichenko in Russian transcriptions) was born in **Ismail** and studied music and composition in St. Petersburg and **Iaşi**. He is the author of numerous compositions of choral music. He eventually settled in **Romania** and, from 1872 until his death, taught at the Iaşi Conservatory. The Gavril Musicescu Music Academy in **Chişinău** is named for him.

-N-

NAMESNIK. Title of the Russian official appointed to govern a local administration. In the 18th through 20th centuries, the title denoted a high-ranking special appointee of the czar with discretionary power to govern over a region, as was the case in **Bessarabia** after 1812.

NATION. A term that generally denotes any sovereign state with political autonomy and a settled territory, such as the Republic of Moldova. In a more detailed definition, a nation can also be described as a community of people sharing a common language, inhabiting a fixed territory, having common customs and traditions, and having become sufficiently conscious to recognize similar interests and a mutual need for a single sovereign leadership. Applied to the vexed issue of the differences and similarities between Moldova and neighboring **Romania**, the first part of the more specific definition carries connotations that may be applied, in twinlike fashion, to Moldova as well as to Romania, as both countries share common ethnic roots, the same **language** and literature, and similar legacies of folklore and traditional beliefs. However, the second part of the definition fails to circumscribe in a similar fashion other fundamental concepts, such as a mutual acknowledgment of common interests and the need for a single leadership. These terms are not conterminous, thus setting Moldova and Romania apart—if not in terms of a broader sense of nationhood, certainly in terms of statehood and separateness as political bodies. *See also* PRO-ROMANIANISM; UNIONIST MOVEMENT.

NATIONAL EMBLEM. Moldova's national emblem is a Roman eagle in gold outlined in black, with a red beak and talons, carrying a yellow cross in its beak, a green olive branch in its right talon, and a yellow scepter in its left talon. On its breast is a blue-and-red shield featuring the stylized black head of a European bison, with star, rose, and crescent. The black bison head has been Moldova's traditional symbol ever since the first foundation of the principality in the 14th century by **Dragoş Vodă**, who, according to legend, crossed the mountains from **Transylvania** in pursuit of a bison he tracked and hunted down to the Moldova River. The legend of a bison hunt as the origin of the **founding of Moldova** was emblazoned in the principality's great seal from the very beginning and was used uninterruptedly as its heraldic sign until the 19th century.

After the 1812 incorporation of the eastern half of the principality into the **Russian Empire**, the symbol was partially preserved, embedded in the inferior field of the arms of the **oblast** of **Bessarabia**, under imperial Russia's black two-headed eagle. The black bison head also became part of modern **Romania**'s coat of arms after the 1859 union of Moldova and **Wallachia**, under the name of the **United Principalities**.

The **Moldavian Soviet Socialist Republic**—a successor of historic Moldova on the latter's eastern territories (1940–1990)—had a different emblem, one featuring the Soviet-style hammer and sickle, with a rising sun inside a rounded garland of grapes and wheat sheaves topped off by a star. The return to Moldova's traditional emblem—which decks the republic's new light blue, yellow, and red flag—became one of the bones of contention in the dispute with the breakaway self-styled **Moldavian Nistrian Republic**, which has preserved the Soviet-style red and green flag with the hammer and sickle emblem.

NATIONAL SECURITY. Moldova's Ministry of National Security replaced the Soviet-era Committee for State Security, the **KGB** branch of the **Moldavian Soviet Socialist Republic**. The local assets and personnel of the former KGB, taking orders from Moscow, were transferred to the new authorities in **Chişinău**. In 1994, Moscow and Chişinău reached an agreement on intelligence cooperation, pledging to work together on a broad range of security issues including exchange of information, combatting terrorism, and illegal arms sales. According to data made public in 1997 by **Tudor Botnaru**, Moldova's minister of national security, only some 30 percent of the officers currently working at the Ministry of National Security were hired as KGB officers before 1990, while the overall staff has been reportedly reduced by 30–40 percent since then. With regard to public access to files of the former KGB in Moldova, the policy of the current government is to keep them secret. Only close relatives of people who suffered **deportation** are permitted access to the files, provided the documents contain no other names.

NATIONAL UNIFICATION. A historical process by which European states gradually achieved unity within specific borders enfolding their own nationhoods, in keeping with shared legacies of culture and political traditions, usually knit together by a common language. Its common underlying premise was the identification of the state or nation with the people, or at least the desideratum of determining the territorial extent of the state according to ethnographic principles. Nineteenth-century Italy (joining together preexisting political entities such as Sardinia, Lombardy, Venice, Parma, Tuscany, Sicily, the kingdom of Naples, and the Papal State) and Germany (joining together preexisting political entities such as Prussia, Bavaria, Hanover, Saxony, Württemberg, and Mecklenburg) are frequently cited as examples of national unification. The **Principality of Moldova** followed a similar path when it joined the Principality of **Wallachia** in 1859 to form the **United Principalities**, later **Romania**. East of the **Prut River**, the Bessarabian districts of **Bolgrad**, **Cahul**, and **Ismail** shared in this 19th-century trend, as components of the United Principalities (1859–1878).

In the 20th century, most especially in the aftermath of World War I— when peace settlements were inspired and in part determined by the **Wilsonian principles** on the people's right to self-determination—aspirations toward national unification gathered specific momentum and gave birth to new territorial configurations on the map of Europe. *See also* NATION.

NEAR ABROAD. The non-Russian successor states of the **Union of Soviet Socialist Republics (USSR)**, in which Moscow has unilaterally expressed a national security interest. The near abroad concept revolves around Russia's ill-defined duty to protect the rights of **Russian ethnics** left behind in the former Soviet republics. The notion emerged in the aftermath of the dissolution of the USSR, which left some 25 million Russians outside the borders of the **Russian Federation**, including some 562,000 Russian ethnics in the Republic of Moldova, where they constitute 13 percent of the total population of the country (1993 est.). Moldova's Russian ethnic minority is mostly made up of an urban, educated population, with larger concentrations in **Chişinău**, **Tiraspol**, **Bălţi**, **Dubăsari**, and **Râbniţa**. A sizable and compact Russian community of about 153,000 people live in the separatist **Nistru** east-bank districts. *See also* COLONIZATION; RUSSIFICATION; SOVEREIGNTY.

NECULCE, ION (1672–1745). Chronicler, historian, and politician; author of *Letopiseţul Ţării Moldovei* (A Chronicle of the Land of Moldova), covering the period 1662–1743. Neculce's *Chronicle* puts special emphasis on the personalities of the princes he knew best, among them, **Constantin** and **Demetrius Cantemir**. An important part of his work describes the beginnings of the Moldova-Russia relationship during the reign of **Peter the Great**, whose 1711 visit to **Iaşi** he portrays in vivid color. Neculce took part in the July 1711 Russo-Moldo-Turkish battle of Stănileşti, which, as a keen eyewitness, he deemed a turning point in the history of 18th-century Moldova.

NEDELCIUC, VASILE (1948–). Chairman of the Foreign Affairs Committee of Moldova's Parliament and of Moldova's delegation to the Council of Europe, as well as one of the leading members of the **Party of Democratic Forces**. A native of Bulboci, **Soroca**, Nedelciuc is a political science expert and a senior researcher in computer sciences. He is a graduate of the Moscow Aircraft Institute, where he earned his Ph.D. in 1979. He entered politics in 1990 and was one of the writers of Moldova's 1991 **Declaration of Independence**. He has authored over 45 publications on a variety of subjects, including a study devoted to Moldova for Stanford University's Center for Russian and East European Studies (1996). Nedelciuc also holds nine patents for personal inventions in the field of informatics.

NEGRUZZI, CONSTANTIN/COSTACHE (1808–1868). Novelist, poet, and publicist; his masterpiece, the historical novella *Alexandru Lăpuşneanul,* is a vivid evocation of the personality of Prince **Alexandru Lăpuşneanu**, who reigned over Moldova in the 16th century. Negruzzi lived in **Chişinău** between 1821 and 1823 and made the acquaintance of the Russian poet **Alexander Pushkin**, then in exile in **Bessarabia**. His Bessarabian impressions, together with a medley of translations, were collected under the title *Zăbavile mele din Basarabia în anii 1821, 1822, 1823 la satul Şărăuţii, în raiaua Hotin* (My Ramblings in Bessarabia in 1821, 1822, 1823 around the Village of Sărăuţi near Hotin). Negruzzi wrote for *Albina românească* and *Spicuitorul moldo-român*, both published by **Gheorghe Asachi**. He pleaded for the Latin alphabet but fought against the exaggerations of his contemporary Eliade Rădulescu, a cultural promoter who led the efforts of the Latinist school in Bucharest, the capital of **Wallachia**. The Negruzzi-Rădulescu polemic was published in the form of an exchange of letters in the latter's *Museu naţional* (1836) under the title "Corespondenţă între doi români, unul din Ţara Românească şi altul din Moldova" (Correspondence between Two Romanians, One from Wallachia, the Other from Moldova). A bronze bust of Constantin Negruzzi decorates the alley of Moldova's literary pantheon in Chişinău's Central Park.

NEW RUSSIA. Southern **oblast**, or border province, of the **Russian Empire**, established in 1824 by Czar **Alexander I**, with the port city of Odessa serving as the headquarters of its general government. In 1828, most of present-day Moldova, then named **Bessarabia**, was included in New Russia (Russian: Novorosiisk), a move that marked the end of its initial status, as defined by the 1818 **Aşezământ**. Bessarabia became a *guberniia* of Russia in 1874. *See also* RUSSIFICATION.

NEWLY INDEPENDENT STATES (NIS). *See* COMMONWEALTH OF INDEPENDENT STATES (CIS).

NEZAVISIMAYA MOLDOVA. **Russian-language** version of the **Chişinău** government's official newspaper, *Moldova Suverană*. *Nezavisimaya Moldova* is one of the wide-readership Russian-language newspapers that began publishing in Chişinău after Moldova's **declaration of independence**.

NICHOLAS I (1796–1855). Czar of Russia between 1825 and 1855. His reign marked the apogee of Russian autocracy, with some lasting effects on the newly acquired province of **Bessarabia**, in which he took aggressive steps to encourage alien immigration. The process altered the pristine ethnic fabric of the land the **Russian Empire** had acquired through **annexation** from the **Ottoman Empire** in 1812. His decree of 26 September 1830 extended privileges for **Jews** from other parts of the empire, inviting them to settle in Bessarabia's towns and cities. In February 1832, he approved the creation of two dozen Bulgarian rural colonies in the southern part of the province. Serbian settlers had already been given privileges in 1826. Between 1825 and 1842, by a series of new imperial privileges, colonists from as far as Switzerland, Bavaria, Württemberg, and other places founded dozens of settlements with German-sounding names across Bessarabia's lowlands and the **Bugeac**. To boost and organize the colonies' expansion, Nicholas I established in 1833 the General Administration of Trans-Danubian Colonists, a body designated to monitor and organize the new settlements in the empire's recently acquired lands. In 1834, he approved the reconstruction of **Chişinău** as a modern city under plans drawn by the province's architects, Pleining and Bogdan Eitner. *See also* COLONIZATION.

NICHOLAS II (1868–1918). Last czar of Russia, reigned from 1894 to 1917; toppled by the Bolshevik Revolution and executed with the entire imperial family in 1918. Under the reign of Nicholas II, the crisis of the czarist system reached an early climax in 1905. At that time, while still retaining the traditional title of "Autocrat of Russia," Nicholas II promised respect for the inviolability of the person, freedom of thought, speech, meetings, and association, and the end of imperial ukases, to be replaced by Western-style laws promulgated by a newly established legislative body, the Duma. The impact of such moves triggered pro-freedom action in **Bessarabia**, where a group of intellectuals started the publication of the periodicals *Basarabia* and *Moldovanul*, asserting the rights of the local population to its own language, traditions, and culture. The short-lived movement was stifled in 1907 under measures taken by Russian Prime Minister Piotr Stolypin. After the March 1917 abdication of Nicholas II, with the mounting pressure of Bolshevik disruption inside Russia's political and military structures, the Moldovan liberation movement flared up once again in **Chişinău**, materializing in the form of the foundation of the Moldovan National Party (Partidul Naţional Moldovenesc), the demand for political autonomy inside Russia, the return to Bessarabia's local traditions, and an end to the Russian system of education. Nicholas II visited Chişinău in June 1914 to unveil a now destroyed statue of his predecessor, **Alexander I**, under whose reign Russia had acquired Bessarabia from the **Ottoman Empire** in 1812.

NIDELCU, DUMITRU (1942–). Former minister of labor, social protection, and the family in Moldova's government of 1997, Nidelcu is a graduate of the Agricultural University of Moldova and of the Moscow Academy of Social Sciences. From 1969 to 1978, he held various positions in the Youth Organization and the **Communist Party** of the **Moldavian Soviet Socialist Republic**. He was deputy minister of agriculture from 1980 to 1984, then secretary and chairman of the Trade Unions of Moldova from 1984 to 1992 (V. N.).

NIKA PRESS. A small **Russian-language** news service based in **Chişinău**, with good contacts in the **Nistru** east-bank breakaway region. It received a grant in 1996 from the U.S. Information and Communication Agency's Democracy Commission.

NISPORENI. Chief town of the former *raion*, or district, of the same name, 70 kilometers west of **Chişinău**. The oldest mention of Nisporeni dates back to the year 1669. The former *raion* was established in 1940, in the aftermath of the Soviet incorporation of **Bessarabia**. Nisporeni had a population of over 81,000 inhabitants (1993 est.). After the 1999 reorganization of Moldova's territory, Nisporeni became part of the newly established *judeţ* of **Ungheni**.

NISTRU. A literary and artistic periodical, first published in **Tiraspol** in 1931 in the form of an almanac-type supplement, under the name *Octombrie* (October). After the foundation of the **Moldavian Soviet Socialist Republic**, it became a monthly. In 1957, its name was changed to *Nistru,* the name of Moldova's main river. Following Moldova's **declaration of independence**, it continued to appear under the name *Basarabia.*

NISTRU/DNESTR/DNIESTER RIVER. The second largest river in the western area of the Black Sea. The Slavic name Dnestr is an apparent adaptation derived from the ancient Latin name Danaster. The vernacular Nistru is a local traditional toponym, also found west of the Carpathians in the Transylvanian region of **Maramureş**.

Some 1,325 kilometers in length, the river rises on the northern slopes of the Carpathian Mountains and drains an area of 47,739 square kilometers before flowing into the Black Sea through a broad estuary, known as **Liman**. Its typical feature is a meandering course determined in part by the geological infrastructure of the Moldovan plateau; the granitic spurs from the Carpathians account for its canyonlike formations on the west bank, which create a higher natural border facing the east bank's mostly lower forms of relief. The average width of the channel is between 150 to 230 meters, but in some places, it attains as much as 420 meters.

Due to the typical elevation of its west bank, which overlooks the plains lying to the east, the Nistru has played the part of a natural frontier of strategic importance for most of its recorded history, with its key points located at the strongholds of **Hotin**, **Soroca**, **Orhei**, **Tighina**, and **Cetatea Albă**. In the wake of the 1940 incorporation of **Bessarabia** into the **Union of Soviet Socialist Republics**, the Nistru River ceased to mark a political boundary, becoming enfolded into the then newly created **Moldavian Soviet Socialist Republic**, which, the same as its successor state, the Republic of Moldova, lies on both of its banks, albeit cut off from Liman. A system of dams and accumulation lakes between **Râbniţa** and **Dubăsari** built during the Soviet era is now part of the northern course of the Nistru.

NKVD. Acronym for the Russian-language Narodny Komissariat Vnutrennikh Del, or the People's Commissariat of Internal Affairs, the political police of the Soviet Union's Communist Party in the 1930s and 1940s. As an instrument of the Communist Party's dictatorship, the NKVD was in charge of domestic security, surveillance of dissidence, repression, arrests, deportations, and extermination of political foes. It was restructured in 1946, when its activities were devolved to a largely identical successor agency, the MVD (for Ministerstvo Vnutrennikh Del, or Russia's Ministry of Internal Affairs).

The NKVD exerted discretionary power over the largely artificial **Moldavian Autonomous Soviet Socialist Republic** between 1924 and 1940 and, after the June 1940 incorporation of **Bessarabia** into the **Union of Soviet Socialist Republics**, over the **Moldavian Soviet Socialist Republic**. Headquartered from 1940 to 1941 in the former Italian consulate building in **Chişinău**, the NKVD conducted interrogations and tortured opponents of the newly installed Communist dictatorship, earmarking many Moldovans for **deportation** and summary execution. Some of the victims were buried in the backyard of the consulate, others in the gardens of Chişinău's Theological Institute or metropolitanate building. The NKVD blew up the Italian consulate in July 1941, before the Red Army's retreat in front of the Romanian army's advance in the first weeks of World War II. With the return of Soviet power in 1944, the NKVD resumed its notorious policies of repression, playing the part of Moscow's chief instrument for crushing dissent, resistance to the liquidation of private property, and any form of opposition to Communist rule in Moldova. Its role was continued by its successor agencies, including the **KGB**.

NONGOVERNMENTAL ORGANIZATIONS (NGOs). A law on NGOs was passed by Moldova's Parliament in 1996. Moldova's several hundred NGOs include the Ecologist Movement of Moldova (Mişcarea Ecologistă din Moldova), Moldova's Disabled Society (Societatea Invalizilor din Moldova), the Pro-Basarabia Pro-Bucovina Association, the Republican Organization for the Empowerment of Moldova's Youth (Organizaţia Republicană pentru Consolidarea Tineretului din Moldova), the Moldovan Scientists Association (Asociatia Oamenilor de Ştiinţă), the AVE-FILM Association, the Foresters Progress Association (Asociaţia Progresul Silvic), the Pro-Moldova Patriotic Movement, the Prosvita Society, the Gromada Society, and the Chişinău Russians' Community.

NORTH ATLANTIC TREATY ORGANIZATION (NATO), RELATIONS WITH. Moldova has distanced itself from the prospects of joining NATO in the foreseeable future since, in keeping with its **Constitution**, it wishes to stay neutral. As emphasized by its officials, Moldova is concerned about NATO expansion because it does not want to end up as a buffer zone between East and West with Russian troops on its territory, which is currently the case: the **Russian Federation** continues to station military units belonging to its former **14th Army** in the **Tiraspol** enclave, where a strong anti-NATO movement was initiated by a council of Russophone war veterans and reservists. In 1998, these servicemen organized a group to create an "Anti-NATO Committee" in the separatist region, which leans toward joining the Russia-Belarus union. The Republic of Moldova participates in the U.S. Partnership for Peace and in the Euro-Atlantic Partnership Council. Addressing the latter's inaugural session in 1997, Moldova's representative declared that **Chişinău** views the council as contributing to Moldovan security through its mechanisms geared at conflict prevention. In 1999, NATO contributed $355,000 in aid for Moldova's participation in various U.S. Partnership for Peace programs. *See also* ARMED FORCES.

NORTHERN BUCOVINA. A 5,489-square-kilometer strip of land at the extreme north of Moldova's historical territory, annexed by the **Union of Soviet Socialist Republics (USSR)** from **Romania** in 1940. The 26 June 1940 Soviet ultimatum referred to the demanded transfer as a "means of compensation for the great losses suffered by the USSR and the people of Bessarabia during the twenty-two years of Romanian rule over Bessarabia." Undertaken at the same time as the incorporation of **Bessarabia**, as spelled out in the secret provisions of the 1939 **Molotov-Ribbentrop Pact**, the move enfolded about 500,000 inhabitants and the city of **Cernăuţi** into the USSR, but it left the ancient capital of **Suceava** and Moldova's historic monasteries south of the border in Romanian territory. Northern Bucovina was integrated into the Ukrainian Soviet Socialist Republic after World War II and is currently part of Ukraine. *See also* ANNEXATION; BUCOVINA.

-O-

OBLAST. Administrative and territorial unit, or province, of the **Russian Empire**. Between 1813 and 1874, most of present-day Moldova, then **Bessarabia**, had the status of an oblast of Russia.

OCNITA. Chief town of the former *raion,* or district, of the same name in northern Moldova, previously in the ancient **Hotin** *judeţ* to which it historically used to belong. Author and poet **Constantin Stamati** spent the last part of his life in the Ocniţa region, where a small village bears his name. The former Ocniţa district, with a population of over 63,000 inhabitants (1993 est.), was established in 1975. After 1999, Ocniţa became part of the newly established *judeţ* of **Edineţ**.

OLVIA PRESS. Official news agency based in **Tiraspol**. Olvia (or Olbia) was the Roman name of an ancient port city on the **Nistru** estuary and the Black Sea, north of **Tyras**.

OPERATIONAL GROUP OF RUSSIAN FORCES. Russian military entity deployed on Moldova's strip of land lying along the east bank of the **Nistru River**, in the self-proclaimed **Moldavian Nistrian Republic**. The Operational Group of Russian Forces in Moldova is a downsized version of Russia's **14th Army**, headquartered in **Tiraspol**.

ORGANIZATION FOR SECURITY AND COOPERATION IN EUROPE (OSCE). Formerly the Conference on Security and Cooperation in Europe, established under its new name in 1995 to address issues of mutual concern to its member countries and to review implementation of the 1975 Helsinki Accord (a.k.a. the Helsinki Final Act). The OSCE is engaged in standard setting in fields including military security, economic and environmental cooperation, and human rights. It also undertakes preventive diplomacy initiatives designed to defuse, manage, and resolve conflict within and among participating states.

Moldova is a member of the OSCE, which has a permanent resident mission in **Chişinău**. The OSCE mission in Moldova has been chiefly concerned with, among other things, the negotiation of a settlement of the **trans-Nistrian conflict** and the withdrawal of Russian troops in the area; indeed, Moldova has repeatedly appealed to the OSCE for assistance with both of these issues, hoping for enforcement of the withdrawal and a peaceful resolution to its internal problems within the **Nistru** east-bank districts. In 1998, the OSCE's chairman expressed the desire to heighten the OSCE profile in Moldova, with help from interested member countries, including Denmark, France, Germany, Italy, the Netherlands, Poland, and **Romania**. The OSCE has also expressed concern over the lack of progress regarding the withdrawal of Russian troops from Moldovan districts.

ORGEYEV. *See* ORHEI.

ORHEI. Chief city of the newly reestablished Orhei *judeţ* in central Moldova, north of **Chişinău** on the east bank of the **Răut River**, close to the confluence with the **Nistru River**. The *judeţ* of Orhei includes the former Soviet-era districts of **Rezina**, **Şoldăneşti**, and **Teleneşti**. The city has a population of over 37,887 inhabitants (1993 est.). Historically, the place used to have a strategic importance, due to its position overlooking the natural borderline of the Nistru. In 1469, Prince **Stephen the Great** fought a **Tatar** invasion in the neighborhood of Orhei and, soon after, erected a fortress to guard the place and give it full control over the adjacent territories lying east, down to the banks of the river. Initially organized as one of old Moldova's key strongholds, Orhei's importance declined after the Russian **annexation** of 1812, when it was renamed Orgeyev.

One of Moldova's most treasured architectural monuments, St. Demetrius Cathedral, was erected in Orhei by Prince **Vasile Lupu** in 1636.

ORTHODOX CHURCH. The Orthodox Church is Moldova's main religious denomination, to which over 98 percent of the population belongs. Despite its many successive incarnations, it represents the oldest and most enduring of all institutions in the country. It was first organized under the jurisdiction of the patriarchate of Constantinople in 1401, when the bishop of **Cetatea Albă** was recognized as metropolitan of Moldova. The bishopric see was later moved to **Suceava** and **Iaşi**, successive capitals of medieval Moldova. Until the 19th century, the Constantinople patriarchy, to which Suceava and Iaşi were canonically subjected, traditionally anointed Moldova's princes according to the tradition of the Byzantine ritual, thus giving them supreme religious consecration as rulers. Moldova's last ruling prince to be anointed in Constantinople was **Grigore Alexandru Ghika V**.

After the 1812 **annexation** of the eastern half of the principality—then known as **Bessarabia**—by the **Russian Empire**, Moldova's ties to the Iaşi metropolitanate were severed, and ecclesiastical jurisdiction over Moldova's eastern lands was devolved to Russia's Orthodox Synod in St. Petersburg, headed by the czar (a title officially assumed since the time of the reign of Paul I, from 1796 to 1801). In 1813, the Russian Orthodox Synod ruled the creation of a new diocese, the eparchy of Kishinev, comprising most of the new **oblast** of Bessarabia, which local Bishop **Gavril Bănulescu-Bodoni** helped organize as an affiliate of the Russian Orthodox Church. Under the leadership of Bănulescu-Bodoni's Russian successors—Archbishops Irinarh Popov (1844–1858), Pavel Lebedev (1871–1882), and Serghei Liapidevski (1882–1891)—the Orthodox

Church of Bessarabia became one of the empire's most powerful instruments in pursuing the policies of **Russification**.

After the 1918 union of the **Moldavian Democratic Federated Republic** with **Romania**, Bessarabia's Orthodox Church came under the jurisdiction of the Romanian Orthodox patriarchate, and a metropolitanate of Bessarabia was created in 1925. It was never canonically abolished, but it technically ceased to exist after the 1940 Soviet occupation.

While pursuing an aggressive atheist propaganda campaign, the Soviet authorities created a Moscow-subordinated metropolitanate of Moldova after World War II, under the jurisdiction of Russia's Orthodox patriarchy. After Moldova's **declaration of independence** in 1991, part of Moldova's clergy, claiming over 300,000 believers, repudiated the authority of the metropolitan of Moldova, Bishop **Vladimir Cantarean**, and put itself under the jurisdiction of the patriarchate of Romania, which recognized it as the canonical successor of the interwar metropolitanate of Bessarabia. The metropolitanate of Bessarabia, headed by **Petru Păduraru**, has repeatedly requested the **Chişinău** authorities to grant its church and clergy official recognition, but the government has postponed a decision on the subject. In 1998, Păduraru's metropolitanate was for the first time invited to attend a general assembly of the World Council of Churches.

In spite of decades of atheist propaganda and destruction of churches under the Soviet rule, present-day Moldova boasts some 853 Orthodox churches and over a dozen monasteries, most of them reopened after the country's accession of independence. *See also* COMMUNIST ATHEISM; RELIGIOUS DENOMINATIONS.

OSTK. Russian acronym for Obedenionye Soiuz Trudovykh Kolektivov (English: United Council of Workers Collective; Romanian: Consiliul Unit al Colectivelor de Muncă), the leading political force in the breakaway **Moldavian Nistrian Republic**, where it practically concentrates all executive powers. The OSTK was formed in 1990, initially as a workers' strike committee, staging protests against the 1989 Language Law adopted in **Chişinău** by the Supreme Soviet of the **Moldavian Soviet Socialist Republic**.

OTTOMAN/OTHMAN EMPIRE. Also known as the Ottoman Porte and the Sublime Porte, the Ottoman Empire was the name applied to the Turkish Empire established by Sultan Osman I (1288–1326). It conquered Constantinople and put an end to the Byzantine Empire in

1453, thereafter gradually imposing its domination over the entire Black Sea basin, the mouths of the **Danube River** and surrounding areas, and westward over part of Central Europe, including to the Pannonian plain, up to the walls of Vienna, unsuccessfully besieged by the Ottomans in 1683. The first Ottoman inroad against the **Principality of Moldova** was the 1420 naval attack on **Cetatea Albă**, followed by another attempt to raid the principality's seaboard and the estuary of the **Nistru River** in 1454. Two years later, the Ottoman Empire, which had already secured sovereignty over neighboring **Wallachia** in 1432, imposed its own conditions on Moldova's Prince **Petru Aron**, who recognized Turkish suzerainty and agreed to pay an annual tribute of 2,000 gold ducats in exchange for peace and the sultan's pledge that "no lands or estates of Moldova will be alienated." Thereafter, with only a few brief interruptions, the Ottoman Empire exerted suzerainty over Moldova throughout the next three centuries, and the principality's strongholds—including **Chilia**, Cetatea Albă, **Tighina**, and **Hotin**—were successively annexed and turned into Ottoman military outposts.

Like Wallachia and **Transylvania**, Moldova was never annexed and turned into a *pashalik*, yet its subjection to the Ottoman Empire was aggravated after 1711, when the sultan assumed the exclusive right to appoint its ruling princes. During the **Phanariote era**, in the wake of several defeats in war, Ottoman Turkey twice dismembered the Principality of Moldova. In 1775, it surrendered to the **Habsburg Empire** the land's northern territories, which Austria renamed **Bucovina**; and in 1812, under the provisions of the Russo-Turkish **Treaty of Bucharest**, it surrendered to the **Russian Empire** the eastern half of the principality, which the Russians renamed **Bessarabia**. Ottoman suzerainty was in part relaxed after the 1826 Russo-Turkish **Convention of Akkerman**, which put an end to Turkey's monopoly over the trade of the **Danubian Principalities** and restored their right to elect local rulers. The Ottoman Empire reluctantly recognized Moldova's 1859 union with Wallachia under Prince **Alexandru Ioan Cuza** while continuing to exert an increasingly nominal suzerainty over the **United Principalities**, later **Romania**, until 1877.

A fundamental history of the Ottoman Empire from its beginnings to the 18th century by Moldova's Prince **Demetrius Cantemir** was published in London in 1734–1735. *See also* SOVEREIGNTY; RUSSO-TURKISH WARS; TURKEY, RELATIONS WITH.

-P-

PADURARU, ION (1961–). Minister of justice in Moldova's governments formed in 1998 and 1999. A native of Ţipleteşti, **Sângerei**, Ion Păduraru is a member of the **Party of Democratic Forces**. He holds a degree in law from the **State University of Moldova** and has been a lawyer in private practice in **Chişinău**. He briefly served as deputy minister of justice in Moldova's government from 1991 to 1992 (V. N.).

PADURARU, PETRU (1946–). Metropolitan of **Bessarabia** and archbishop of the pro-Romanian branch of the **Orthodox Church** of Moldova. A native of Ţiganca, **Cantemir**, Petru Păduraru graduated in 1973 from the Odessa Theological Seminary. Between 1973 and 1988, he served as a country priest in the Romanian-speaking villages of trans-Carpathian Ukraine: Biserica Albă, Slatina, Plăiuţi, Apşa de Jos, and Apşa de Mijloc. Back in Moldova in 1988, he served at the Chişinău Orthodox Cathedral and as abbot of **Căpriana**. Anointed bishop in 1989, he started a campaign to sever Moldova's church from Russia's patriarchy and to reestablish the pre–World War II status of the metropolitanate of Bessarabia as a suffragan of Romania's Orthodox Church. In 1995, the Bucharest Synod named him archbishop of **Chişinău**, metropolitan of Bessarabia, and exarch of its neighborhoods (i.e., *exarh al plaiurilor*). The move triggered strife between the clergy of Russian canonical obedience, headed by rival Bishop **Vladimir Cantarean**, and Păduraru's pro-Romanian clergy, which claims over 300,000 believers and over 100 parishes. In 1997, the Chişinău Court of Appeals ruled that the government must recognize and register Păduraru's Metropolitan Church as a religious denomination in the Republic of Moldova, but the government refused to do so. Later on, Moldova's Supreme Court turned down Păduraru's appeal against the government's refusal. The case is slated to appear before the European Court of Human Rights (V. N.).

PAN-SLAVISM. A movement advocating a closer union among the peoples speaking Slavic languages that emerged in 19th-century Russia. It inspired the czarist expansionist ideas during the last decades of the century, more especially during the 1860s and 1880s. In conjunction with **Russification**, Pan-Slavism was influential in non-Slavic areas as well, particularly in provinces incorporated into the **Russian Empire** in the 19th century, such as **Bessarabia**.

PANZARU, IURIE (1965–). Economist and foreign relations adviser to Moldova's president, Pânzaru is an international economics graduate of Keio University, Tokyo, where he studied between 1993 and 1997. Earlier in his career, Pânzaru worked in Moldova's embassy in Moscow. He also holds a degree in economics from the Moscow Lomonosov State University (V. N.).

PARASCA, VASILE (1948–). Minister of health in Moldova's government formed in December 1999. A native of Clocuşna, **Edineţ**, Parasca graduated from Moldova's State Medical Institute, where he specialized in dentistry. Since 1970, he has worked as a dentist and, with few interruptions, as hospital director. From 1989 to 1999 he served as chief physician at the Chişinău municipal hospital no. 5 (V. N.).

PARIS, CONGRESS OF. Convened in Paris between 25 February and 30 March 1856, after the defeat of the **Russian Empire** in the Crimean War (1853–1856). Its concluding document, the Treaty of Paris of 1856, placed the **Principalities of Moldova** and **Wallachia** with their existing privileges under the collective guarantees of Europe's powers, thus ending the Russian protectorate that had been in effect after the 1829 Russo-Turkish **Treaty of Adrianople** and the 1849 Russo-Turkish **Convention of Balta Liman**. It retained the nominal suzerainty of the **Ottoman Empire** over the two entities. The 1856 Treaty of Paris removed Russia from the mouths of the **Danube** and restored Moldova's access to the **Chilia** arm of the river by returning to its jurisdiction **Bolgrad**, **Cahul**, and **Ismail**, three Danubian districts of the lands that the Russian Empire had incorporated in 1812 under the name of **Bessarabia**.

PARIS, CONVENTION OF. Signed in Paris on 19 August 1858 by Great Britain, France, Austria, Prussia, Russia, Turkey, and the kingdom of Sardinia to set the guidelines for the future reorganization of the **Danubian Principalities** of Moldova and **Wallachia** after the defeat of the **Russian Empire** in the Crimean War (1853–1856). It established the political and administrative status of Moldova and Wallachia as twin political entities, under the name of the **United Principalities**. The two principalities were to have in common a central legislative commission and a common Supreme Court of Appeals, maintaining, however, separate governments and separate ruling princes, under the nominal suzerainty of the **Ottoman Empire**.

PARIS PEACE TREATY. Signed in Paris on 10 February 1947, its provisions restored the 1 January 1941 borders between **Romania** and the **Union of Soviet Socialist Republics (USSR)**, and thus sanctioned the incorporation of **Bessarabia** into the Soviet Union. Except for the Romanian wartime occupation (June 1941–March 1944), the de facto incorporation of Bessarabia into the USSR had been in effect since its 1940 **annexation** by the Soviet Union, enforced in keeping with the Soviet ultimatum of 26 June of that year, which implemented one of the secret provisions of the **Molotov-Ribbentrop Pact**.

PARTY FOR A DEMOCRATIC AND PROSPEROUS MOLDOVA / PARTIDUL PENTRU O MOLDOVA DEMOCRATICA SI PROSPERA (PMDP). A party established in June 1998 by **Dumitru Diacov**, on the organizational basis of the previously founded Movement for a Democratic and Prosperous Moldova. It is centrist in its policies and social democratic in its ideological orientation. It served as the linchpin of the centrist **Bloc for a Democratic and Prosperous Moldova**, which came in third in the 1998 parliamentary elections when it garnered over 18 percent of the vote. In the center-right coalition government formed in the aftermath of the 1998 elections, PMDP members were entrusted with several key positions, for example, the ministers of economy, finance, and agriculture. In October 1998, the PMDP formed a separate political alliance with other centrist parties. *See also* POLITICAL BLOCS AND PARTIES.

PARTY OF DEMOCRATIC FORCES / PARTIDUL FORTELOR DEMOCRATICE (PFD). Centrist right-wing political party first organized in 1993 under the name of the Congress of Intellectuality (Congresul Intelectualității). In 1994, it changed its name to the United Democratic Congress (Congresul Democrat Unit) before adopting its current name in 1995. **Alexandru Moşanu**, former speaker of the Parliament of Moldova, was the party's first leader, followed by **Valeriu Matei**, who won 8.90 percent of the vote in the first round of the 1996 presidential elections. In the 1998 parliamentary elections, the PFD won 8.84 percent of the national vote and joined the **Democratic Convention of Moldova** and the **Bloc for a Democratic and Prosperous Moldova**, with which it formed the **Alliance for Democracy and Reforms**, holding a center-right majority of 61 out the 101 seats of the **Chişinău** Parliament. *See also* POLITICAL BLOCS AND PARTIES.

PARTY OF MOLDOVA'S COMMUNISTS / PARTIDUL COMU-NISTILOR DIN MOLDOVA (PCDM). *See* COMMUNIST PARTY.

PASAT, VALERIU (1958–). Minister of defense in Moldova's governments of 1997, 1998, and 1999. A native of Scumpia, **Făleşti**, Pasat is a graduate of the history department of the **State University of Moldova** and of the Moscow Diplomatic Academy. Before 1992, he served as a researcher with the Chişinău Institute of History and as chief of the Ideology Direction of the Chişinău Committee of the **Communist Party** of the **Moldavian Soviet Socialist Republic**. From 1992 to 1994, he served as ministerial counselor of the embassy of Moldova to the **Russian Federation** and, after 1994, as Moldova's ambassador to Moscow (V. N.).

PASHALIK. Under the Ottoman rule, a province governed by or under the jurisdiction of a pasha, a high-ranking Turkish officer. As the **Ottoman Empire** expanded through successive territorial conquests, *pashaliks* were established in various lands fallen under Turkish military and civil authority, which included Bulgaria, Serbia, and, for a shorter time, Hungary, after the 1541 fall of Buda. Although subject to the Turkish sultan's suzerainty after 1456, the **Principality of Moldova** was never annexed by the Ottoman Empire and never had the status of a *pashalik. See also* SOVEREIGNTY.

PELIVAN, IOAN (1876–1954). A native of Răzeni, a village near **Chişinău**, Ioan G. Pelivan was a historian and jurist. His study on **Bessarabia** as part of the **Russian Empire** was published in Paris in 1919. He was a member of Moldova's 1917 **Sfatul Ţării** (General Assembly), and after Bessarabia's 1918 union with **Romania**, he served as minister of justice in that country's government. Pelivan died in a Communist prison in Romania.

PERESTROIKA. A political concept launched by **Mikhail Gorbachev** in August 1986, at the 27th Congress of the **Communist Party** of the Soviet Union. It called for a restructuring of the economy and society by adjusting and modernizing the political, economic, and social mechanisms of communism, while preserving its basic doctrinal tenets and structures. The perestroika policies gradually spun out of control and ended up in the dissolution of the Soviet Union on 26 December 1991. The impact of perestroika policies carried crucial consequences for the social and political developments in the **Moldavian Soviet Socialist**

Republic, culminating with its **declaration of independence** as the Republic of Moldova on 27 August 1991. *See also* GLASNOST.

PETER THE GREAT / PETER I (1672–1725). Sole autocrat and czar of Russia from 1696 to 1725. From 1682 to 1696, he shared the throne with his mentally deficient half brother, Ivan V, holding the subordinate position of junior czar. After assuming full power, he undertook a series of fact-finding trips to Prussia, the Netherlands, England, and Austria and returned home with the determination to forcefully modernize Russia and to pursue war against the **Ottoman Empire**. As a part of that design, he concluded the 1711 **Lutsk Treaty** with the **Principality of Moldova**, by which Russia guaranteed Moldova's perpetual integrity and independence under the hereditary dynasty of Prince **Demetrius Cantemir**. In exchange, Moldova was to join the anti-Ottoman struggle as an ally of Russia.

Peter the Great made a triumphant entry in Moldova's capital city of **Iaşi** on 24 June 1711. He and Demetrius Cantemir went to war against the Ottoman armies deployed on the **Prut River**, but their coalition was defeated at Stănileşti (18–22 July 1711). Peter the Great granted asylum, properties, and support to Prince Cantemir and his family and made him a private counselor at his imperial court in Russia. Peter played a seminal role in laying the foundations for Russia's territorial conquests at the expense of Ottoman Turkey and of other neighboring countries, such as Poland and Sweden. In 1721, Peter the Great proclaimed himself "Father of the Fatherland and Great Emperor of All Russia."

PETRU ARON (?–1469). Prince of Moldova during the period of upheaval and war that preceded the reign of **Stephen the Great**, Petru Aron reigned three times (1451–1452, 1454–1455, and 1455–1457). In 1456, he bowed to Turkish pressure and agreed to pay an annual tribute of 2,000 golden ducats in exchange for an end to Ottoman incursions on Moldova's Black Sea shores. Petru Aron was overthrown by Stephen the Great, who resumed the fight against the **Ottoman Empire** in an attempt to preserve the principality's independence. *See also* SOVEREIGNTY.

PETRU MUSAT I (?–1391). Prince of Moldova (ca. 1375–1391). The family name of Muşat was derived from the surname of Petru's mother, Margareta ("Muşata," i.e., "the Beautiful"), and was adopted as a patronymic for a dynasty that included **Alexander the Good**, **Stephen the Great**, and **Petru Rareş**.

PETRU RARES (?–1546). Prince of Moldova in 1527–1538 and 1541–1546. Under his reign, the country's army was crushed by the Turks, who stormed the capital of **Suceava** and occupied Moldova's southern hinterland between the **Danube** and the **Nistru Rivers**, including the strategic citadel of **Tighina**, renamed Bender. Petru Rareş's defeats were followed by an increasingly severe enforcement of the suzerainty of the **Ottoman Empire** over the **Principality of Moldova**. *See also* SOVEREIGNTY.

PHANARIOTE ERA. The name Phanariote was applied to high-ranking members of the Greek community living in Phanar (the Greek quarter in Istanbul) who—sporadically before 1711 and on an almost regular basis until 1821—provided the **Ottoman Empire** with a pool of administrative appointees, handpicked by the sultan to be ruling princes, or *hospodars,* of Moldova or of **Wallachia**, or successively of both. The Istanbul-appointed princes reigned for short periods of time (the average duration of an administration was two to three years), and several were occasionally interchanged between the two **Danubian Principalities**.

Moldova had 36 Phanariote rulers between 1711 and 1821. Whereas not all of them were ethnic Greeks (notable exceptions were the members of the **Racoviţă, Ghika**, and **Callimachi** families), these rulers were generally bent on gaining as many advantages as possible in the shortest period of time—hence a derogatory connotation usually given to the term "Phanariote." The **Convention of Akkerman**, signed by the **Russian Empire** and the Ottoman Empire in the aftermath of the 1820–1821 Greek uprising, reinstated the appointment of local rulers as princes of Moldova and Wallachia. The last Phanariote prince of Moldova was **Mihail Suţu**. *See also* IPSILANTI, ALEXANDRU; IPSILANTI, CONSTANTIN; MAVROCORDAT, CONSTANTIN; MAVROCORDAT, NICOLAE; MORUZI, ALEXANDRU; MORUZI, CONSTANTIN; MORUZI, DUMITRACHE.

PLACE-NAMES. Moldova's place-names reflect the country's linguistic and cultural traditions and are similar to those encountered in other regions where Romanian ethnics live and the **Romanian language** is spoken. Renaming places (e.g., Kishinev for **Chişinău**, Orgeyev for **Orhei**, Kotovsk for **Hânceşti**, Kutuzov for **Ialoveni**, Lazovsk for **Sângerei**, Suvorov for **Ştefan Vodă**) was part of the **Russification** process. Especially under Soviet rule, the number of Russified place-names grew abnormally (including the renaming of scores of villages), sometimes by duplication and repeated duplication, which led to a multiplication of identical toponyms. Given the smallness of the country, the number of renamed places bearing identical Russified toponyms has tended to create confusion, especially in the rural areas where, as of 1998, Moldova's territory had eight villages by the name of Nikolaevka, six Ivanovkas, five Aleksandrovkas and Mihailovkas, four Alekseevkas and Konstantinovkas, three Bogdanovskas, Kirilovskas, and Vladimirosvskas, and two Antonovkas, Elisavetovskas, Petrovkas, and Popovskas. Moldova has been considering changing these and other altered toponyms, slated for renaming or a return to their original native forms. *See also* the "Note on Toponyms" in the introductory material of this volume.

PLAMADEALA, MIHAI (1945–). Former minister of internal affairs in the government formed in 1997 and secretary of Moldova's Supreme Security Council in the cabinet formed after the 1998 elections, Plămădeală is a graduate of the Kharkov Law Institute in Ukraine. From 1972 to 1984, he held different appointments in the Department of the Public Prosecutor of the **Moldavian Soviet Socialist Republic (MSSR)**. He was prosecutor of the Buicani district of **Chişinău** between 1984 and 1985 and deputy prosecutor of the MSSR from 1988 until the breakup of the **Union of Soviet Socialist Republics** in 1991 (V. N.).

POGROM. A Russian word borrowed by other languages some time around 1903–1905. It originally denoted a storm or devastation brought about by a storm. The event that established the word as a synonym for looting, destruction of property, and slaughter of innocents was the massacre of the **Jews** of Kishinev on Passover in April 1903 (*see* EASTER MASSACRE). It was the first in a series of planned rapine and mass murder, implementing an anti-Semite program initially devised by Konstantin Pobedonostsev, procurator of Russia's Holy Synod under Czar **Alexander III**, and carried out by successive ministers of state. The Kishinev pogrom was followed by that at Gomel (in present-day Belarus) and, later on, by the "mobilization pogroms" in the context of the **Russian Empire**'s unpopular war with Japan and by the "patriotic pogroms" led by the Black Hundreds extremist group, under the battle cry "The foes of Christ are the foes of the czar."

POLITICAL BLOCS AND PARTIES. The 1998 parliamentary elections triggered the formation of a number of political blocs and alliances from among the over 50 registered parties and movements, out of which, in hindsight, about a dozen appear to have significance in defining the basic orientations in Moldova's fluctuating **political spectrum**. As some names have undergone changes and some political entities have regrouped, the following is a selective freeze-frame of some of the main political parties whose actions proved relevant at the time of the last electoral campaign and, in one way or another, in its aftermath.

The primary right-wing organization is the **Democratic Convention of Moldova / Convenţia Democrată din Moldova (CDM)**, set up by the **Christian Democrat Popular Front / Frontul Popular Creştin Democrat**, led by **Iurie Roşca**; the Moldovan Party of Revival and Accord / Partidul Renaşterii şi Concilierii din Moldova, led by **Mircea Snegur**; the Ecological Party of Moldova / Partidul Ecologist din Moldova, led by Ion Dediu; the Moldovan Women's Christian Democratic League / Liga Creştin-Democrată a Femeilor din Moldova, led by Ala Mândâcanu; the Democratic Convention National Peasant Party / Partidul Naţional Ţărănesc–Convenţia Democrată, led by Ion Untilă; and the Christian Democrat Party of Moldova / Partidul Creştin Democrat din Moldova, led by Vladimir Reuş.

The main centrist party is the social democratic **Bloc for a Democratic and Prosperous Moldova / Blocul pentru o Moldovă Democratică şi Prosperă (BMDP)**, set up by the Movement for a Democratic and Prosperous Moldova / Mişcarea pentru o Moldovă Democratică şi Prosperă, led by **Dumitru Diacov**; the Civic Party of Moldova / Partidul Civic din Moldova, led by **Vladimir Solonari**; the Popular Democratic Party / Partidul Popular Democratic, led by Serghei Scripnic; the New Force Movement / Mişcarea Noii Forţe, led by Valeriu Pleşca; the National League of Moldova's Youth / Liga Naţională a Tineretului din Moldova, led by Valeriu Streleţ; and the **Chişinău** intellectuals' Democratic Party for Rebirth and Prosperity / Partidul Democrat pentru Renaştere şi Prosperitate. A splinter group of the BMDP calling itself the Social-Democrat Furnica-Speranţa Union was formed in 1999.

On the center right is the **Party of Democratic Forces / Partidul Forţelor Democratice (PFD)**, led by **Valeriu Matei, Alexandru Moşanu**, and **Vasile Nedelciuc**.

The left wing consists of the **Party of Moldova's Communists / Partidul Comuniştilor din Moldova (PCDM)**, led by **Vladimir Voronin**, and the **United Social Democratic Party / Partidul Social Democrat Unit,** a center-left entity based on the alliance among the **Social Democrat Party / Partidul Social Democrat**, the Party of Social Progress / Partidul pentru Progres Social, the Republican Party / Partidul

Republican, the Party of Socialist Action / Partidul Acţiunii Socialiste, and the Party of Economic Rebirth / Partidul Renaşterii Economice.

More to the left is the Bloc of Popular Patriotic Forces / Blocul Forţelor Popular-Patriotice, established by the **Unity-Edinstvo Movement / Mişcarea Unitate-Edinstvo** and led by **Piotr Sornikov**; the **Union of Moldova's Communists / Uniunea Comuniştilor din Moldova**, led by Florin Hristev; and the Socialist Party of Moldova / Partidul Socialist din Moldova, led by Victor Morev.

Also on the political scene is the social democratic Union of Justice / Uniunea Dreptăţii, organized by the leftist Social Democrat Party of Moldova / Partidul Social Democrat din Moldova, led by Andrei Ţurcanu; the Moldovan Party for Social-Economic Justice / Partidul Dreptăţii Social-Economice din Moldova, led by Maricica Leviţchi; and the Radical Youth Organization / Organizaţia Tineretului Radical, led by Mihai Ţăruş.

More to the right is the Peasant Liberal Bloc / Blocul Ţărănesc Liberal, set up by the National Peasant Party / Partidul Naţional Ţărănesc, led by Simion Certan; the Liberal Party of Moldova / Partidul Liberal din Moldova, led by Mircea Rusu; and the National Liberal Party / Partidul Naţional Liberal, led by Andrei Iuri-Apostol.

In the wake of the 1998 elections, a new political bloc, the center-right **Alliance for Democracy and Reforms / Alianţa pentru Democraţie şi Reforme**, emerged from a political agreement among the CDM, the PFD, and the BMDP, together holding 61 seats in the Chişinău Parliament, versus the left-wing minority of 40 seats held by the PCDM.

The BMDP was also reshuffled in October 1998 as an alliance, with support from 10 smaller political allies, including the Party of Progressive Forces and the New Force Party (V. N.).

POLITICAL RISKS GUARANTEE. A project of the Republic of Moldova, sponsored by the **World Bank**, designed to attract foreign private finance for imports of raw materials and for intermediate inputs and capital goods by Moldovan industrial, commercial, and agricultural enterprises through guarantees backed by the Internationale Nederlanden Bank acting as the agent bank. By providing guarantees protecting against political risks, the government of Moldova hopes to attract trade and credit flows, which are expected to stimulate economic growth in Moldova. *See also* INVESTMENT.

POLITICAL SPECTRUM. In a 1997 survey conducted by the **Chişinău** publication *Moldova Notes,* Moldova's political sense of "left" and "right" was defined as follows: the left includes parties that are Russophone and against economic reform, with at least some yearning for a reconstituted **Union of Soviet Socialist Republics**. These include the new incarnations of the **Communist Party**, the **Unity-Edinstvo Movement**, and some smaller groups. The right, on the other hand, consists of parties that are Romanophone and pro-reform, with at least some degree of desire to see Moldova united with **Romania** at some time down the road. The main standard-bearer on this wing is the **Democratic Convention of Moldova**. The "center" comprises three tendencies: the right-wing centrists (such as the **Party of Democratic Forces**), the left-wing centrists (such as the **Democratic Agrarian Party of Moldova**), and the centrists proper, among them the **Bloc for a Democratic and Prosperous Moldova** and the Social Democrat Party. This middle group includes pro-reform Russophones and Romanophones who are favorable to economic renewal but who show no interest in union with Romania.

Although precise ethnic polling statistics cannot be deduced, it would appear that the left, in its broader sense, commands the loyalty of most of the **Russian**-speaking Slavic population (30–35 percent), while the right and center right is the province of Moldovans whose mother tongue is **Romanian** (ca. 65 percent). *See also* POLITICAL BLOCS AND PARTIES; PRO-ROMANIANISM.

POLLING ORGANIZATIONS. Moldova's fledgling opinion research initiatives include four major polling organizations: Opinia, **Flux**, Fakt, and Moldova Modernă. Opinia conducts polls on government policies, the economy, social protection, family issues, problems of democracy, and the environment. The mostly Russophone Fakt conducts its polls by telephone, which narrows its ability to reach respondents beyond people in the higher-educated segment of the population. Its focus is on the social and political situation of the country. Flux publishes a weekly bearing its name, which carries information primarily on political and military affairs. Moldova Modernă is connected with the centrist press agency **Basa-Press**, which finances its polls. It conducts about a dozen polls per year from four territorial centers based in the universities of **Chişinău**, **Bălţi**, **Comrat**, and **Tiraspol**. Moldova Modernă's focus is on the economy, politics, and social problems.

POPOV, MIHAI (1949–). Diplomat and politician, Popov holds a Ph.D. in history and is a graduate of the Philology Department of the **State University of Moldova**. He also holds a degree from the Moscow

Diplomatic Academy. Between 1973 and 1983, he held several positions with the Youth Organization and the **Communist Party** of the **Moldavian Soviet Socialist Republic**. From 1986 to 1992, he was first counselor of the Soviet (subsequently Russian) embassy to **Romania**. He then served as minister counselor of the Moldovan embassy to Moscow (1992–1993), followed by another year-long position as Moldova's ambassador to Belgium. After serving as Moldova's minister of foreign affairs between 1994 and 1997, Popov was appointed ambassador of the Republic of Moldova to Paris.

POPOVICI, IACOB (1939–). Minister of education in Moldova's government formed in 1997, Popovici is a graduate of the Pedagogical Institute in **Bălți**. His professional career includes various teaching positions. Prior to becoming a minister, he was deputy director of the Bălți Technical College and chairman of Moldova's Teachers Trade Union.

POPULAR FRONT OF MOLDOVA / FRONTUL POPULAR DIN MOLDOVA (FPM). Formed in May 1989 by leading members of the Alexie Mateevici Literary Musical Club, named for the poet **Alexie Mateevici**. The founding congress issued a 20-point program calling for sovereignty, political restructuring, return to the language of the majority, and a new environmental policy. In the 1990 elections, the FPM garnered 27 percent of the seats in Moldova's legislature and broke for the first time the monopoly of the **Communist Party** over the country's political life. With support from deputies favorable to its political platform, the FPM proved able to control over half of the votes in the legislature. Soon afterward, mostly because of its **pro-Romanianist** and **unionist** views, it began to lose part of its initial appeal; by 1993, it was reduced to a minority. Later that year, it was re-formed as the **Christian Democrat Popular Front**, which regained momentum as one of the main components of the **Democratic Convention of Moldova**. *See also* POLITICAL BLOCS AND PARTIES; POLITICAL SPECTRUM.

PRESS. Moldova's daily newspaper circulation is about 24 copies per 1,000 persons. The main official newspapers are the **Chișinău** daily *Moldova suverană*, published by the government, and its **Russian-language** version, the quasi-daily *Nezavisimaya Moldova*. The country's largest **Romanian-language** publications are the independent weekly *Săptămâna*; *Mesagerul*, a weekly published by the **Party of Democratic Forces**; *Țara*, published twice weekly by the **Christian Demo-**

crat Popular Front; the large-circulation independent daily *Flux* and its accompanying publication, the weekly *Flux magazin săptămânal*; and *Tineretul Moldovei*, published by the Ministry of Youth. Other print media include *Sfatul Țării*, published by the Parliament; *Viața satului*, a government publication that targets Moldova's rural readers; the weekly *Literatura și arta*, published by the Writers Union; and *Femeia Moldovei*, a popular independent publication for women. Minority-language publications include **Kishinyovskye Novosti**, *Telegraf*, *Russkoye slovo*, and *Kodry*, all published in Russian; also in Russian is *Komratskie vedemosti*, published in the administrative center of **Gagauz Yeri**, where *Ana Sozu* and *Kârlangaci* are also published in **Gagauz**. Other ethnic minorities' publications include *Prosvita* and *Homin* (in Ukrainian), *Rodno slovo* (in Bulgarian), and *Undser Kol / Nash Golos* (published in Yiddish and Russian).

In all, Moldova's print media include over 200 newspapers (out of which over 90 are in the Romanian language) and over 60 magazines (out of which over 30 are in the Romanian language). Periodical circulation by postal delivery has lately been on the increase, rising to about 260,000 as of March 1997. The most popular publication delivered is *Săptămâna* (over 24,000 subscribers), followed by *Mesagerul* (over 19,000 subscribers), *Literatura și arta* (over 17,000 subscribers), *Țara* (over 16,000 subscribers), and *Nezavisimaya Moldova* (over 10,000 subscribers). The total also includes subscriptions to **Commonwealth of Independent States** publications (ca. 56,000 subscriptions, mostly to Russian publications) and over 2,300 subscriptions to publications from **Romania**. **Tiraspol** separatist publications include *Rabochyi Tiraspol* and **Dnestrovskaya pravda**, the newspaper of the Tiraspol soviet.

PRIVATIZATION. Moldova's privatization effort is governed by the Privatization Act of 1991, according to which all Moldovans have the right to privatize state property by using their National Patrimonial Bonds to purchase shares of major, midsized, and small enterprises, as well as state-owned homes. Moldova's privatization program has been tailored in a way somewhat similar to the Czech Republic's voucher privatization process. National Patrimonial Bonds were issued to each citizen in proportion to the number of years worked in the economy. Some 90 percent of Moldovans participated in the program, and until 1998, about half of the Soviet-era state-owned enterprises were sold.

As of 1 April 1995, the privatization program had resulted in the privatization of 657 state-owned enterprises, including 323 large and midsized enterprises and 334 smaller enterprises. As of the end of 1997, over 85 percent of all state-owned residences had also been privatized. Of these, 70 percent were privatized free of charge, 28 percent with National Patrimonial Bonds, and 2 percent with cash. In the agricultural sector, more than 30 percent of agrarian industries had been organized as joint-stock companies and agricultural associations. About 70 percent of Moldova's **trade** and services had become private by the end of 1998.

Whereas privatization programs continue to be under way, economic downturns in **industry** and **agriculture** and the lack of control over the economy of the breakaway **Nistru** east-bank districts, where most of the country's industry is located, have generated dysfunctions, resulting in a slowing down of the pace of reform. Downturns of privatization efforts are also due to counterforces in the **Chişinău** legislature, where the Communists have publicly stated their will to press for a review of Moldova's privatization policies. Moldova's privatization efforts have the support of the **International Monetary Fund** and the **World Bank**. *See also* ECONOMY, NATIONAL.

PRO-ROMANIANISM. A concept denoting the aspirations of a minority of Moldova's society—mostly historians, writers, and other members of the intelligentsia—who advocate the view that "Moldovan" should simply be a semantic label applied to regional identity, not one connoting nationhood. They also hold that, in the end, Moldova should work toward integration with **Romania**. This view is based on the notion that the two countries share common historical roots, the same language, literature, and folklore, and the same inherited myths and symbols of culture. Insofar as it represents a polarity in Moldova's movement of ideas, pro-Romanianism is set into clearer relief when assessed as a counterreaction to the cultural and political legacies of **Russification**. The pro-Romanianist views were succinctly put forth in a 1994 open letter to Moldova's presidency titled "The Danger of the Political Enslaving of Eternal Truths," signed by 43 Moldovan scholars who wrote: "We know that we are Moldovans . . . just as the Italians are Milanese, Venetians, Piedmontese. . . . That is why it is not hard to understand that the name 'Moldovan' denotes not the people as such, but merely a part of the Romanian nation. It comes from the topographic name Moldova and is geographic, not ethnic, in essence—just like the names denoting Romanians living in other areas of the national territory. Simply put, while being Moldovans by virtue of the place where we were born, as an integral part of the Romanian people, we are at the same time Romanians, whether we like it or not" ("Pericolul aservirii politice a veşnicelor adevăruri," in *Plus-Minus* [Chişinău, February 1994]).

A terse statement lending balance to that angle of approach was made in 1999 by Moldova's president, **Petru Lucinschi**, who put it this way in a February 1999 Reuters interview: "We are ethnic Romanians by inheritance but Moldovans by citizenship."

Pro-Romanianists who advocate Moldova's eventual union with Romania are more numerous in academic circles and cultural institutions, such as the Writers Union, Chişinău **State University of Moldova**, and some institutes of Moldova's Academy of Sciences. In 1998, the leaders of the breakaway **Moldavian Nistrian Republic** lashed out at the **Chişinău** government, accusing it of aiming at "Romanianizing the Moldovan Republic and unifying it with Romania."

Nonetheless, the government and most of Moldova's society seem aware of the advantages of preserving the country's internationally recognized nationhood and political identity as separate from Romania. Political and cultural figures who had earlier pressed for unification with Romania seem too to have realized that such a step does not currently enjoy significant public support. Furthermore, reunification is strongly opposed by Slavic and other minorities. The realistic view among those who favor pro-Romanianism is that reunion might possibly lie ahead, but it could happen only in some largely unpredictable future. *See also* ANNEXATION; NATION; UNIONIST MOVEMENT.

PRUT RIVER. A 950-kilometer river belonging to the basin of the Black Sea. It rises on the northern slope of the Ukrainian Carpathians and drains longitudinally along the midland of historical Moldova before entering the **Danube River**, west of that river's delta. For most of its length—between Lipcani in the north and **Giurgiuleşti** on the Danube—the Prut marks the some-700-kilometer natural boundary between the Republic of Moldova and **Romania**. Two crossing points on the Prut link the two nations: the railway checkpoint of **Ungheni** and the through-route checkpoint of Leuşeni. The Prut became a political boundary in May 1812, at the time of the acquisition of the eastern part of Moldova by the **Russian Empire**, when the river started to separate west-bank Moldova from the east-bank territories, renamed **Bessarabia**. Ancient Moldova's territorial units of **Fălciu** and **Iaşi**, which used to straddle both banks of the Prut before 1812, were then cut in two.

PUIU, VISARION (1879–1964). Prelate of the **Orthodox Church**, Puiu became director of the Chişinău Theological Seminary in 1918, bishop of **Hotin** in 1921, and metropolitan of **Bucovina** for five years, between 1935 and the Soviet occupation of 1940. From 1942 to 1944, Puiu served as head of the short-lived diocese of **Transnistria**, with the bishopric's see in Odessa. He authored a number of books on **Bessarabia**, including a collection of documents in two volumes published in **Chişinău** in 1928–1938. He was tried as a war criminal by a Soviet tribunal and sentenced to death in absentia in 1946.

PUSHKIN, ALEXANDER (1799–1837). Russia's most famous romantic poet. He was banished from St. Petersburg for his revolutionary epigrams and exiled to **Chişinău** between September 1820 and August 1823. While in **Bessarabia**, he wrote some 100 poems and made the acquaintance of local writers **Constantin Negruzzi** and **Constantin Stamati** and nobleman **Matei Krupenski**. Pushkin showed interest in Moldova's local customs and folklore, which he captured in some of his works, including a Russian adaptation of the old Moldovan love song "Arde-mă, frige-mă" (Burn Me, Roast Me) and "The Black Shawl." His stay at the Dolna estate of landowner Zamfirache Rally (1767–1831) inspired the writing of *The Gypsies,* one of his best-known masterpieces. In his poem "To Ovid," he compared his fate in Bessarabia to that of the Latin writer Ovid, whose legendary place of banishment—Tomis, on the Black Sea—was not far distant. A bronze monument to Alexander Pushkin, erected in 1886, which graces Chişinău's downtown park, is inscribed with verses from "To Ovid."

-R-

RABNITA/RIBNITA. Chief city of the former *raion,* or district, of the same name, on the east bank of the **Nistru River**, 110 kilometers northeast of **Chişinău**, across from the west-bank town of **Rezina**. Râbniţa was first mentioned as a village in 1657, as a possession of the Polish Crown, the southern borders of which extended at that time to the banks of the Nistru. In the wake of the 1792 **Treaty of Iaşi**, the region became part of the **Russian Empire**.

The Râbniţa district was formed in 1924 as part of the **Moldavian Autonomous Soviet Socialist Republic**, carved out by the **Union of**

Soviet Socialist Republics from Soviet Ukraine. It became integrated in the **Moldavian Soviet Socialist Republic** after the 1940 **annexation of Bessarabia**.

Present-day Râbniţa has over 61,800 inhabitants (1993 est.), preponderantly Ukrainians and Russians. Both the district and the city (which has a population of over 32,000 inhabitants) are currently under the authority of the self-proclaimed **Moldavian Nistrian Republic (MNR)**. Râbniţa is a heavily industrial agglomeration and the site of Moldova's largest and most successful industrial complex of metallurgical works. Most of its steel exports go to the United States and other Western destinations. The Râbniţa steel mill provides more than 50 percent of the MNR's average yearly budget.

RACOVITA, CONSTANTIN (?–1764). Son of Mihail Racoviţă and prince of Moldova in 1749–1753 and 1756–1757. Constantin also reigned twice in **Wallachia**, from 1753 to 1756 and from 1763 to 1764.

RACOVITA, MIHAIL (?–ca. 1745). Prince of Moldova from 1707 to 1709 and from 1715 to 1726. Mihail Racoviţă also occupied the throne of **Wallachia** from 1730 to 1731 and from 1741 to 1744.

RAION. The Soviet-era name of Moldova's administrative districts (plural: *raioane*). Before the reorganization of the territory, the Republic of Moldova included 40 small-sized districts, each of them roughly the size of a small county. An administrative-territorial reform began in 1991 but was stalled by political uncertainties stemming from the secessionist movements in the **Nistru** east-bank districts and in **Gagauz Yeri**. In November 1998, Moldova's Parliament reestablished the division of the territory into larger units, called *judeţe*—namely, **Bălţi**, **Cahul**, **Chişinău**, **Edineţ**, **Lăpuşna**, **Orhei**, **Soroca**, **Tighina-Căuşeni**, and **Ungheni**, plus the autonomous Gagauz Yeri territorial unit (**Gagauzia**); an additional *judeţ*, **Taraclia**, carved out of Cahul, was established later, in 1999. A virtual **Dubăsari** *judeţ* is supposedly designed to include, in the future, the Nistru east-bank territories as an autonomous entity enjoying special status, once the **trans-Nistrian conflict** is resolved.

Enforced in 1999, the new administrative structure that eliminated the *raion* as its basic element is, by and large, similar to the one dismantled by Soviet rule in 1940. The 1999 administrative and territorial reform has been a precondition for continued **International Monetary Fund** and **World Bank** loans to the Republic of Moldova.

RANDUNICA. Short form or nickname of one of Moldova's main electoral organizations, **Dumitru Diacov**'s **Bloc for a Democratic and Prosperous Moldova**, whose both long and clumsy name and acronym (i.e., BMDP) were replaced in usage by the name of its electoral symbol, a lark (Romanian: Rândunica), which became the hallmark of Diacov's political platform in the 1998 elections.

RASCANI. Chief town of the former *raion*, or district, of the same name, northwest of **Bălți**. Râşcani (also spelled Răşcani) has over 13,000 inhabitants. A 1993 estimate placed the number of inhabitants in the former district at 83,456. In keeping with the 1999 reorganization of Moldova's territory, Râşcani has become part of the reestablished *judeţ* of Bălți.

RAUT RIVER. A river in northern Moldova 286 kilometers in length, tributary to the **Nistru River**.

RELIGIOUS DENOMINATIONS. The main religious denomination in the Republic of Moldova is the **Orthodox Church**, to which about 98.5 percent of the country's population belong. Moldova is thus one of the most homogeneous Orthodox countries in the world. The Orthodox Church has over 850 churches and a dozen monasteries in Moldova, but the denomination is canonically split between the metropolitanate of Moldova, subject to the jurisdiction of Russia's patriarchy, and the metropolitanate of **Bessarabia**, which put itself under the jurisdiction of **Romania**'s patriarchy.

Soon after Moldova's 1991 ascension to independence, over 200 churches were under reconstruction or were being built anew across Moldova. Other denominations include Baptists (184 communities), Adventists (61 communities), Pentecostals (34 communities), Roman Catholics (11 communities), and **Jews** (6 communities). *See also* RUSSIFICATION.

RENI. Port city of historic Moldova on the maritime **Danube**, east of the river's confluence with the **Prut**, about 7 kilometers southeast of **Giurgiuleşti**. Reni was first mentioned in 1593 in an act of donation of Moldova's Prince **Aron Vodă**. After the 1940 Soviet **annexation**, together with the rest of **Bessarabia**'s historic seaboard, Reni was detached from the remainder of the province and awarded by the **Union of Soviet Socialist Republics** to Soviet Ukraine. *See also* BORDERS OF MOLDOVA.

RENITA, ALECU (1954–). President of the Ecologist Movement of Moldova and a member of Moldova's Parliament, Reniţă graduated from the Chişinău State University of Moldova in 1975. He is chairman of the Parliament's Subcommittee for Ecological Issues and an active member of several **nongovernmental organizations**. Reniţă has been actively involved in the protection of Moldova's **environment** and **water resources** since 1983. In 1999, in recognition of his achievements in the area of environmental protection, the Cambridge Biography Institute awarded him the title of "Man of the 21st Century."

REVENCO, VALERIAN (1939–). Minister of labor, social protection, and the family in Moldova's government formed in December 1999. A native of the city of **Bălţi**, Revenco is a graduate of Moldova's State Medical Institute, where he specialized in pediatrics. Beginning in 1992 he served as deputy minister of labor, social protection, and the family in Moldova's preceding cabinets (V. N.).

REZINA. Chief town of the former Rezina *raion,* or district, 97 kilometers north of **Chişinău** on the **Nistru River.** The village was first attested to in a document in the 15th century. The former district had over 55,000 inhabitants (1993 est.). Rezina is part of the reestablished *judeţ* of **Orhei.**

ROMAN I (?–1394). Prince of Moldova from 1391 to 1394. In a written act defining the **borders of Moldova** in 1392 (the first official document of the principality preserved in its entirety), Roman I proclaimed himself "by the grace of God the Almighty, great ruler of Moldova's land from the Mountains to the Sea."

ROMANIA, CONTEMPORARY. Western neighbor of the Republic of Moldova, with which it shares a 681-kilometer border along the **Prut River.** Romania (capital: Bucharest) covers a surface of 238,391 square kilometers and has a population of 21,545,925 inhabitants (1997 est.). Between 1947 and 1989, under the name of the Romanian People's Republic, later on the Socialist Republic of Romania, the country was ruled by a Soviet-imposed Communist regime.

Despite the continuing difficulties in moving away from the totalitarian command economy that left its powerful imprint on the first six years of the post-1989 era, reforms started to be introduced in a more sustained way after 1997, with a growing private sector, especially in agriculture and in services. Such changes started to take place after the November

1996 general and presidential elections, when the democratic opposition defeated the former Communists and won the presidency and the majority in Romania's bicameral Parliament.

According to the 1998 atlas of the **World Bank**, Romania's 1996 gross national product per capita was $1,600. External trade data available indicated an increasing trade deficit caused by the paucity in exports and a jump in imports. At the end of 1998, Romania's trade deficit exceeded $3 billion. Romania's main trade partners in exports are Germany (18.1 percent), Italy (16.7 percent), France (5.6 percent), Turkey (5.0 percent), the Netherlands (4.2 percent), and the United States (2.3 percent). In terms of imports, the country's main partners are Germany (18.5 percent), Italy (16.9 percent), the **Russian Federation** (13.7 percent), France (5.4 percent), and South Korea (4.2 percent). Romania is Moldova's second trade partner in exports (13.9 percent of Moldova's total exports) and its third partner in imports (6.7 percent of Moldova's total imports).

Because of the slow pace of reform, Romania has been faced with economic woes. According to data released in February 1999 by Romania's National Statistical Board, Romania's gross domestic product dropped by 7.3 percent in 1998 compared to 1997. Industrial production declined by 17 percent in 1998 compared to the previous year, and grain production dropped by slightly more than 30 percent. At the end of 1998, inflation was up 40.6 percent from the December 1997 level, and unemployment reached a peak of 10.3 percent of the workforce. *See also* ROMANIA, RELATIONS WITH.

ROMANIA, HISTORICAL SPHERE. Romania as a unitary state emerged in two stages, influenced by the interplay of political-historical forces at work in three areas of pressure. The first one involved ethnic Romanians in the **Habsburg Empire**; the second one, ethnic Romanians in the **Principalities of Moldova** and **Wallachia**, both at that time under the nominal suzerainty of the **Ottoman Empire**; and the third, eastern Moldovans detached from the Principality of Moldova who became subjects of the **Russian Empire** in 1812.

Russia's growing sway over Eastern Europe and the successive defeats it inflicted on Ottoman Turkey during the course of the **Russo-Turkish Wars** played an important part in creating the premises for both the union of Moldova and Wallachia (which Russia tried to thwart) and Romania's declaration of independence (which Russia subscribed to, albeit exacting from it territorial gains at that juncture).

The first step in Romania's assertion as a unitary state—begun while part of its lands were still under nominal suzerainty of the Ottoman Empire—was the union of Wallachia and Moldova joined in a single state as the **United Principalities** in 1859 (renamed Romania after 1862) under the rule of Moldova's Prince **Alexandru Ioan Cuza**. Although most of what constitutes the current-day Republic of Moldova, previously annexed by Russia in 1812 under the name of **Bessarabia**, was no longer part of historic Moldova at that time, three of the latter's southern districts—**Bolgrad, Cahul,** and **Ismail**, which the 1856 **Congress of Paris** had returned to the Principality of Moldova—became part of Romania between 1859 and 1878. Under the provisions of the **Congress of Berlin**, Romania had to surrender them to Russia, which reincorporated them into Bessarabia.

Romania formally declared its independence as a nation in 1877, fought as an ally of Russia in the Russo-Romanian-Turkish War of 1877–1878, and became a kingdom in 1881 under **Carol I**. It entered World War I, one more time as an ally of Russia. It unsuccessfully fought the Central Powers on two fronts, along the **Danube River** and in **Transylvania**. As Russia's army began to flag down amid the crisis triggered among its ranks by disorder and mutiny at the outbreak of the 1917 revolution, Romania was defeated on both fronts, and most of the country was occupied by the enemy. The capital and the government were moved to **Iaşi**, and between 1917 and 1918, the area controlled by Romania's authorities was reduced to a small tract of land west of the Prut, with its last lines of defense stabilized on the Carpathians and the bend of the Danube. Rump Romania's only secure border was on the Prut, east of which lay Bessarabia, a backyard already engulfed by the turmoil of the revolution, as the czars' empire was collapsing. At the end of 1917, under the name of the Moldavian Democratic Republic (*see* **Moldavian Democratic Federated Republic**), Bessarabia proclaimed itself a republic, severed all links with Russia, and tried to counter on its own the ascent of **Bolshevik power**, which was gathering momentum in **Chişinău** and all across the land. Under mounting pressure from Bolshevik paramilitary units, the Chişinău governing body, **Sfatul Ţării**, turned for help to rump Romania's government in Iaşi. In January 1918, a Romanian **anti-Bolshevik military intervention** helped reestablish a fragile state of political stability at the rear of Romania's front lines, while World War I continued unabated on all fronts.

The second step in Romania's **national unification** was achieved at the end of World War I, starting with the Moldavian Democratic Republic's decision to join rump Romania in the wake of growing revolutionary turmoil in Ukraine, its eastern neighbor. Under those circumstances, on 27 March 1918, Sfatul Țării proclaimed a conditioned union with Romania. Later in the year, soon after the 11 November armistice, Sfatul Țării declared the unconditioned union of the former Russian province of Bessarabia with the kingdom of Romania. On 27 November, the same day as Bessarabia, **Bucovina** declared its own unconditioned union with Romania. The former Habsburg province of Transylvania followed suit on 1 December 1918, as the Allies' victory in World War I eventually brought Romania into the victors' camp.

The 1918 unification of all provinces with Romanian ethnic majorities was part of the surge for self-determination of Central Europe's nationalities in the wake of the collapse of the Habsburg, Russian, and Ottoman Empires. It was inspired and supported by the **Wilsonian principles**, spelled out by U.S. President Woodrow Wilson as the basis of territorial settlements at the end of the war. The **Versailles Conference**, which enforced those principles, established the borders of interwar Romania. In keeping with the post–World War I Versailles settlement, most of present-day Moldova was part of Romania between 1918 and 1940.

With the Versailles system of treaties collapsing and the outbreak of World War II, Romania surrendered Bessarabia and **Northern Bucovina** to the **Union of Soviet Socialist Republics (USSR)**, under the conditions of Moscow's 48-hour ultimatum pronounced on 26 June 1940.

At the end of World War II, under the provisions of the 1947 **Paris Peace Treaty**, Bessarabia and Northern Bucovina remained incorporated in the USSR. Romania was occupied by the Soviet army in the aftermath of the war, but it remained formally a kingdom until 30 December 1947, when its last king, **Michael I**, was forced to abdicate under Communist pressure. Between 1947 and 1989, under the name of the Romanian People's Republic, later on the Socialist Republic of Romania, the country was ruled by a Soviet-imposed Communist regime. The last leader of Communist Romania was dictator Nicolae Ceaușescu, overthrown in a popular uprising and executed by firing squad in December 1989.

See also ROMANIA, CONTEMPORARY; ROMANIA, RELATIONS WITH.

ROMANIA, RELATIONS WITH. Romania was the first state to recognize the independence of Moldova on the day it was proclaimed, 27 August 1991. However, as of 1998, a basic treaty between **Chișinău** and Bucharest had not been signed because of disagreement on a number of points, most of them related to the way of describing the nature of the relationship between the two countries, which, while being separate political entities, share identical origins and a common history, the same language, and quasi-identical cultural legacies.

Visiting Bucharest soon after his election, in December 1997, Moldovan President **Petru Lucinschi** pointed out that despite their similar historical and cultural legacies and the fact that they do share a common language, a merger of the two countries must be ruled out. Integration, as he put it, should best take the form of the two states' joint effort to integrate into a united Europe. On the other hand, in a January 1999 interview with Radio Romania, Lucinschi acknowledged that the major part of Moldova's population is made up of "ethnic Romanians of Moldovan citizenship."

In another statement on the vexed matter of an eventual merger, **Tudor Botnaru**, Moldova's former minister of national security, said that, if at all envisaged, such a hypothetical move could not be based on the 1918 or 1941 unification models, but rather on the feasibility of some future step-by-step process, starting with members of the present generation and concluding, perhaps, with their children and grandchildren.

Among the disputed issues in drafting a Moldova-Romania treaty were such sticking points as the Romanian side's initial insistence on mentioning the **Molotov-Ribbentrop Pact** in the document and such linguistic points as the use of the word "fraternal" in describing the two states or naming them "the two Romanian states." In 1998, describing his country's position, former Prime Minister **Ion Ciubuc** praised Moldova's ties with Romania and expressed hope for the future, but he also pointed out that the pending Friendship and Cooperation Treaty should reflect today's realities, the interests of both countries, and the specific provisions of each state's respective Constitution.

While a Soviet republic (according to its first Constitution, "an inalienable part of the whole Soviet people"), the **Moldavian Soviet Socialist Republic (MSSR)** was practically devoid of the right to establish foreign relations, and the Soviet republic's ties with neighboring Romania—particularly in the areas of language, arts, and culture—were drastically cut, all contacts between Chişinău and Bucharest having to go through Moscow. The 1978 Soviet-style Constitution of the MSSR admitted the republic's virtual right to establish foreign relations, but it stipulated that such a right should be guided by the goals, tasks, and principles of the foreign policy established by the Constitution of the **Union of Soviet Socialist Republics**. In the case of Moldova, the chief objective of these policies remained that of rescinding or reducing to a minimum linguistic, cultural, and artistic contact with neighboring Romania, a goal whose implementation was facilitated by the barrier of the **alphabet issue** and many other hindrances. As a rule, books and publications printed in Romania could not be found and purchased in Chişinău, people interested in buying them having to go Moscow to do so. Printing the local language in the Roman alphabet was prohibited. Public **libraries** in the MSSR were strictly deprived of the right to directly acquire books and publications from neighboring Romania.

At the time of the 1964 ideological conflict that brought to a freeze the relations between Moscow and Beijing—as the Chinese Communist leaders questioned Soviet Russia's right to **Bessarabia**—Romania's Communist leaders tried to take advantage of the Sino-Soviet rift by assuming a veiled confrontational attitude. Among other things, under the title *Notes on the Romanians,* four unpublished manuscripts of Karl Marx's, preserved in the Marx-Engels Archives of the Amsterdam International Institute for Social History, were published for the first time in Bucharest. In them, the author of the *Communist Manifesto* criticized Russia's imperialism and, more directly, the **annexation** of Bessarabia as rapine. The book irritated the Soviet leadership in Chişinău and Moscow. Later on, relations were mended as, in August 1976, Romania's Communist dictator, Nicolae Ceauşescu, paid a carefully staged visit to Chişinău, the first ever by a Romanian head of state to the MSSR. The move was widely interpreted as a sign of improved relations and of Communist Romania's implicit recognition of the legitimacy of Moscow's rule over the formerly Romanian territory of Bessarabia. During the late 1970s and throughout the **glasnost** era of the 1980s, there was a relative relaxation of Moscow's cultural tutelage over the MSSR, and a partial thaw in the Soviet republic's cultural and artistic relations with Romania occurred. Such contacts played a part in preparing the ground for what was to become the cultural reawakening that triggered the country's eventual disentanglement from Soviet rule, culminating in the 1991 **declaration of independence**.

After the December 1989 downfall of the Communist regime in Romania and the first free elections in the MSSR (held in February–March 1990), a new era began in Moldova's relations with Romania. On 6 May 1990, a mass demonstration dubbed the "Bridge of Flowers" was staged across the **Prut River** by both Moldovans and Romanians, with thousands of people crossing the river in both directions and flocking together on both banks to celebrate the demise of totalitarian rule.

Currently, Moldova's relations with Romania include several areas of cooperation. Romania is Moldova's second largest **trade** partner in exports, with 13.9 percent of Moldova's exports going to Romania, and its third largest partner in imports, with 6.7 percent of Moldova's imports coming from Romania. In matters of **energy**, Romania has offered Moldova some degree of participation in the construction of the second reactor of the nuclear energy-producing complex of Cernavoda, but high-cost investment considerations have so far prevented materialization of a joint venture. In November 1998, as Ukraine stopped providing about 60 percent of Moldova's imported energy, Romania started to provide electricity to Moldova, pumping 120 MW per hour through three energy links across the Prut. As a stopgap measure taken in an emergency situation, the initial import of 120 MW per hour from Romania's grid ensured about 15 percent of the total of Moldova's power needs. Moldovan authorities said Romania will decide if it wants to be paid in cash or receive instead a stake in **Moldtelecom**, the national telecommunications agency. A 1991 plan—temporarily delayed after 1994—envisioned the establishment of a permanent energy link between the two countries. Such an arrangement would eventually be able to provide about 60 percent of Moldova's power needs.

Educational cooperation has been intense since 1991, with Romania's Ministry of Education providing thousands of grants and scholarships for Moldovan students to study at Romanian universities or spend their vacations in camps, many of them on the Black Sea coast. For the 1999–2000 academic year, about 7,000 graduate and undergraduate students from Moldova were scheduled to study in Romania.

As with educational cooperation, cultural cooperation is by and large a one-way process. Romania has supplied Moldova with financial aid for the publication of periodicals and newspapers. Other forms of cooperation have included large donations of books for Moldova's libraries, which under Soviet rule had been dispossessed of practically all **Romanian-language** collections. Between 1990 and 1999, Romania's Ministry of Education provided the Republic of Moldova with about five million books in the Romanian language.

Moldova's railroad communication with Romania is carried through one checkpoint linking **Ungheni** to **Iaşi**, but the railway connection continues to be somewhat cumbersome because of Moldova's inherited Russian-style broad-gauge rail system, not used anywhere else in Europe, with the exception of former Soviet Eurasia and the Iberian Peninsula. Road traffic currently includes three through-route checkpoints on the Prut, at Ungheni, Leușeni, and **Costești**, which provide west-bank links to Iași and Albița. The future reconstruction of the bridge connecting the east-bank town of Lipcani to Rădăuți-on-the-Prut is designed to improve road traffic between the northern districts of the Republic of Moldova and their territorial counterparts in Romania. On the other hand, regular flights by Moldovan and Romanian airlines connect Chișinău and Bucharest on an almost daily basis.

Military cooperation between Moldova and Romania has been sporadic. Alongside other nations, both countries have taken part in joint military exercises conducted in various countries (including the United States), under the U.S. Partnership for Peace. In 1998, the Chișinău Parliament ratified a Moldo-Romanian cooperation agreement in the area of military transportations. *See also* BESSARABIA; NATION.

ROMANIAN LANGUAGE. The native language of the majority of Moldova's population. Like the other Romance languages (i.e., French, Italian, Spanish, Portuguese, Catalan, Provençal, Sardinian, and Romansh), Romanian is a lineal descendant of Vulgar Latin, the nonliterary speech of the legionaries and colonists drawn from various parts of the Roman Empire who began the Romanization of **Dacia** in the second century of the Christian Era. Romanian developed from the lingua franca spoken around the lower **Danube** and the Carpathian Mountains from about the middle of the first millennium of the present era. Unlike the group of Romance languages having evolved in the rest of Europe, Romanian represents the only offspring of the Latin language spoken in the eastern provinces of the Roman Empire, and its basic features embody the changes that language went through in isolation, during over 1,800 years of separate development.

The frequency of the Latin lexical element in modern Romanian amounts to about 85 percent. The non-Latin lexical elements fall into two categories: the numerically small but semantically important Thraco-Dacian substratum (connected but not identical with elements found in Albanian); and the manifold loanwords borrowed over the course of centuries of political, cultural, and ethnic contacts with other languages. The most numerous element in the second category is Slavonic, Church Slavonic written in **Cyrillics** having been for centuries the vehicle of written communication in Eastern Orthodox cultures. By virtue of the **Orthodox Church** affiliation applied to the writing of the language between the early Middle Ages and the 19th century, the Slavonic alphabet played an instrumental role in creating the visual appearance that Romanian was distinct and separate from the Romance languages spoken in Western Europe, normally written in the Latin alphabet.

The Romanian language absorbed a considerable number of Slavic words at the time of the Slavic populations' invasion of former Dacia and East-Central Europe, beginning with the seventh and eighth centuries. Many of these borrowings entered the basic word stock of Romanian and were assimilated, giving the Romanian language its specific flavor in the family of the Romance languages. The Slavic influence over Romanian has been compared, in terms of linguistic consequences, to the absorption and assimilation of Arabic borrowings in the basic word stock of the Spanish language. Other borrowings in the Romanian language are of Hungarian, Greek, and Turkish origin.

Four technical distinctions apply to dialects pertaining to the wider sphere of generic Romanian, as defined by modern linguistics: Daco-Romanian, spoken in the Republic of Moldova and Romania; Macedo-Romanian, spoken sparsely in the Balkan Peninsula, in Greece's Pindus and Thessaly regions, and in parts of Bulgaria and the former Yugoslav republic of Macedonia; Megleno-Romanian (or Vlasi), an almost extinct dialect still spoken by about 20,000 people in the mountains northwest of Thessaloniki in Greece; and Istro-Romanian, a now extinct idiom spoken until the beginning of the 20th century in the Istra Peninsula of present-day Croatia. Unlike the three Balkan dialects (in fact remnant samples of Romance patois, spoken in mountainous enclaves south of the **Danube** River), Daco-Romanian (or Common Romanian), spoken north of the Danube, is a unitary language spoken by some 27 million people, differentiated only by hues of regional accents that fall into three broad categories—Moldavian, Transylvanian, and Muntenian—comparable to the differences in accents between English spoken in Massachusetts and, for example, Texas or Vermont. *See also* ALPHABET ISSUE; LANGUAGE ISSUE.

ROSCA, IURIE (1961–). Deputy Speaker of Moldova's Parliament, co-chairman of the **Democratic Convention of Moldova (CDM)**, and president of the **Christian Democrat Popular Front (FPCD)**, Roşca is a graduate in journalism from the **State University of Moldova**. His career includes training courses as a journalist with the cultural and literary programs of Chişinău TV (1985–1988) and brief employment as a researcher with the Demetrius Cantemir Literary Museum (1988–1989). Beginning in 1988, he played an important role in Moldova's cultural, linguistic, and political reawakening and the upsurge of its movement for national emancipation, chiefly by the leadership provided to the **Popular Front of Moldova**, re-formed as the FPCD in 1992. In 1997, Roşca's FPCD entered a political alliance with other right-wing parties to form the CDM. In the wake of the 1998 general elections, wherein the CDM won 19.42 percent of the national vote, Roşca's political organization joined hands with other antileftist forces to form the majoritarian **Alliance for Democracy and Reforms**, a center-right parliamentarian coalition from which it withdrew in 1999. *See also* POLITICAL BLOCS AND PARTIES.

RUSSIA. *See* RUSSIAN EMPIRE; RUSSIAN FEDERATION; UNION OF SOVIET SOCIALIST REPUBLICS.

RUSSIAN EMPIRE. Historical entity comprising Russia and the territories of the Eurasian continent that gradually expanded between the 9th and the 19th century to eventually constitute a multifaceted polity headed by czars or emperors. After the 15th century—under the slogan "Moscow, the Third Rome"—Russia's czars claimed the mission and inheritance of the Greek Orthodox Empire of Byzantium, fallen to the Turks in 1453. Throughout the 18th and 19th centuries, the Russian Empire gradually grew to include a blend of several alien peoples: Mongolian, Finno-Ugric, and Tatar-Turkic, among several others.

Russia became a neighbor of the **Principality of Moldova** under **Catherine the Great** in 1792, when, in the wake of several victories in the 1787–1792 **Russo-Turkish War**, the empire's southwestern border was moved to the **Nistru River**. Under the name of **Bessarabia**, the eastern half of the historical Principality of Moldova became part of the Russian Empire during the reign of **Alexander I** in 1812. It was an **oblast**, then a *guberniia*, of Russia until 1917, when the empire of the czars was disbanded in the aftermath of the Bolshevik Revolution.

The earliest political act linking the Russian Empire with Moldova was an anti-Ottoman alliance, the 1711 **Lutsk Treaty** signed by envoys of Czar **Peter the Great** and Prince **Demetrius Cantemir**. Begun under Peter the Great, Russia's expansionist drive at the expense of the **Ottoman Empire** played a key role in determining the political orientation of the Principality of Moldova throughout the 18th century and the early decades of the 19th, as Moldovan rulers attempted in various ways to regain **sovereignty** and shed Ottoman Turkey's vassalage. In the initial phase, as spelled out in the Lutsk Treaty, the Russian Empire recognized Moldova's right to exist as an independent entity, free from Ottoman Turkey's suzerainty, within its original historical borders. Under Catherine the Great, Russian interest in Moldova included, among other things, the unfulfilled **Greek Project**, which called for a union of Moldova and **Wallachia** in the form of a reconstituted kingdom of **Dacia**, to serve under Russian and Austrian protection as a buffer state against Ottoman Turkey, north of the **Danube River**. The Russo-Turkish Wars of the last decades of the 18th century entailed several military occupations of Moldova and ended in important territorial conquests for Catherine the Great.

At that juncture, an already weakened Ottoman Empire made the portentous first step toward the partition of its vassal Principality of Moldova by awarding the northern territories of the land, henceforth known as **Bucovina**, to the **Habsburg Empire**. In step with that precedent, in the wake of the 1806–1812 Russo-Turkish War, Catherine's successor, **Alexander I**, demanded from Turkey the eastern half of Moldova, incorporated into the czarist empire as Bessarabia under the provisions of the 1812 **Treaty of Bucharest**, which also gave Russia direct access to the mouths of the Danube. The newly acquired land of Bessarabia became the object of sustained policies of **Russification** and **colonization** under **Nicholas I**. The 1856 Treaty of Paris (*see* PARIS, CONGRESS OF), which marked the end of the Crimean War in which Russia's Czar **Alexander II** was defeated, returned southern Bessarabia to the Principality of Moldova, which, three years later, united with Wallachia and formed the kernel of modern **Romania** (1859–1862).

As a result of the Russo-Romanian-Turkish War of 1877–1878, the Russian Empire reannexed southern Bessarabia from Romania. Under the reign of Alexander II, Bessarabia underwent a number of notable economic and social transformations. His imperial statute of 1868 promulgated an agrarian reform that changed Bessarabia's structure of landholding by bestowing property rights to individual families. His successor, **Alexander III**, pursued aggressive policies inspired by the Pan-Slavist determination to make the newly acquired provinces of the empire as homogeneous as possible in terms of language, religion, and administration. Russification of the **Orthodox Church** of Bessarabia was dramatically increased under his reign. The next ruler, **Nicholas II**, was forced to undertake more dramatic changes in policies, as the downfall of Russia's original imperial system reached an early first climax in 1905. Still retaining the title of "Autocrat of Russia," Nicholas I pledged respect for the inviolability of the person and freedom of thought, speech, meetings, and association, and he allowed the establishment of the Duma, a Western-style legislative body that brought to an end the imperial system of governing by virtue of imperial ukases.

The impact of these moves triggered pro-freedom action in Bessarabia, where a group of intellectuals started the publication of several **Romanian-language** periodicals advocating the rights of the majority of the province's local population to its own language, traditions, and culture. In 1907, these actions were stifled by Russia's central government, and Romanian-language publications were severely reined in.

The Russian Empire crumbled in March 1917, when Nicholas II abdicated in favor of his brother Mikhail, who declined to take over the succession to the throne. Amid revolutionary turmoil and the gradual ascent of **Bolshevik power** to the helm, Russia was proclaimed a republic on 2 September 1917. In October–November 1917, the Bolsheviks conquered power in Petrograd and Moscow and proclaimed the devolving of all authority to the Communist soviets. On 15 November 1917, the revolutionists proclaimed "The Declaration of Rights of the Peoples," acknowledging the rights to self-determination of all peoples that had been part of the czarist empire, including their right "to separate from Russia." On 20 November, Bessarabia's neighbor Ukraine announced the convocation of a freely elected Ukrainian Constituent Assembly. Bessarabia's General Assembly, **Sfatul Ţării**, followed suit on 2 December 1917, when it proclaimed the establishment of the **Moldavian Democratic Federated Republic**. A free and sovereign Ukrainian republic was proclaimed on 22 January 1918. After having repelled several Bolshevik attempts to grab power in **Chişinău**, the fledgling Moldavian republic proclaimed its own independence and broke all ties with Russia on 24 January 1918. East of the Nistru, the short-lived independence of Ukraine was marred by the mounting tide of revolutionary turmoil, and the country's chief people's commissariats eventually united with Russia's soviets on 28 December 1920.

Between 1919 and 1920, the multiethnic legacy of the Russian Empire, a blend of several alien peoples, was revived as Bolshevik power was gradually established in all but a few former czarist possessions—Finland, the Baltic countries, and Bessarabia being the notable exceptions. The Russian Empire's successor state in full-fledged existence was the **Union of Soviet Socialist Republics**, proclaimed in Moscow on 30 December 1922. *See also* RUSSIAN FEDERATION, RELATIONS WITH; SOVEREIGNTY.

RUSSIAN ETHNICS. Moldova's Russian ethnics make up a population of about 562,000, out of which about 36 percent are recent immigrants, born in other parts of the former Soviet Union. About 153,000 ethnic Russians (27 percent of the group) live in the five districts of the self-styled **Moldavian Nistrian Republic (MNR)**, where they constitute the military, technical, cultural, and administrative elite. In 1998, Russian nationalist leader Vladimir Zhirinovsky urged Russian ethnics in the separatist MNR to take up Russian citizenship in order to make it easier for Moscow to protect them.

Most of Moldova's Russian ethnics are post–World War II settlers. They grew from a low 6 percent of the total population in 1940, to 10.2 percent in 1959, attaining a maximum of 13 percent in 1989. The greatest influx of ethnic Russians into Moldova occurred between the 1950s and the late 1980s and brought about dramatic changes in the demographic balance of Moldova's cities. *See also* RUSSIFICATION.

RUSSIAN FEDERATION. The Russian Federation was created in the aftermath of the 1991 dissolution of the **Union of Soviet Socialist Republics**. It is the most important successor state of the former Soviet Union and one of the key member states of the **Commonwealth of Independent States**. The Russian Federation maintains a military presence in the Republic of Moldova in the form of the **Operational Group of Russian Forces** headquartered in **Tiraspol**, deployed in the separatist, self-styled **Moldavian Nistrian Republic**. A basic treaty between the Russian Federation and the Republic of Moldova, signed in September 1990 and ratified by the Moldovan Parliament that same year, has not yet been ratified by Russia. *See also* RUSSIAN FEDERATION, RELATIONS WITH.

RUSSIAN FEDERATION, RELATIONS WITH. A basic treaty between Moldova and the **Russian Federation**, signed in September 1990 and ratified by Moldova's Parliament that same year, has never been ratified by Russia's State Duma. In July 1998, Egor Stroev, president of the Russian Federation's Assembly, and Genadii Seleznev, president of Russia's Duma, officially asked for a renegotiation of the treaty. The Russophone leadership of the breakaway **Tiraspol** enclave on the east bank of the **Nistru River**—which entertains strong ties with the Duma's left-wing majority—has strongly opposed the ratification of the 1990 treaty by Russia, which continues to station troops in the self-proclaimed **Moldavian Nistrian Republic**. Since Moldova's independence (*see* DECLARATION OF INDEPENDENCE) and territorial integrity have been recognized by Russia, according to Moldova's President **Petru Lucin-**

schi, the attitude of the Duma deputies should not be confused with Russia's official position vis-à-vis Moldova, which Moldova's president described as correct. In June 1998, Russian President Boris Yeltsin stated that Moscow wants the sides involved in the **trans-Nistrian conflict** to strictly abide by the May 1997 memorandum on normalizing relations between **Chişinău** and Tiraspol and the March 1998 Odessa Accord.

As far as economic relations are concerned, with Moldova producing only a very small percentage of its own national **energy** needs, the country continues to rely heavily on Russian imports of coal, oil, and gas, the Russian company **Gazprom** being the main provider of Moldova's energy firms. In 1998, about 60 percent of Moldova's exports were directed to the Russian Federation, and Moldova paid for 90 percent of its gas and petrol imports from Russia with agricultural and wine industry products. A program of economic cooperation between Moldova and the Russian Federation for the years 1999–2000 included provisions aimed at partly clearing Moldova's debt to Russia and Gazprom by barter. It also stipulated that the withdrawal of Russian troops from Moldovan territory will continue as the necessary conditions for it are being created. The Moldo-Russian statement further declared that the two countries would continue efforts toward a political settlement of the Nistru east-bank districts' **separatism**, including granting special status to the region while preserving the independence and territorial integrity of the Republic of Moldova. *See also* FOURTEENTH ARMY; RUSSIFICATION; SOVEREIGNTY.

RUSSIAN LANGUAGE. A Slavic language closely related to Belarussian and Ukrainian. During the 19th century, it was imposed as the language of official communication and the language of liturgy in Russian-held **Bessarabia** as part of the czarist policies of **Russification**.

As of 9 August 1940, soon after the Soviet **annexation** of Bessarabia and its transformation into a Soviet republic, Russian was decreed the official language of the **Moldavian Soviet Socialist Republic (MSSR)**. The dominance of Russian increased dramatically over the post–World War II decades, as can be seen in statistical data showing that while in 1970 only 33.8 percent of native Moldovans used Russian as their second language, in 1979 that proportion went up to 46.1 percent and in 1989 to 53.3 percent. The linguistic Russianization of the MSSR included the Russianization of the important Ukrainian ethnic group as well, which currently makes up 13.8 percent of the population of Moldova. For example, the proportion of Ukrainians holding Russian as their mother tongue in Moldova grew from 12.2 percent in 1959, to 19.4

percent in 1970, and to over 30 percent in 1979. Moreover, as indicated by 1989 statistics, some 43 percent of Soviet Moldavia's Ukrainians consider Russian their second language. Soviet Russia's long-standing policies of imposing Russian as both the official language of the MSSR and the prime language of education to all nationalities, including the **Gagauz** group, resulted in bilingualism, which is currently one of the most widespread cultural features not only of urban Moldova, but of some of the rural areas as well. *See also* LANGUAGE ISSUE; MOLDAVIAN; ROMANIAN LANGUAGE.

RUSSIFICATION. A political doctrine and administrative practice applied across time to Moldova as well as to other non-Russian peoples under the jurisdiction of the **Russian Empire** and, later, of the **Union of Soviet Socialist Republics (USSR)**, in order to disjoin them from their prior ethnic and cultural allegiances. Administrative Russification consisted of introducing Russian institutions and laws and extending the use of the **Russian language** in bureaucracies and schools. Cultural Russification consisted of coercing local populations to adopt Russian culture, language, and religious forms as their own. Imperial Russia's Russification policy was initially driven by Orthodox messianism and Russian expansionism, which professed the aim of freeing Orthodox peoples then held under Ottoman rule. Its main moving force throughout the 19th century, more especially after 1856, was embedded in the tenet *"Pravoslaviie i Narodnost"* (Orthodoxy and Nationhood).

In Moldova, in conjunction with state administrative measures such as the imposition of Russian as the language of all official business after 1834, the **Orthodox Church** was one of the main institutional instruments in the Russification process, particularly after **Bessarabia**'s incorporation into **New Russia**. As early as 1813, the local church's links with its traditional canonical contact in **Iaşi** had been severed and Bessarabia's clergy placed under the jurisdiction of Russia's Holy Synod of St. Petersburg, with Russian soon to become the compulsory language of liturgy. At the province's theological seminary in **Chişinău**, from 1840 on, all disciplines were taught in Russian, and before the end of the century, knowledge of Russian became a precondition to priesthood.

Soviet rule (1940–1941 and 1944–1989) renewed and intensified the Russification policies. Soon after the 28 June 1940 **annexation**, Russian was officially decreed the language of the country (on 9 August 1940), while Great Russian nationalism and Slavophile ideas were resurrected—this time, under the cloak of Communist internationalism.

Post–World War II policies intensely predicated Russia's preeminence inside the Soviet Union. The doctrine was officially spelled out in a 1949 ideological speech by **Joseph Stalin**, who proclaimed the Russian people "the most eminent nation of the USSR" and the unparalleled champion of economic, intellectual, and moral progress worldwide. In the case of Moldova, Russification was pursued in parallel by cultural containment policies, including drastic administrative measures devised to prevent cultural, literary, and artistic communication with neighboring **Romania** and increasing the instrumental role of the Russian language in **education**. Before 1991, instruction beyond the primary levels in urban Moldova was conducted in Russian. For instance, in kindergarten education, only 10 percent of the schools used the language of the autochthonous population (called "**Moldavian**") as the language of instruction; and in 1987, in Moldova's medical and agricultural institutes, not a single subject was taught in Moldavian. As a consequence, before Moldova's **declaration of independence**, only 11 percent of the Chişinău Russian elite spoke Moldavian, while Russian culture was pervasively present and dominant in all urban, technical, and educational realms.

These long-range policies resulted in Russian cultural hegemony over Moldova's mostly rural indigenous culture. Across time, coupled with **colonization**, the cultural and demographic outcome of the process became obvious and is easily assessed by comparing the systematic decline of Moldova's autochthonous population as reflected in census figures throughout the 19th century and—with the exception of the interwar period—during the second half of the 20th century.

According to the first Russian census (conducted in 1817), 87 percent of the newly acquired province's inhabitants (419,420 out of 482,630) were described as native "Moldavians," with a Russian minority amounting to only 1.5 percent of the total population. Some 6.5 percent were registered as Ukrainians and 4.2 percent as **Jews**. By 1858, the proportion of the autochthonous Romanian-speaking population had fallen to 74 percent, while Ukrainians and Jews had risen to constitute, respectively, 12 and 8 percent of Bessarabia's population. According to the 1897 czarist census, which distinguished the population by native language rather than nationality, of the total population of 1,936,012, 47.6 percent (over 900,000 persons) were speakers of "Romanian" (this was the term used), 19.6 percent of Ukrainian, 8.1 percent of Russian, and 11.8 of Yiddish. The Soviet nationality census conducted in 1941, after Bessarabia's incorporation into the USSR, indicated a balance of 65.5 percent Moldavians, versus 6 percent Russians and 16.4 percent Ukrainians. The last Soviet-era census (conducted in 1989) recorded 64.5 percent of the population as Moldavian, over 13 percent as Ukrainian, and 13 percent as Russian. *See also* LANGUAGE ISSUE.

RUSSO, ALECU (1819–1859). Writer, civic activist, and folklore collector, born in **Strășeni**, **Lăpușna**. Russo is credited with having discovered and collected one of the most elaborate forms of the national folk ballad **"Miorița."** He was also a contributor to the **Iași** periodical *Zimbrul*, in which he published one of his best-known works, *Studie Moldovană* (Moldovan Studies), in 1851–1852. A statue of Alecu Russo graces the alley devoted to Moldova's classical writers in **Chișinău**'s Central Park. The Alecu Russo State University of Bălți is named for him.

RUSSO-ROMANIAN-TURKISH WAR OF 1877–1878. *See* RUSSO-TURKISH WARS.

RUSSO-TURKISH WARS. A series of historic conflicts for domination of the Black Sea basin and the Balkans in which the **Russian Empire** expanded southward, reaching the **Nistru** border with the **Principality of Moldova** in 1792 and gaining access to the mouths of the **Danube** in 1812 and domination of the entire Danube Delta thalweg between 1829 and 1856. Most of these wars involved, in some fashion, the Principalities of Moldova and **Wallachia**, which lay along the route of the Russian armies into the Balkans. One of Russia's several aims in the Russo-Turkish Wars was to gain the right of protection over the Greek Orthodox subjects living in the Balkans and other parts of the **Ottoman Empire**.

The Russo-Turkish War of 1710–1711, which ended in Russia's defeat, was fought with the participation of the Principality of Moldova as an ally to Russia. The following Russo-Turkish Wars (1735–1739, 1768–1774, 1787–1792, 1806–1812, 1828–1829, 1853–1856, and 1877–1878) entailed, most of the time, successive spans of Russian occupation of Moldova. Moldova was under Russian military occupation briefly in 1739 and, later on, together with Wallachia, during the 1768–1774 Russo-Turkish War, which ended with the **Kuchuk Kainarji Peace Treaty**. Russia's armies again occupied Moldova between 1787 and 1792, during the Russo-Turkish War that ended with the **Treaty of Iași**.

Alongside Wallachia, Moldova once again came under Russian military occupation between 1806 and 1812, at the time of the first Russo-Turkish War of the 19th century. The 1812 **Treaty of Bucharest**, which ended the third occupation of Wallachia and Moldova by Russia, resulted in the partition of the latter, the eastern half of which was incorporated into Russia as **Bessarabia** and remained part of the czars' possessions until the 1917 Bolshevik Revolution (*see* BOLSHEVIK POWER). The 1829 Russo-Turkish **Treaty of Adrianople** incorporated the Danube Delta into Russian-held Bessarabia, and the 1849 **Convention of Balta Liman** reinforced Russia's protectorate over the **Danubian Principalities**.

After the Crimean War (1853–1856), the **Convention of Paris** removed Russia from the mouths of the Danube and returned to the Principality of Moldova part of southern Bessarabia, comprising the lowland districts of **Bolgrad, Cahul**, and **Ismail**. The Russo-Turkish War waged between 1877 and 1878, with the participation of Romania on Russia's side, ended with the Treaty of Berlin (*see* CONGRESS OF BERLIN), by which Bolgrad, Cahul, and Ismail were reincorporated into the Russian Empire. *See also* ANNEXATION.

RUSSU, ION (1941–). Minister of agriculture in Moldova's government formed in December 1999. A native of Făleştii-Noi, **Bălţi**, Russu holds an agronomic degree from the Agricultural Institute of Herson (**Ukraine**). Between 1969 and 1991 he served in various positions on collective farms in the **Nistru** east-bank districts and in Moldova's **Communist Party**. At the time of the outbreak of the **Transnistrian conflict** (1991–1992), Ion Russu served as president of the State Committee for Transnistrian issues in Moldova's government. Between 1994 and 1998 he served as Moldova's ambassador to Ukraine (V. N.).

-S-

SAKA, SERAFIM (1935–). Novelist, playwright, and scriptwriter, Saka coauthored, with **Valeriu Matei**, a biography of Moldovan polymath **Nicolae Milescu**, which was turned into a successful historical film. He is the author of several volumes of prose, including *Vămile* (The Customs) in 1972 and *Linia de plutire* (Keeping Afloat) in 1987. In 1996, Saka was elected president of the Moldova PEN (International Association of Poets, Playwrights, Editors, Essayists, and Novelists).

SANGEREI. Chief town of the former Sângerei *raion,* or district, on the **Chişinău-Bălţi-Cernăuţi** highway, included in the reestablished *judeţ* of Bălţi after 1999. Under Soviet rule, the traditional name of Sângerei was changed to Lazovsk, after the name of the Bolshevik leader **Serghei Lazo.** The village of Sângerei was first mentioned in an official document in 1586. The former district had a population of over 91,000 inhabitants (1993 est.).

SANGHELI, ANDREI (1944–). Politician and former prime minister of Moldova (1992–1997). A native of Grinăuţi-Moldova, **Ocniţa,** Sangheli is a graduate of the agronomy department of Moldova's Agricultural Institute in **Chişinău** (1971). He served in leading positions in the **Moldavian Soviet Socialist Republic**'s Council of Ministers (1986-1992) and, after the country's **declaration of independence,** helped organize the **Democratic Agrarian Party** of Moldova, on the list of which he unsuccessfully ran as a candidate in Moldova's 1996 presidential elections (V. N.).

SAPTAMANA. One of Moldova's most popular publications, *Săptămâna* is an independent weekly with a circulation of around 25,000 copies. It is pro-independence and generally embraces the centrist view along Moldova's **political spectrum.**

SARBU, IOAN (1830–1868). Fabulist and poet born in Măşcăuţi, **Orhei.** One of his earliest poems, titled "Moldova," was published in the **Iaşi** biweekly *Zimbrul* in 1851. His chief books, *Fabule alcătuite în limba moldovenească* (Fables Composed in the Moldavian Language) and *Alcătuirele* (Compositions), printed in **Chişinău** (1851–1852), are among the earliest literary works published by local authors in Russian-held **Bessarabia** who called their own language "**Moldavian.**" *See also* LANGUAGE ISSUE.

SAS (?–ca. 1358). Second *voivode,* or ruler, of Moldova (ca. 1354–1358) under the suzerainty of the Hungarian Crown. He built one of medieval Moldova's oldest shrines, the Holy Trinity Church of **Siret.**

SEPARATISM. Policy advocated by the Russophone minority in Moldova's trans-Nistrian districts, calling for separation from the country's central authority in **Chişinău.** A separate pro-Russian political entity was proclaimed on 2 September 1990 in the five districts of the Republic of Moldova lying on a narrow corridor east of the **Nistru River,** adjacent to the country's border with Ukraine, but it gained no international recognition. In a 1998 declaration made in **Tiraspol**, Russian nationalist leader Vladimir Zhirinovsky said that he considers the separatist region to be a province of Russia. *See also* AUTONOMY; FEDERALIZATION; MOLDAVIAN NISTRIAN REPUBLIC.

SEREBRIAN, OLEG (1969–). Historian, diplomat, and political scientist; one of the representatives of Moldova's new generation of politicians and cultural animators. A native of **Ocniţa**, Serebrian is a graduate of the **State University of Moldova** and holds an M.A. in international relations from the Institut Européen de Hautes Études Politiques in Nice, France. His career highlights include several assignments in Moldova's Ministry of Foreign Affairs, where he worked in the West Europe and North America section (1991–1992) and in the East Europe section (1993–1994). Between 1994 and 1995, he headed the **Romania** section. Serebrian, who is the author of a study on the geopolitics of the Black Sea basin, held the position of deputy rector of the **Free International University of Moldova** in **Chişinău** and of coordinator of **Soros Foundation Moldova** programs for the republic. In 1998, Serebrian served as spokesperson of Moldova's Ministry of Foreign Affairs.

SEVEROVAN, MIHAI (1947–). Minister of territorial development, public utilities, and constructions in Moldova's governments formed in 1997, 1998, and 1999. A native of Gura Camencii, **Floreşti**, Severovan is a graduate of the Chişinău Technical Institute and of the Moscow Party High School. His political career includes leading positions in the executive apparatus of the city of **Chişinău** between 1979 and 1985. He was deputy minister of public utilities from 1987 to 1990 and chairman of the Executive Council of Chişinău between 1990 and 1991. Severovan also served as minister of public utilities in Moldova's 1992 government (V. N.).

SFANTUL GHEORGHE. An independent anticollectivist farmers association affiliated with the **Christian Democrat Popular Front** wing of the **Democratic Convention of Moldova**. It was founded in February 1996 with the help of **Valentin Dolganiuc**, with its declared mission of acting as a "ministry for landowning farmers," lobbying for them in **Chişinău**, offering them legal help and material assistance, and providing them with seeds, agricultural machinery, and means of transportation for their produce. The name of the association (English: Saint George) draws its inspiration from the local tradition that holds Saint George as the patron saint of farmers (the Greek source name *Gheorghios* means farmer).

SFATUL TARII. A traditional institution (also called Adunarea Ţării), first mentioned in 1441 under the reign of Princes Iliaş and Ştefan, as Moldavia's convocational General Assembly. It was revived as a legislative body in 1917, when Sfatul Ţării convened in **Chişinău** to proclaim the establishment—and, soon after, the independence—of the former Russian province of **Bessarabia** under the name of the **Moldavian Democratic Federated Republic.** Described by Soviet historians as "counterrevolutionary" and "anti-Soviet" in orientation, the assembly initially had 120 deputies (21 November 1917), of which there were 84 Romanophone Moldavians and 36 Ukrainians, Russians, Jews, Bulgarians, Gagauz, Germans, and others. On 27 March 1918, when Sfatul Ţării voted for the union with Romania, the assembly had 138 deputies. The vote was 86 in favor of the union and 3 against; 36 deputies abstained (26 of whom represented ethnic minorities) and 13 deputies were not present. Conditions for the union included the preservation of a certain degree of autonomy and the right to maintain Sfatul Ţării as a regional Diet. These conditions were dropped by Sfatul Ţării in November 1918, when the assembly proclaimed the unconditioned union with Greater Romania and voted for its own dissolution.

On 18 March 1918, a publication titled *Sfatul Ţării: The Organ of the Moldavian Republic's Parliament* became the official mouthpiece of the Chişinău legislative body, published first as a biweekly, then as a daily, until Sfatul Ţării as a body ceased to exist.

SIRET. According to tradition, one of the chief cities of medieval Moldova, established as a residence of the court by *voivode* **Sas** around 1360. The town is located on the Siret River, an affluent of the **Prut**. It enjoyed greater importance in early times as a strategic stronghold east of the Carpathians. A Roman Catholic bishopric was founded in Siret in March 1371 as part of an attempt by **Laţco Vodă** to turn Moldova's religious allegiance away from Byzantium toward the Church of Rome. The Holy Trinity Church of Siret, erected by his successor, **Petru Muşat I**, is the earliest example of a trefoil structure in Moldovan medieval architecture.

SLOBOZIA. Chief town of the former *raion,* or district, of the same name, the territory of which lay on the west and east banks of the **Nistru River**. The town of Slobozia is located 88 kilometers southeast of **Chişinău** and 13 kilometers south of **Tiraspol**. As the district straddles both banks of the Nistru, part of its territory is currently under the authority of the self-proclaimed **Moldavian Nistrian Republic**, while the west-bank portion is under the jurisdiction of the newly reestablished *judeţ* of **Tighina**. The Nistru flows across Slobozia's maritime lowlands down to the river's estuary, or **Liman**, from which they are separated by only several hundred meters of land, south of the west-bank town of Palanca. The former district of Slobozia had over 113,000 inhabitants (1993 est.).

SLOPAC, EUGENIU (1951–). First deputy prime minister in Moldova's government formed in December 1999, Eugeniu Şlopac held a number of positions in the **agriculture** sector before Moldova's **independence**. Since 1991 he has served as director of the international insurance company QBE Asito. A native of Mălăieşti, **Orhei**, he graduated from the Chişinău Technical University, where he earned a degree in economics (V. N.).

SMIRNOV, IGOR (1941–). Political leader of the Russophone movement in the trans-Nistrian separatist districts of the Republic of Moldova. In 1990, he became president of the self-proclaimed Moldavian Nistrian Soviet Socialist Republic, later renamed the **Moldavian Nistrian Republic**. He was reelected in 1996, when he won 71.94 percent of the vote, out of a low 57.1 percent turnout. A member of the **Communist Party** of the Soviet Union since 1960, Smirnov held the office of director of several electrical machinery plants in Zaporozhie until 1979 and, later on, in **Tiraspol**, where he served as chairman of the City Council from 1989 to 1990 (V. N.).

SMOCHIN, AFANASIE (1945–). Minister of transportation and communications in Moldova's government formed in December 1999. A native of Utkonosovka, **Ismail**, Smochin holds a degree in mechanical engineering from the Harkov (**Ukraine**) Institute of Cars and Roads Transportation. He worked in several transportation-related governmental positions from 1973 to 1990. After 1990 Smochin became executive director of the company ASOIO (V. N.).

SNEGUR, MIRCEA (1940–). Former president of Moldova (1990–1996), co-chairman of the **Democratic Convention of Moldova**, and one of the leaders of the **Alliance for Democracy and Reforms**, the governing center-right coalition formed in the wake of the 1998 national elections. Before becoming independent Moldova's first chief of state, Snegur was chairman of the Supreme Soviet of the **Moldavian Soviet Socialist Republic**, and in that capacity, he played an important role in the country's opening via the **glasnost** policies inaugurated in Moscow by **Mikhail Gorbachev**. By 1990, he associated himself with the **Popular Front of Moldova** and became the country's first democratically elected leader. In the December 1996 elections, although backed by two parties—his own Moldovan Party of Revival and Accord, a centrist splinter group from the **Democratic Agrarian Party of Moldova**, and the **Christian Democrat Popular Front (FPCD)**—he garnered only 46.86 percent of the vote and lost to **Petru Lucinschi**. In 1997, Snegur's political formation formally entered into an alliance with the Christian Democrats, and at that point he became the co-chairman of the FPCD, together with that formation's leader, **Iurie Roşca**.

By profession, Snegur is an agronomist and, prior to entering politics in 1985, held various positions in Moldova's agricultural research and production field. At the time of Moldova's **declaration of independence**, Snegur played an important role in charting Moldova's course as a free nation, as the **Union of Soviet Socialist Republics** was disintegrating. *See also* POLITICAL BLOCS AND PARTIES.

SOCIAL DEMOCRAT PARTY / PARTIDUL SOCIAL DEMOCRAT (PSD). A centrist political formation that initially participated in the **Popular Front of Moldova** but later distanced itself from what it perceived as the too nationalistic orientation of that organization. Its constituency is multiethnic, made up of educated, white-collar professionals and managerial decision-making groups with strong representation in the cities of **Chişinău** and **Bălţi**. *See also* POLITICAL BLOCS AND PARTIES; POLITICAL SPECTRUM.

SOCIALIST UNITY / UNITATEA SOCIALISTA (US). A left-wing electoral bloc and political alliance among the **Unity-Edinstvo Movement**, the Socialist Party of Moldova, the Union of Moldova's Communists, and leftist formations in **Gagauz Yeri**. Established in **Bălţi** on 21 June 1997, the bloc welcomed the Belarus-Russia union and demanded that Lenin's mausoleum in Moscow be left untouched. The US bloc has criticized the policies of the **Chişinău** government, calling them "destructive." The alliance, which did not gain representation in the 1998 elections, had at that time four co-chairmen: Valeriu Senic, Victor Morev, Florin Hristev, and **Piotr Sornikov** (V. N.). *See also* POLITICAL BLOCS AND PARTIES.

SOLDANESTI. Chief town of the former *raion,* or district, of the same name, Şoldăneşti is situated east of **Rezina** on the Ciorna River. It was first mentioned in an official document in the 15th century. The former district, which had a population of over 46,000 inhabitants (1993 est.), is part of the reestablished *judeţ* of **Orhei**.

SOLONARI, VLADIMIR (1959–). Leader and founder of the Civic Party of Moldova, established in 1997, Solonari is a historian by training. Born in **Chişinău**, he graduated from the **State University of Moldova** (1981) and earned his doctoral degree from the Moscow Lomonosov State University (1986). His political career began in 1990, when he contributed to the founding of the left-wing **Unity-Edinstvo Movement / Mişcarea Unitate-Edinstvo (MUE)**, which opposed Moldova's bid for independence and the adoption of the language of its native majority as the official language of the country. In 1996, he became a supporter of the policies of President **Petru Lucinschi** and relinquished the MUE and the **Socialist Unity** parliamentary group. He is a member of Moldova's Parliament and of Moldova's delegation in the Council of Europe, as well as the vice president of the Council of Europe's Parliamentary Assembly (V. N.).

SORNIKOV, PIOTR (1949–). Political leader and president of the socialist **Unity-Edinstvo Movement**, which entered the left-wing Bloc of Popular Patriotic Forces in 1997. Born in Peresecina, **Orhei**, Sornikov is a historian by training. He is an adept of Moldova's full integration into the **Commonwealth of Independent States** and a critic of pro-Western policies. Between 1991 and 1992, he taught as a lecturer at the Tiraspol State University (V. N.).

SOROCA. Chief city of the reestablished *judeţ* of the same name, 160 kilometers north of **Chişinău** on the west bank of the **Nistru River**. It comprises the former Soviet-era districts of Soroca, **Drochia**, and **Floreşti**. First mentioned in 1499, Soroca had strategic importance as a border checkpoint on the Nistru and an outpost facing the Podolyan plains on the eastern bank of the river. A citadel erected by Prince **Stephen the Great**, which overlooks the river, played an important part in the defense of the **Principality of Moldova** against the **Tatars**. At Lipnic, north of Soroca, a Tatar invasion was crushed by Stephen the Great in 1469. Soroca's strategic importance declined after 1550. Under Russian and Soviet rule, Soroca was renamed Soroky. The city of Soroca has over 41,400 inhabitants. The former Soroca *raion* had a population of over 58,000 inhabitants (1993 est.).

SOROKY. *See* SOROCA.

SOROS FOUNDATION MOLDOVA. A nonpolitical, nongovernmental, private organization established in **Chişinău** in 1992 with the aim of contributing to the promotion of democracy and civil society in Moldova. Its manifold programs are aimed at fostering the establishment of independent mass media, forming high-quality educational and health care systems, sustaining economic reforms (with special emphasis on **agriculture**), supporting law and public administration reforms, and assisting artistic and literary creation. The publishing program of the Soros Foundation has supported book publishing for the promotion of critical thinking and the values of an open society, and it has also encouraged the development of a viable, diverse, and independent publishing industry in Moldova. From the time of its establishment to 1997, the Soros Foundation has provided over $10 million in assistance to the development of Moldovan society.

SOVEREIGNTY. Moldova proclaimed its sovereignty in a declaration adopted by the **Chişinău** legislative body on 23 June 1990, while the country was still nominally a part of the Soviet Union. On 27 August 1991, a few months before the dissolution of the Soviet Union, Moldova solemnly declared its national independence (*see* DECLARATION OF INDEPENDENCE).

Historically, Moldova enjoyed various degrees of sovereignty, beginning with its early foundation as a principality, a unilateral act of independence vis-à-vis the Crown of Hungary, the vassalage of which was rejected by **Bogdan I**. Before the advent of Ottoman suzerainty—first established in 1456 under **Petru Aron** and soon rejected by his successor, **Stephen the Great**, and, intermittently, by other princes—Moldova's status as a European principality was governed by the medieval principle of *nexus feudalis,* a bond of allegiance ensuring the alliance between the *voivode,* otherwise *domn* or *domnitor,* on the one hand, and a higher protector on the other, with the latter acting as a personal warrant of the right of the lesser prince to govern as a sovereign over his own territory, to mint money, to run foreign commerce independently, and to assist his protector with armies in wartime. An example of that type of allegiance was sought by Stephen the Great from Poland's King Casimir IV in 1485 and by several of his successors.

Turkish suzerainty was of a different kind. It entailed the principality's obligation to pay an annual tribute in gold and a strict monopoly over its trade, Moldova having to sell its crops and livestock to only the **Ottoman Empire** at marginal and noncompetitive prices. However, Moldova enjoyed some degree of incomplete sovereignty under the Turkish rule, in that it was never annexed and integrated as a *pashalik*, or province, into the Ottoman Empire, as were, for instance, Bulgaria, Serbia, and, for a shorter time, Hungary.

While Moldova's external sovereignty was practically lost, internal sovereignty was by and large ensured by virtue of the fact that the Ottoman Empire had no internal jurisdiction over Moldova, and Turkish subjects had no right to own property, open mosques, or interfere in the country's customs, language, worship services, and traditions in the administration of the land. After 1711 and throughout the **Phanariote era**, Moldova's sovereignty became increasingly nominal, with its princes having less and less power to act independently.

It was under the terms of that status that, abusing its rights, the Ottoman Empire ceded the northern lands of the **Principality of Moldova**, or **Bucovina**, to Austria in 1775. In a similar way, the eastern half of Moldova was surrendered by the Turks to the **Russian Empire** in 1812. The 1812 partition of Moldova created an entirely new status for its eastern lands, renamed **Bessarabia** and turned into a province of Russia. The czar of Russia became the sovereign of the land, exerting full jurisdiction over Bessarabia through his governors. Russia's last governor of Bessarabia was Mikhail M. Voronovich, who fled **Chişinău** in 1917. A return to partial sovereignty was proclaimed in Chişinău on 2 December 1917, when the province's General Assembly, **Sfatul Ţării**, voted for an end to Bessarabia's status as a province of Russia and the establishment of the **Moldavian Democratic Federated Republic**, a constituent of the ephemeral Federation of Russian Republics, proclaimed in the wake of the downfall of the czar.

As early as 15 November 1917, Russia's new Bolshevik leadership adopted "The Declaration of Rights of the Peoples," which included their right to separate themselves from Russia. Amid the increasing anarchy triggered by the Bolshevik Revolution, Moldova took advantage of that provision and claimed full sovereignty on 24 January 1918, renouncing all ties with the successor state of the Russian Empire. On 27 March 1918, in the wake of attempts at a Communist takeover in Chişinău and threats of absorption by Ukraine, Sfatul Ţării gave up most of the country's recently proclaimed sovereignty, voting for a conditioned union with neighboring **Romania**. Conditions included the preservation of a certain degree of autonomy and the right to maintain a regional Diet in Chişinău.

Moldova's sovereignty was entirely devolved to Romania on 27 November 1918, when Sfatul Ţării voted for Bessarabia's unconditioned union with the kingdom of Romania, the successor state to the **United Principalities** of Moldova and **Wallachia** and a subject of international law as a sovereign state since 1878. Upon its 1940 incorporation into the **Union of Soviet Socialist Republics**—when Bessarabia was renamed the **Moldavian Soviet Socialist Republic**—all legal and coercive powers were devolved to the Soviet state, which in its own capacity as a subject of international law, exercised from Moscow full sovereignty and jurisdiction over the land until Moldova's 1990–1991 declarations of sovereignty and independence.

SOVIET MOLDAVIA. *See* MOLDAVIAN SOVIET SOCIALIST REPUBLIC.

SOVIET UNION. *See* UNION OF SOVIET SOCIALIST REPUBLICS.

STALIN, JOSEPH (1879–1953). Communist revolutionary during the 1917 Bolshevik Revolution and subsequent dictator of the **Union of Soviet Socialist Republics (USSR)**, under a variety of official titles: secretary-general of the **Communist Party** (1922–1953), president of the Council of Ministers (1941–1953), chairman of the State Defense Committee, and supreme commander in chief of the USSR armed forces (1941–1945). Stalin's early policies with regard to Moldova included the creation of the **Moldavian Autonomous Soviet Socialist Republic** in 1924 and the 1939 nonaggression pact concluded with Nazi dictator Adolf Hitler, known as the **Molotov-Ribbentrop Pact**, which secretly established the right of the USSR to incorporate **Bessarabia**, eastern Poland, and the Baltic states. The June 1940 **annexation** of Bessarabia by the USSR led to the creation of the **Moldavian Soviet Socialist Republic (MSSR)**, the immediate historical predecessor of today's Republic of Moldova. Stalin's rule over Moldova exemplified a form of state despotism the main characteristics of which were notorious police control over the population, political purges, complete control over the media for propaganda purposes, **Russification**, systematic stifling of any form of opposition, and the personality cult of the supreme leader presented as a benevolent ruler protecting a happy and prosperous people.

During the Stalinist rule begun in Moldova in June 1940, the main forms of suppression were arrests and **deportations**. The first wave of deportations from the newly founded MSSR began immediately after the annexation and comprised exterminations and mass relocations to Siberia and other parts of the USSR in the 1940–1941 interval. Other waves of brutal deportations ordered by Stalin followed in 1944 and 1949, when huge numbers of Moldovans were resettled in the Astrakhan and Rostov regions of the Russian Soviet Federated Socialist Republic, Siberia, and Kazakhstan. Stalin's notorious personality cult, despotic rule, and atrocities were denounced by Nikita Khrushchev in his "secret speech" to the 20th Congress of the Communist Party in 1956. *See also* BOLSHEVIK POWER.

STAMATI, CONSTANTIN (1786–1869). Author and translator; he settled in **Chişinău** after the 1812 partition of Moldova but made his literary debut in **Iaşi**, in the magazine *Albina românească* published by **Gheorghe Asachi**. Constantin Stamati became a *titularnyi sovetnik* (civil servant) and official translator under the first Russian administration of **Bessarabia**. He was rewarded by the czar with the Medal of Saint Ann and became a knight of that order. According to his own testimony, he made the acquaintance of the Russian poet **Alexander Pushkin** at the time of the latter's exile to Chişinău (1820–1823). Stamati's most important work, *Povestea povestelor* (A Tale of Tales), featuring in verse an idealized description of Moldova's beginnings, was published in Iaşi in 1843. His other works include contemporary satires and glorifications of Moldova's past, such as "Geniul vechi al românilor şi românii de astăzi" (The Presiding Spirit of the Romanians of Yore and the Romanians Today), "Domnul Moldovei Marele Stefan al VI-lea şi bravul său hatman Arbore" (The Great Prince of Moldova Stephen VI and His Gallant Hetman Arbore), and other shorter pieces. Stamati travelled frequently across the **Prut River**, where most of his pieces were published in *Albina românească* (1830–1834), *Dacia Literară* (1840), *Almanah pentru români* (1853), and *Foiletonul Zimbrului* (1855). His collected works were first published in *Muza românească* (Iaşi, 1868).

STAMATI-CIUREA, CONSTANTIN (1828–1898). Son of **Constantin Stamati**, he followed in his father's footsteps as an author of prose, poetry, plays, and translations. A versatile polyglot, equally fluent in Romanian, Russian, and French, he served as secretary at Russia's embassies in Paris, Berlin, and London.

STATE UNIVERSITY OF MOLDOVA. Moldova's largest higher-education institution, founded in 1946 and reorganized after the country's

declaration of independence. In 1996, it had about 9,000 students taking courses in over a dozen departments, including mathematics, cybernetics, physics, chemistry, biology, history, law, literature, foreign languages and comparative literature, journalism, philosophy and psychology, and political science. Courses are taught in both the **Romanian** and the **Russian language**. The State University of Moldova has relations of partnership and cooperation with over half a dozen European universities and, in America, with the University of Florida and Lafayette College, Pennsylvania. *See also* EDUCATION.

STEFAN CEL MARE. *See* STEPHEN THE GREAT.

STEFANUCA, PETRE (1906–1942). Ethnographer and folklore collector, Ştefănucă taught in **Tighina**, **Cetatea Albă**, and **Chişinău** and was a member of the team of ethnographers who studied the traditional culture and folklore of **Bessarabia**'s countryside, including the village of Cornova, **Orhei**, in 1931–1932. In 1940, he was tried and sentenced to death by the Soviet authorities and died in **deportation** in the Tatar Soviet Autonomous Republic. His contributions to the study of Moldova's folklore and social traditions were published posthumously in two volumes in 1991.

STEFAN VODA. Named for **Stephen the Great**, Ştefan Vodă was the chief town of the former *raion,* or district, of the same name (under Soviet rule, dubbed Suvorov), 120 kilometers southeast of **Chişinău**. The former district was established in 1964 and had a population of over 76,000 inhabitants (1993 est.). After 1999, it became part of the reestablished *judeţ* of **Tighina**. South of Ştefan Vodă is Palanca, Moldova's southernmost point next to the estuary of the **Nistru River**, controlled by Ukraine.

STEPHEN THE GREAT / STEFAN CEL MARE / STEPHEN III (?–1504). Prince of Moldova between 1457 and 1504 and champion of the principality's independence against the **Ottoman Empire**, the suzerainty of which he rejected. His 47-year reign epitomized in many ways the apogee of Moldova's history as a fully sovereign principality. During most of Stephen's rule, Moldova was in control of all of its natural borders, stretching eastward from the Carpathian Mountains to the **Nistru River** and southward down to the **Danube River** and the Black Sea. Stephen's victories at **Chilia** on the Danube (1465) and **Baia** in the north of the country (1467), where Moldova defeated the armies of King

Matthias Corvinus, put a temporary end to Hungary's older claims of suzerainty over its former vassal principality. At the battle of Lipnic on the Nistru (1469), Stephen the Great inflicted a severe defeat on the **Tatar** Golden Horde and drove its armies back across the river, the west bank of which he further fortified by erecting new defenses at **Orhei** and **Soroca**. While the Turkish military threat was continuously putting pressure on neighboring **Wallachia**, Stephen waged several wars against that principality's rulers and contributed, among other things, to the toppling of Vlad Țepeș ("Vlad the Impaler," alias Dracula) in 1462.

In 1474, Stephen called on Pope Sixtus IV, pleading for a common crusade of Europe's kings and princes against the Turks, whose pressure over the princes and kingdoms of southeastern Europe was on a dramatic increase after the fall of Byzantium. The pope acknowledged Stephen's merits, naming him "Athleta Christi" (the "Athlete of Christ"), but no coalition materialized. As an invading Ottoman army led by Sultan Mehmed II ("Mehmed the Conqueror") attacked **Țara de Jos**, Stephen went to war and won a resounding victory at Vaslui in 1475. One year later in the battle of Valea Albă, the Turks defeated Stephen's army, which retreated applying scorched earth tactics, eventually entrenching itself in the northern fortresses that defended the capital city of **Suceava** and the cities of Neamț and **Hotin** and that proved impregnable. Mehmed II eventually withdrew south into Wallachia.

In 1484, with help from the Tatars, Sultan Bayezid II started a new war against Stephen and captured Moldova's key port cities, the fortresses of Chilia and **Cetatea Albă**, thus gaining control of the principality's seaboard, a critical turnaround that landlocked the country, gave the Ottoman Empire control of the mouths of the Danube and Nistru Rivers, and turned the Black Sea into a "Turkish lake" for the next three centuries. After turning for help to King Casimir IV of Poland—whom he recognized as overlord (1485)—Stephen was finally compelled to agree to the sultan's terms in a treaty of capitulation (*ahdname*) that made Moldova tributary to the Sublime Porte, with the Turks pledging to respect the autonomy of the principality and to refrain from interfering in the framework of church and state in exchange for the tribute. A war with Poland ensued, marked in 1497 by Moldova's victories over the Poles at Codrii Cosminului, Lențești, and **Cernăuți**.

The Putna (1469) and Voroneț (1488) Monasteries are among the 46 churches and monasteries built across Moldova during Stephen the Great's reign. In a first personal overture of a Moldova prince to a then distant ruler of Russia, Stephen gave the hand of his daughter Olena to Ivan, son of

Moscow's autocrat Ivan III. Revered as a legendary hero and even a saintly figure, Stephen the Great is considered to be Moldova's greatest medieval ruler. A bronze monument dedicated to him in **Chişinău** in 1927 (Alexandru Plămădeală, sculptor) is one of the best-known historic landmarks of Moldova's capital. **Stefan Vodă**, named for Stephen the Great (under Soviet rule dubbed Suvorov), is a former district on the Nistru in southern Moldova, now part of the reestablished *judeţ* of **Tighina**.

STERE, CONSTANTIN (1865–1936). Leading political and cultural activist. A native of Horodiştea, **Soroca**, Stere shared the nonconformist views of many young intellectuals of his time and joined Narodnaya Volya (the People's Will Party) against Russia's authoritarian regime. He was arrested in 1883 and exiled to Siberia for eight years. Upon his return from exile, he moved to **Romania**, where he became one of the propounders of the Poporanist current, the main tenets of which were to defend the common people's interests by promoting land reform and universal suffrage and raising the underprivileged through education. In 1906, he returned to **Chişinău** to support the movement for liberalization launched in czarist Russia under reform-minded Prime Minister S. Y. Witte.

Stere founded *Basarabia*, a short-lived publication with an editorial program that aimed to fight for social and national justice. He called for the recognition of a special status for **Bessarabia**'s Romanian-speaking majority and for granting the province autonomy in accordance with its traditional historical character. In 1918, after the proclamation of the **Moldavian Democratic Federated Republic**, **Sfatul Ţării** elected Constantin Stere as its first chairman. Stere's eight-volume autobiographical novel, *In preajma revoluţiei* (Around the Revolution), contains a vast panorama of Bessarabian society, including a vivid picture of the author's own **deportation** to Siberia and the birth pangs of his native land trying to break loose from Russia in the context of the 1917 Bolshevik Revolution.

STIRBET, VALERIA (1946–). Minister of justice in Moldova's government formed in December 1999. A native of Miciurin, **Bălţi**, Valeria Ştirbet holds a degree in law from the **State University of Moldova**. She served as a local and national judge from 1973 until 1997, when she became vice president of Moldova's Supreme Court of Justice (V. N.).

STRASENI. Chief town of the former *raion*, or district, of the same name, 23 kilometers north of **Chişinău** on the **Bâc River** and the Chişinău-**Ungheni** railway. Străşeni was first mentioned in an official document in

1545. The district was formed in 1940 in the wake of the Soviet **annexation of Bessarabia**. The relief of the Străşeni district is part of the Codri natural region (*see* CODRU), graced by a string of accumulation lakes on the Bâc, the most important of which is Lake Ghidighici. The former district, now part of the reestablished *judeţ* of Chişinău, had a population of over 96,000 inhabitants (1993 est.).

STRATULAT, OLEG (1957–). Deputy prime minister in Moldova's governments of 1998 and 1999. A native of Slobozia-Horodişte, **Rezina**, Stratulat is a member of the **Party of Democratic Forces** and an economist by training. He holds a Ph.D. in economics from the **State University of Moldova**. Before being appointed deputy prime minister in Moldova's cabinet, Stratulat's career included various teaching positions at the Chişinău Polytechnic Institute (1984–1991) and dean of the College of Finance, Credit, and Currency at Moldova's Academy of Economic Studies (1991–1997). Ministries subordinate to Stratulat's deputyship in Moldova's cabinet include the Ministry of Social Policy and Science, the Ministry of Education and Science, the Ministry of Health, the Ministry of Labor, Social Protection, and Family, the Ministry of Culture, and the Ministry of National Relations (V. N.).

STURDZA, ALEXANDRU SCARLAT (1791–1854). Writer, publicist, and cultural activist in the service of Russia's czars, Alexandru Scarlat Sturdza served in St. Petersburg in the Ministry of Foreign Affairs Chancery and as a diplomat in Vienna and Paris. A fervent supporter of Eastern Orthodoxy, he published, among other things, an essay defending the spirit and teachings of the Eastern Orthodox Church (1816), the ideals and cause of which were being vindicated by the **Russian Empire** as part of its anti-Ottoman policies in the Balkans.

STURDZA, ION SANDU (?–1842). The first local-born nobleman to occupy the throne of the **Principality of Moldova** after the **Phanariote era**, Ion Sandu Sturdza reigned between 1822 and 1828.

STURDZA, MIHAIL (1795–1884). Prince of Moldova between 1834 and 1849, Mihail Sturdza had been elected to reign for life but was forced to leave the throne in the aftermath of the 1848 revolution.

STURDZA, SCARLAT (?–1816). Civil governor of **Bessarabia** from July 1812 to May 1813, appointed by Czar **Alexander I** on an interim basis to run the day-to-day business in the newly acquired province after its **annexation** by the **Russian Empire** in May 1812, pursuant to the **Treaty of Bucharest**. Scarlat Sturdza exerted his short-lived authority under guidance from Russian military governor General I. M. Harting, who took over and cumulated all civil, judicial, and military attributions over Bessarabia after 20 May 1813. Scarlat Sturdza was the first and the last native governor of Bessarabia during the province's over 100 years of Russian rule.

STURZA, ION (1960–). Prime minister of Moldova's government formed in early 1999. He served as deputy prime minister and minister of economy and reforms in Moldova's 1998 cabinet. A native of Pârjolteni, **Călăraşi**, Ion Sturza is by training an economist and a graduate in economics from Moscow Lomonosov State University. A member of the **Party of Democratic Forces**, reform-minded Sturza was one of the chief executives of Moldex, Moldova's state company for foreign trade. In 1991, he became the founder and president of the canned-food production joint-stock company Incom, which was later transformed into a financial-industrial group. One of the latter's shareholders is the International Financial Corporation. Sturza also served as chairman of the board of directors of Fincombank (V. N.).

STURZA, VASILE (1953–). Former minister of justice in Moldova's government formed in 1997, Vasile Sturza is a graduate of the **State University of Moldova's** Institute of Law. Between 1977 and 1981, he served as an investigator in the former district of **Nisporeni**, and from 1981 to 1985, he was a prosecutor in Moldova's General Prosecutor's Office. After that, in 1985–1988, he served as a prosecutor in the city of **Râbniţa**. Sturza was also deputy prosecutor of Moldova from 1991 to 1994 (V. N.).

SUCEAVA. Medieval capital of the **Principality of Moldova**, first mentioned in an official document in 1388. From 1401, it was the seat of the metropolitan of Moldova and, until 1565, the official residence of Moldova's princes. The citadel was erected there (ca. 1375–1391) by **Petru Muşat I** and rebuilt by **Stephen the Great**. It was many times besieged by Poles, Hungarians, **Tatars**, and Ottoman Turks. It resisted the attack of Sultan Mehmed II in 1476.

SURUCENI MONASTERY. Historic monastery founded in 1785 by landowner Casian Suruceanu in the neighborhood of **Chişinău**. Its precincts served as a refuge and rallying place for anti-Bolshevik Moldovans in 1917–1918.

SUTU, ALEXANDRU (?–1821). Prince of Moldova between 1801 and 1802. A typical ruler of the **Phanariote era**, Alexandru Suţu also reigned for a few months in **Wallachia**, in 1802 and 1806, and again for three years between 1818 and 1821.

SUTU, MIHAIL (?–?). Last **Phanariote-era** ruler of Moldova, where he reigned twice, 1792–1795 and 1819–1821. He is the only prince to have occupied the throne of the principality both before and after the 1812 partition of its territory under the terms of the Russo-Turkish **Treaty of Bucharest** by which the eastern half, renamed **Bessarabia**, was incorporated into Russia. Mihail Suţu also reigned three times in **Wallachia,** 1783–1786, 1791–1793, and 1801–1802.

SUVOROV. *See* STEFAN VODA.

-T-

TABACARU, NICOLAE (1955–). Minister of foreign affairs of the Republic of Moldova, named by presidential decree in July 1997, then reappointed to the same position in Moldova's governments formed in 1998 and 1999. A native of Cioara-Mârza, in the **Bugeac**, Tăbăcaru is a member of the **Democratic Convention of Moldova.** He studied in Moldova and Russia and took diplomatic courses at the Swedish Foreign Ministry. Before joining the administration as foreign affairs adviser to President **Petru Lucinschi**, Tăbăcaru served at various Moldovan diplomatic representations abroad, including the United Nations and Belgium, and was director of the Europe and North America Section in Moldova's Ministry of Foreign Affairs (V. N.).

TABUNSCIC, GHEORGHI (1939–). Governor, or *bashkan*, of the autonomous territorial unit of **Gagauz Yeri**. A native of Copceac, **Taraclia**, Gheorghi Tabunscic was elected *bashkan* in 1995 with Communist backing. He graduated from the Chişinău Agricultural Institute and holds a doctoral degree from Moscow State University. Between 1975 and 1987, he served as the **Communist Party**'s first secretary in **Comrat**, and from 1987 to 1990, he was vice president of the **Moldavian Soviet Socialist Republic**'s State Planning Commission (V. N.).

TAMBLAC, GRIGORIE (ca. 1367–1419). Ecclesiastical personality, active in Moldova after 1401. Bishop Ţamblac was sent to **Cetatea Albă** and **Suceava** by the head of the **Orthodox Church** of Constantinople to settle the canonic status and jurisdiction of the country's metropolitan, Bishop Iosif I. Țamblac later became metropolitan of Kiev and was one of the representatives of the Eastern Church at the 1414–1418 Council of Constance. Țamblac's homilies delivered in Moldova between 1401 and 1406 contain vivid descriptions of the court of Prince **Alexander the Good**. He played an important role in reinforcing the influence of Slavonic rite Orthodoxy over medieval Moldova's culture and literacy. His writings and sermons were translated into Romanian by **Metropolitan Varlaam** and published in 1643.

TANASE, ION (1950–). Minister of industry and commerce in Moldova's government formed in 1998. A native of Lebeinskoe, Russia, Tănase is a member of the **Democratic Convention of Moldova**. An engineer by profession, he entered politics in 1990, when he was first elected to the **Chișinău** Parliament (V. N.).

TARA. **Romanian-language** newspaper published twice a week by the **Christian Democrat Popular Front** and one of Moldova's influential right-wing papers. *Țara* (English: The Country) has a circulation of over 10,000, out of which about 4,000 copies are distributed in **Chișinău**.

TARACLIA. Chief town of the former *raion*, or district, of the same name. Taraclia was founded by Christian Turk settlers coming from Bulgaria in the wake of the 1812 **Treaty of Bucharest**, when eastern Moldova, renamed **Bessarabia**, became part of the **Russian Empire**. In a 1993 estimate, the Taraclia district had a population of 45,912 inhabitants, among whom there are numerous ethnic **Gagauz** and Bulgarians. In 1999, the Taraclia local authorities held an unofficial referendum on the district's local administrative independence, thus seeking to preserve its old status apart from the new *județ* of **Cahul**. In October 1999, complying with the wishes of the zone's Gagauz and Bulgarian ethnic minorities, Moldova's central authorities eventually granted Taraclia the status of a separate *județ*. It partially overlaps the surface of the former *raion* and has become Moldova's smallest territorial unit.

TARA DE JOS. Old administrative division of the **Principality of Moldova**, established after the reign of **Alexander the Good**. Țara de Jos, literally "The Lower Country," ran horizontally across historic Moldova's southern part, from the foot of the Carpathians to the **Nistru River** and the Black Sea lowlands, stretching down from the Nistru estuary to the **Chilia** mouth of the **Danube River**. The chief city of Ţara de Jos was Bârlad, on the west bank of the **Prut River**. Southerners were called "Moldoveni-Joseni."

TARA DE SUS. Old administrative unit of the **Principality of Moldova**. It ran horizontally across northern Moldova, from the Carpathian Mountains down to the banks of the upper course of the **Nistru River**. The principality's division into "upper" and "lower" Moldova dates back to the 15th century. The chief city of Ţara de Sus was Dorohoi, on the west bank of the **Prut River**.

TATARBUNAR. A village on the shore of the Sasâc lagoon in historical **Bessarabia**'s seaboard, or **Bugeac**, now part of Ukraine. An armed rebellion against Romanian-held Bessarabia put Tatarbunar on the map in 1924, when, assisted by local Communists, a detachment of Soviet-trained infiltrators marched into the multiethnic village, occupied it by force, and proclaimed there a "Moldavian Soviet republic" on 16 September. About 6,000 people joined in the Bolshevik riot, which ended on 22 September, crushed with heavy casualties by the intervention of the Romanian army and police. *See also* BOLSHEVIK POWER.

TATARS. Migrating people of Asian origin whose invasion of Europe in the 13th century devastated many lands, including most of present-day Moldova. During their retreat, Tatar tribes settled in the steppes along the shores of the Black Sea, especially around the mouths of the Bug River and in the Crimean Peninsula. Several times during the following centuries the Tatars attempted to invade Moldova, frequently as allies of the **Ottoman Empire**. The Tatar invasion of Moldova in 1469 was crushed by **Stephen the Great** at the battle of Lipnic. The stronghold of **Orhei** was built in its aftermath to complete Moldova's defenses along the banks of the **Nistru River**. After the Turkish conquest of Moldova's lower lands lying between the mouths of the Nistru and the **Danube**, Tatar tribes were settled in that territory, which they called *budjiak,* or "the nook." *See also* BUGEAC.

TAU, NICOLAE (1948–). Politician and diplomat, Moldova's first minister of foreign affairs after the country's proclamation of **sovereignty** and **declaration of independence** (1990–1993), and Moldova's ambassador to the United States (1993–1998). A native of Andruşu de Jos, **Cahul,** Ţâu is a graduate of the State Agrarian University of Moldova

(1970) and holds a Ph.D. in economics from the Academy of Social Sciences of Sofia, Bulgaria. Highlights of his career include executive functions in the capital city of **Chişinău**, where he helped organize a number of important housing and construction projects between 1986 and 1990.

TCACENCO, PAVEL (1901–1926). Revolutionary activist in czarist **Bessarabia**, Soviet Russia, Soviet Ukraine, and **Romania**, Pavel Tcacenco, by his true name Iakov Antipov, took part in the 1915 **Tighina** (or Bender) riot and, later on, in 1919, became the leader of a Soviet-led Bolshevik clandestine organization of **Chişinău**. In 1921, he was arrested and sentenced to two years in prison by the Romanian authorities. Freed in 1923, he fled to Moscow, where he was given the mission to help organize the **Moldavian Autonomous Soviet Socialist Republic**, a political formation carved out of Soviet Ukraine on the east bank of the **Nistru River**. The Soviets sent Tcacenco on yet another clandestine revolutionary mission to Romania between 1925 and 1926. He was arrested in Bucharest and was eventually shot under controversial circumstances at a railway station near Chişinău in 1926. Tcacenco was revered by the Communists as a hero of two parties—both the **Communist Party** of Soviet Moldavia and the Romanian Communist Party.

TELECOMMUNICATIONS. Moldova has direct telecommunications lines to all successor states of the **Union of Soviet Socialist Republics**, **Romania**, Bulgaria, and Greece. Lines to the rest of the world are supported via satellite links through transit telephone exchange units in Montreal, Canada, and Copenhagen, Denmark. Moldova's telecommunications networks serve 1.1 million users.

TELENESTI. Chief town of the former *raion,* or district, of the same name, 91 kilometers north of **Chişinău**. The place was first mentioned in 1497. The former district was established in 1940 in the wake of the Soviet **annexation** of **Bessarabia**. After 1999, Teleneşti became part of the newly reestablished *judeţ* of **Orhei**.

TESTEMITEANU, NICOLAE (1921–1986). Physician, surgeon, and hygienist, Dr. Testemiţeanu was one of Moldova's chief decision makers in the field of public health while the republic was still a part of the Soviet Union. He served as minister of health in the government of the **Moldavian Soviet Socialist Republic** between 1963 and 1968, after which point he was demoted for allegedly promoting too many autochthonous medical personnel contrary to the Soviet **Russification** policies. The Nicolae Testemițeanu State University of Medicine and Pharmacy in **Chișinău** is named for him.

TIGHECI. Historical region of Moldova stretching amid thick forests among the Lăpușna, **Ialpug**, Sărata, and Larga Rivers. Its highest elevation, Mount Tigheci (310 meters), rises between the Ialpug and the **Prut River**. In the 16th century, this woodland-rich province was part of the **Fălciu** district. The Tigheci region was first described by **Demetrius Cantemir** in his 1714–1716 *Descriptio Moldaviae*. In present-day Moldova, this is also the name of a village in **Leova**.

TIGHINA/BENDER (CITY). Moldova's fourth largest city. It occupies a strategic position on the west bank of the **Nistru River**, about 51 kilometers southeast of **Chișinău**, and is currently under the authority of the east-bank breakaway leadership in **Tiraspol**. The place was first mentioned as a checkpoint on the Nistru in 1408. Conquered by the **Ottoman Empire** in the 16th century, Tighina was dubbed Bender (Turkish for "port" or "water gate"). With several brief interruptions, it remained under Ottoman domination from 1538 to 1806, when it was eventually conquered by Russia. Sweden's King Charles XII took refuge there (1709–1713) under Turkish protection after his defeat by Russia's **Peter the Great** at Poltava. The Tighina fortress, erected by Turkey's Suleiman the Magnificent in 1558, was disaffected as a military stronghold in 1897. However, part of the extant fortifications are still used by military units controlled by the separatist **Moldavian Nistrian Republic (MNR)**.

An important bridge over the Nistru links Tighina with Tiraspol, the capital of the self-proclaimed MNR. Tighina was the scene of fierce fighting in 1992, when the separatist forces of the Tiraspol Russophile government, with help from Russia's **14th Army**, captured the city. Tighina has a population of over 137,400 inhabitants (42.4 percent Russians, 28.8 percent Romanian-speaking Moldovans, 18.5 percent Ukrainians). Tighina is said to have been increasingly active as a regional center of arms production after it came under the control of the Tiraspol breakaway authorities. One of its factories, the Pribor plant, is reportedly manufacturing ammunition, including Grad jet-rocket equipment for Russian troops deployed in the breakaway Nistrian region.

TIGHINA (DISTRICT). New *județ* established in 1999, with the **Nistru** west-bank city of **Căușeni** as its administrative center. Since 1992, the city of Tighina, which gives the name to the district, has been under the control of the **Tiraspol** east-bank separatist authorities. The reestablished *judeţ* of Tighina comprises, in addition to Căuşeni, the former Soviet-era districts of **Căinari** and **Ştefan Vodă.**

TINUT. Administrative and territorial unit of historic Moldova, first mentioned as such in 1408 under **Alexander the Good**. In 1566, the **Principality of Moldova** comprised 24 such units (plural: *ţinuturi*). In his 1714–1716 *Descriptio Moldaviae*, **Demetrius Cantemir** listed 19 such units. The eastern half of the principality incorporated into the **Russian Empire** in 1812, which currently covers most of present-day Moldova, included nine *ţinuturi* in 1814: **Iaşi, Orhei, Hotin, Soroca, Codru,** Bender, Hotărniceni, Greceni, and **Ismail**. In the early stages of the **annexation**, the Russians respected the name of Moldova's traditional territorial unit, reapplying it to the recovered coastal areas (e.g., Akkerman) that had been held by the **Ottoman Empire** since the 16th century. *See also JUDET.*

TIRASPOL. City on the east bank of the **Nistru River**, 64 kilometers southeast of **Chişinău,** currently the capital of the self-proclaimed breakaway **Moldavian Nistrian Republic**. Tiraspol was founded by the Russians in 1793 near the outskirts of the ancient Moldovan village of Sucleia and was originally meant to serve as a military outpost on the then new boundary of the **Russian Empire**, which had been moved from the Bug River to the **Nistru,** under the provisions of the **Treaty of Iaşi.**

The strategic importance of the place stemmed from its geographic position, across from the Turkish stronghold of **Tighina,** or Bender, on the west bank of the Nistru, inside the borders of the **Principality of Moldova,** at that time under the suzerainty of the **Ottoman Empire.** The city grew steadily throughout the 19th century, both as the district center of the Kherson province of the czarist empire and as a key railway link with Moscow, on the one hand, and the Black Sea port of Odessa, on the other. Under Soviet rule, in 1929, Tiraspol became the capital of the **Moldavian Autonomous Soviet Socialist Republic** and started to play an important part as a beachhead in preparing the cultural and political groundwork for the establishment of the future **Moldavian Soviet Socialist Republic,** founded by the **Union of Soviet Socialist Republics** in 1940, to straddle both banks of the Nistru River. Such institutions as the Tiraspol **Romanian-language** publishing houses and the Tiraspol Pedagogical Institute (established in 1930) were instrumental in disseminating Communist ideology and preparing Soviet-style instructors and educators.

With its population steadily increasing—due mainly to a strong influx of immigrants from Russia and Ukraine—the city developed during the Soviet era into a multiethnic community and, next to Chişinău, the main industrial hub and energy producer of Soviet Moldavia. The seat and headquarters of Russia's **14th Army**, currently downgraded to the status of an operational group under the name **Operational Group of Russian Forces**, the Tiraspol enclave constitutes the southernmost outpost of Russia's military power in the proximity of the Balkans and the only extant deployment of Russian forces outside the borders of the **Russian Federation** in Europe. With a population of over 203,000 inhabitants (41.3 percent Russians, 32.2 percent Ukrainians, and a minority of 17.7 percent Romanian-speaking Moldovans), Tiraspol is the second largest city in the Republic of Moldova. *See also* SEPARATISM; TRANS-NIS-TRIAN CONFLICT.

TOPAL, STEPAN (1938–). Former leader of the **Gagauz** separatist movement and first governor, or *bashkan,* of **Gagauz Yeri**, Topal is a native of **Comrat**. By training a transportation engineer, he was the chief executive of Gagauz Yeri between 1991 and 1994. He was defeated in the 1995 elections and, no longer a public servant, chose to move to Russia (V. N.).

TRADE. Moldova trades with over 80 countries worldwide. Since early 1994, most import-export limitations have been liberalized. Bilateral agreements providing most-favored-nation status have been effected with Austria, Bulgaria, China, Hungary, India, Iran, Latvia, Poland, Turkey, Ukraine, and the United States. Free trade agreements have also been adopted with Armenia, Belarus, **Romania**, the **Russian Federation**, Turkmenistan, and Uzbekistan. A Generalized System of Preferences arrangement, which provides a duty-free regime for nonsensitive goods, is in force with the **European Union (EU)**.

Russia's 1998 economic crisis had a negative impact on Moldova's foreign trade and determined a reorientation of priorities toward markets outside the **Commonwealth of Independent States (CIS)**. In 1998, Moldova's trade with the CIS was down 23.7 percent, while trade with all other nations increased by 7.4 percent. Moldova is the only CIS state whose textile exports to the EU are not subject to quotas. Moldova's main trading partners are the Russian Federation (50 percent), Ukraine (15 percent), Romania (10 percent), Germany (4 percent), Belarus (4 percent), and the United States (approx. 2 percent). During the first half of 1997, Moldova's foreign trade amounted to $754 million, a total comparable to the 1996 figure, but the import-export balance worsened, exports falling to some $294 million (a drop of about 6.9 percent) and imports rising to some $460 million (an increase of 5.5 percent). In 1998, Moldova's imports went down by 8.4 percent and its exports down by 22.5 percent, as compared to 1997. Most of the decrease was generated by exports to the CIS falling by 26.1 percent, while exports to other countries grew by 4.2 percent.

Moldova's main exports are wines and brandies, preserves, canned food, tobacco, fruits, vegetables, grapes, textiles and garments, carpets, furniture, footwear, dairy products, sunflower oil, sugar, raw skins, and corn. Moldova's main imports are fuel and energy, followed by chemical products and machinery. *See also* AGRICULTURE; ECONOMY, NATIONAL; INDUSTRY.

TRAJAN'S WALL. A series of ancient defense vestiges in southern Moldova known to locals as "Valul lui Traian" and attributed by tradition to Roman Emperor Trajan (A.D. 98–117), the conqueror of **Dacia**. Other interpretations credit Trajan's successor, Hadrian, with building these defenses as part of the well-known fortified chain of walls, ditches, and forts the latter ordered erected from northern England down to Rome's Continental possessions, starting north along the Rhine River, east along the **Danube**, and down to the Black Sea. Hadrian's grand design was indeed to divide the Roman Empire from the barbarians in the form of a *vallum*. The extant Moldova segment facing east and northeast between the **Prut** and **Nistru Rivers** was apparently designed as an outpost of the newly conquered province of Dacia. Opposing views hold that much of what is known as Valul lui Traian was in fact built at a later date, as a defense against the Goth or **Tatar** invasions, its attribution to Trajan being mythical and legendary.

The wall's northern structure ("Verchnyi Trojany" in Russian topography) stretches in the form of mounds and earthworks cutting across the southern part of present-day Moldova from **Leova** on the Prut to Copanca, near the junction of the **Botna River** with the Nistru. A second line stretches farther south, with segments running roughly parallel to the Danube River thalweg between **Vulcăneşti** and **Bolgrad** and farther on—following an upward direction—abutting the **Bugeac** seaboard, south of the mouth of the Nistru. Villages like Troian, in the **Lăpuşna** district, or Novi Trojany (Noul Troian), south of Moldova's current border with Ukraine, corroborate a persistence of the local tradition connecting Emperor Trajan with the vestiges.

In terms of language history, it is relevant to note that the Roman emperor's name is also the source word of the common noun *troian,* which denotes in Romanian a wall or any long crest of earth, sand, or snow in the form of a protracted elevation. The Moldova vestiges were first described in a scholarly work by French military engineer Philippe Masson du Pont in 1686 and later on by Prince **Demetrius Cantemir**, who, in a note to his *History of the Growth and Decay of the Othman Empire,* cited numismatic evidence and a Latin inscription with the text: "Imp. Caesari, Div. filio Nervae Trajano, Augusto, Ger. Dacico, Pont. Max. Fel. B. dict. XVI. Imp. VI Cons. VII. PP. Calpurnio, Publio, Marco, C. Aurelio Rufo" (London, 1734–1735, I, III, 4, n. 30, pp. 187–188). Transcribed by the author from a marble stela dug up in the *vallum* vestiges in his own lifetime, the now lost Latin inscription appears to corroborate the Roman origin of the works.

TRANSNISTRIA. The wartime area between the **Nistru River** and the Bug River, dubbed Transnistria and passed over by Germany to Romanian administration under the Tighina Convention of 30 August 1941, with **George Alexianu** as governor-general. According to the German-Romanian agreement, the province was placed under Romanian civil administration, with the German army's High Command in charge of giving instructions in the areas of security and the economic utilization of the territory.

The territory of Transnistria was organized by **Romania** into 13 administrative districts: Ananiev, **Balta**, Berezovca, **Dubăsari**, Golta, Jugastru, Moghilev, Odessa, Oceacov, Ovidiopol, **Râbniţa**, **Tiraspol**, and Tulcin. Mass deportations of **Jews** from **Bessarabia** and **Northern Bucovina** were conducted in Transnistria between 1941 and 1943. Reportedly, about 130,000 local Jews were exterminated during the wartime occupation of Transnistria, to which statistics add at least 85,000 deaths or exterminations of nonlocal Jews, most of them deported from Romanian-held territory. Presumably, approximately 50,000 Jews survived the Transnistria **war deportations**.

In contemporary usage, used in hyphenated form as a common noun, "trans-Nistria" is loosely applied to the self-proclaimed east-bank secessionist **Moldavian Nistrian Republic**.

TRANS-NISTRIAN CONFLICT. This conflict broke out in the sliver of land with a Russophone majority on the east bank of the **Nistru River**, where, in an act of secession, a Russia-aligned Moldavian Nistrian Soviet Socialist Republic was proclaimed on 2 September 1990. Ethnic Russians and Ukrainians form together an almost 60 percent majority of the over 700,000 population of the area, an internationally unrecognized entity currently named the **Moldavian Nistrian Republic.** The trans-Nistrian conflict was triggered by ideological and political differences, but it took the initial form of a cultural protest against laws promulgated in **Chişinău** regarding Moldova's return to the Latin script, the establishment of the native local language **(Moldavian)** rather than **Russian** as the official language of the country, and the change of the country's Soviet-style symbols. A powerful backlash ensued that led to the 1992 armed conflict between Moldova's central authorities in Chişinău and the **Tiraspol** separatist forces. Russia's **14th Army** sustained the separatist forces, which in turn were able to maintain control over the Nistru east-bank districts and the west-bank city of **Tighina.**

Since the signing of a cease-fire agreement (at Limanskoe, on the Moldova-Ukraine border, on 7 July 1992), negotiations have been going on between the Chişinău authorities and the self-appointed authorities in Tiraspol in a series of sporadic attempts to settle the conflict by granting expanded autonomy to the left-bank districts. In October 1994, a Russian-Moldovan agreement was signed stipulating the withdrawal of Russian troops from the region. That accord has never gone into effect owing to the Russian State Duma's refusal to ratify it. On 13 November 1996, the State Duma adopted a resolution declaring the region a zone of "special strategic interest for Russia." In February 1997, after an official visit to Moldova by **North Atlantic Treaty Organization (NATO)** Secretary-General Javier Solana, Russian Defense Council Secretary Yurii Batunin promised that Russia would reduce the number of its troops in the trans-Nistrian region of Moldova but that it would not do so at NATO's behest—rather, only "when the political conflict is solved." Reportedly downsized, the **Russian Federation**'s military base in the trans-Nistrian districts of Moldova continues to be Moscow's only permanent armed forces deployment outside Russia's borders in Europe.

A 1998 **Organization for Security and Cooperation in Europe (OSCE)** meeting on "Military Transparency in Moldova" held in Vienna stated that due to Russia's lack of cooperation, OSCE monitors have been unable to check the real level of the presence of Russian troops in the area. The meeting concluded that the process of Russian troop withdrawal from the east-bank districts is in fact stagnating and needs to be expedited. However, because of its strong political and ideological underpinnings, the trans-Nistrian conflict appears to be a long-term problem that is likely to take years to resolve, while a negotiated solution is not likely to be found unless Russia changes its attitude.

In 1997, a memorandum on normalizing the relations between Chişinău and Tiraspol was signed in Moscow, with the Russian Federation and Ukraine as guarantors. The memorandum called for future talks on the status of the Nistru east-bank region. According to a statement made that same year by Moldovan Minister of National Security **Tudor Botnaru**, the key to the trans-Nistrian conflict is neither in Chişinău nor in Tiraspol, but in Moscow. *See also* FEDERALIZATION; SEPARATISM.

TRANS-NISTRIAN PRINT MEDIA. The **Russian-language** *Pridnestrovye* and the "**Moldavian**"-language version *Adevărul nistrean* (The Nistrian Truth), printed in **Romanian** in Russian **Cyrillics**, were launched in 1994 as leftist press organs of **Tiraspol**'s Supreme Soviet and of the **Moldavian Nistrian Republic**'s government. The oldest Tiraspol newspaper is *Dnestrovskaya Pravda*. Other trans-Nistrian publications include *Tighina,* published in the west-bank city of **Tighina**, and *Znamya pobedy* (The Flag of Victory), published in the east-bank city of **Dubăsari**.

TRANSPORTATION. Moldova's network of railways covers a total length of 1,318 kilometers in common carrier service. They use the broad-gauge system, compatible with the traditional lines built by Russia and still in use in the **Commonwealth of Independent States (CIS)**. Automobile, bus, and truck transport accounts for most local transportation—96 percent of the cargo movement and over 80 percent of the means of conveyance for passengers. Moldova's highways total about 20,100 kilometers, out of which 13,900 kilometers are paved or gravelled and 6,100 kilometers are unpaved. Most of Moldova's land transportation is provided by means of bus routes that connect 90 percent of Moldova's cities, towns, and villages.

The **Nistru River** is navigable for most of its course, but water transport is of only local and touristic importance. There is one major airport in **Chişinău**, and its urgently needed modernization is being undertaken by the Turkish firm Axen. By the year 2010, the Chişinău airport will have the capacity to handle an annual traffic of over 600,000 passengers (compared to the 1998 figure of only 160,000). There are 18 other airports of lesser importance across the country, seven of them with paved runways. Air transportation is provided by two carriers—Air Moldova and Moldavian Airlines—that have direct flights to and from Bucharest, Budapest, Moscow, Paris, Tel Aviv, Vienna, and a number of other capital cities in the CIS.

TRANSYLVANIA. A region and historical principality central to the Carpathian basin, west of historical Moldova. In ancient times, the region formed the fortified nucleus of the Dacian kingdom, which was to become the Romanized province of **Dacia** under Emperor Trajan in A.D. 106. It was overrun by successive barbarian tribes in the interval between the end of the 3rd century and the 12th century, during which time it was eventually conquered by the Hungarians. Transylvanian local chieftains, or *voivodes,* resisted, but they were finally brought to recognize the king of Hungary as their overlord.

During the first centuries after the Hungarian conquest, the province preserved the *voivodate* as the central political institution of the land, while the traditional title of *voivode,* as ruler of Transylvania, was perpetuated under Hungarian suzerainty until 1541. In the 12th century, the Hungarian Crown invited colonies of Saxon settlers to Transylvania, entrusting them with the task of building the land's new fortified cities, the seven urban centers that gave the province its German name, Siebenbürgen ("Seven Cities").

On the eve of the **Tatar** invasion of 1241, Transylvania's population was estimated to consist of a melting pot of local Wallachians, Szeklers, Hungarians, and Saxons. The Tatar invasions determined the need for a border mark east of Transylvania, a strategic task assigned by the king of Hungary to Wallachian nobleman **Dragoş,** who, like his successor, **Bogdan I,** hailed from the northern Transylvanian land of **Maramureş.** Dragoş Vodă is considered the founder of Moldova (ca. 1352); Bogdan I (1359–ca. 1365) is Moldova's first recorded sovereign ruler.

After having been ruled for most of its history by Hungary and, later on, by the **Habsburg Empire,** Transylvania joined **Romania** at the end of World War I, in keeping with the **Wilsonian principles** of self-determination. *See also* NATIONAL UNIFICATION.

TRILATERAL AGREEMENT. A document signed in **Ismail** in July 1997, stipulating the creation of a Euro-Region encompassing the border areas of Moldova, **Romania,** and Ukraine. These areas include the **Lower Danube,** with a free trade zone designed to include the cities of Galaţi (Romania), **Reni** (Ukraine), and the future facilities of **Giurgiuleşti** in southern Moldova, and the **Upper Prut.** The agreement went into effect in August 1998. The Lower Danube segment includes the **Cahul** *judeţ* in southern Moldova, three maritime **Danube** districts in Romania—the *judeţe* of Brăila, Galaţi, and Tulcea—and Ukraine's Black Sea region of Odessa. The Upper Prut segment is expected to include the new Moldovan *judeţe* of

Bălți and **Edineț, Suceava** and Botoșani in Romania, and the Chernovtsy (*see* CERNAUTI) region in Ukraine.

TURCANU, ANDREI (1948–). Literary critic, poet, and cultural-political activist, Țurcanu is the author of a study on the evolution of poetry in post–World War II Moldova. He served as a deputy in independent Moldova's first Parliament from 1990 to 1993.

TURCANU, VLADIMIR (1954–). Minister of internal affairs in Moldova's government formed in December 1999, and first deputy minister in the same ministry from 1997 to 1999. A native of the **Nistru** eastbank town of Slobozia, Vladimir Țurcanu holds a degree in law from the Moscow Lomonosov State University. Earlier in his career he worked as a prosecutor and held legal positions in the hierarchy of the **Communist Party**. After Moldova's **declaration of independence** he headed the Moldo-Belarus Association Zubr (1991–1993) and served as counselor in Moldova's embassy to Belarus (1993–1997) (V. N.).

TURKEY, RELATIONS WITH. Moldova's relations with Turkey have ancient historical roots. In 1812, while the whole of the **Principality of Moldova** was a vassal of the **Ottoman Empire**, the latter ceded its eastern half to Russia, which renamed it **Bessarabia**. Today's Moldova covers most of the territory then acquired by the **Russian Empire** from Ottoman Turkey, by virtue of the 1812 **Treaty of Bucharest**. After Moldova's 1991 **declaration of independence**, good relations with Turkey were boosted by an exchange of visits between the presidents of the two countries. Several negotiations were signed in 1996, including a defense and cooperation agreement and accords providing for cooperation in science and technology, culture, trade, and the legal sphere. Moldova's policy toward its Turkophone Christian minority, the **Gagauz**, was praised by Turkey. Turkey pledged to invest $35 million in the **Gagauz Yeri** autonomous region of Moldova, via Moldova's central authorities in **Chișinău**. Moldova envisages strengthening its special military cooperation with Turkey by using the U.S. Partnership for Peace format to increase joint action in the area of training and in mutual sharing of military expertise and experience.

TYRAS. A colony and port city founded by the Greek city of Miletus around 600 B.C. at the mouth of the **Nistru River** (named Tyras by the Greeks). Numismatic evidence indicates that its inhabitants traded wine, wheat, and fish. Destroyed by local Dacian warlords around 50 B.C., it was restored by the Romans in the aftermath of the conquest of **Dacia** and was turned into one of the most prosperous cities of the Roman province of Moesia Inferior, on the western shore of the Black Sea. Tyras was governed by five elected archons, a senate, a popular assembly, and a registrar. Recovered coins in the area display effigies of Roman emperors from Domitian to Alexander Severus (A.D. 235). Its scanty site is covered by successive layers of cities built in the course of time by the Byzantine Empire, which renamed it Maurokastron; by the Genoese, who called it Monocastro; and by the Moldovans, to whom it was **Cetatea Albă**. Northwest of the ancient port city, 18th-century **Tiraspol** was named by the Russians after Tyras.

-U-

UKRAINE, RELATIONS WITH. Moldova ratified a Friendship and Cooperation Treaty with Ukraine in 1996. The **Trilateral Agreement** among Moldova, Ukraine, and **Romania** signed in **Ismail** in 1997 laid the groundwork for the parties' cooperation within the framework of two proposed Euro-Regions, the **Lower Danube** and the **Upper Prut**, as well as in a future free trade zone meant to include the port cities of Galați in Romania, **Reni** in Ukraine, and Moldova's **Giurgiulești**—the latter designated to become the site of a future oil terminal on the **Danube River**. Moldova and Ukraine were scheduled to implement a unified procedure for collection of customs duties as agreed in April 1998.

Moldova's past relationship with Ukraine has been marked by the fact that several areas that used to belong to historic Moldova and, between 1812 and 1918, to Russian-held **Bessarabia** were awarded after World War II by the **Union of Soviet Socialist Republics** to Soviet Ukraine. These include part of the northern lands, enfolding such historic places as **Cernăuți** and **Hotin**, and most of the southern seaboard, or **Bugeac**, with the **Nistru** estuary, which used to give ancient Moldova access to the Black Sea and the port cities of **Chilia**, Ismail, and Reni on the maritime Danube. About one-fifth of the inhabitants of the southern region speak **Romanian** and are considered Moldovans, but they constitute a majority only in the district of Reni. In the other part of historic Moldova, now part of Ukraine (i.e., **Northern Bucovina**), Gluboka,

Storojineţ, and Noua Suliţă are the only districts with Romanian-speaking Moldovan majorities.

Territorial claims between Moldova and Ukraine revolved around the borderline between the two countries in the Bugeac, drawn under Soviet rule in such a way as to criss-cross several times the railway between Palanca in Moldova and **Bolgrad** in Ukraine. A separate item on the agenda was a patch of land several hundred meters in size south of Giurgiuleşti, which, in 1999, restored Moldova's access to the maritime course of the Danube, west of Reni. *See also* BORDERS OF MOLDOVA.

UKRAINIAN ETHNICS. Ukrainian ethnics constitute about 13.8 percent of the total population of Moldova and number about 600,000 people. This is the largest single ethnic group in the country, with Russians coming in second. Moldova is the only successor state of the Soviet Union in which Russians as an ethnic group are outnumbered by another group. About 30 percent of Moldova's Ukrainians—most of them urban dwellers—are not natives of Moldova, having been born in Ukraine or other parts of the former Soviet Union. *See also* COLONIZATION/ MIGRATION; RUSSIAN ETHNICS.

UNGHENI. Chief city of the newly established *judeţ* of the same name, 107 kilometers west of **Chişinău** on the **Prut River**. The new *judeţ* of Ungheni includes, in addition to Ungheni proper, the former districts of **Călăraşi** and **Nisporeni**. The city of Ungheni has a population of over 38,000 inhabitants (1993 est.). First mentioned in 1462 as a village across from the west-bank city of **Iaşi**, Ungheni gained importance after the 1812 Russian **annexation** of **Bessarabia**. A strategically important railway between Chişinău and Ungheni was built by Russia in 1875 in preparation for the **Russo-Turkish War** of 1877–1878. After World War II, Ungheni became the main railway link between the **Union of Soviet Socialist Republics** and **Romania**. The Ungheni-Iaşi transit link across the Prut is currently the main line of land communication between Moldova and Romania. The former Ungheni *raion* had a population of over 79,000 inhabitants (1993 est.).

UNION OF MOLDOVA'S COMMUNISTS / UNIUNEA COMUNIS-TILOR DIN MOLDOVA (UCM). *See* COMMUNIST PARTY.

UNION OF SOVIET SOCIALIST REPUBLICS (USSR). Proclaimed in Moscow on 30 December 1922, its core was the Russian Soviet Federated Socialist Republic, which comprised essentially most of the territories of the former **Russian Empire**. The notable exceptions were Finland, the Baltic countries, and **Bessarabia**, which had declared their independence. Bessarabia subsequently proclaimed its union with **Romania** in the wake of the threat of a **Bolshevik power** takeover. The federative form of the USSR was kept together by the rigid discipline and centralized authority of the **Communist Party**, which tightly controlled each Soviet republic. Ukraine, Belarus, Georgia, Armenia, and Azerbaijan were among the first republics incorporated into the USSR. The powers of their governing bodies were strictly limited by the overriding authority of Soviet Russia, which included not only the defense apparatus and the right to conduct foreign policy, but also the right to dictate economic policies from the center.

At the outbreak of World War II, in addition to the Russian Soviet Federated Socialist Republic, the USSR comprised 10 Soviet Socialist republics: Ukraine, Belarus, Azerbaijan, Georgia, Armenia, Turkmenistan, Uzbekistan, Tajikistan, Kazakhstan, and Kyrgyzstan, as well as a number of small autonomous Soviet Socialist republics, including the largely artificial **Moldavian Autonomous Soviet Socialist Republic**, carved out of Soviet Ukraine in 1924 on the east bank of the **Nistru River**. In 1940, pursuant to the Secret Additional Protocol of the 1939 **Molotov-Ribbentrop Pact**, four more republics were created by the Soviet Union and enfolded into the USSR: the former independent republics of Estonia, Latvia, and Lithuania, and Bessarabia, incorporated under the terms of the ultimatum issued to Romania on 26 June 1940. Less than 48 hours later, 32 Red Army divisions, including two tank brigades, an assault regiment, and two special reserve regiments, marched across the Nistru, took possession of the province, and completed its occupation by the early afternoon of 3 July. On 2 August 1940, the Supreme Soviet of the USSR passed into law the creation of the **Moldavian Soviet Socialist Republic (MSSR)** on most of the territory of Bessarabia, while the occupied land's seaboard and northern region were enfolded into Soviet Ukraine.

Decades later, in the aftermath of Soviet Russia's liberalizing policies of **glasnost** and **perestroika**, the MSSR changed its name to the Republic of Moldova and declared its independence (*see* DECLARATION OF INDEPENDENCE) on 27 August 1991. The USSR officially broke up on 26 December 1991. *See also* GORBACHEV, MIKHAIL; RUSSIAN FEDERATION.

UNIONIST MOVEMENT. In 19th-century Moldova, name given to a political movement born in the aftermath of the Crimean War (1853–1856) seeking the rapprochement and ultimately the union of that principality with **Wallachia** under the terms of the **Convention of Paris**. The unionist movement attained its goal in 1859, when Moldova, which included the Bessarabian districts of **Bolgrad**, **Cahul**, and **Ismail**, was united with Wallachia under Moldovan Prince **Alexandru Ioan Cuza**. The rest of **Bessarabia**, at that time a province of the **Russian Empire**, was not involved in that movement.

A unionist movement was revived in post-Soviet Moldova, where the term "unionist" is loosely applied to the pro-Romanian orientation of a number of Moldovan politicians and public figures, especially members of the cultural intelligentsia who advocate a future union of Moldova with **Romania** intended to reflect the two countries' common cultural and linguistic heritage. Its main exponents were leaders of the **Popular Front of Moldova**, who expressed their views in that organization's 1992 political program, which defined its status as that of a "national, unionist movement." *See also* POLITICAL BLOCS AND PARTIES; POLITICAL SPECTRUM; PRO-ROMANIANISM.

UNITED PRINCIPALITIES. Twofold 19th-century political entity made up of the **Principalities of Moldova** and **Wallachia**. The United Principalities were established in accordance with the provisions of the 1858 **Convention of Paris**, which stipulated the creation of common institutions for the two Romanian-speaking countries, with a central commission in the city of Focşani and two separate princes with their respective capitals in **Iaşi** and Bucharest. However, by virtue of the 1859 double election of Moldova's Prince **Alexandru Ioan Cuza** as prince of Wallachia too, the two executives were joined de facto in a personal union. In 1862, Cuza made Bucharest his capital city and changed the name of the country to **Romania.** The United Principalities were also known in the 19th century as the **Danubian Principalities**. *See also* NATIONAL UNIFICATION.

UNITED SOCIAL DEMOCRATIC PARTY / PARTIDUL SOCIAL DEMOCRAT UNIT (PSDU). Political formation founded in 1997 that includes the Social Democrat Party of Moldova, the Party of Social Progress, the Republican Party, the Party of Socialist Action, and the Party of Economic Rebirth. The PSDU claims to be center-left oriented. It rejects shock therapy in the pursuit of economic reform and the concentration of property and capital in the hands of what it perceives as a small social group. It supports Moldova's neutrality and opposes the country's **federalization**. *See also* POLITICAL BLOCS AND PARTIES.

UNITED STATES, RELATIONS WITH. Related to Moldova's population and compared to U.S. assistance going to other former Soviet republics, American assistance going to Moldova ranks second among that received by other member states of the **Community of Independent States**. Through the United States Agency for International Development, Washington, D.C., provides Moldova with a variety of programs to support land privatization reforms, agricultural yield growth, democratization, and market reform programs. The Bilateral Investment Treaty concluded between the United States and Moldova guarantees nondiscriminatory treatment for American investments and operations, hard currency repatriation rights, and expropriation compensation. By 1995, American investments in Moldova totalled almost $2 million, with the United States coming in as the third largest investor, after Italy and Switzerland. Moldova has enjoyed most-favored-nation status in its trade relations with the United States since 1992. U.S.-Moldova relations also include cultural and academic agreements and Peace Corps operations.

Moldova takes an active part in the programs of the U.S. Partnership for Peace and is also a signatory of the U.S. Cooperative Threat Reduction Agreement. In keeping with that agreement and to prevent high-tech weaponry ending up in the hands of rogue nations, the United States quietly purchased from Moldova 21 Soviet-made MiG-29C aircraft, some of them capable of carrying nuclear weapons. The deal, concluded in 1997, was described as an important step forward in improving the bilateral relationship. In January 1999, on the occasion of the presentation of credentials by Moldova's new ambassador to Washington, the White House emphasized the fact that the United States is interested in urging an early, orderly, and complete removal of Russian troops, weapons, and ammunition from the east-bank districts of the **Nistru River**, as well as Russia's full cooperation for expediting a peaceful, negotiated final settlement of the **trans-Nistrian conflict**.

In 1998, the Republic of Moldova was included in the South-East Europe Action Plan, launched by the United States to intensify technical cooperation with southeastern European countries, including Bulgaria, the former Republic of Macedonia, **Romania**, and Slovenia. In 1998, American technical assistance to Moldova stood at about $25 million. Also in 1998, the United States provided an extra $5 million in humanitarian assistance to help Moldova's needy groups face the hardships of the 1999 winter.

UNITY-EDINSTVO MOVEMENT / MISCAREA UNITATE-EDIN-STVO (MUE). A left-wing political organization that emerged from the **Interfront** movement in 1991, in the wake of Moldova's minorities' campaign against the Language Law adopted by the **Chişinău** Parliament, which established the local language of the majority, rather than **Russian**, as the official language of Moldova. It has strong constituencies in **Tiraspol** and the **Nistru** east-bank districts, as well as among ethnic communities elsewhere, including in **Gagauz Yeri** and the urban conglomerates of Chişinău and **Bălţi**. MUE members include Russians, Ukrainians, Bulgarians, and other Russophone residents of Moldova. Politically conservative and pro-Russian, it maintains an ambiguous stance vis-à-vis Tiraspol. In 1998, one of its former deputies in the Chişinău Parliament, Serghei Gradinari, who had also been nominated to serve as deputy foreign minister by the propresidential **Bloc for a Democratic and Prosperous Moldova**, took up citizenship in the self-proclaimed **Moldavian Nistrian Republic** and was appointed finance minister in the Tiraspol separatist government. *See also* POLITICAL BLOCS AND PARTIES.

UPPER PRUT. A Euro-Region that includes two *judeţe* of Moldova (**Bălţi** and **Edineţ**), two *judeţe* of **Romania** (**Suceava** and Botoşani), and Ukraine's Chernovtsy region (*see* CERNAUTI; *JUDET*). A protocol of association of the chambers of commerce and industry of the three regional entities was signed in 1999.

URECHE, GRIGORE (ca. 1590–1647). One of the earliest chroniclers of Moldova's history, Ureche spent his early years in Poland, where he received part of his education. After his return to Moldova, he took an active part in the country's political life. His *Letopiseţul Ţării Moldovei* (A Chronicle of the Land of Moldova) is a vivid personal description of the events leading from the **founding of Moldova** up to the year 1595. It was translated into French by Emile Picot (*Chronique de Moldavie depuis le milieu du XIV-eme siècle jusqu'à l'an 1595* [Paris: Leroux, 1878–1879]). In addition to being acknowledged by historians as an important testimony marking the beginnings of Moldova's historiography, Ureche's *Chronicle* is considered by critics a valuable literary work shining with intrinsic linguistic and stylistic qualities.

URECHEANU, SERAFIM (1950–). Mayor of the city of **Chişinău** after 1994. A native of Larga, **Briceni**, Urecheanu is a graduate of the Chişinău Polytechnic Institute. He served as a government official in various capacities between 1978 and 1990 and was for some time a member of Moldova's Parliament. As mayor of Moldova's capital, Urecheanu earned the reputation of an efficient and pragmatic leader (V. N.).

-V-

VADUL LUI VODA. A town 23 kilometers northeast of **Chişinău** on the west bank of the **Nistru River** on one of the traditional trade routes linking the two banks of the river. The place—in literal translation, the "Crossing of the Prince" (*see* VODA), was first mentioned as a village in 1466 under the reign of **Stephen the Great.** The Vadul lui Vodă camping facilities are one of the main touristic attractions in the Chişinău area.

VALCOV/VYLKOVO. Fishing port city on the **Chilia** arm of the **Danube River**, integrated into Soviet Ukraine by the **Union of Soviet Socialist Republics (USSR)** after the 1940 incorporation of **Bessarabia** into the USSR.

VARLAAM, METROPOLITAN (?–1657). By his lay name Vasile Moţoc, Metropolitan Varlaam was educated as a young monk at the Secu Monastery and became head of Moldova's **Orthodox Church** in 1632. In 1637, he was one of the three bishops on the short list of candidates competing for the seat of the patriarchy of Constantinople. A polyglot and scholar, Varlaam authored and published an anthology titled *Carte românească de învăţătură, dumenecele preste an şi la praznice împărăteşti şi la svînţi mari* (Romanian Book of Teachings for Sundays and Other Major Feasts and Religious Holidays), printed in **Iaşi** in 1643. Varlaam's *Carte românească,* also known as *Cazania,* consists of Romanian adaptations of religious texts translated from Slavonic. In his preface, Varlaam explained that his intention had been to offer the fruit of his endeavors "to the entire Romanian kin" (*"cătră toată seminţia românească"*), his translations being "a gift to the Romanian language" (*"un dar limbii româneşti"*). Credited to be the first book printed in the **Romanian language**, it enjoyed a wide circulation in all Orthodox churches of Moldova, **Wallachia**, and **Transylvania**. Metropolitan Varlaam headed the Church of Moldova for almost a quarter of a century.

VARNITA. A village on the outskirts of suburban **Tighina**, on the west bank of the **Nistru River** facing **Tiraspol**. The Tighina-Tiraspol bridge passes through Varniţa, which is a key checkpoint next to the east-bank territory controlled by the self-proclaimed **Moldavian Nistrian Republic**.

VARZARESTI MONASTERY. One of Moldova's most ancient monasteries, first mentioned in 1420 in an official act of donation by Prince **Alexander the Good.** Destroyed several times during the 18th-century **Russo-Turkish Wars,** the Vărzăreşti Monastery's church was twice restored (in 1770 and 1796). The village that gives the name to the monastery is located northwest of **Chişinău** in historic **Lăpuşna.**

VERSAILLES CONFERENCE. Peace conference (1919–1920) that officially ended World War I and redrew the map of Europe, in the aftermath of the dissolution of the **Habsburg, Russian,** and **Ottoman Empires.** Its provisions regarding the status of **Bessarabia** were signed into the Treaty of St. Germain by the Council of the Ambassadors on 28 October 1920, with Great Britain, France, Italy, and Japan as signatories. The document acknowledged Bessarabia's proclamations of union with **Romania** of March–November 1918 and gave recognition to Romania's eastern border on the **Nistru River,** while providing that the successor state of Russia—at that time still in a state of revolutionary turmoil—would be invited to adhere to it, once its situation stabilized. Great Britain ratified the treaty in 1921, France in 1924, and Italy in 1927; Japan never ratified it. Russia's successor state, established on 30 December 1922 as the **Union of Soviet Socialist Republics (USSR),** refused to adhere to its provisions, seeking instead to pursue one of its articles that called for Romania and Russia to negotiate at a later stage on any matters of dispute, through the arbitration of the League of Nations.

At negotiations conducted in Vienna in April 1924, such talks ended in deadlock over the USSR's insistence that a referendum be held in Russia's former province. A thaw intervened later on, when several pacts and international agreements to which Soviet Russia and Romania jointly adhered were interpreted as tacit status quo recognitions by the USSR of the Versailles provisions regarding Bessarabia. Such were the Moscow Protocol of adhesion to the Kellogg-Briand Peace Pact (9 February 1929), the London Convention regarding aggression (3–5 July 1933), and the Montreux Protocol between the USSR and Romania (20 July 1936).

The USSR and Romania established full diplomatic relations, with recognition of each country's sovereignty, on 9 June 1934. The Nistru border between the two countries was opened on 18 October 1935, when a bridge that established the railway junction between **Tighina** on the Romanian bank and **Tiraspol** on the Soviet bank was inaugurated with lavish official festivities on both sides. The Versailles system of treaties, including its Bessarabia component, was openly called into question at the outbreak of World War II, when both Germany and the Soviet Union sought to redraw the post–World War I borders of Europe. *See also* BORDERS OF MOLDOVA; MOLOTOV-RIBBENTROP PACT; WILSONIAN PRINCIPLES.

VIERU, GRIGORE (1935–). Poet and civic activist. A native of Pererâta, **Hotin**, Vieru made his literary debut in 1957 with the volume *Numele tău* (Your Name), a veiled allusion to the conundrum of Soviet Moldova's language and language-name controversies. Vieru is the author of numerous books that earned him the reputation of one of Moldova's main literary personalities. One of his most recent books, *Acum şi în veac* (Now and Across Time), was published in 1997.

VOCEA POPORULUI. A weekly newspaper published nationally in **Romanian** and **Russian** in **Chişinău**. It has been in print since early 1990 and covers economic issues and national and international human rights.

VODA. *See VOIVODE.*

VOIVODE. A Slavic synonym for ***domn*** or ***domnitor*** and a medieval title initially denoting a military leader in charge of a smaller territory called a *voivodate*. In central-southeastern Europe, the rulers of Moldova, **Wallachia**, and **Transylvania** were the only ones to hold the rank of *voivode* as a sign of power exerted over entire countries, not merely over small local administrative units. Its shortened form, *vodă,* was the usual title of Moldova's rulers, from the country's founders **Dragoş Vodă** and Bogdan Vodă (*see* BOGDAN I) down to its last ruling prince, Cuza Vodă (*see* ALEXANDRU IOAN CUZA).

VOLOCH/VOLOKH. Slavic form for "Wallachian" ("Volokh" is the Russian variation) denoting a cluster of Romanic people, mostly pastoral in occupation, unevenly spread out from the Carpathian basin over a geographical area extending both north and south of the **Danube River**, as far south as the mountainous regions of Macedonia, Albania, and northern Greece, and as far north as **Maramureş**. In different variants, the noun was used in the post-Roman world and the Byzantine epoch to denote such populations (other forms: Vlach, Valach, Wallach, Olah, Iflak). The Slavs appear to have borrowed the term from the generic name given by Germanic tribes in the fourth and fifth centuries to people who spoke non-Germanic languages. In his 1714–1716 *Descriptio Moldaviae,* **Demetrius Cantemir** observed that, in Slavic usage, Moldovans were

Volochs or Wallachians: "Poloni et Russi Moldavos Volochos . . . appellarunt" (Bucharest: Editura Academiei, 1973, p. 52).

An instance that illustrates the bivalent denotation of the term before 1812 is found in the Turkish denotation "Ak-Iflak" ("white" or northern Volochs) applied to Moldovans, while "Kara-Iflak" ("black" or southern Volochs) was applied to the population of **Wallachia**. Russia named two regiments of Moldo-Wallachian volunteers the "Black Volokh Hussars" and the "Volokh Ulans," organized by Marshal Kutosov to fight against the Turks in the last stages of the 1806–1812 **Russo-Turkish War**. In later Soviet interpretations, they were described as the ancestors of Moldova's first inhabitants and the founders of the land's customary laws, or **Jus Vallachicum**, after the establishment of the **Principality of Moldova** in the 14th century by Wallachian noblemen from Maramureș—**Dragoș** and **Bogdan I**.

VORNIC. An official nobility title in ancient Moldova (also spelled *dvornic*). The traditional units of **Țara de Sus** and **Țara de Jos** were each run by a *vornic,* exerting administrative authority in the territory in the name of Moldova's ruler, the *domn* or *voivode.*

VORONIN, VLADIMIR (1941–). Left-wing politician, former presidential candidate, and secretary of the Party of Moldova's Communists, born in Corjovo, in the district of **Dubăsari**. Voronin is a graduate of the Academy of Social Studies of the **Communist Party** of the Soviet Union (1983) and of the Moscow Academy of Internal Affairs (1991). In 1989, he was promoted to major general in the Soviet army. He garnered 13 percent of the vote in the 1996 presidential elections. In the 1998 parliamentary elections, his party came in first, garnering 30.01 percent of the national vote and winning 40 seats in the **Chișinău** Parliament. Short of an absolute majority, Voronin's Communists were eventually outnumbered in Parliament by the **Alliance for Democracy and Reforms**, a center-right coalition of three parties holding 61 seats in the legislature (V. N.). *See also* POLITICAL BLOCS AND PARTIES.

VORONTSOV, MIKHAIL (1782–1856). Russian military leader and statesman, Vorontsov was appointed in 1823 governor of the region of **New Russia**, which included, under a special status, the newly acquired **oblast** of **Bessarabia**. Under Czar **Nicholas I**, General Vorontsov was given discretionary power as *namesnik* of the province, to which he applied a set of new edicts known as the "Vorontsov Regulations." These regulations abolished the oblast's traditional statutes—still preserved in part under the 1818 statute, or "Aşezământul Obrazovaniei Oblastiei Basarabiei" (*see* ASEZAMANT)—and fully integrated Bessarabia into the general government of New Russia (Russian: Novorossiisk). Article 63 of the Vorontsov Regulations outlawed the use of the local language (called "**Moldavian**") in public documents and transactions and made the **Russian language** compulsory in Bessarabia's public administration. From 1844 to 1854, General Vorontsov was reassigned as *namesnik* over the Caucasus region. *See also* LANGUAGE ISSUE; RUSSIFICATION.

VULCANESTI. Chief town of the territorial unit of the same name, located about 200 kilometers southwest of **Chişinău** on the Cahul River, in **Gagauz Yeri**. Vulcăneşti was founded in the 17th century. In July 1770, an important battle of the 18th-century Russo-Turkish-Tatar Wars (*see* RUSSO-TURKISH WARS) was fought near Vulcăneşti. The district has a population of over 62,000 inhabitants (1993 est.).

-W-

WALLACHIA/VALLACHIA. Name given by foreigners to Ţara Românească or Muntenia, a former principality lying south of **Transylvania**'s Carpathian Mountains and bordered by the **Danube River**. Founded in 1330 by Basarab I (*see* BASARAB), it fell under Turkish suzerainty in 1417. It merged with the post-1812 **Principality of Moldova** in 1859, when its General Assembly elected Moldova's Prince **Alexandru Ioan Cuza** to reign over the **United Principalities**, later renamed **Romania**. Romania shook off Turkish suzerainty in 1877. Wallachia's last ruling prince before its union with the post-1812 Principality of Moldova was Barbu Stirbey (1854–1856). *See also* NATIONAL UNIFICATION.

WALLACHO-MOLDAVIAN LANGUAGE. Coined label used by Russian authorities in the early 19th century to denote the **Romanian language** without naming it. At the University of St. Petersburg (founded in 1819), where emphasis was put on the study of the languages of Russia's newly acquired provinces, such as Armenia, Georgia, and **Bessarabia**, the chair of Romanian was listed as the "Wallacho-Moldavian Chair" in the Foreign Languages Department. *See also* LANGUAGE ISSUE; MOLDAVIAN.

WAR DEPORTATIONS. During the first part of World War II (1941–1942), while battling the Soviet Union as an ally of Nazi Germany, under orders from Marshal **Ion Antonescu**, **Romania** deported huge numbers of Bessarabian **Jews** from the territory of present-day Moldova to **Transnistria**, at that time under Nazi military authority. According to Jewish statistics, between 55,867 and 56,089 Jews were taken from **Bessarabia** across the **Nistru River** and sent to concentration camps in occupied Ukraine, where they were used as labor corps, under the terms of the German-Romanian Tighina Convention of 30 August 1941. Many of them died or were exterminated in the process, which included many documented atrocities, war crimes, and crimes against humanity. Statistics that add to the number of Jews deported from Bessarabia, those deported from Romania and **Northern Bucovina**, say that a total of over 85,000 Romanian Jews died or were exterminated in the World War II deportations to Transnistria. Romanian leaders held responsible for ordering deportations and exterminations during the war were sentenced to death for crimes against humanity and executed by firing squad in June 1946. After the war, approximately 90,000 Bessarabian Jews returned to their places of origin in the towns and cities of the **Moldavian Soviet Socialist Republic**.

WATER RESOURCES. Moldova's water resources have been adversely affected by the extensive utilization and irrational exploitation of the natural **environment** that occurred during the Soviet era. Average water resources amount to 6.3 cubic kilometers in a normal year, 4.9 cubic kilometers in a dry year, and 3.4 cubic kilometers in a year of drought. Most of the total comes from the annual flow of the **Nistru** and **Prut Rivers**. Annually, about 11.5 percent of the total is regenerated. There are 3,621 permanent and periodic water sources in Moldova, with some 90 percent of them less than 10 kilometers in length. The territory comprises over 60 lakes, with a total water surface of 62.2 square kilometers. The largest meadow lakes—Beleu, Dracele, and Rotunda—are located near the inferior waterways of the Prut River. Moldova's main artificial reservoirs are in the **Costeşti**-Stânca sector of the Prut and in the **Dubăsari** segment of the Nistru.

WILSONIAN PRINCIPLES. These principles were contained in the famous Fourteen Points Speech delivered on 8 January 1918 to the U.S. Congress by President Woodrow Wilson, to provide America's guidelines for future territorial settlements, as World War I was nearing its end.

The Wilson doctrine advocated, among other things, that every nation had the right to "the freest opportunity of autonomous development," that "peoples and provinces are not to be bartered about from sovereignty to sovereignty as if they were chattels or pawns in a game," and that "well-defined national aspirations shall be accorded the utmost satisfaction that can be accorded them without introducing new or perpetuating old elements of discord."

The agreements reached at the **Versailles Conference**, which put an end to World War I, attempted to settle all territorial disputes in the spirit of the Wilsonian principles, which aimed "to put an end to all wars." With the expansionist rise in the 1930s and 1940s of Adolf Hitler's Nazi dictatorship in Germany and of **Joseph Stalin**'s dictatorship in the Soviet Union, they eventually failed to ensure lasting peace in Europe.

WORLD BANK. Moldova joined the World Bank in 1992, and in March 1995, the World Bank opened its Moldovan office in **Chişinău**. In conjunction with the World Bank, the government of Moldova established that same year a $30 million preexport guarantee organization, the **Guarantee Administration Unit**, which provides coverage against special political risks. Since Moldova joined the World Bank, the latter's commitments to Moldova have totalled over 10 multimillion-dollar projects, including two Private Sector Development Projects ($14 million), a General Education Project ($16.8 million), a 1998 Rural Finance Project ($5 million), and the 1998 First Cadastre Project ($11.5 million) designed to promote **privatization** of land and the development of real estate markets in Moldova.

In the aftermath of the 1998 national elections, the World Bank's regional director for Moldova expressed satisfaction with the prospects of Moldova's cooperation in implementing a new "partnership accord" to finance several projects, in keeping with documented evidence of progress in the way the country's economy performs. In July 1998, the World Bank granted Moldova a loan of $175 million meant to boost reforms helping the country stabilize its economic growth, improve its social security and insurance systems, and contribute to a radical transformation of its health, **energy**, and **agriculture** sectors. Also in 1998, 11 projects—including those for bridges, roads, medical facilities, and rehabilitation of schools—were implemented with World Bank assistance in Moldova. *See also* ECONOMY, NATIONAL.

-Y-

YEVNEVICH, VALERII (1951–). Commander in chief of the **Operational Group of Russian Forces** in Moldova, General Yevnevich is a graduate of the Ryazan Aviation College. He participated in the Afghan war, served in Soviet Turkmenistan, and was later promoted to command the Taman Division in the Moscow Military District. His division took part in the October 1993 suppression of a coup attempt in Moscow, for which he was awarded the title of "Hero of the Russian Federation." Yevnevich took over the command of the **Tiraspol**-based former **14th Army** of the **Russian Federation** in May 1995.

-Z-

ZEMSTVA. Administrative body in Russian-held **Bessarabia**. The *zemstva* system was created by Czar **Alexander II** as part of his emancipation and administrative reforms. Promulgated in 1864, the system was applied to the **oblast** of Bessarabia beginning in 1869. The competence of a *zemstva,* akin to a county council, included public service welfare, roads, food, education, hospitals, and medical and veterinary services. *Zemstvas* were dominated by landowners who held an ex officio majority over other categories of the czar's subjects, such as peasants and town inhabitants. The authority of the *zemstva* was limited and fell under the control of Russia's Ministry of the Interior and of the czar's governor, who was entitled to rescind any of its decisions.

ZUBCU-CODREANU, NICOLAE (1850–1927). Bessarabian revolutionary and a member of the Narodnik socialist movement that arose in Russia in the latter part of the 19th century. Zubcu-Codreanu was educated in **Chişinău**, where he graduated from the Orthodox Theological Seminary (1874). In 1875, due to czarist persecution of the Narodnik movement, he emigrated to neighboring **Romania**, where, together with **Zamfir Arbore-Rally** and other social democrats, he took an active part in the dissemination of leftist ideas.

ZUBRESTI. Village in the historic **Lăpuşna** region, included after 1999 in the newly reestablished *judeţ* of **Chişinău**.

Bibliography

INTRODUCTION

This bibliography reflects contrasting views of Moldova and the various assessments of it in works many times inspired by diverging historical perspectives—Western, Romanian, Russian, and, of course, Moldovan.

English-language scholarly literature on Moldova is sparse, as are works written on this subject in other languages of wider circulation. Most works on Moldova are in Romanian and Russian. This situation fittingly reflects the two main historic and cultural polarizations in the country's long march toward self-assertion.

A noticeable volume of Soviet literature on Moldova written in Russian (also in Romanian, but in the Russian alphabet) has been included in this bibliography. Its very bulk exemplifies the Soviet and pro-Russian perspective and will prove useful in establishing comparative reference fields apt to lead, in objective fashion, to a deeper understanding of Moldova's historic plight, first as an independent principality, then successively as a province of Russia, an odd member of the Union of Soviet Socialist Republics (USSR), and, lastly, in recent years, an independent republic of post-totalitarian Eastern Europe. A considerable amount of scholarly literature on Moldova is in the country's language, Romanian. Most of it reflects the other historical views on Moldova, either pro-independence or pro-Romanian.

In the spirit of objectivity, it was deemed appropriate to list this wide range of sources and trends of interpretation, an option that seems particularly proper in light of the fact that an overwhelming amount of Moldova's intellectual and academic life under the Russian and Soviet rules was expressed in Russian. Numerous works published in Russian during the Soviet era will be found to be out-of-date. Many of them reflect the tenets and dictates of Communist Russia's totalitarian ideology applied to other nationalities. Such works may still serve as a marker of Moldova's cultural history as drawn by imperial Russia in the 19th century and by Soviet Russia in part of the 20th.

As mentioned previously, before the country's proclamations of sovereignty and independence, the Russian Cyrillic alphabet was applied by the Soviet authorities to obfuscate the obvious Romance aspect of the Romanian language spoken in Moldova. For reasons of consistency, titles of works published under the Soviet rule in the Romanian language have been transliterated according to Western bibliographical practice, using Roman equivalents of Russian Cyrillics instead of the normal Roman alphabet of Romanian. The appearance of two versions of the same language in this bibliography is one more striking fact worth noting by the reader interested in deciphering the many facets of Moldova's culture and history.

The first section of this classified bibliography lists the principal tools of general access to information about Moldova. The interested reader will find works providing sources on periodicals, library science, toponymics, education, the economy, and other domains. Unfortunately, there is no standard bibliography for Moldova's history encompassing all of its events and transformations across time.

Section I.2, "General Information," on Moldova provides several strongly politicized Soviet-era encyclopedias. The chief work in this category is Iakim S. Grosul et al.'s eight-volume *Encyclopedia of Soviet Moldavia* (in Romanian in Russian Cyrillics, 1970–1981). A penetrating, balanced analysis of that work is Michael Bruchis's study "Moldavian National History, Ancient and Modern, as Presented in the Moldavian Soviet Encyclopedia," published in Donald L. Dyer's edited volume *Studies in Moldovan* (1996).

The "Guidebooks" section (I.3) offers samples of publications useful as general orientations. With a few notable exceptions, among them Nicola Williams's *Romania and Moldova* (1998) and Nicolae Cernomaz and Ion Pasecinic's *The Republic of Moldova Album* (1998), most of them reflect the Soviet-era angle.

Statistical information, both old and new, is provided by works listed under the heading "Statistics" (sec. I.4). Several titles in this category offer useful insights for anyone interested in drawing comparisons among official statistics, from a variety of viewpoints, in 1862, 1902, 1923, 1984, and 1994.

The "Travel and Description" section (I.5) provides sketches of places of touristic and historic interest, including Chişinău (Moldova's capital), Drochia, Căuşeni, Orhei, Soroca, and Tighina (Moldova's largest city on the Nistru River). Most of these books describe the places as an integral part of the old Soviet order.

For readers interested in the general coordinates of Moldova's beleaguered history, a comprehensive selection of titles will be found in the history section's "General Context" classification, which serves as an introduction to the detailed subsequent sections that reflect the main stages of Moldova's progressive history: ancient, medieval, premodern, as a province of imperial Russia, as part of Romania in the 1918–1940 interwar period, as part of the USSR during World War II and after, and, last but not least, as an independent state in the new, post-Soviet era. Several works treat Moldova's history as part of the multifaceted history of the Romanians; others treat Moldova's history as part of the history of Russia, later Soviet Russia.

An early description of Moldova as an object of Russia's great-power interest is found in Karl Marx's *Notes on the Romanians,* written in German—interspersed with English and French annotations—and published with a line-by-line accompanying Romanian translation in 1964. In this pamphlet, the circulation of which was prohibited in the USSR, the father of the Communist doctrine harshly condemns the czarist annexation of Bessarabia and its incorporation into the Russian Empire in 1812.

Comprehensive, factual approaches to that controversial subject are provided by American historian Keith Hitchins in two books: *The Rumanians, 1774–1866* (1996) and *Rumania, 1866–1947* (1994), particularly in the sections devoted to the 1812 annexation by Russia and the history of Romanians outside Romania. Useful for understanding the general context of Moldova's ancient and modern history are Charles Upson Clark's *Bessarabia: Russia and Roumania on the Black Sea* (1927) and Wim P. van Meurs's more recent work, *The Bessarabian Question in Communist Historiography: Nationalist and Communist Politics and History-Writing* (1994).

An early Russian viewpoint can be found in Pavel Krushevan's general *Bessarabia* (1903), in Antony Babel's *La Bessarabie: Étude historique, ethnographique, et économique* (1926), and in more recent books expounding Soviet Russia's perspective, such as Dmitrii Shemiakov's *History of the Moldavian SSR* (1971) and V. I. Tsaranov et al.'s six-volume work of the same name (1988).

The opposing viewpoint has been spelled out in such older works as Alexandre Boldur's *La Bessarabie et les relations russo-roumaines* (1927, reprinted in 1973), Nicolae Iorga's *La vérité sur le passé et le présent de la Bessarabie* (1922), and Gheorghe Bratianu's posthumous synthesis, *La Moldavie et ses frontières historiques* (1997).

For the reader interested in specifics of each and every relevant period of Moldova's history, the section on ancient history (II.2) offers specialized studies in the country's archeology, from the most remote ages, to the foundation of Moldova as an independent state in the 14th century, to the partition of the principality in 1812. A classic work on Moldova's history from ancient times through the 18th century is *Descriptio Moldaviae* (see sec. II.3), written in Latin in 1714–1716 by respected Moldovan scholar Demetrius Cantemir, a member of the Berlin Academy and a private adviser of Russia's Peter the Great. The work was first published in German as *Beschreibung der Moldau* in 1771.

The engaging and controversial subject of Moldova's history under Russian rule has been treated at length by Russian, Moldovan, and Romanian historians alike. The Soviet Russian perspective is evinced by virtually all works written in Russian (or in Romanian in the Russian Cyrillic alphabet) under Russian, later Soviet, rule. For those interested in the urbanization of Bessarabia under the czarist regime (an essential component of both modernization and Russification), V. I. Zhukov's *Goroda Bessarabii, 1861–1900* (1975) provides useful information, while the province's economic development under Russia before the advent of Soviet rule is described in D. E. Shemiakov's *Ocherki ekonomicheskoi istorii Bessarabii epokhi imperializma* (1980). For the reader looking for an overview of the main stages of Moldova's history, *Rossiia, Rumyniia, i Bessarabiia: 1812, 1918, 1924, 1940* (1976–1980) by Israeli historian Michael Bruchis is a useful instrument of access to the basics of factual knowledge on the subject.

Solid work on Bessarabia under the czarist rule has also been done by Barbara Jelavich, whose *Russia's Balkan Entanglements, 1806–1914* (1991) offers a balanced view of how Russia came to incorporate the province and, eventually, make it part of its empire. George Jewsbury's *The Russian Annexation of Bessarabia, 1774–1828: A Study in Imperial Expansion* (1976) is a helpful introduction to the 19th-century turning point that has shaped Moldova's history to the present day. For a factual assessment of the pro-Romanian viewpoint, Andrei Popovici's *Facts and Comments concerning Bessarabia, 1812–1940* (1941) provides a useful source. Conversely, a synthesis of the pro-Russian viewpoint can be found in I. A. Antsupov, D. M. Dragnev, and colleagues' work on the historic significance of Bessarabia's incorporation into Russia in 1812, which is also included in the list of works constituting the subsection titled "Under Imperial Russia."

Literature on the history of Bessarabia while a part of Romania during the 1918–1940 interval is generally included in histories of modern Romania. An exposition of the anti-Romanian viewpoint is to be found in J. Okhotnikov and N. Batchinsky's *La Bessarabie et la paix européenne* (1927). The pro-Romanian angle has been expounded by Emmanuel de Martonne in *What I Have Seen in Bessarabia* (1919) and by Andrei Popovici in *The Political Status of Bessarabia* (1931). Ion Ţurcanu's *Relaţii agrare din Basarabia în anii 1918–1940* (1991) presents an overview of Moldova's agricultural relations, a main component of its economy during the interwar years.

Books in Russian on Moldova as a Soviet Republic attempt to justify the Soviet rule as beneficial to Moldova. This viewpoint was defended in Semen K. Grossu's *La Moldavie soviétique* (1987) and, conspicuously, in Artem M. Lazarev's *Moldavskaya sovetskaia gosudarstvennost' i bessarabskiy vopros* (1974). The latter triggered several polemical responses, including Petre Moldovan's *A. M. Lazarev: Un faux-monnayeur de l'histoire* (1976) and

George Ciorănescu's *Bessarabia: Disputed Land between East and West* (1993). A well-documented study on the Moldavian Autonomous Soviet Socialist Republic as a launching pad for the Sovietization of Moldova after the 1940 annexation is Charles King's "The Moldovan ASSR on the Eve of the War: Cultural Policy in 1930s Transnistria," published in the collective volume *Romania and World War II* (1996).

Helpful introductions to post-Soviet Moldova are Matei Cazacu and Nicolas Trifon's *La Moldavie ex-Soviétique: Histoire et enjeux actuels* (1993), Michael Bruchis's *The Republic of Moldavia: From the Collapse of the Soviet Empire to the Restoration of the Russian Empire* (1996), and Charles King's *Post-Soviet Moldova: A Borderland in Transition* (1997). Ample factual information is offered in Helen Fedor's edited volume *Belarus and Moldova* (1995), in the Country Studies series published by the Library of Congress.

Under the heading "Politics" (sec. III), the reader will find three separate sections. "Government and Law" lists a selection of fundamental legal documents, such as independent Moldova's Constitution, promulgated in 1994. For the reader interested in drawing historical comparisons, Moldova's old-style Soviet Constitution of 1978 is a useful marker. The titles grouped under the subheading "Political Issues, Political Parties, Elections" offer a sampling of some of the significant studies describing Moldova's political arena today. Karen Dawisha and Adeed Dawisha's *The Making of Foreign Policy in Russia and the New States of Eurasia* (1995) brings together a solid set of studies addressing the general context of Moldova's situation as a successor state of the Soviet Union. In *Democratic Changes and Authoritarian Reactions in Russia, Ukraine, Belarus, and Moldova* (1997), Karen Dawisha and Bruce Parrott provide sharp analyses of the politics at work in the successor states of the USSR, including Moldova. The U.S. Commission on Security and Cooperation in Europe's reports on Moldova's parliamentary elections of 1992, 1994, and 1998 are also helpful tools in accessing the events that laid part of the groundwork for Moldova's democracy in the making.

The works listed under the subheading "Ethnic Groups, Minorities, Nationalism" are of particular importance to those interested in the complexity of Moldova's multiethnic patchwork. An informed introduction to the subject is Michael Bruchis's *Nations, Nationalities, Peoples: A Study of Nationalities Policy of the Communist Party in Soviet Moldavia* (1984), which explains Soviet Russia's dominance in preindependence Moldova. The context of the reverse situation, of Russians as a minority, has been aptly described in Jeff Chinn's *Russians As the New Minority: Ethnicity and Nationalism in the Soviet Successor States* (1996). Professor Chinn's study on "Ethnic Mobilization and Reactive Nationalism" (1995) focusses on the specifics of the case in post-Soviet Moldova. Another good approach to the specifics of the subject is found in William Crowther's "Nationalism and Political Transformation in Moldova" (1996), and Charles King's "Moldovan Identity and the Politics of Pan-Romanianism" (1994) is a solid analysis of one of the most relevant post-Soviet reactions to the prior process of forced Russification. Information on particular minorities such as the Gagauz and the Bulgarians, colonized by Russia in the 19th century, is also proffered by King in his "Gagauz Yeri and the Dilemmas of Self-Determination" (1995), as it is in A. Skal'kovskii's historic presentation of the Bulgarian colonization, *Bolgarskie kolonii v Bessarabii i Novorossiiskom krae* (1848).

The plight of the Jewish population of Bessarabia (where one of the earliest pogroms of the 20th century took place in 1903) has been aptly described in many works. *Easter in Kishinev: Anatomy of a Pogrom* by Edward Judge (1992) is a useful introduction to this long history of persecution. An overall view of the Russian persecution will be found in Michael Davitt's *Within the Pale: The True History of Anti-Semitic Persecutions in Russia* (1975). The tragic fate of Bessarabia's Jewry in World War II is amply documented in *Bessarabia, Bukovina, Transnistria*, volume 5 of Jean Ancel's *Documents concerning the Fate of Romanian Jewry during the Holocaust* (1986).

Finally on this subject, good introductions to ethnic discrimination and conflict in present-day Moldova are Erika Dayley's *Human Rights in Moldova: The Turbulent Dniester* (1993) and J. Stuart Kaufman's "Spiraling to Ethnic War: Elites, Masses, and Moscow in Moldova's Civil War" (1996).

In the section "Economy," the reader researching Moldova's main productive asset will find the first subsection useful for specific information on agriculture, although most works listed here are outdated Soviet-era studies devoted to farming, vine growing, crops, and harvesting regulated by the collective farm system of kolkhozes. The titles grouped under the subheading "Development, Industries, Market Economy" provide a useful presentation of post-Soviet Moldova's economic priorities. Publications on Moldova by the International Monetary Fund and the World Bank are primary tools of information and introduction to statistics. Arcadie Capcelea's *The Republic of Moldova on the Way to Sustainable Development* (1996) and Deborah Mabbett's *Social Insurance in the Transition to a Market Economy* (1996) offer useful insights into the coordinates of some of the most urgent issues confronting Moldova's current transition to a market economy.

The titles in the fifth main section, "Society," begin by addressing the issue of Moldova's ethnography. Iakim S. Grosul's collections (1977 and 1992) reflect the pro-Russian viewpoint, according to which Moldova's ethnographical background is to be interpreted as a separate entity of its own, distinct from common Romanian folklore and traditions. The pro-Romanian viewpoint is posited in Gheorghe Postică's work *Civilizaţia veche românească din Moldova* (1995), which focusses on the Romanian common denominator to Moldova's folk traditions and ethnographical background.

The subsection "Sociology, Education, Religion" lists titles that attempt to encompass three unequally represented areas. Since religion is playing an important part in present-day Moldova's rebirth to its traditional values, such works as Boris Buzilă's historical survey *Din istoria vieţii bisericeşti din Basarabia* (1996) and Paul Mihail's *Mărturii de spiritualitate românească din Basarabia* (1993) are helpful introductions to the specifics of this particularly topical area of societal expression, long suppressed under the Soviet rule. For those interested in the effects this aspect of the Communist regime had on mentalities, an interesting approach can be found in the collective work *Novyie grazhdanskie prazdniki, obriady, i rituraly: Prakticheskie rekomendatsii* (Zelenchuk and Loskutova, 1984), which illustrates militant atheism at work in Moldovan society in the post–World War II period. For a sociological incursion into rural life, before the advent of the Soviet era, a helpful tool is Boris Malski's *Viaţa moldovenilor de la Nistru, studiu sociologic al unui sat nistrean* (1939). The changing role of public opinion in shaping societal attitudes is expounded in Andrei Timush's *Opiniia publike: Aspekte sochiale* (1990). Assessments of the post-totalitarian perception of values are found in T. Comendant's study on the evolution of moral and spiritual values, "Evoluţia valorilor moral-spirituale în concepţia tineretului rural," published in *Buletinul Academiei de ştiinţe a Republicii Moldova* (1995), and in Andrei Eşanu's collection of essays *Valori şi tradiţii culturale în Moldova* (1993).

Under the general heading "Culture" (sec. VI), deemed of paramount importance in the Moldovan context, a first selection of titles focusses on linguistics and the landmark issue of the language. Dennis Deletant's "Language Policy and Linguistic Trends in the Republic of Moldavia, 1924–1990," Donald L. Dyer's "The Making of the Moldavian Language," and Charles King's "The Politics of Language in the Moldovan Soviet Socialist Republic" (published in the already mentioned *Studies in Moldovan*, 1996) and "The Ambivalence of Authenticity, or How the Moldovan Language Was Made" (*Slavic Review,* 1999) are essential reading. Also by Charles King, *The Moldovans: Romania, Russia and the Politics of Culture* (1999) provides an updated synthesis of the most relevant aspects of the political uses of culture in the Moldovan context.

On the subject of "Literature," a recent anthology by Mihai Cimpoi, *O istorie deschisă a literaturii române din Basarabia* (1996), is useful as a good introduction.

Lastly, under the general heading "Science" (sec. VII), this bibliography offers a few glimpses of the fields in which, not surprisingly, specific literature published during the decades when Moldova was part of the Soviet Union and, to a certain extent after 1991 as well, is mostly in Russian, the common instrument of scientific and technical communication in the former USSR. A sizable part of that earlier information has become outdated and was invalidated in recent years. The reader interested in current scientific research and studies in the areas of geography, ecology, geology, and public health will find them in the various publications sponsored by the Moldovan Academy of Sciences.

I. GENERAL

1. Bibliographies

Bodrug, Vera D., N. Ia. Grekova, and A. K. Karazanu. *Ekonomika Moldavii: Bibliograficheskii ukazatel' literatury za 1975–1986 gody* (Moldavian economy: Bibliographical reference for 1975–1986). Chișinău: Kishinyovskii Godudarstvennii Universitet (KGU), 1988–1989.

Ceaicovschi-Mereșanu, G. *Compozitori și muzicologi din Moldova: Lexicon biobibliografic* (Composers and musicologists of Moldova: A biographical and bibliographical lexicon). Chișinău: Universitas, 1992.

Chirtoagă, Valentina, et al. *Publicațiile periodice ale Moldovei Sovietice: Indice bibliografic, 1975–1985* (Periodical publications of Soviet Moldova: A bibliographical index). Chișinău: Cartea Moldovenească, 1990.

David, Alexandru. *Bibliografia lucrărilor privitoare la Basarabia apărute de la 1918 încoace* (A bibliography of works on Bessarabia published after 1918). Chișinău: n. p., 1933.

———. *Tipăriturile românești sub stăpânirea rusă (1814–1918)* (Romanian-language publications printed under the Russian rule [1814–1918]). Chișinău: n. p., 1934.

Grimsted, Patricia Kennedy. *Archives and Manuscript Repositories in the USSR: Ukraine and Moldavia.* Princeton, NJ: Princeton University Press, 1988.

Matei, N. P., et al. *Kartia Moldovei: Catalog jeneral* (Moldova's books in print: A general catalog). Chișinău: Shtiintsa, 1990–.

Nicu, Vladimir. *Localitățile Moldovei în documente și cărți vechi: Îndreptar bibliografic* (Moldova's towns and villages in ancient documents and books: A bibliographical directory). Chișinău: Universitas, 1991.

Pavlik, T. F., ed. *Razvitie knizhnogo dela bibliotechno-bibliograficheskoi deiatel'nosti v Moldove* (Development of printing, libraries, and bibliographic activity in Moldova). Chișinău: Shtiintsa, 1991.

Shaffner, Bradley L. *Bibliography of the Soviet Union, Its Predecessors and Successors.* Metuchen, NJ: Scarecrow Press, 1995.

Shpak, Ion. *Unele aspecte ale bibliografiei literare moldovenești* (Aspects of Moldovan literary bibliography). Chișinău: Shtiintsa, 1990.

Sleahtițchi, Mihai, ed. *Literatura istorico-pedagogica din Republica Moldova, 1940–1990: Indice bibliografic* (Historical and pedagogical literature of the Republic of Moldova, 1940–1990: A bibliographical index). Chișinău: Shtiintsa, 1992.

Spitalnic, S. *Evreii în literatura, arta și știința Moldovei: indreptar bibliografic* (The Jews in Moldova's Literature, Arts, and Science: A bibliographical directory). Chișinău: n. p., 1995.

Stoicescu, Nicolae. *Repertoriul bibliografic al localităților și monumentelor medievale din Moldova* (A bibliographical catalogue of places and monuments of medieval Moldova). Bucharest: Direcția Patrimoniului Cultural Național, 1974.

Sullivan, Helen F. *Russia and the Former Soviet Union: A Bibliographic Guide to English Language Publications, 1986–1991.* Englewood, CO: Libraries Unlimited, 1994.

Tkachuk, Z. K. *Zhivotny mir Moldavii: Bibliograficheskii ukazatel' literatury za 1969–1978 gody* (Animals in Moldavia: Bibliographical reference for 1969–1978). Chișinău: Shtiintsa, 1982.

2. General Information

Andrunakievich, Vladimir A., ed. *Sovetskaia Moldaviia: Kratkaia entsiklopediia* (Soviet Moldavia: A small encyclopedia). Chișinău: Glavnaia redactsiia Moldavskoi Sovetskoi entsiklopedii, 1982.

———. *Diktsionar enchiklopedik Moldovenesk* (A Moldovan encyclopedic dictionary). Chișinău: Redactsia Princhipale a Enchiklopediei Sovetice Moldoveneshti, 1989.

Batalden, Stephen K., and Sandra L. Batalden. *The Newly Independent States of Eurasia: Handbook of Former Soviet Republics.* Phoenix, AZ: Oryx, 1997.

Bezviconi, Gheorghe G. *Contribuții la istoria relațiilor româno-ruse* (Contributions to the history of Russo-Romanian relations). Bucharest: n. p., 1962.

Bruchis, Michael. "Moldavian National History, Ancient and Modern, as Presented in the Moldavian Soviet Encyclopedia." In *Studies in Moldovan,* Donald L. Dyer, ed. Boulder, CO: East European Monographs; distributed by Columbia University Press, 1996.

The Cambridge Encyclopedia of Russia and the Former Soviet Union. Cambridge: Cambridge University Press, 1995.

Ciobanu, Ștefan. *La Bessarabie, sa population, son passé, sa culture.* Bucharest: Imprimerie Nationale, 1941.

Colesnic, Iurie. *Basarabia necunoscută* (Unknown Bessarabia). Chişinău: Universitas, vol. 1: 1993; vol. 2: 1997.

———. *Sfatul Ţării: Enciclopedie* (An encyclopedia of Moldova's General Assembly). Chişinău: Casa Cărţii Petru Movilă, 1998.

Dragnev, Demir, et al., eds. *Istoria Moldovei: Din cele mai vechi timpuri pînă în epoca modernă: Aspecte din viaţa politică, socială, şi a culturii* (A history of Moldova from the most ancient times to the modern epoch: Aspects of political, social, and cultural life). Chişinău: Shtiintsa, 1992.

Eremia, Anatol, et al. *Nomenclatorul localităţilor din Republica Moldova* (A classified list of place-names of the Republic of Moldova). Chişinău: Fundaţia Culturală Grai şi Suflet, 1996.

Gosnell, Kelvin. *Belarus, Ukraine, and Moldova.* Brookfield, CT: Millbrook Press, 1992.

Grosul, Iakim S., et al. *Enchiklopediia Sovetike Moldoveniaske* (Encyclopedia of Soviet Moldavia). 8 vols. Chişinău: Akademiia de Shtiintse a Republichii Sovetiche Sochialiste Moldoveneşht', 1970–1981.

Olson, James, et al., eds. *An Ethnographical Dictionary of the Russian and Soviet Empires.* Westport, CT: Greenwood Press, 1994.

Timush, Andrei I., ed. *Literatura shi arta Moldovei: Enchiklopedie yn 2 volume* (Moldova's literature and art: A two-volume encyclopedia). Chişinău: Redacţia Principale a Enchiklopediei Sovetiche moldovenesht', 1985–1986.

Varo Inform's Directory: Moldova, 1997. Chişinău: Varo Inform SRL, 1997.

Vartichan, I. K., ed. *Moldavskaia Sovetskaia Sotsialisticheskaia Respublica: Entsiklopedicheskii spravochnik* (The Moldavian Soviet Socialist Republic: Encyclopedic guidebook). Chişinău: Glavnaia redaktsiia Moldavskoi Sovetskoi entsiklopedii, 1979.

Who's Who in Russia and the CIS Republics. New York: Henry Holt, 1995.

Who's Who in Russia and the New States. London: I. B. Tauris, 1993.

3. Guidebooks

Angeli, F. A. *Moldove, myndriia mia* (Moldova, my pride). Chişinău: Timpul, 1984.

Cernomaz, Nicolae, and Ion Pasecinic, eds. *The Republic of Moldova Album.* Chişinău: Litera, 1998.

Ghid de monumente şi situri istorice din Republica Moldova (A guide to Moldova's monuments and historic sites). Chişinău: Editura Shtiintsa, 1998.

Grossu, Semen K. *Sovetskaia Moldaviia* (Soviet Moldavia). Moscow: n. p., 1982.

Livshin, Moisei I. *Acquaint Yourselves: Moldavia.* Chişinău: Kartia Moldoveniaske, 1968.

The Moldavian Soviet Socialist Republic. Moscow: Novosti Press Agency Publishing House, 1974.

Moldova. Prepared by Geography Department, Lerner Publications. Minneapolis, MN: Lerner Publications Co., 1993.

Moldova: Open to the World—A Practical Business Guide. Chişinău: n. p., 1995.

Shuhat, M. *Moldavia: A Guide.* Moscow: Raduga Publishers, 1986.

Stoilik, Georgii V. *Moldavia.* Moscow: Novosti Press Agency Publishing House, 1987.

Twining, David T. *Guide to the Republics of the Former Soviet Union.* Westport, CT: Greenwood Press, 1993.

Williams, Nicola. *Romania and Moldova: From Tarzan's Birthplace to Ovid's Grave.* Melbourne: Lonely Planet Publications, 1998.

4. Statistics

Caracteristica social-economică a oraşelor şi raioanelor Republicii Moldova / Sotsial'no-ekonomicheskaia kharakteristika gorodov i raionov Respubliki Moldova, 1990–1992 (Romanian and Russian) (Social-economic characteristics of the towns and districts of the Republic of Moldova). 2 vols. Chişinău: Departamentul de Stat pentru Statistică al Republicii Moldova, 1993.

Dicţionarul statistic al Basarabiei, întocmit pe baza recensământului populaţiei din anul 1902, corectat prin datele actuale statistice ale primarilor şi prin tabelele birourilor de populaţie centralizate în 1922–1923 (A statistical dictionary of Bessarabia on the basis of the 1902 population census, updated with statistical data of current municipalities and population centers, tabulated in 1922–1923). Chişinău: Glasul Ţării, 1923.

Egunova, A. N., ed. *Zapiski Bessarabsksovo Oblastnovo Statistichestkovo Komiteta* (Notes of the Bessarabian oblast's statistical committee). 3 vols. Chişinău: Pechatatano v tipografii Oblastnovo Pravleniia, 1864–1868.

Larionova, V., ed. *Moldavskaia SSR v tsifrakh, 1924–1984* (The Moldavian SSR in numbers). Chişinău: Kartia Moldoveniaske, 1984.

———. *Narodnoe khoziaistvo Moldavskoi SSR, 1924–1984* (The national economy of the Moldavian SSR, 1924–1984). Chişinău: Kartia Moldoveniaske, 1984.

Lewis, Robert A., et al. *Nationality and Population Change in Russia and the Soviet Union: An Evaluation of Census Data, 1897-1970.* New York: Praeger, 1976.

Moldova. *Anuar statistic: Economia naţională a Republicii Moldova* (Statistical yearbook: The national economy of the Republic of Moldova). Chişinău: Universitas, 1990.

———. *Economia naţională a Republicii Moldova* (The national economy of the Republic of Moldova). Chişinău: Departamentul de Stat pentru Statistică al Republicii Moldova, 1992.

———. *Chişinăul în cifre: Culegere de informaţii* (The city of Chişinău in figures: A selection of information). Chişinău: Departamentul de Stat pentru Statistică al Republicii Moldova, 1993.

Republica Moldova în cifre (The Republic of Moldova in figures). Chişinău: Departamentul de Stat pentru Statistică al Republicii Moldova, 1993.

———. *Anuarul statistic al Republicii Moldova* (Statistical yearbook of the Republic of Moldova). Chişinău: Universitas, 1994.

———. *Report of the Government of Moldova for the World Social Summit, 6–12 March 1995, Copenhagen.* Chişinău: n. p., 1995.

Murgoci, Gheorghe. *La population de la Bessarabie: Étude démographique avec cartes et tableaux statistiques.* Paris: n. p., 1920.

Pashina, Ludmilla, and John Dunlop. *Newly Independent States of the Soviet Union: Statistical Materials.* Washington, DC: International Programs Center, Population Division, Bureau of Census, 1996.

Robertson, Lawrence R., ed. *Russia and Eurasia Facts and Figures Annual.* 24 vols. Gulf Breeze, FL: Academic International Press, 1977–1998.

The Republic of Moldova in Figures 1998: Statistical Pocket Book. Chişinău: Department for Statistical and Sociological Research of the Republic of Moldova, 1999.

Zaschik, A. *Materialy dl'a gheografii i statistiki Rossii sobrannye ofitserami gheneralnovo shtaba, Bessarabskaia Oblast* (Data provided for the Russian geography and statistics by the officers of the General Office, Bessarabian oblast). 2 vols. St. Petersburg: n. p., 1862.

5. Travel and Description

Bezviconi, Gheorghe G. *Mănăstirea Japca din judeţul Soroca* (The Japca Monastery in Soroca County). Bucharest: Fântâna Darurilor, 1942.

———. *Călători ruşi în Moldova şi Muntenia* (Russian travellers in Moldova and Muntenia). Bucharest: Institutul de Istorie Naţională, 1947.

Bogza, Geo. *Basarabia, ţară de pământ* (Bessarabia's landscapes of clay). Bucharest: Editura Ara, 1991.

Byrnia, P. P. *Orkheiul Vek'* (with French translation: *L'ancien Orhey*). Chişinău: Timpul, 1986.

Chelyshev, Boris D. *Itinerare literare din Moldova* (Literary travels across Moldova). Chişinău: Timpul, 1988.

Chirkov, Vadim A. *Mirakolele kanioanelor verzi* (with English translation: *Miracles of the Green Canyons*). Chişinău: Timpul, 1982.

Ciobanu, Constantin. *Biserica Adormirii Maicii Domnului din Căuşeni* (The Dormition of the Virgin Church in Căuşeni). Chişinău: Shtiintsa, 1997.

Colesnic, Iurie, ed. *Chişinău.* Chişinău: Museum, 1997.

Dorofeev, N. A. *Drokiia* (Drochia). Chişinău: Timpul, 1986.

Grekov, Iurii. *Puteshestvie domoi* (Travelling back home). Chişinău: Kartia Moldoveniaske, 1985.

Khazin, Mikhail. *Pushkin la Dolna* (Pushkin at Dolna). Chişinău: Timpul, 1989.

Korolitskii, A. N. *Soroki, gorod turistov* (Soroca for tourists) (with English and French translations). Chişinău: Timpul, 1984.

Korytnik, N. F. *Bendery* (Bender). Chişinău: Timpul, 1988.

Orlov, Naum A. *Kishineu—strezile povestesc: Yndreptar keleuze* (Chişinău's streets and their stories: A tourist's guide). Chişinău: Timpul, 1983.

Postică, Gheorghe, and Nicolae Constantinescu. *Căpriana.* Chişinău: Shtiintsa, 1996.

Sadoveanu, Mihail. *Orhei şi Soroca* (Orhei and Soroca). Chişinău: Glasul Ţării, 1921.

———. *Drumuri basarabene* (Travels across Bessarabia). Chişinău: Shtiintsa, 1992.

Tarasenko, Larisa V. *Moldova, sekvense chinematografiche* (Moldova in film snapshots). Chişinău: Timpul, 1984.

Viktorovna, Elena. *Across Moldavia*. Moscow: Foreign Languages Publishing House, 1959.

II. HISTORY

1. General Context

Adauge, Mihai, and Alexandru Furtună. *Basarabia şi Basarabenii* (Bessarabia and the Bessarabians). Chişinău: Uniunea Scriitorilor din Moldova, 1991.

Babel, Antony. *La Bessarabie: Étude historique, ethnographique, et économique.* Paris: Alcan, 1926.

Boldur, Alexandre. *La Bessarabie et les relations russo-roumaines.* Munich: Verlag Rumänische Studien, 1973 (reprint of 1927 ed.).

Bratianu, Gheorghe I. *La Moldavie et ses frontières historiques.* Bucharest: Semne, 1997.

Brzezinski, Zbigniew, and Paige Sullivan, eds. *Russia and the Commonwealth of Independent States: Documents, Data, and Analysis.* Armonk, NY: M. E. Sharpe, 1997.

Bugnion, M. *La Bessarabie ancienne et moderne.* Lausanne: G. Bridel, 1846.

Cherepnin, I. V., et al., eds. *Istoriia Moldavskoi SSR* (A history of the Moldavian SSR). Chişinău: Akademiia Nauk Moldavskaia SSR, 1965.

Ciorănescu, George, et al. *Aspects des relations russo-roumaines, rétrospective et orientations.* Paris: Minard, 1967.

Clark, Charles Upson. *Bessarabia: Russia and Roumania on the Black Sea.* New York: Dodd, Mead, 1927.

Colson, Felix. *De l'état présent et de l'avenir des Principautés de Moldavie et de Valachie.* Paris: A. Pougin, 1839.

Deletant, Dennis. "A Shuttlecock of History: Bessarabia." In *Studies in Romanian History.* Bucharest: Editura Enciclopedică, 1991.

Dvornik, Francis. *The Slavs in European History and Civilization.* New Brunswick, NJ: Rutgers University Press, 1962.

Florescu, Radu R. *The Struggle against Russia in the Romanian Principalities: A Problem in Anglo-Turkish Diplomacy, 1821–1854.* Iaşi: Center for Romanian Studies, 1997.

Giurescu, Constantin C., and Dinu C. Giurescu. *Istoria Românilor* (A history of the Romanians). Bucharest: Editura Albatros, 1971.

Gonţa, Alexandru. *Relaţiile românilor cu slavii de răsărit până la 1812* (The relations between the Romanians and the Eastern Slavs until 1812). Chişinău: Universitas, 1993.

Hitchins, Keith. *Rumania, 1866–1947.* Oxford: Clarendon Press, 1994.

———. *The Rumanians, 1774–1866.* Oxford: Clarendon Press, 1996.

Hughes, Lindsey. *Russia in the Age of Peter the Great.* New Haven, CT: Yale University Press, 1998.

Hupchick, Dennis P., and Harold E. Fox. *A Concise Historical Atlas of Eastern Europe.* New York: St. Martin's Press, 1996.

Ieremia, I., ed. *Moldova în contextul relaţiilor politice internaţionale, 1387–1858: Tratate* (Moldova in the context of international relations, 1387–1858: The treaties). Chişinău: Universitas, 1992.

Iorga, Nicolae. *La vérité sur le passé et le présent de la Bessarabie.* Paris: Champion, 1922.

———. *A History of Roumania.* New York: AMS Press, 1970 (reprint of 1925 ed.).

———. *Românii de peste Nistru* (The Romanians across the Nistru). Bucharest: Excelsior, 1990.

Jelavich, Barbara. "Russia, the Great Powers, and the Recognition of the Double Election of Alexander Cuza: The Letters of A. P. Lobanov-Rostovskii to N. K. Giers, 1858–1859." *Rumanian Studies,* vol. 1 (1970): 3–34.

Jewsbury, George F. "An Overview of the History of Bessarabia." In *The Tragic Plight of a Border Area: Bessarabia and Bucovina,* Maria Manoliu-Manea, ed. Los Angeles: Humboldt State University Press, 1983.

King, Charles. *The Moldovans: Romania, Russia, and the Politics of Culture.* Stanford, CA: Hoover Institution Press, 1999.

Krushevan, Pavel A., ed. *Bessarabiia: Geograficheskii, istoricheskii, statistichestkii, ekonomicheskii, etnograficheskii, literaturnyi, i spravochnyi sbornik* (Bessarabia: Geographical, historical, statistical, economical, ethnographic, literary, and reference source). Moscow: Tip. A. V. Vasil'eva, 1903.

Litvak, K. "The Role of Political Competition and Bargaining in Russian Foreign Policy: The Case of Russian Policy toward Moldova." *Communist and Post-Communist Studies,* vol. 29, no. 2 (1996): 213–229.

Marx, Karl. *Insemnări despre români: Manuscrise inedite* (Notes on the Romanians: So-far unpublished manuscripts), Andrei Oţetea and S. Schwann, eds. Bucharest: Editura Academiei Republicii Populare Române, 1964.

Meurs, Wim P. van. *The Bessarabian Question in Communist Historiography: Nationalist and Communist Politics and History-Writing.* Boulder, CO: East European Monographs; distributed by Columbia University Press, 1994.

Moraru, Anton. *Istoria Românilor: Basarabia şi Transnistria (1812–1993)* (A history of the Romanians: Bessarabia and Transnistria [1812–1993]). Chişinău: Editura Aiva, 1995.

Nedelciuc, Vasile. *The Republic of Moldova: Moldova, Basarabia, Transnistria: A Short History: State Organization, National Problem.* Chişinău: n. p., 1992.

Nistor, Ion. *Istoria Basarabiei* (A history of Bessarabia). Bucharest: Humanitas, 1991.

Oprea, Ion M. *România şi Imperiul Rus, 1900–1924* (Romania and the Russian Empire, 1900–1924). Bucharest: Editura Albatros, 1998.

Osservazioni storiche naturali e politiche intorno la Valachia e Moldavia. (Dal Signor Raicevich di Ragusa, consulo d'Austria in Moldavia.) Naples: G. Raimondi, 1788.

Riassanovsky, Nicholas. *A History of Russia*. New York: Oxford University Press, 1993.

Ruzé, Alain. *La Moldova entre la Roumanie et la Russie: De Pierre le Grand à Boris Eltsine*. Paris: L'Harmattan, 1997.

Rywkin, Michael. *Moscow's Lost Empire*. Armonk, NY: M. E. Sharpe, 1994.

Scurtu, Ioan, et al., eds. *Istoria Basarabiei de la începuturi până în 1998* (A history of Bessarabia from its beginnings to 1989). Bucharest: Semne, 1998.

Seton-Watson, R. W. *A History of the Romanians*. Cambridge: Cambridge University Press, 1934.

Shemiakov, Dmitrii E. *Istoriia Moldavskoi SSR* (A history of the Moldavian SSR). Chişinău: n. p., 1971.

Ţaranov, V. I., et al. *Istoria Republicii Moldova din cele mai vechi timpuri până în zilele noastre* (A history of the Republic of Moldova from the most ancient times to our days). Chişinău: Ministerul Învăţământului, Tineretului, şi Sportului, 1998.

Tsaranov, V. I., et al. *Istoriia RSS Moldovenesht'yn shase volume* (A history of the Moldavian SSR in six volumes). Chişinău: Kartia Moldoveniaske, 1988.

Vernadsky, George. *A History of Russia*. New Haven, CT: Yale University Press, 1961.

Voyage en Valachie et en Moldavie, avec des Observations sur l'histoire, la physique, et la politique: Augmenté de notes et additions pour l'intelligence de divers points essentiels. Translated from the Italian by M. N.-M. Lejeune. Paris: Masson, 1822.

Waldron, Peter. *The End of Imperial Russia, 1855–1917*. New York: St. Martin's Press, 1997.

Wilkinson, William. *An Account of the Principalities of Wallachia and Moldavia*. New York: Arno Press, 1971 (reprint of 1820 ed.).

Zhukov, V. I., et al. *Istoricheskoe znachenie prisoedineniia Bessarabii i Levoberezhnogo Podnestrovia k Rossii* (The historical significance of attaching Bessarabia and the Dnester region to Russia). Chişinău: Shtiintsa, 1987.

2. Ancient

Bichir, Gh. *The Archaelogy and History of the Carpi from the Second to the Fourth Century A.D.* Oxford: British Archaeological Reports, 1976.

Chaplygina, Nelli A. *Naselenie Dnestrosko-Karpatskikh zemel'i Rim v I-nachale III v.n.e.* (The population of the Dnester Carpathian area and Rome between the first and early third centuries A.D.). Chişinău: Shtiintsa, 1990.

Dergacev, Valentin. "Arheologia Republicii Moldova: Retrospectivă istorică" (The archeology of the Republic of Moldova: A historical retrospective appraisal). *Thraco-Dacica*, vol. 15, nos. 1–2 (1994): 7–18.

———, ed. *Arkheologiia, etnografiia, i iskusstvovedenie Moldavii: Itogi i perspektivy: Tezisy dokladov respublikanskoi nauchno-teoreticheskoi konferentsii, 8-9 augusta 1989* (Archeology, ethnography, and the arts in Moldavia: Conclusions and perspectives: Papers presented at the Scientific Theoretical Conference, 8–9 August 1989). Chişinău: Shtiintsa, 1989.

———. *Culturi din epoca bronzului în Moldova* (Bronze Age cultures in Moldova). Chişinău: Shtiintsa, 1994.

Dvoichenko Markov, Demetrius. "The Vlachs: The Latin-speaking Population of Eastern Europe." *Byzantion,* vol. 54, no. 2 (1984): 508–527.

Ghendiuc, Ion. *Populaţia Moldovei centrale în secolele XI–XIII* (The population of central Moldova in the 11th–13th centuries). Iaşi: Helios, 1996.

Ketraru, Nicolai A. *Din istoria arheologiei Moldovei: Basarabia şi Transnistria* (Selections from the history and archeology of Moldova: Bessarabia and Transnistria). Chişinău: Shtiintsa, 1994.

Khynku, Ivan A. *Vestijii stremoshesht'* (Inherited ancient vestiges). Chişinău: Shtiintsa, 1990.

Larina, Olga. *Culturi din epoca neolitică* (Cultures from the Neolithic Age). Chişinău: Shtiintsa, 1994.

Leviţki, Oleg. *Culturile Hallstattului timpuriu şi mijlociu în Moldova* (Early and middle Hallstatt cultures in Moldova). Chişinău: Shtiintsa, 1994.

Manzura, I. V. *Kamenskie kurgany* (The Kamensk hills). Chişinău: Shtiintsa, 1992.

Markevich, Vsevolod I. *Merturii ale trekutului* (with English translation: *These Remote Near Ages*). Chişinău: Timpul, 1985.

Popescu, Em. "Câteva consideraţii cu privire la rolul episcopiilor din Dobrogea (Scythia Minor) în viaţa creştină a Moldovei în secolele IV–XIV" (Annotations on the role played by the bishops of Dobrogea (Scythia Minor) in the Christian life of Moldova between the 4th and 14th centuries). *Studii teologice,* 2nd ser., nos. 5–6 (1991): 105–110.

Rafalovich, Isak A. *Dancheny: Mogil'nik cherniakhoskoi kul'tury III–IV v.n.e.* (Third- and fourth-century burial grounds of the Dănceni Cherniakov culture). Chişinău: Shtiintsa, 1986.

Sanie, Silviu. *Civilizaţia romană la est de Carpaţi şi romanitatea pe teritoriul Moldovei: Secolele II i.e.n.–III e.n.* (Roman civilization east of the Carpathians and the Roman presence on Moldova's territory in the second and third centuries A.D.). Iaşi: Junimea, 1981.

Smilenko, A. T., et al., eds. *Dnestro-Dunaiskoe mezhdurech'e v I–nachale II tys. n.e.* (The lands between the Dnester and Danube Rivers in the first and early second century A.D.). Kiev: Nauk, 1987.

Spinei, Victor. *Moldova în secolele XI–XIV* (Moldova between the 11th and 14th centuries). Chişinău: Universitas, 1994.

Teodor, Dan Gh. *Teritoriul est-carpatic în veacurile V–XI e.n.* (The territory east of the Carpathians from the fifth century to the 11th century A.D.). Iaşi: Junimea, 1978.

Vulpe, Radu. "La Valachie et la basse Moldavie sous les Romains." *Dacia,* n.s., vol. 11 (1961): 365–394.

3. Preannexation by Russia

Bătrâna, L. "Contribuţia cercetărilor arheologice la cunoaşterea arhitecturii ecleziastice din Moldova în secolele XIV-XV" (The contribution of archeological evidence to the knowledge of Moldova's church architecture in the 14th to 15th centuries). *Studii și cercetări de istorie veche și arheologie,* no. 2 (1994): 145–169.

Butnariu, V., ed. *Tezaure din muzeele orașului Chișinău: Secolele XV–XVIII* (Treasures in the museums of the city of Chișinău: 15th–18th centuries). Chișinău: Universitas, 1994.

Cantemir, Demetrius. *Descriptio Moldaviae* (A description of Moldavia) (Latin with Romanian translation). Bucharest: Editura Academiei, 1973; first published in book form in Frankfurt and Leipzig in 1771 as *Beschreibung der Moldau.*

———. "De antiquis et hodiernis Moldaviae nominibus" (On the ancient and modern names of Moldavia). *Manuscriptum,* vol. 4 (1976): 14–37.

Celac, T., ed. *Letopisețul Țării Moldovei: Grigore Ureche, Miron Costin, Ion Neculce* (A chronicle of the land of Moldova: Grigore Ureche, Miron Costin, Ion Neculce). Chișinău: Hyperion, 1990.

Chebotarenko, G. F. *Naselnie tsentral'noi chasti Dnestrovsko-Prutskogo mezhdurech'ia v X–XII vv* (The population of the midland between the Dnester and Prut Rivers in the 10th to 12th centuries). Chișinău: Shtiintsa, 1982.

———. *Sorokskaia krepost': Pamiatnik stariny* (The Soroca fortress: A monument to the past). Chișinău: Shtiintsa, 1984.

Cocârlă, Pavel. *Târgurile sau orașele Moldovei în epoca feudală: Secolele XV–XVIII* (The towns and cities of Moldova during the feudal age). Chișinău: Universitas, 1991.

Costin, Miron. *Chronicon Terrae Moldavicae ab Aarone Principe* (A chronicle of the land of Moldova from the times of Prince Aaron), E. Barwinski, ed. Bucharest: Socec, 1912.

———. *Grausame Zeiten in der Moldau: Die Moldauische Chronik des Miron Costin, 1593–1661,* A. Armbruster, ed. Graz: Verlag Styria, 1980.

Deletant, Dennis. "Some Considerations on the Emergence of the Principality of Moldavia in the Middle of the 14th Century." In *Studies in Romanian History.* Bucharest: Editura Enciclopedică, 1991.

Dragnev, Demir, et al. *Evul mediu timpuriu în Moldova* (The early Middle Ages in Moldova). Chișinău: Academia de Științe a Republicii Moldova, Institutul de Istorie, 1994.

———. *Moldova yn epoka feudalizmului* (Moldova in the feudal age). 6 vols. Chișinău: Shtiintsa, 1978–1992.

Dvoichenko-Markov, Demetrius. "Byrlad, the First Moldavian Principality." *American-Romanian Christian Literary Studies,* vol. 1 (1980): 92–116.

———. "Gheorghe Duca Hospodar of Moldavia and Hetman of the Ukraine, 1678–1684." *Balkan Studies,* vol. 31, no. 1 (1990): 73–84.

Elian, Al. "Moldova și Bizanțul în secolul al XV-lea" (Moldova and Byzantium in the 15th century). In *Cultura moldovenească în timpul lui Ștefan cel Mare* (Moldova's culture under Stephen the Great), M. Berza, ed. Bucharest: Editura Academiei Republicii Populare Române, 1964.

Episcopul Melchisedec [Bishop Melchizedech, in English]. *Viața și scrierile lui Grigorie Țamblac* (The life and the writings of Grigorie Țamblac). Bucharest: Tipografia Academiei, 1884.

Eşanu, Andrei. *Cultură şi civilizaţie medievală românească* (Medieval Romanian culture and civilization). Chişinău: Arc, 1996.

Fedorov, G. B., et al. *Braneshtskii mogil'nik X–XI vv* (The Brăneşti 10th- to 11th-century burial grounds). Chişinău: Shtiintsa, 1984.

Giurescu, Constantin C. *Le voyage de Niccolo Barsi en Moldavie, 1633*. Paris: n. p., 1925.

———. *Târguri sau oraşe şi cetăţi moldovene: Din secolul al X–lea pînă la mijlocul secolului al XVI–lea* (Moldova's towns or cities and fortresses from the 10th to the middle of the 16th century). Bucharest: Editura Enciclopedică, 1997.

Giurescu, Dinu C. *Ion Vodă cel Viteaz* (Prince Ion Vodă the Brave). Chişinău: Universitas, 1992.

Gonţa, Gh. *Ţara Moldovei şi Imperiul Osman—secolele XV–XVI* (The land of Moldova and the Ottoman Empire in the 15th and 16th centuries). Chişinău: Shtiintsa, 1990.

Grigoraş, Nicolae. *Ţara românească a Moldovei de la întemeierea statului pînă la Ştefan cel Mare, 1359–1457* (The Romanian land of Moldova from its foundation as a state to Stephen the Great, 1359–1457). Chişinău: Universitas, 1992.

Henry, Paul. "Le régne et les constructions d'Etienne la Grand, Prince de Moldavie, 1457–1504". *Mélanges Charles Diehl*, vol. 2 (1930): 43–58.

Holban, Theodor. "Contribuţii la problema originii şi localizării bolohovenilor" (Contributions to the question of the origin and localization of the Bolohoveni). *Studii Revistă de istorie,* vol. 21, no. 1 (1968): 21–26.

Iorga, N. *Studii istorice asupra Chiliei şi Cetăţii Albe* (Historical studies on Chilia and Cetatea Albă). Bucharest: n. p., 1899.

Kasso, L. *Bizantinskoe pravo v Bessarabii* Byzantine (Law in Bessarabia). Moskva: n. p., 1907.

Kirtoage, I. G. *Iug Dnestrovsko-Prutskogo mezhdurechia pod osmanskim vladichestvom: 1484–1595* (The southern lands of the territory between the Dnestr and Prut Rivers under the Ottoman rule: 1484–1595). Chişinău: Shtiintsa, 1992.

Kogălniceanu, Pseudo-Enache. *Letopiseţul Ţării Moldovei . . . , 1733–1774* (A chronicle of the land of Moldova . . . , 1733–1774), A. Ilieş and I. Zmeu, eds. Bucharest: Minerva, 1987.

Laurent, V. "Aux origines de l'Église moldave: Le métropolite Jéremie et l'évêque Joseph." *Revue des Études Byzantines,* vol. 5 (1947): 158–170.

Marieş, Stela. *Supuşii străini din Moldova în perioada 1781–1862* (Foreign residents in Moldova, 1781–1862). Iaşi: n. p., 1985.

Mokhov, Nikolai, and Demir Dragnev. *Rossia i osvoboditel'naia bor'ba moldavskogo naroda protiv osmanscogo iga, 1769–1812* (Russia and the liberation movement of the Moldavian People against the Ottoman Yoke, 1769–1812). Chişinău: Shtiintsa, 1984.

Nistor, Ion I. "Vechimea aşezărilor româneşti dincolo de Nistru" (The antiquity of Romanian settlements across the Nistru River). *Academia Română; Memoriile Secţiunii Istorice* [Romanian Academy; Memoirs of the History Section], seria a III-a, tomul XXI. Bucharest (1939), pp. 203–225.

Papacostea, Serban. "La Moldavie état tributaire de l'Empire Ottoman au XVe siècle." *Revue Roumaine d'Histoire,* vol. 13 (1974): 445–461.

———. *Stephen the Great, Prince of Moldavia, 1457–1504.* Bucharest: Editura Enciclopedică, 1996.

Podgradskaia, E. M. *Ekonomicheskie sviazi Moldovy so stranami Tsentral'noi i Vostochnoi Evropi v XVI–XVII vv* (Moldova's economic relations with the Central and Western European countries in the 16th to 17th centuries). Chişinău: Shtiintsa, 1991.

Postică, Gheorghe. *Românii din codrii Moldovei în evul mediu timpuriu* (Romanian settlements in Moldova's Codri in the early Middle Ages). Chişinău: Universitas, 1994.

Spinei, V. "La genèse des villes du sud-est de la Moldavie et les rapports commerciaux des XIIIe–XIVe siècles." *Balkan Studies*, vol. 35, no. 2 (1994): 197–269.

Sugar, Peter F. *Southeastern Europe under Ottoman Rule, 1354–1806.* Seattle: University of Washington Press, 1977.

Toma, Stela, ed. *Demetrii Cantemir Historia Moldo-Vlachica* (Latin and Romanian) (Demetrius Cantemir's Moldo-Wallachian history). Bucharest: Editura Albatros, 1981.

Velikanova, Marina S. *Antropologiia srednevekogo naselaniia Moldavii: Po materialam pamiatnika Staryi Orkhei* (Anthropology of the Middle Ages population of Moldova: Materials from the old Orhei monument). Moscow: Institut etnologii i antropologii RAN, 1993.

4. Under Imperial Russia

Antsupov, I. A., D. M. Dragnev, et al., eds. *Istoricheskii akt 1812 goda i ego znachenie v sud'bakh moldavskogo naroda: K 170-letiiu osvobozhdenia Bessarabii ot osmansgo iga i prisoedineniia ee k Rossii* (The year 1812 as a historical event and its meaning for the Moldavian people: A paper devoted to the 170th anniversary of the liberation of Bessarabia from under the Ottoman Yoke and the joining with Russia). Chişinău: Shtiintsa, 1982.

Bezviconi, Gheorghe G., ed. *Boierimea Moldovei dintre Prut şi Nistru: Actele Comisiei pentru cercetarea documentelor nobilimii din Basarabia la 1821* (Nobility of Moldova between the Prut and Nistru Rivers: The papers of the Committee for Researching Bessarabia's Nobility Documents in 1921). Bucharest: Fundaţia Regele Carol I, vol 1: 1940; vol. 2: 1943.

Bruchis, Michael. *Rossiia, Rumyniia, i Bessarabiia: 1812, 1918, 1924, 1940* (Russia, Romania, and Bessarabia: 1812, 1918, 1924, 1940). Tel Aviv: Nauchno-issl. tsentr Rosii i Vostochnoi Evropi Tel'-Avivskogo Universiteta, 1976–1980.

Casso, Leon. *Rusia şi basinul dunărean* (Russia and the Danube basin). Iaşi: Tipografia Alexandru Ţerek, 1940.

Cazacu, Petre. *Moldova dintre Prut şi Nistru: 1812–1918* (Moldova between the Prut and Nistru: 1812–1918). Chişinău: Shtiintsa, 1992.

Cernăvodeanu, Paul. *Basarabia: Drama unei provincii istorice româneşti în context politic internaţional, 1806–1920* (Bessarabia: Drama of a Romanian historical province in its international political context, 1806–1920). Bucharest: Editura Albatros, 1993.

Ciachir, Nicolae. *Basarabia sub stăpânire ţaristă: 1812–1917* (Bessarabia under czarist rule: 1812–1917). Bucharest: Universitatea din Bucureşti, Facultatea de Istorie, 1992.

Ciobanu, Ştefan. *Cultura românească în Basarabia sub stăpînirea rusă* (Romanian culture in Bessarabia under the Russian rule). Chişinău: Uniunea Culturală Bisericească, 1923.

Durandin, Catherine. *Révolution à la française ou à la russe: Polonais, Roumains, et Russes au XIX-ème siècle.* Paris: Presses Universitaires de France, 1989.

Dvoichenko Markov, Demetrius. "The Impact of Russia in the Danubian Principalities, 1806–1812." *South-European Monitor,* vol. 1, nos. 3–4 (1994): 24–51.

Eklof, Ben, et al. *Russia's Great Reforms, 1855–1881.* Bloomington: Indiana University Press, 1994.

Focas, Spiridon G. "Bessarabia in the Political Order of Southeast Europe in the 19th Century." *Acta Historica* (Rome), vol. 8 (1968): 119–144.

Grossul, Vladislav Ia., and Evghenii E. Chertan. *Rossia i formirovanie rumynskogo nezavisimogo gosudarstva* (Russia and the Constitution of the independent Romanian state, 1821–1878). Moscow: Izdatel'stvo Nauka, 1969.

Grosul, Ia. S., and I. G. Budak. *Ocherki istorii narodnogo khoziaistva Bessarabii, 1861–1905* (Reports on the history of the province of Bessarabia's economy, 1861–1905). Chişinău: n. p., 1972.

Jelavich, Barbara. *Russia and the Formation of the Romanian National State, 1821–1878.* Cambridge: Cambridge University Press, 1984.

———. *Russia's Balkan Entanglements, 1806–1914.* Cambridge: Cambridge University Press, 1991.

Jewsbury, George F. *The Russian Annexation of Bessarabia, 1774–1828: A Study of Imperial Expansion.* Boulder, CO: East European Monographs; distributed by Columbia University Press, 1976.

Jurasco, D. D. *L'influence russe dans les pays Moldo-Valaques depuis Koutchouk-Kainardji jusqu'à la Paix de Bucarest.* Chateauroux: Badel, 1913.

Kasso, L. *Rossiia na Dunae i obrazovanie Bessarabskoi oblasti* (Russia on the Danube and the establishment of the Bessarabian oblast). Moscow: n. p., 1913.

Kellog, Frederick. *The Road to Romanian Independence.* West Lafayette, IN: Purdue University Press, 1995.

Krupenskii, Aleksandr, and Charles Schmidt. *Pamphlets on Events in Bessarabia, 1917–1918.* Paris: Lahure, 1919.

LeDonne, John. *The Russian Empire and the World, 1700–1917: The Geopolitics of Expansion and Containment.* New York: Oxford University Press, 1997.

Marx, Karl. *Insemnări despre Români: Manuscrise inedite* (Notes on the Romanians: Unpublished manuscripts), Andrei Oţetea and S. Schwann, eds. Bucharest: Editura Academiei Republicii Populare Române, 1964.

Mihail, Paul, and Zamfira Mihail. *Acte în limba română tipărite în Basarabia (I) 1812–1830, precedate de bibliografia tipăriturilor româneşti din Basarabia 1812–1830* (Documents in the Romanian language printed in Bessarabia [I] 1812–1830, preceded by a bibliography of materials printed in the Romanian language printed in Bessarabia, 1812–1830). Bucharest: Editura Academiei Române, 1993.

Moraru, Anton. *Istoria Românilor: Basarabia şi Transnistria, 1812-1993* (A history of the Romanians: Bessarabia and Transnistria, 1812–1993). Chişinău: Universul, 1995.

Oprea, Ion M. *România şi imperiul rus, 1900–1924* (Romania and the Russian Empire, 1900–1924). Bucharest: Editura Albatros, 1998.

Pearson, Raymond, ed. and comp. *Russia and Eastern Europe, 1789–1985*. Manchester: Manchester University Press, 1989.

Pelivan, Ioan G. *La Bessarabie sous le Régime Russe: 1812-1918*. Paris: Lahure, 1919.

Popovici, Andrei. *Facts and Comments concerning Bessarabia: 1812–1940*. London: G. Allen and Unwin, 1941.

Popovschi, Nicolae. *Istoricul şi activitatea zemstvelor în Basarabia în curs de 50 de ani, 1869–1919* (The history and activity of Bessarabia's zemstvas across 50 years, 1869–1919). Chişinău: Tipografia Sfatul Ţării, 1920.

———. *Istoria bisericii din Basarabia în veacul al XIX-lea supt ruşi* (A history of the Church of Bessarabia under the Russian rule in the 19th century). Chişinău: Tipografia Eparhială Cartea Românească, 1931.

Poştarencu, Dinu. *O istorie a Basarabiei în date şi documente: 1812–1940* (A history of Bessarabia in dates and documents: 1812–1940). Chişinău: Cartier Istoric, 1998.

Seton-Watson, Hugh. *The Russian Empire, 1801–1917*. Oxford: Clarendon Press, 1990.

Shemiakov, D. E. *Ocherki ekonomicheskoi istorii Bessarabii epokhi imperializma* (Reports on the Bessarabian economical history during the imperialist epoch). Chişinău: Shtiintsa, 1980.

Trubetskoi, B. A. *Iz istorii periodicheskoi pechati Bessarabii 1854–1916* (Selections from the history of Bessarabia's periodicals, 1854–1916). Chişinău: Shtiintsa, 1989.

Urusov, Serghei. *Zapiska gubernatora* (Notes of a governor). Berlin: J. Ladyschnikow, 1907.

Văratec, Vitalie. "Sudul Basarabiei revenit în componenţa Principatului Moldovei la 1857" (Southern Bessarabia returned to the Principality of Moldova in 1857). *Destin românesc,* vol. 2, no. 6 (1955): 13–31.

Waldron, Peter. *The End of Imperial Russia, 1855–1917*. New York: St. Martin's Press, 1997.

Zalyshkin, Mikhail. *Vneshniaia politika Rumynii i rumyno-russkie otnosheniia, 1875–1878* (Romania's foreign policy and Russo-Romanian relations, 1875–1878). Moscow: n. p., 1974.

Zharkutskii, I. I., and Vladimir Mischevca. *Pacea de la Bucureşti: Din istoria diplomatică a încheierii tratatului de pace ruso-turc de la 16 (28) mai 1812* (The Peace of Bucharest: Diplomatic history of the Russo-Turkish Peace Treaty of 16 [28] May 1812). Chişinău: Shtiintsa, 1993.

Zhukov, V. I. *Goroda Bessarabii, 1861–1900* (The towns of Bessarabia, 1861–1900). Chişinău: n. p., 1975.

Zhukov, V. I., et al. *Voprosy istorii Moldavii XIX–nachala XX v* (Moldovan history issues in the 19th century and early 20th century). Chişinău: Shtiintsa, 1989.

5. Between the Two World Wars

Babii, Aleksandr I. *Moldavsko-russkie ideinye sviazi v epokhu revoliutsionnogo narodnichestva* (Moldovan-Russian ideological relations during the Narodnik revolutionary movement). Chişinău: Shtiintsa, 1991.

Bogos, Dimitrie. *La răspântie, Moldova de la Nistru: 1917–1918* (Moldova on the Nistru at a crossroads: 1917–1918). Chişinău: Shtiintsa, 1998.

Ciorănescu, George. *Bessarabia: Disputed Land between East and West.* Bucharest: Editura Fundaţiei Culturale Române, 1993.

Constantin, Ion. *România, marile puteri, şi problema Basarabiei* (Romania, the great powers, and the Bessarabia problem). Bucharest: Editura Enciclopedică, 1995.

Dobrinescu, Valeriu Florin. *Bătălia pentru Basarabia, 1918–1940* (The battle for Bessarabia, 1918–1940). Iaşi: Junimea, 1991.

———. *The Diplomatic Struggle over Bessarabia.* Iaşi: Center for Romanian Studies, 1996.

Donici, Leon. *Revoluţia rusă: Amintiri, schiţe, şi impresii* (The Russian Revolution: Recollections, sketches, and impressions). Chişinău: Universitas, 1992.

Esaulenko, A. S., and N. D. Roitman. *V. I. Lenin i pobeda Velikogo Oktiabria v Moldavii* (V. I. Lenin and the victory of the great October Revolution in Moldavia). Chişinău: Kartia Moldoveniaske, 1985.

Ghibu, Onisifor. *In vâltoarea revoluţiei ruseşti, însemnări din Basarabia anului 1917* (In the whirlpool of the Russian Revolution, notes from 1917 Bessarabia). Bucharest: Editura Fundaţiei Culturale Române, 1993.

Halippa, Pantelimon. *Testament pentru urmaşi* (A testament for the future generations). Chişinău: Hyperion, 1991.

Hitchins, Keith. "The Russian Revolution and the Romanian Socialist Movement, 1917–1918." *Slavic Review,* vol. 27, no. 2 (1968): 271–275.

Husărescu, Z. I. *Mişcarea subversivă în Basarabia* (The subversive movement in Bessarabia). Chişinău: Imprimeriile Statului, 1925.

King, Charles. "The Moldovan ASSR on the Eve of the War: Cultural Policy in 1930s Transnistria." In *Romania and World War II,* Kurt W. Treptow, ed. Iaşi: Center for Romanian Studies, 1996.

Martonne, Emmanuel de. *What I Have Seen in Bessarabia.* Paris: Imprimerie des Arts et des Sports, 1919.

Moisuc, Viorica, ed. *Basarabia, Bucovina, Transilvania, şi Unirea din 1918* (Bessarabia, Bucovina, Transylvania, and the 1918 Union). Bucharest: DIP, 1996.

Okhotnikov, J., and N. Batchinsky. *La Bessarabie et la paix européenne.* Paris: Association des Émigrés Bessarabiens, 1927.

Popovici, Andrei. *The Political Status of Bessarabia.* With an introduction by James Brown Scott. Washington, DC: Ransdell, 1931.

Stănescu, Marin C. *Moscova, Cominternul, filiera comunistă balcanică, şi România, 1919–1944* (Moscow, the Comintern, the Communist Balkan network, and Romania, 1919–1944). Bucharest: Silex, 1994.

Tatuiko, V. T., ed. *Vosstanavlivaia pravdu istorii: 1937, 1938, 1940* (Reestablishing historical truth: 1937, 1938, 1940). Chişinău: Kartia Moldoveniaske, 1989.

Ţurcanu, Ion. *Relaţii agrare din Basarabia în anii 1918–1940* (Land relations in Bessarabia, 1918–1940). Chişinău: Universitas, 1991.

Weber, Max. *The Russian Revolutions,* Gordon C. Wells and Peter Baehr, eds. and trans. Ithaca, NY: Cornell University Press, 1995.

Wojstomski, Stefan Witold. *Russia and the Principle of Self-Determination (1917–1918).* London: n. p., 1955

6. World War II and After

Afteniuk, Semen I. *RSS Moldoveniaske yn marele rezboi al Uniunii Sovetiche pentru aperarea patriei, 1941–1945* (The Moldavian SSR in the Great War for the defense of the Soviet fatherland, 1941–1945). Chişinău: Kartia Moldoveniaske, 1961.

Afteniuk, Semen I., et al. *Istoriografiia istorii kommunisticheskoi partii Moldavii* (Historiography of the history of the Communist Party of Moldavia). Chişinău: Kartia Moldoveniaske, 1985.

Andrushchak, Viktor E. *Sovetskaia Moldaviia v sotrudnichestve SSR s osvobodivshimisia i kapitalisticheskimi stranami* (Soviet Moldavia and its role in cooperating with the USSR in the area of liberated and capitalist countries). Chişinău: Kartia Moldoveniaske, 1987.

Brânceanu, Lidia, and Adina Berciu-Drăghicescu. *Basarabenii şi bucovinenii între drept internaţional şi dictat: Documente 1944-1945* (Bessarabians and Bucovinians between international law and the policies of diktat: 1944–1945 documents). Bucharest: Casa de Editură şi Presă Sansa, 1997.

Bulat, L., ed. *Basarabia, 1940.* Chişinău: Cartea Moldovenească, 1991.

Constantin, Ion. *Basarabia sub ocupaţie sovietică: De la Stalin la Gorbaciov* (Bessarabia under Soviet occupation: From Stalin to Gorbachev). Bucharest: Editura Fiat Lux, 1994.

———. *România, marile puteri, şi problema Basarabiei* (Romania, the great powers, and the Bessarabia problem). Bucharest: Editura Enciclopedică, 1995.

Dima, Nicholas. *From Moldavia to Moldova.* Boulder, CO: East European Monographs; distributed by Columbia University Press, 1991.

Dobrinescu, Valeriu-Florin. *Basarabia în anii celui de-al doilea război mondial: 1939–1945* (Bessarabia during World War II: 1939–1945). Iaşi: Institutul European, 1995.

Fischer-Galati, Stephen. "Moldavia and the Moldavians." In *Attitudes of Major Soviet Nationalities* (vol. 5). Cambridge, MA: MIT Press, 1974.

Gafenco, Grégoire. *Préliminaires de la Guerre a l'Est, de l'accord de Moscou (21 aout 1939) aux hostilités en Russie (22 Juin 1941)*. Paris: Egloff, 1944–1945.

Gill, Graeme. *Stalinism*. New York: St. Martin's Press, 1998.

Graham, W. Malbone. "The Legal Status of Bukovina and Bessarabia." *American Journal of International Law*, vol. 38 (October 1944): 667–773.

Grekul, Andrei. *Ynfloriria natsiei sochialiste moldovenesht'* (The flourishing of the Moldavian socialist nation). Chişinău: Kartia Moldoveniaske, 1978.

Gribincea, Mihai. *Basarabia în primii ani de ocupaţie sovietică: 1945–1950* (Bessarabia in the first years of Soviet occupation: 1945–1950). Cluj-Napoca: Dacia, 1995.

Grossu, Semen K. *La Moldavie soviétique*. Moscow: Editions du Progres, 1987.

Lazarev, Artem M. *Moldavskaya sovetskaia gosudarstvennost' i bessarabskiy vopros* (The Moldavian Soviet state and the Bessarabian question). Chişinău: Kartia Moldoveniaske, 1974.

Lebedev, Nikolai I. *Rumyniia v gody vtoroi mirovoi voiny, vneshnepoliticheskaia i vnutrepoliticheskaia istoriia Rumynii v 1938–1945* (Romania in World War II and Romania's foreign policy, 1938–1945). Moscow: Izdatelstvo Imo, 1961.

Loupan, Nicolas. *Bessarabie Terre Roumaine*. Brussels: n. p., 1982.

Manoliu Manea, Maria, ed. *The Tragic Plight of a Border Area: Bessarabia and Bucovina*. Los Angeles: Humboldt State University Press, 1983.

Matei, Valeriu, ed. *The Molotov-Ribbentrop Pact and Its Consequences*. Chişinău: Universitas, 1991.

Moldovan, Petre. *A. M. Lazarev: Un faux-monnayeur de l'histoire*. Milan: Nagard, 1976.

Mosely, Philip E. "Is Bessarabia Next?" *Foreign Affairs*, vol. 18 (April 1940): 557–562.

Pasat, V. I. *Trudnye stranitsy istorii Moldovy: 1940–1950* (A hard time in Moldova's history: 1940–1950). Moscow: Terra, 1994.

Pop, Adrian, ed. *Sub povara graniţei imperiale: Românii de dincolo de Prut de la ultimatumul anexării la proclamarea independenţei de stat* (Under the yoke of the imperial border: The Romanians across the Prut from the annexation ultimatum to the Declaration of Independence and statehood). Bucharest: Recif, 1993.

Postică, Elena. *Rezistenţa anti-sovietică în Basarabia, 1944–1950* (Anti-Soviet resistance in Bessarabia, 1944–1950). Chişinău: Shtiintsa, 1997.

Roman, Aleksandr T. *Partiinoe rukovodstvo sovetami Moldavii v period postroeniia sotstializma, 1924–1950* (The Communist Party leadership over Moldova's soviets during the era of socialist construction). Chişinău: Shtiintsa, 1988.

Sişcanu, Elena. *Basarabia sub regimul bolşevic, 1940–1952* (Bessarabia under the Bolshevik regime, 1940–1952). Bucharest: Semne, 1998.

Sişcanu, Ion. *Uniunea Sovietică-România, 1940: Tratative în cadrul comisiilor mixte* (The 1940 Soviet-Romanian Joint Commission negotiations). Chişinău: Arc, 1995.

Suga, Alexander. *Die völkerrechtliche Lage Bessarabiens in der geschichtlichen Entwicklung des Landes.* Cologne: n. p., 1958.

Tsaran, A. M., et al., eds. *Golod v Moldove, 1946–1947* (The 1946–1947 famine in Moldova). Chişinău: Shtiintsa, 1993.

Verenca, Olivian. *Administraţia civilă română în Transnistria* (The Romanian civil administration in Transnistria). Chişinău: Universitas, 1993.

7. Post-Soviet Moldova

Barbour, William, and Carol Wekesser, eds. *The Breakup of the Soviet Union: Opposing Viewpoints.* San Diego: Greenhaven Press, 1994.

Bater, James H. *Russia and the Post-Soviet Scene: A Geographical Perspective.* London: Arnold, 1996.

Berton-Hogge, Roberte, and Marie-Agnes Crosnier, eds. *Ex-URSS, les États du divorce.* Paris: La Documentation Française, 1993.

Bruchis, Michael. *The Republic of Moldavia: From the Collapse of the Soviet Empire to the Restoration of the Russian Empire.* Boulder, CO: East European Monographs; distributed by Columbia University Press, 1996.

Bucătaru, L., ed. *Istoricul an 1989* (The historic year 1989). Chişinău: Universitas, 1991.

Cazacu, Matei, and Nicolas Trifon. *La Moldavie ex-Soviétique: Histoire et enjeux actuels.* Paris: Editions Acratie, 1993.

Dawisha, Karen, and Bruce Parott, eds. *Democratic Changes and Authoritarian Reactions in Russia, Ukraine, Belarus, and Moldova.* New York: Cambridge University Press, 1997.

Fedor, Helen, ed. *Belarus and Moldova: Country Studies.* Washington, DC: Library of Congress, 1995.

Gosnell, Kelvin. *Belarus, Ukraine, and Moldova.* Brookfield, CT: Millbrook Press, 1992.

Gribincea, Mihai. "Challenging Moscow's Doctrine on Military Bases." *Transition,* vol. 1, no. 19 (1995): 4–8.

Karatnycky, Adrian, Alexander Motyl, and Boris Shor, eds. *Nations in Transit: Civil Societies, Democracy, and Markets in East-Central Europe and the Newly Independent States.* New York: Freedom House, 1999.

King, Charles. *Post-Soviet Moldova: A Borderland in Transition.* Iaşi: Center for Romanian Studies, 1997.

Knight, Amy. *Spies without Cloaks: The KGB's Successors.* Princeton, NJ: Princeton University Press, 1996.

Kurti, Lazslo, and Juliet Langman, eds. *Beyond Borders: Remaking Cultural Identities in New East and Central Europe.* Boulder, CO: Westview Press, 1997.

Lebed, Alexander. *My Life and My Country.* Washington, DC: Regnery, 1997.

Lucinschi, Petru. *Ultimele zile ale URSS* (The last days of the USSR). Bucharest: Editura Evenimentul Românesc, 1999.

Mikhailov, Valerii A. *Sub'ektivnye osnovy natsional'nogo dvizheniia* (Subjective foundations of the national movement). Saratov: Izd-vo Saratovskogo Universiteta, 1993.

Serebrian, Oleg. *Va exploda oare Estul? Geopolitica spaţiului pontic* (Will the East explode? The geopolitics of the Pontic Space). Cluj-Napoca: Dacia, 1999.

Sunley, Johnathan. "The Moldovan Syndrome." *World Policy Journal,* vol. 11, no. 2 (Summer 1994): 87–91.

———. "Post-Communism: An Infantile Disorder." *National Interest,* no. 44 (Summer 1996): 3–15.

Tomikel, John. *Russia and the Near Abroad.* Elgin, PA: Allegheny Press, 1996.

Tsurkan, Ivan A. *Basarabia din nou în faţa opţiunii istorice: Impresii şi mărturii privind mişcarea naţională a românilor basarabeni la sfârşitul anilor 80 şi începutul anilor 90* (Bessarabia one more time confronted with a historic option: Impressions and testimonies on the national movement of Bessarabian Romanians in the 1980s and 1990s). Chişinău: Universitas, 1994.

Twining, David T. *Strategic Surprise in the Age of Glasnost.* New Brunswick, NJ: Transaction Publishers, 1992.

Vinogradov, V. N. *Bessarabiia na perekrestke Evropeiskoi diplomatii: Dokumenty i materialy* (Bessarabia at the crossroads of European diplomacy: Documents and materials). Moscow: Izd-vo Indrik, 1996.

Wilson, Andrew. *Russia and the Commonwealth A to Z.* New York: HarperPerennial, 1992.

III. POLITICS

1. Government and Law

Actele legislative ale RSS Moldoveneşti cu privire la decretarea limbii moldoveneşti limbă de stat şi revenirea la grafia latină / Zakonodatel'niye akti Moldavskoi SSR o pridanii moldavskomu yaziku statusa gosudarstvennogo i vozvrate emu latinskoi grafiki (Romanian and Russian) (Legislation of the Moldavian SSR regarding the Moldavian language decreed the state language and the return to the Latin alphabet). Chişinău: Cartea Moldovenească, 1990.

Borodac, Alexandru, et al. *Drept penal* (Criminal code). Chişinău: Shtiintsa, 1994.

Constituţia Republicii Moldova adoptată la 29 iulie 1994 (The Constitution of the Republic of Moldova passed into law 29 July 1994). Chişinău: Moldpress, 1994.

Goria, N. K., et al. *Naznachenie nakazaniia po delam o nasilstvennykh prestupleniiakh* (Criminal punishment against violent crimes). Chişinău: Shtiintsa, 1991.

Gretsu-Livitski, Marichika. *Iuridicheskaia zashchita: L'goty i sotsialnye uslugi invalidam* (Legal defense: Benefits and social assistance for the handicapped). Chişinău: n. p., 1992.

Kirby, M. D. "Establishment of an Independent Judiciary in the States of the Former USSR: The Case of Moldova." *International Commission of Jurists* (Geneva), no. 51 (1995): 38–44.

Konstitutstiia (lejia fundamentale) a Republichii Sovetiche Sochialiste Moldovenesht' adopatate la sesiia a opta ekstraordinare a Sovetului Suprem al RSS Moldovenesht' de lejislatura a noua, la 15 aprilie 1978 (The Constitution [Fundamental Law] of the the Moldavian Soviet Socialist Republic . . . passed into law 15 April 1978). Chişinău: Kartia Moldoveniaske, 1984.

Moldova. *Acte normative cu privire la problemele economice si bugetare, 1990–1992: Legi şi hotarâri adoptate de Parlament şi decretele Preşedintelui Republicii Moldova* (Normative legislation regarding economic and budget issues, 1990–1992: Laws and decisions of the Parliament and executive orders by the president of the Republic of Moldova). Vols. 1–2. Chişinău: Universitas, 1992–1993.

———. *Normativnye akty po voprosam ekonomiki i biudzheta: 1990–1992 gody: Zakony i Postanovleniia Parlamenta, ukazy Prezidenta Respubliki Moldova, mai 1990–ianvar' 1993* (Normative acts on the economy and the budget: 1990–1992: Laws and decisions of the Parliament, decrees of the president of the Republic of Moldova, May 1990–January 1993). Vols. 1–2. Chişinău: Universitas, 1992–1993.

———. *Nalogi Respubliki Moldova* (Taxes in the Republic of Moldova). Chişinău: Tsentr issl. i razrabotok, 1993.

———. *Legislaţia ecologică a Republicii Moldova* (Ecological legislation of the Republic of Moldova). Chişinău: Biotica, 1999.

Moldova, Departamentul de Stat pentru Privatizare. *Acte normative cu privire la problemele privatizării: Legi şi hotărâri adoptate de Parlament, decrete ale Preşedintelui, hotărâri ale guvernului Republicii Moldova* (Normative legislation regarding the issues of privatization: Laws and decisions of the Parliament and executive orders by the president of the Republic of Moldova), V. Cesuev, V. Gitlan, and V. Guţu, eds. Chişinău: Shtiintsa, 1993.

Tsurkanu, V. I., P. G. Tostogan, and V. D. Kataraga, eds. *Spravochnik predprinimatelia: Normative akty i bukhgalterskii uchet* (The enterpreneur's handbook: Normative acts and accounting). Chişinău: Hyperion, 1992.

2. Political Issues, Political Parties, Elections

Carothers, Thomas, et al. *The Moldovan Parliamentary Elections: February 27, 1994.* Washington, DC: International Foundation for Electoral Systems, 1994.

Dawisha, Adeed, and Karen Dawisha, eds. *The Making of Foreign Policy in Russia and the New States of Eurasia.* Armonk, NY: M. E. Sharpe, 1995.

Dawisha, Karen, and Bruce Parrott. *Russia and the New States of Eurasia: The Politics of Upheaval.* Cambridge: Cambridge University Press, 1994.

———. *The End of Empire? The Transformation of the USSR in Comparative Perspective.* Armonk, NY: M. E. Sharpe, 1997.

Dawisha, Karen, and Bruce Parrott, eds. *Democratic Changes and Authoritarian Reactions in Russia, Ukraine, Belarus and Moldova.* Cambridge, England: Cambridge University Press, 1997.

Fischer-Galati, Stephen. "The Moldavian Soviet Socialist Republic in Soviet Domestic and Foreign Policy." In *The Influence of East Europe and the Soviet West on the Soviet Union,* Roman Szporluk, ed. New York: Praeger, 1976.

Jonson, Lena, and Clive Archer, eds. *Peacekeeping and the Role of Russia in Eurasia.* Boulder, CO: Westview Press, 1996.

Socor, Vladimir. "Moldova's Political Landscape: Profiles of the Parties." *RFE/RL [Radio Free Europe / Radio Liberty] Research Report,* vol. 11 (March 1994).

U.S. Congress. *Staff Delegation Trip Report on Moscow, Georgia, Moldova, and Belarus, June 25–July 4, 1992.* Washington, DC: U.S. Commission on Security and Cooperation in Europe (CSCE), 1992.

————. *Report on the Moldovan Parliamentary Elections, February 27: Chişinău, Northern Moldova, Transdniestria, Varnitsa.* Washington, DC: CSCE, 1994.

————. *Report on the Moldovan Parliamentary Elections: Southern Moldova, the "Security Zone," and Gagauzia, March 22, 1998.* Washington, DC: CSCE, May 1998.

3. Ethnic Groups, Minorities, Nationalism

Adler, Cyrus, ed. *The Voice of America in Kishineff.* Philadelphia: Jewish Publication Society of America, 1904.

Ancel, Jean. *Transnistria.* Bucharest: Atlas, 1998.

————, ed. *Bessarabia, Bucovina, Transnistria.* Vol. 5 of *Documents concerning the Fate of Romanian Jewry during the Holocaust.* New York: Beate Klarsfeld Foundation, 1986.

Aroni, Samuel. *Memories of the Holocaust: Kishinev (Chişinău), 1941–1944.* Los Angeles: University of California Press, 1995.

Banac, Ivo, and Catherine Verdery, eds. *National Character and National Ideology in Interwar Eastern Europe.* Yale Russian and East European Publications, no. 13. Columbus, OH: Slavica Publishers, 1995.

Barkey, Karen, and Mark Von Hagen, eds. *After Empire: Multi-ethnic Societies and Nation-Building: The Soviet Union and the Russian, Ottoman, and Habsburg Empires.* Boulder, CO: Westview Press, 1997.

Bârsan, Victor. *The Ilaşcu Trial: White Paper of the Romanian Helsinki Committee.* Bucharest: Editura Fundaţiei Culturale Române, 1994.

————. *Masacrul inocenţilor: Războiul din Moldova, 1 martie–29 iulie 1992* (The massacre of the innocents: The war in Moldova, 1 March–29 July 1992). Bucharest: Editura Fundaţiei Culturale Române, 1994.

Bollerup, Soren Rinder, and Christian Dans Christensen. *Nationalism in Eastern Europe: Causes and Consequences of the National Revivals and Conflicts in Late-20th-Century Eastern Europe.* New York: St. Martin's Press, 1997.

Bremmer, Ian, et al., eds. *Nations and Politics in the Soviet Successor States.* New York: Cambridge University Press, 1993.

Brubaker, Rogers. "National Minorities, Nationalizing States, and External Homelands in the New Europe." *Daedalus,* vol. 24, no. 2 (Spring 1995): 107–132.

Bruchis, Michael. *Nations, Nationalities, Peoples: A Study of Nationalities Policy of the Communist Party in Soviet Moldavia.* Boulder, CO: East European Monographs; distributed by Columbia University Press, 1984.

Budeanu, Gheorghe. *Transnistria în flăcări* (Transnistria ablaze). Chişinău: Universitas, 1993.

Carp, Matatias. *Cartea neagră: Fapte şi documente* (The black book: Actions and documents). 3 vols. Bucharest: Socec, 1946–1948.

Chebotar, Petr A. *Gagauzkaia khudozhestvennaia literatura: 50-80 e gg. XX v* (Gagauz literature in the 20th century, 1950s and 1980s). Chişinău: Shtiintsa, 1993.

Chinn, Jeff. "Ethnic Mobilization and Reactive Nationalism: The Case of Moldova." *Nationalities Papers,* vol. 23, no. 2 (1995): 291–325.

———. *Russians As the New Minority: Ethnicity and Nationalism in the Soviet Successor States.* Boulder, CO: Westview Press, 1996.

Ciobanu, Ştefan. *Unirea Basarabiei: Studiu şi documente cu privire la mişcarea naţională din Basarabia în anii 1917–1918* (The union of Bessarabia: Studies and documents regarding the national movement of Bessarabia, 1917–1918). Chişinău: Universitas, 1993.

Crowther, William E. "Moldova after Independence." *Current History,* vol. 93, no. 585 (October 1994): 342–347.

———. "Nationalism and Political Transformation in Moldova." In *Studies in Moldovan,* Donald D. Dyer, ed. Boulder, CO: East European Monographs; distributed by Columbia University Press, 1996.

Davitt, Michael. *Within the Pale: The True History of Anti-Semitic Persecutions in Russia.* New York: Arno Press, 1975.

Dayley, Erika. *Human Rights in Moldova: The Turbulent Dniester.* New York: Helsinki Watch, 1993.

Drobiszheva, Leokadia, ed. *Ethnic Conflict in the Post-Soviet World: Case Studies and Analyses.* Armonk, NY: M. E. Sharpe, 1996.

Duplain, Julian. "Chişinău and Tiraspol's Faltering Quest for Accord." *Transition,* vol. 1, no. 19 (1995): 10–13.

Dvoichenko Markov, Demetrius. "Transnistria: A Romanian Claim in the Ukraine." *Südost-Forschungen,* vol. 16, no. 2 (1957): 375–388.

Erich, Renata. *Ojtser: Das Schtetl in der Moldau und Bukovina heute.* Vienna: C. Brandstatter, 1988.

Feldman, Eliyahu. *Ba'ale melakhah Yehudim be-Moldavyah* (Jewish artisans in Moldavia). Jerusalem: Hotsa'at Sefarim'a sh. Y. L. Magnes, ha-Universitatah ha-'Ivrit, 1982.

Fisher, Julius. *Transnistria: The Forgotten Cemetery.* South Brunswick: Yoseloff, 1969.

Goberman, David Noevich. *Jewish Tombstones in Ukraine and Moldova.* Moscow: Image Publishing House, 1993.

Gradeshliev, Ivan. *Gagauzite* (Gagauz papers). Dobrich: Izdatelska kushta Liudmil Beshkov, 1993.

Hajda, Lubomyr, and Mark Beissinger. *The Nationalities Factor in Soviet Politics and Society.* Boulder, CO: Westview Press, 1990.

Hill, Ronald J. *Soviet Political Elites: The Case of Tiraspol.* New York: St. Martin's Press, 1977.

Iakovlev, Vasilii, et al., eds. *Bessarabskii vopros i obrazovanie Pridnestrovskoi Moldavskoi Respubliki: Sbornik ofitsial'nykh dokumentov* (The Bessarabian question and the Constitution of the Moldavian Nistrian Republic: A collection of official documents). Tiraspol: Respublikanskii Informatsionii Otdel-Gosudarstvennii Pridnestrovskii Korporativnii Universitet (RIO PGKU), 1993.

Institutul de Istorie şi Teorie Militară, Arhivele Statului Bucureşti, Arhiva Ministerului Apărării Naţionale. *Al doilea război mondial: Situaţia evreilor din România, 1939–1941* (World War II: The situation of Romania's Jews, 1939–1941). Bucharest: Fundaţia Culturală Română, 1994.

Ioanid, Radu. *Evreii sub regimul Antonescu* (The Jews under the Antonescu regime). Bucharest: Hasefer, 1997.

Ionescu, Dan. "Media in the 'Dnester Moldovan Republic': A Communist Era Memento." *Transition,* vol. 1, no. 19 (1995): 16–20.

———. "Russia's Long Arm and the Dnester Impasse." *Transition,* vol. 1, no. 19 (1995): 14–15.

Judge, Edward H. *Easter in Kishinev: Anatomy of a Pogrom.* New York: New York University Press, 1992.

Kaufman, J. Stuart. "Spiraling to Ethnic War: Elites, Masses, and Moscow in Moldova's Civil War." *International Security Series Reader* (MIT Press), vol. 21, no. 2 (Fall 1996): 108–138.

Kellog, Frederick. "The Structure of Romanian Nationalism." *Canadian Review of Studies on Nationalism,* vol. 11, no.1 (1984): 21–50.

Khazanov, Anatoly. *After the USSR: Ethnicity, Nationalism, and Politics in the Commonwealth of Independent States.* Madison: University of Wisconsin Press, 1995.

King, Charles. "Moldovan Identity and the Politics of Pan-Romanianism." *Slavic Review,* vol. 53, no. 2 (1994): 345–368.

———. "Eurasia Letter: Moldova with a Russian Face." *Foreign Policy,* no. 97 (1994–1995): 106–120.

———. "Gagauz Yeri and the Dilemmas of Self-Determination." *Transition,* vol. 1, no. 19 (1995): 21–25.

Kolstoe, P., with a contribution by Andrei Edemsky. *Russians in the Former Soviet Republics.* Bloomington: Indiana University Press, 1995.

Kolstoe, P., et al. "The Dnester Conflict: Between Irredentism and Separatism." *Europe-Asia Studies,* vol. 45, no. 6 (1993): 985ff.

Koprov, Ariel. *Jewish Life in Bessarabia.* Toronto: n. p., 1995.

Kuroglo, Stepan S. *Proshloe i nastoiashchee gagauzkoi zhenshchiny* (Past and present and the Gagauz woman). Chişinău: Kartia Moldoveniaske, 1976.

Lepidus, Gail, ed. *The "Nationality" Question in the Soviet Union.* New York: Garland, 1992.

Levin, Dov. *The Lesser of Two Evils: Eastern European Jewry under Soviet Rule, 1939–1941.* Philadelphia: Jewish Publication Society of America, 1995.

Lisetskii, A. M., et al. *Pravo na samobytnost'* (The right to native culture). Briansk: Grani, 1993.

Livezeanu, Irina. "Moldavia, 1917–1990: Nationalism and Internationalism Then and Now." *Armenian Review,* vol. 43, nos. 2–3 (Summer/Autumn 1990): 153–193.

——. *Cultural Politics in Greater Romania: Regionalism, Nation Building, and Ethnic Struggle, 1918–1930.* Ithaca, NY: Cornell University Press, 1995.

Marinov, Vasil A. *Na gosti u besarabskite bulgari: Istoriko-etnografski belezhki* (Visiting Bessarabia's Bulgarians: Historical and ethnographical notes). Sofia: Izd-vo Otechestvo, 1988.

Marunevich, Mariia V. *Material'naia kul'tura gagauzov, XIX-nachalo XX v* (The material culture of the Gagauz people in the 19th and the early 20th century). Chişinău: Shtiintsa, 1988.

Nistor, Ioan Silviu. *Istoria românilor din Transnistria: Organizarea, cultura, şi jertfa lor* (The history of the Romanians in Transnistria: Their organization, culture, and sacrifices). Bucharest: Editura Eminescu, 1995.

Oliner, Samuel P. "The Non-Russian Peoples in the USSR: An Unsolved Problem." *Ukrainian Review,* vol. 32 (Autumn 1976): 261–285.

Ozhiganov, Edward. "The Republic of Moldova: Transdnester and the 14th Army." In *Managing Conflict in the Former Soviet Union: Russian and American Perspectives,* Alexei Arbatov, et al., eds. Cambridge, MA: MIT Press, 1997.

Pogolşa, Nadejda. "Istoricul comunităţii evreieşti din judeţul şi oraşul Tiraspol până la 1917" (A history of the Jewish community in the city and district of Tiraspol before 1917). *Tyragetia,* nos. 6–7 (1998): 317–321.

Radova, O. K. "Gagauzy Bessarabii Rasselenie i chislennost' v XIX v" (The Gagauz people of Bessarabia, location area and numbers in the 19th century). *Etnograficheskiie obozrenie,* vol. 1 (1997): 121–128.

Saka, Serafim. *Basarabia în Gulag* (Bessarabia in the gulag). Chişinău: Meridianul 28, 1995.

Seymore, Bruce. *The Access Guide to Ethnic Conflicts in Europe and the Former Soviet Union.* Washington, DC: Access, 1994.

Shachan, Avigdor. *Burning Ice: The Ghettos of Transnistria.* Boulder, CO: East European Monographs; distributed by Columbia University Press, 1996.

Skal'kovskii, A. A. *Bolgarskie kolonii v Bessarabii i Novorossiiskom krae* (The Bulgarian colonies of Bessarabia and the New Russia province). St. Petersburg: V tipografii Ministerstva vnutrennikh del, 1848.

Smith, Graham, ed. *The Nationalities Question in the Post-Soviet States.* London: Longman, 1996.

Starr, Frederick, ed. *The Legacy of Russia and the Post-Soviet States of Eurasia.* Armonk, NY: M. E. Sharpe, 1994.

Steinberg, Fannie. *Birthday in Kishinev.* Philadelphia: Jewish Publication Society of America, 1978.

Stoenescu, Alex Mihai. *Armata, mareşalul, şi evreii* (The army, the marshal, and the Jews). Bucharest: Editura RAO, 1998.

Sugar, Peter. *Nationality and Society in Central and South-Eastern Europe, 18th and 19th Centuries.* Brookfield, VT: Variorum, 1997.

Szporluk, Roman, ed. *National Identity and Ethnicity in Russia and the New States of Eurasia.* Armonk, NY: M. E. Sharpe, 1994.

Troebst, Stefan. "Die bulgarische Minderheit Moldovas zwischen national-staatlichem Zentralismus, gagausischem Autonomismus und transnistrichem Separatismus (1991–1995)." *Südeuropa,* vol. 44 (1955): 560–584.

Ursu, Valentina. *Rîul de sânge* (A river of blood). Chişinău: Editura Basarabia, 1993.

Urussov, S. P. *Memoirs of a Russian Governor, Prince Serge Dmitriyevici Urussov: The Kishinev Pogrom,* H. Rosenthal, ed. New York: Bergman Publishers, 1970.

Weiss, Immanuel. *Bessarabian Knight: A Peasant Caught between the Red Star and the Swastika.* Lincoln, NE: American Historical Society of Germans from Russia, 1991.

IV. ECONOMY

1. Agriculture, Farming

Chertan, S. I., et al. *Agrarnaia ekonomika v usloviiakh rynochnykh otnoshenii* (The development of agricultural economy under conditions of free market relations). Chişinău: Shtiintsa, 1992.

Dumitrashko, Mikhail I. *Sistema udobreniia v intensivnom polevodstve na chernozemakh* (Fertilization systems in intensive farming of chernozem soils). Chişinău: Shtiintsa, 1992.

Fedoriaka, V. P., et al., eds. *Nauchnoe obespechenie zhivotnovodstva Moldavii* (Scientific support for cattle raising in Moldavia). Chişinău: Shtiintsa, 1989.

Ganenko, V. P. *Gumus pochv Moldovy i ego transformatsiia pod vliianiem udobrenii* (Humus in Moldova's soils and changes caused by fertilizers). Chişinău: Shtiintsa, 1991.

Gribincea, Mihai. *Agricultural Collectivization in Moldavia: Basarabia during Stalinism, 1944–1950.* Boulder, CO: East European Monographs; distributed by Columbia University Press, 1996.

Grosul, Iakim S. *Istoriia narodnogo khoziaistva Moldavskoi SSR* (A history of the national economy of the Moldavian SSR). Chişinău: Academiia de Shtiintse a RSSM, 1976.

Komanich, I. G. *Otdalennaia gibridizatsiia vidov orekha* (Remote irrigation techniques for walnut orchards). Chişinău: Shtiintsa, 1989.

Konstantinova, T. S., ed. *Regional'nye ekologicheskie problemy* (Regional ecological issues). Chişinău: Shtiintsa, 1992.

Kozhokar, Evghenia V. *Organizatsionno-pravovye problemy agrokhimicheskogo obsluzhivaniia v Respublike Moldova* (Organizational and legal issues of the agro-chemical service in the Republic of Moldova). Chişinău: Shtiintsa, 1991.

Kozub, Georgii I. *Marochnye i igritsie vina Moldavii* (Table wines and sparkling wines of Moldova). Chişinău: Kartia Moldoveniaske, 1983.

Krupenikov, I. A. *Pochvennyi pokrov Moldovy: Proshloe, nastoiashchee, upravlenie, prognoz* (Moldova's soils: Past, present, management, prognosis). Chişinău: Shtiintsa, 1992.

Levadniuk, Andrei T., et al., eds. *Geograficheskie aspekty issledovannia APK Moldavii* (Geographical aspects of Moldavian studies). Chişinău: Shtiintsa, 1986.

Mishchenko, Z. A., ed. *Agroklimaticheskie resursy i mikroklimat Moldavii* (Agroclimatic resources and microclimate conditions in Moldavia). Chişinău: Shtiintsa, 1988.

Osadchii, V. K. *Optimal'noe planirovanie material'no-tekhnicheskoi bazy sel'skokhoziaistvennogo proizvodstva* (Optimal methods for planning supplies of agricultural production). Chişinău: Shtiintsa, 1990.

Paskall, V. A., ed. *Kukuruza v Moldavii* (Corn crops of Moldova). Chişinău: Kartia Moldoveniaske, 1985.

Talda, Nikolai E. *Soiuri de viţă de vie în Moldova* (Moldova's vine species). Chişinău: Cartea Moldovenească, 1990.

Targon, P. G., ed. *Pochvy Moldovy i ikh izmenenie v usloviiakh intensivnogo zemledeliia* (Moldova's soils and the changes they underwent under intensive farming). Chişinău: Shtiintsa, 1991.

Tsopa, A. G., O. A. Byrlad, and L. S. Bulat. *Pomikultura Moldovei, 1918–1982* (Fruit growing in Moldova, 1918–1982). Chişinău: Kartia Moldoveniaske, 1988.

Tsurkan, I. A. *Satul basarabian yn anii 1918–1940: Studii sochial-ekonomiche* (Bessarabian villages, 1918–1940: Social-economic studies). Chişinău: Kartia Moldoveniaske, 1980.

Ursu, Viacheslav A. *Matochniki privoinykh loz intensivnogo tipa i uskorennoe razmnozhenie vinograda* (Intensive methods for vine cutting and expanding vineyard production). Chişinău: Shtiintsa, 1989.

2. Development, Industries, Market Economy

Agapova, A. L., et al. *Rynok i sovremennaia ekonomika* (Modern market economy). Chişinău: Shtiintsa, 1992.

Averbukh, R. S. *Sistemnyi analiz problem ekonomicheskogo razvitiia regiona* (System analysis of the economical development of a region). Chişinău: Shtiintsa, 1990.

Belarus and Moldova (Country Report). Second Quarter 1998. London: Economist Intelligence Unit, 1998.

Bran, P. "Preocupări economice şi monetare în Republica Moldova" (Economic and monetary issues in the Republic of Moldova). *Tribuna economică*, no. 35 (1995): 5–6.

Capcelea, Arcadie. *The Republic of Moldova on the Way to Sustainable Development.* Chişinău: Shtiintsa, 1996.

Ciobanu, Gh. "Crearea şi funcţionarea pieţei de capital în Republica Moldova" (Creating and operating capital markets in the Republic of Moldova). *Tribuna economică*, no. 20 (1996): 20.

Comendant, I. *Proiectul strategiei de dezvoltare a complexului energetic al Republicii Moldova pînă în anul 2005* (The project for developing the energy-producing sector of the Republic of Moldova until the year 2005). Chişinău: Analele Institutului de Energetică al Academiei de Ştiinţe a Republicii Moldova, 1996.

Darakhovskii, I. S., et al. *Organizatsionnye problemy upravleniia proizvodstvom: Na materialakh pishchevoi promyshlennosti* (Issues dealing with organizational management: The case of food-processing industries). Chişinău: Shtiintsa, 1991.

D'iakonova, M. E., P. V. Kozhukhar, and I. A. Novoselskii. *Modeli i metody planirovaniia mezhotraslevykh proportsii* (Interdisciplinary planning models and methods). Chişinău: Shtiintsa, 1990.

Graham, G. "Taking Pledges in Moldova." *East European Business Law,* vol. 12 (1995): 5–7.

Guţu, Ion. *Republica Moldova: Economia in tranziţie* (The Republic of Moldova: An economy in transition). Chişinău: Litera, 1998.

International Monetary Fund. *Common Issues and Interrepublic Relations in the Former USSR.* Economic Review series. Washington, DC: IMF, 1992.

———. *Moldova.* Economic Review series. Washington, DC: IMF, 1994.

———. *Moldova's Reforms Emphasize Post-Privatization Restructuring. Surveys,* vol. 25, no. 12. Washington, DC: IMF, 1996.

Iuferev, O. V., V. A. Samusaenko, and V. F. Shakhmatov. *Biznes karta: Moldova, Ukraina, Iuzhnyi raion: Promyshlennost'* (Business map of the industries of Moldova, Ukraine, and the southern areas). Moscow: Nauka, 1992.

Kaminski, Bartolomiej, ed. *Economic Transition in Russia and the New States of Eurasia.* Armonk, NY: M. E. Sharpe, 1996.

Kazakov, Leonid. *Logos press predstavliaet Moldavskii biznis: Kto est' kto?* (Logos Press introduces Moldovan business: A business who's who). Chişinău: Litera, 1995.

Khrishchev, E. I., et al. *Intensifikatsiia i rezervy ekonomicheskogo rosta: Sushchnost', faktory, stimuly* (Intensification and resources of economical growth: Components and stimulation). Chişinău: Shtiintsa, 1991.

Kosinova, Ekaterina F. *Vsenarodnoe dvizhenia za vosstanovlenie i razvitie promyshlesnnosti Moldavskoi SSR, 1944–1950* (Popular movements for industrial rehabilitation and development of the Moldavian SSR, 1944–1950). Chişinău: Shtiintsa, 1988.

Mabbett, Deborah. *Social Insurance in the Transition to a Market Economy: Theoretical Issues with Application to Moldova.* Washington, DC: World Bank, 1996.

"Moldova: The Fruits of Peace." *Euromoney* (September 1996): 428–438.

Nikolskii, I. V., et al. *Ekonomiko-geograficheskie problemy transporta Moldavskoi SSR* (Economical and geographical problems of transportation in the Moldavian SSR). Chişinău: Shtiintsa, 1981.

Novikova, L. I. *Ekonomicheskie problemy razvitiia promyshlennosti stroitel'nykh matrialov i konstruktsii* (Issues dealing with economical development in the construction and construction supplies industry). Chişinău: Shtiintsa, 1991.

Palmieri, Deborah Anne, ed. *Russia and the NIS in the World Economy: East-West Investment, Financing, and Trade.* Westport, CT: Praeger, 1994.

Roşca, A., et al., eds. *Tineretul Republicii în perioada de tranziție la economia de piață: Probleme și soluții* (Moldova's youth in the period of transition to a market economy: Issues and solutions). Chişinău: Institutul de Filosofie, Sociologie, și Drept al Academiei de Științe a Republicii Moldova, 1993.

Rossiia i SNG: Dezintegratsionnye i integratsionnye protsessy (Russia and the NIS in the world economy: East-West investment, financing, and trade). Pod redaktsiei G. D. Kostinskogo (Russian for "under the editorship of G. D. Kostinsko"). Moscow: Vash Vybor, 1995.

Rozhko, A. A. "Metodicheskie voprosy identifikatsii maloobespechennosti naseleniia v usloviiakh perekhoda k rynochnoi ekonomike" (Issues dealing with the methodological identification of impoverished population during the transition to the market economy). *Izvestia Akademii nauk Respubliki Moldova. Ekonomika i sotsiologiia,* no. 1 (1995): 22–31.

Safronov, Iu. M., et al. *Problemy povysheniia urovnia zhizni naseleniia Moldavskoi SSR* (Problems dealing with ways to improve the living standards of the population of the Moldavian SSR). Chişinău: Shtiintsa, 1989.

Sheiko, N. "Nekotorye problemy tsenoobrazovaniia v toplivno-energeticheskom komplekse Moldovy" (Some issues dealing with the price policies in the fuel and energy sector of Moldova). *Izvestia Akademii nauk Respubliki Moldova, Ekonomika i sotsiologiia,* no. 3 (1995): 57–65.

Timuş, Andrei. "Motivarea muncii și protecția socială a oamenilor" (Motivation on the job and the social protection of people). *Buletinul Academiei de științe a Republicii Moldova,* no. 1 (1995): 65–67.

———. "Transformările economice și presiunea lor asupra intensificării relațiilor sociale ale populației" (Economic transformations and the pressure they exert on intensifying the social relations between people). *Buletinul Academiei de științe a Republicii Moldova,* no. 2 (1995): 62–73.

Timuş, Andrei, et al. *Tranziția la economia de piață: Probleme sociale* (Social problems in the transition to a market economy). Chişinău: n. p., 1991.

Timush, A. "Sotsiologiia ekonomicheskoi zhizni: Problemy i perspecktivy" (Sociology of economics: Problems and perspectives). *Buletinul Academiei de științe a Republicii Moldova,* no. 3 (1995): 66–77.

World Bank. *Moldova: Moving to a Market Economy* (Country Study). Washington, DC: World Bank, 1994.

V. SOCIETY

1. Ethnography

Botezatu, Grigore, et al. *Folklor din Bujiak* (Folklore of the Bugeac). Chişinău: Shtiintsa, 1982.

Furtune, Aleksandr T. *Ovtsevodstvo u moldovan v XIX–nachale XX v: Istoriko-etnograficeskii aspekt* (Moldovan sheep breeding in the 19 to 20th centuries: Historical and ethnographic aspects). Chişinău: Shtiintsa, 1989.

Gagauz, O. "Sotsial'nye probelmy razvitiia dukhovnykh potrebnostei truzhenits promyshlennykh predpriatiiatii Moldovy" (Issues dealing with the social development and spiritual needs of female workers in Moldova's enterprises). *Ekonomika i sotsiologiia*, no. 1 (1993): 85–91.

Golopenţia, Sanda. "Love Charms in Cornova, Bessarabia." In *Studies in Moldovan*, Donald L. Dyer, ed. Boulder, CO: East European Monographs; distributed by Columbia University Press, 1996.

Grosu, V. I., et al. *Materialy i issledovaniia po arkheologii i etnografii Moldovy* (Research materials in Moldova's archeology and ethnography). Chişinău: Shtiintsa, 1992.

Grosul, Iakim S., et al. *Moldovane* (Moldovaniana). Chişinău: Academiia de Shtiintse a RSSM, 1977.

Khynku, A. S., and V. S. Zelenchuk. *Folklorul obicheiurilor de familie* (Folklore of family customs). Chişinău: Shtiintsa, 1979.

Luk'ianets, Olga S. *Russkie issledovateli i moldavskaia etnograficheskaia nauka v XIX–nachale XX v* (Russian researchers and Moldavian ethnographic science in the 19th and the early 20th century). Chişinău: Shtiintsa, 1986.

Pavel, Emilia. *Portul popular moldovenesc* (The Moldovan folk costume). Iaşi: Junimea, 1976.

Postică, Gheorghe. *Civilizaţia veche românească din Moldova* (The ancient Romanian civilization of Moldova). Chişinău: Shtiintsa, 1995.

Sharanutsa, Silvia N. *Ornamente populare moldovenesht'* (Moldavian folk ornaments). Chişinău: Timpul, 1984.

Stefănucă, Petre V. *Folclor şi tradiţii populare* (Folklore and popular traditions), G. Botezatu and A. Hîncu, eds. Chişinău: Shtiintsa, 1991.

Vetavu, Mitrofan, and Mihai Potyrnike, eds. *Norok, satule* (Good luck, my village). Chişinău: Kartia Moldoveniaske, 1982.

Zelenchuk, Valentin, and Natalia M. Kalashnikova. *Vestimentaţia populaţiei orăşeneşti din Moldova: Secolele XV–XIX* (Costumes and apparel of Moldovan townspeople: 15th–19th centuries). Chişinău: Shtiintsa, 1993.

Zhungietu, E., and A. Furtune. *Folklor pestoresk* (Pastoral folklore). Chişinău: Shtiintsa, 1991.

2. Sociology, Education, Religion

Bolgov, V. I., and V. G. Gutsu. *Sotsiologiia vremeni* (The sociology of time). Chişinău: Shtiintsa, 1993.

Buzilă, Boris. *Din istoria vieţii bisericeşti din Basarabia (1812–1918; 1918–1944)* (Notes on the history of the life of the church in Bessarabia [1812–1918; 1918–1944]). Bucharest: Editura Fundaţiei Culturale Române, 1996.

Byrka, G. I. *Podgotovka kadrov vysshei i srednei kvalifikatsii v Moldavskoi SSR* (Preparing high- and middle-level qualification specialists in the Moldavian SSR). Chişinău: Shtiintsa, 1981.

Cibotaru, T. T., ed. *Istoria învăţământului şi a gândirii pedagogice în Moldova* (A history of education and pedagogical thought in Moldova). Chişinău: Lumina, 1991.

Comendant, T. "Evoluţia valorilor moral-spirituale în concepţia tineretului rural" (Evolution of moral-spiritual values in the mind-set of youths in the countryside). *Buletinul Academiei de Ştiinţe a Republicii Moldova*, no. 3 (1995): 86–93.

Crăciun, Maria. *Protestantism şi Ortodoxie în Moldova secolului al XVI-lea* (Protestantism and Orthodoxy in 16th-century Moldova). Cluj-Napoca: Presa Universitară Clujană, 1996.

Dima, Nicholas. "Politics and Religion in Moldova: A Case Study." *Mankind Quarterly*, vol. 34, no. 3 (Spring 1994): 175–194.

Dragnev, Demir, et al. *Iz istorii sotsial'nykh otnoshenii i obshchestvenno-politichesskogo dvizheniia: XIV–nachalo XX v* (Pages from the history of the social relations and sociopolitical movements between the 16th century and the early 20th century). Chişinău: Shtiintsa, 1991.

Eşanu, Andrei, ed. *Valori şi tradiţii culturale în Moldova: Culegere de studii* (Values and cultural traditions in Moldova). Chişinău: Shtiintsa, 1993.

Gutsu, Vladimir G. *Kul'turnyi uroven' zhizni naseleniia Respubliki Moldova: Teoria, metody, i opyt sotsiologicheskogo issledovaniia* (The level of the population's cultural activity in the Republic of Moldova: Theory, methods, and practices of sociological research). Chişinău: Assotsiatsiia sotsiologov Respubliki Moldova, 1993.

Hassard, Daniel A. *From Russia to Romania: Three Generations of Women and Translocation—Two Studies in Human Adaptability.* Youngstown, OH: n. p., 1994.

Livezeanu, Irina. "Urbanization in a Low Key and Linguistic Change in Soviet Moldavia." *Soviet Studies,* vol. 33, no. 3 (July 1981): 327–351.

Malcoci, L. "Televiziunea în spaţiul socio-cultural al Republicii Moldova" (Television in the social and cultural space of the Republic of Moldova). *Buletinul Academiei de ştiinţe al Republicii Moldova,* no. 3 (1995): 78–85.

Malski, Boris. *Viaţa moldovenilor de la Nistru, studiu sociologic al unui sat nistrean—Olăneşti* (The life of the Moldovans on the Nistru, sociological study of a Nistrian village—Olăneşti). With a preface by Professor D. Gusti. Cetatea Albă: Tipografia Prefecturii, 1939.

Mihail, Paul. *Mărturii de spiritualitate românească din Basarabia: Aşezăminte, scrieri, personalităţi* (Expressions of Romanian spirituality in Bessarabia: Institutions, writings, personalities). Chişinău: Shtiintsa, 1993.

Mocanu, V. "Şomajul în oraşe şi sate" (Unemployment in cities and the countryside). *Buletinul Academiei de ştiinţe a Republicii Moldova,* no. 2 (1995): 74–80.

Nica, Antim. *Monahismul în Basarabia, 1812–1918* (Monastic life in Bessarabia, 1812–1918). Bălţi: Tipografia Eparhială, 1940.

Pocitan, Vasile. *Biserica românească din Basarabia* (The Romanian Church in Bessarabia). Bucureşti: Albert Baer, 1914.

Puiu, Visarion. *Mănăstirile din Basarabia* (Monasteries of Bessarabia). Chişinău: Luceafărul, 1919.

Puiu, Visarion, Constantin Tomescu, Stefan Berechet, and Stefan Ciobanu, comps. *Documente din Basarabia* (Bessarabian documents). Chişinău: Tipografia Eparhială Cartea Românească, 1928.

Roshka, Aleksandr N., et al., eds. *Sem'ia i semeinyi byt v Moldove* (Family and family culture in Moldova). Chişinău: Shtiintsa, 1991.

Stadnitski, A. *Gavriil Banulescu-Bodoni, ekzarkh Moldo-Vlachiiskii (1808–1812) i Mitropolit Kishinevskii (1813–1821)* (Gavril Bănulescu-Bodoni, exarch of Moldo-Wallachia [1808–1812] and metropolitan of Kishinev [1813–1821]). Chişinău: n. p., 1894.

Tarlapan, Efim. *De ce v-aţi dus de-acasă? Convorbiri nostalgice cu unii moldoveni statorniciţi în Moscova temporar sau pentru totdeauna* (Why have you left home? Nostalgic conversations with Moldovans having settled in Moscow, temporarily or permanently). Chişinău: Basarabia, 1991.

Timush, Andrei I., ed. *Opiniia publike: Aspekte sochiale* (Public opinion: Social aspects). Chişinău: Shtiintsa, 1990.

———. *Problemy sotsial'noi zhizni SSR Moldova: Analiz obshchestvennogo mneniia* (Issues dealing with social life in the Moldovan SSR: A questionnaire). Chişinău: Akademia Nauk SSR Moldova, 1990.

Topilina, Valentina. *Religioznaia filosofiia v Moldavii nachala XX v* (Religious philosophy in early-20th-century Moldavia). Chişinău: Shtiintsa, 1990.

Varlaam. *Opere* (Works by Metropolitan Varlaam of Moldova). Chişinău: Hyperion, 1991.

Zelenchuk, Valentin S., and Liudmila D. Loskutova. *Novyie grazhdanskie prazdniki, obriady, i rituly: Prakticheskie rekomendatsii* (New secular holidays, traditions, and rituals: Practical recommendations). Chişinău: Kartia Moldoveniaske, 1984.

VI. CULTURE

1. Linguistics

ALM—Atlasul lingvistik moldovenesk (I-II) (Moldavian linguistic atlas, vols. 1-2). Chişinău: Kartia Moldoveniaske, 1968.

Atlasul lingvistic român pe regiuni: Basarabia, Nordul Bucovinei, Transnistria (Linguistic atlas of the Romanian language by regions: Bessarabia, Northern Bucovinia, and Transnistria) vol. 1. Chişinău: Stiinţa, 1993.

Avram, Mioara. "Consideraţii asupra situaţiei limbii române în Republica Moldova" (Considerations on the situation of the Romanian language in the Republic of Moldova). *Limba română*, no. 5 (1992): 249–260.

Boldur, Alexandru V. "Originea numelui Moldova: O ipoteză nouă" (The origin of the name Moldova: A new hypothesis). *Revista de Istorie,* vol. 28, no. 6 (1977): 935–940.

Bruchis, Michael. *One Step Back, Two Steps Forward: On the Language Policy of the Communist Party of the Soviet Union in the National Republics: Moldavian, a Look Back, a Survey and Perspective, 1924–1980.* Boulder, CO: East European Monographs; distributed by Columbia University Press, 1982.

————. *The USSR: Language and Realities: Nations, Leaders, and Scholars.* Boulder, CO: East European Monographs; distributed by Columbia University Press, 1988.

Chebotar, Petr A. *Chto voskliknul turetskii pasha* (What the Turkish pasha said). Chişinău: Shtiintsa, 1990.

Corlăteanu, Nicolae. "Româna literară în Republica Moldova: Istorie şi actualitate" (The Romanian literary language in the Republic of Moldova: History and actuality). *Revista de lingvistică şi ştiinţă literară,* no. 5 (1995): 14–23.

Deletant, Dennis. "Slavonic Letters in Moldavia, Wallachia, and Transylvania from the 10th to the 17th Centuries." In *Studies in Romanian History.* Bucharest: Editura Enciclopedică, 1991.

————. "Language Policy and Linguistic Trends in the Republic of Moldavia, 1924–1992." In *Studies in Moldovan,* Donald L. Dyer, ed. Boulder, CO: East European Monographs; distributed by Columbia University Press, 1996.

Dumbrevianu, A. N. *Mik dikstionar de prenume dialektale moldovenesht'* (Small dictionary of dialectal Moldovan first names). Chişinău: Shtiintsa, 1983.

Dyer, Donald L. "The Making of the Moldavian Language." In *Studies in Moldovan,* Donald L. Dyer, ed. Boulder, CO: East European Monographs; distributed by Columbia University Press, 1996.

Eremiia, Anatolie. *Graiul pemyntului: Skitse de toponimie moldoveniaske* (The language of the land: Notes on Moldovan toponymy). Chişinău: Shtiintsa, 1981.

Guboglu, Mikhail N. *Razvitie dvuiazychiia v Moldavskoi SSR* (The development of a bilingual environment in the Moldavian SSR). Chişinău: Shtiintsa, 1979.

Heitmann, Klaus. *Limbă şi politică în Republica Moldova* (Language and politics in the Republic of Moldova). Chişinău: Arc, 1998.

King, Charles. "The Politics of Language in the Moldovan Soviet Socialist Republic." In *Studies in Moldovan,* Donald L. Dyer, ed. Boulder, CO: East European Monographs; distributed by Columbia University Press, 1996.

————. "The Ambivalence of Authenticity, or How the Moldovan Language Was Made." *Slavic Review,* vol. 58, no. 1 (Spring 1999): 117–142.

Kosnichianu, M. A. *Dicţionar de prenume şi nume de familie purtate de moldoveni* (Dictionary of Christian and family names borne by Moldovans). Chişinău: Redacţia Principală a Enciclopediei Sovietice Modoveneşti, 1991.

Lupan, Ilie, ed. *Povare sau tezaur sfynt?* (A burden or a holy treasure?). Chişinău: Kartia Moldoveniaske, 1989.

Niculescu, Alexandru. *Outline History of the Romanian Language.* Bucharest: Editura Stiinţifică şi Enciclopedică, 1981.

Oancea, D. "Tezaurul toponimic al Moldovei" (Moldova's treasury of toponyms). *Academica,* vol. 1, no. 7 (1991): 5.

Palii, Alexei. *Calchierea ca aspect al interferenței limbilor: Contacte moldo-ruse* (Linguistic transfer, an aspect of languages in contact: The Moldo-Russian interference). Chișinău: Shtiintsa, 1991.

Roman, A. T. "Evoluția opiniei publice în problema instituirii limbii de stat în Republica Moldova" (The evolution of public opinion on the issue of establishing the official language of the Republic of Moldova). *Sociologie românească*, no. 6 (1992): 655–658.

Rosetti, Alexandru. *Istoria limbii române de la origini pînă în secolul al XVII-lea* (A history of the Romanian language from its origins to the 17th century). Bucharest: Editura Stiințifică și Enciclopedică, 1978.

Tomescu, D. "Lucrări de onomastică românească din Republica Moldova" (Studies in the Romanian anthroponyms in the Republic of Moldova). *Limba română*, no. 5 (1992): 283–286.

2. Arts

Andon, V., et al., eds. *Kinoiskusstvo Moldovy: Istoriia, teoriia, praktika* (Moldova's movie industry: History, theory, practice). Chișinău: Shtiintsa, 1991.

Balan, Pavel, and Vlad Druk. *Poliptik moldav: Arte moldoveniaske din viakurile XIV–XIX* (with English translation: *Moldavian Polyptich: Moldavian Art in the 14th–19th Centuries*). Chișinău: Timpul, 1985.

Ciobanu, Constantin, ed. *Arta '92: Studii, cercetări, și documente* (Art '92: Studies, analyses, and documents). Chișinău: Litera, 1992.

Kolotovkin, Anatolii V., et al. *Arkhitektura Sovetskoi Moldavii* (Soviet Moldavia's architecture). Moscow: Stroiizdat, 1987.

Koroleva, E. A. *Moldavskii baletnyi teatr* (Moldavian ballet theater). Chișinău: Shtiintsa, 1990.

Kotliarov, Boris Ia. *Moldavskie leutary i ikh iskusstvo* (Moldavian folk musicians and their art). Moscow: Sovet Kompozitor, 1989.

Marin, G., ed. *Moldaviia fotoal'bom* (Moldavia, a photo album). Moscow: Planeta, 1980.

Miliutina, I. B., ed. *Muzyka v Moldove: Voprosy istorii i teorii* (Music in Moldova: Issues concerning its history and musical theories). Chișinău: Shtiintsa, 1991.

Muzeul artistik de stat din RSS Moldoveniaske (The state art museum of the Moldavian SSR). Chișinău: Timpul, 1982.

Pennington, Anne Elizabeth. *Music in Medieval Moldavia*. Bucharest: Musical Publishing House, 1985.

Stoianov, Petr F. *Ritmika moldavskoi doiny* (Rhythmics of the Moldavian *doina*). Chișinău: Shtiintsa, 1980.

Tarasenko, Larisa V. *Poeziia moldavskogo ekrana* (The poetry of Moldavia's movies). Chișinău: Literatura Artistike, 1980.

Vangeli, M. S., ed. *Aktual'nye problemy stroitel'stva i arkhitektury Moldavii* (Current issues in Moldavia's constructions and architecture). Chișinău: Shtiintsa, 1989.

Vasiliu, Anca. *Monastères de Moldavie, XIVe–XVIe siècles: Les Architectures de l'image*. Bucharest: Humanitas, 1998.

Zhosul, Viktor I. *Na puti k teatru: Iz istorii teatral'nogo stroitel'stva v Moldove v pervye gody Sovetskoi vlasti, 1917–1924* (A theater in progress: Pages from the history of the theater of Moldova in the first years of the Soviet regime). Chişinău: Shtiintsa, 1990.

3. Literature

Alecsandri, Vasile. *Mioritsa*. Chişinău: Editura pentru Literatură Artistike, 1983.

Asachi, Gheorghe. *Dochia şi Traian dupre zicerile populare a românilor* (Dochia and Trajan after the popular sayings of the Romanians). Iaşi: Institutul Albinei, 1840.

Babii, A. I., et al. *Nicolae Milescu Spătarul şi problemele culturii Moldovei* (Nicolae Milescu Spatharius and the issues of Moldova's culture). Chişinău: Shtiintsa, 1991.

Bezviconi, Gheorghe. *Cărturari basarabeni* (Bessarabian scholars). Chişinău: Colecţia Scriitorilor din Basarabia, 1940.

Bogach, G. F., et al., eds. *Istoriia literaturii moldovenesht', de la ynceputuile ei pyne la revolutsiia din Oktombrie* (A history of Moldavian literature from its beginnings to the October Revolution). Chişinău: Editura de Stat a Moldovei, 1958.

Botezatu, Grigore, et al., eds. *Literatura moldoveniaske shi folclorul* (Moldavian literature and folklore). Chişinău: Shtiintsa, 1982.

Chibotaru, Simion S. *Literatura sovetike moldoveniaske din anii 1924–1960* (Soviet Moldavia's literature, 1924–1960). Chişinău: Shtiintsa, 1982.

Chobanu, Lazer. *Kertsile populare yn Moldova: Viakurile XVII–XVIII: Romane, lejende, povestir', istorioare, fabule, parabole, ynvetsetyr'* (Popular literature in 17th- and 18th-century Moldova: Novels, legends, tales, sketches, fables, parables, didactic pieces). Chişinău: Literatura Artistike, 1989.

Cimpoi, Mihai. "Panorama literaturii basarabene postbelice" (A panorama of Bessarabia's post–World War II literature). *Forum*, nos. 11–12 (1993): 78–91.

———. *Basarabia sub steaua exilului* (Bessarabia in exile). Bucureşti: Viitorul Românesc, 1994.

———. *O istorie deschisă a literaturii române din Basarabia* (An open history of Romanian literature in Bessarabia). Chişinău: Arc, 1996.

Constelaţia lirei: Antologia poeţilor din RSS Moldovenească (The constellation of the Lyra: An anthology of poetry written by poets from the Moldavian SSR). Bucharest: Univers, 1987.

Coval, Dumitru, ed. *Ecouri dintr-un secol: Pagini din presa periodică moldovenească a secolului XIX: Articole-program, manifeste, recenzii, portrete literare, pamflete* (Echoes from the 19th century: Selections from Moldavian periodicals, editorials, manifestos, reviews, literary portraits, pamphlets). Chişinău: Universitas, 1991.

Dimitrie Cantemir [Cantemir, Demetrius]. *Cele mai frumoase pagini* (A selection from Dimitrie Cantemir's most beautiful pages). Chişinău: Hyperion, 1992.

Dvoichenko-Markova, E. M. *Russko-Rumynskie literaturnye sviazi* (Russo-Romanian literary relations). Moscow: Nauka, 1966.

———. *Pushkin v Moldavii i Valakhii* (Pushkin in Moldavia and Wallachia). Moscow: Nauka, 1979.

Haneş, Petre V. *Scriitorii Basarabiei (1850–1940)* (Writers from Bessarabia [1850–1940]). Bucharest: Editura Casei Şcoalelor, 1942.

Korbu, Kh. G., ed. *Pajin' din istoriia literaturii shi kulturii moldovenesht': Studii shi materiale* (Selections from the history of Moldavian literature and culture: Studies and documents). Chişinău: Shtiintsa, 1979.

Korbu, Kh., et al., eds. *Istoriia literaturii moldovenesht'yn trei volume* (with a summary in English and in French) (A history of Moldavian literature in three volumes). Chişinău: Shtiintsa, 1986–1990.

———, eds. *Literatura moldoveniaske shi problema istorismului: Studii shi materiale* (Moldavian literature and the issue of historicism: Studies and documents). Chişinău: Shtiintsa, 1990.

Korbu, Kharalambie G. *Yn lumia klasicilor: Sinteze shi interpreter'* (In the world of the classics: Syntheses and interpretations). Chişinău: Literatura Artistike, 1990.

Lungu, Eugen, ed. *O altă imagine a literaturii basarabene* (A different image of Bessarabia's literature). Chişinău: Arc, 1995.

Michelson, Paul E. "That Was Then, This Is Now: Animadversions on Alecu Russo's *Studie Moldovană*." In *Studies in Moldovan,* Donald L. Dyer, ed. Boulder, CO: East European Monographs; distributed by Columbia University Press, 1996.

Shpak, I. I., et al. *Kritika shi shtiintsa literare yn Moldova, 1976–1980* (Literary criticism and literary knowledge in Moldova, 1976–1980). Chişinău: Shtiintsa, 1982.

———. *Kritika i literaturovedenie Moldavii, 1981–1985* (Literary criticism and literary knowledge in Moldova, 1981–1985). Chişinău: Shtiintsa, 1988.

———. *Kritika i literaturovedenie Moldavii, 1924–1965* (Literary criticism and literary knowledge in Moldova, 1924–1965). Chişinău: Shtiintsa, 1989.

Smochină, N. P. "Din cultura naţională în republica moldovenească a Sovietelor" (Gleanings from the national culture of the Moldavian Soviet republic). *Revista Fundaţiilor Regale,* vol. 4, no. 4 (1937).

Stere, Constantin. *In viaţă, în literatură* (In life and in literature). Chişinău: Hyperion, 1991.

VII. SCIENCE

1. Geography, Geology, Ecology

Bazarin, N. A., et al. *Poisk predvestnikov zemletriasenii v Moldavii* (Identifying early warning signals of earthquakes in Moldavia). Chişinău: Shtiintsa, 1986.

Bilinkis, G. M., et al. *Geomorfologiia Moldavii* (Geomorphology of Moldavia). Chişinău: Institutul de Jeofizike shi Jeolojie, Academiia de Shtiintse a RSSM, 1978.

Capcelea, Arcadie M. *Hârtoapele Moldovei* (Moldova's ravines). Chişinău: Shtiintsa, 1992.

Constantinov, Tatiana, ed. *Studii geo-ecologice in Republica Moldova / Geo-ekologicheskie issledovaniia v Respublike Moldova* (Geo-ecological studies in the

Republic of Moldova). Chişinău: Academia de Ştiinţe a Republicii Moldova, Institutul de Geografie, 1994.

Dediu, I. *Strategia protecţiei mediului în Republica Moldova* (A strategy for protecting the environment in the Republic of Moldova). Chişinău: Anul European de Conservare a Naturii, 1995.

Eremiia, Anatolie. *Geograficheskie nazvaniia raskazyvaiut* (What geographical names tell us). Chişinău: Shtiintsa, 1982.

Gania, I. M., et al., eds. *Ekologiia i okhrana ptits i mlekopitaiushchikh v antropogennom landshafte* (Ecology and the protection of birds and mammals in an anthropogenic environment). Chişinău: Shtiintsa, 1992.

Katser, R. P., ed. *Problemy kachestva, ispol'zovaniia, i okhrany vodnykh resursov SSR Moldova* (Issues dealing with the quality, use, and protection of water resources in the Moldovan SSR). Chişinău: Shtiintsa, 1991.

Konstantinova, Tatiana S., ed. *Regional'nye ekologicheskie problemy* (Regional ecological problems). Chişinău: Shtiintsa, 1992.

Laking, Phyllis N. *The Black Sea, Its Geology, Chemistry, Biology.* Woods Hole, MA: Woods Hole Oceanographic Institution, 1974.

Levandiuk, Andrei T., ed. *Opolzneopasnye teritorii Moldavii i ikh ratsional'noe ispol'zovanie* (Controlling landslide-prone soils in the territory of Moldova). Chişinău: Shtiintsa, 1990.

Maiatskii, I. N., ed. *Lesorazvedenie v Moldavii* (The woods of Moldova). Chişinău: Shtiintsa, 1985.

Matei, Konstantin, et al. *Geografiia naseleniia Moldavskoi SSR i demograficheskie protsessy* (Geography of the population and demographical processes in the Moldavian SSR). Chişinău: Shtiintsa, 1985.

Mel'nichuk, O. N., N. V. Lalykin, and A. I. Filippenkov. *Iskusstvennye vodoemy Moldovy: Sostoianie, ispol'zovanie, okhrana, gidrologicheskie raschety* (Man-made water reservoirs in Moldova: Conditions, usage, protection, and hydrological estimates). Chişinău: Shtiintsa, 1992.

Mishchenko, Z. A., ed. *Klimaticheskie i mikroklimaticheskie issledovaniia v Moldavii* (Climate and microclimate research in Moldavia). Chişinău: Shtiintsa, 1985.

Myrlian, N. F., et al. *Ekologo-geokhimicheskii atlas Kishineva* (Ecological and geochemical map of Kishinev). Chişinău: Shtiintsa, 1992.

Nikora, Vladimir I., ed. *Gidrologiia malykh rek* (The hydrology of small rivers). Chişinău: Shtiintsa, 1991.

Polevoi, Lazar L. *Ocherki istoricheskoi geografii Moldavii XIII–XV vv* (Historical geography of Moldavia in the 13th to 15th centuries). Chişinău: Shtiintsa, 1979.

Rymbu, Nikolai L. *Prirodno-geograficheskoe raionirovanie Moldavskoi SSR* (Geographical disposition of the Moldavian SSR's districts). Chişinău: Shtiintsa, 1982.

Sokolov, V. E., et al., eds. *Fauna zapovednika "Kodry": Operativno-informatsionnyi material* (The Codri wildlife: Information and action materials). Moscow: n. p., 1989.

Tarasov, Oleg Iu. *Nauka i ee organizatsiia v Moldavskoi SSR* (Science and its organization in the Moldavian SSR). Chişinău: Shtiintsa, 1966–1970.

2. Public Health

Kozliuk, A. S., and V. S. Iakim, eds. *Immunostruktura naselniia i zabolevaemost'* (Immunostructure of the population and diseases). Chişinău: Shtiintsa, 1991.

Martynchik, Evghenii G., ed. *Bor'ba s narkomaniei: Problemy i perspektivy* (The war against illegal drugs: Problems and perspectives). Chişinău: Shtiintsa, 1990.

Prisakar', Ivan F., and Mikhail S. Chekan. *Sotsial'no-gigienicheskie aspekty zdorov'ia rabotnikov agropromyshlennogo kompleksa* (Social and hygiene aspects of agricultural workers' health). Chişinău: Shtiintsa, 1991.

Remizov, V. B., et al., eds. *Aktual'nye voprosy klinicheskoi i teoreticheskoi meditsiny* (Current issues in clinical and theoretical medical science). Chişinău: Shtiintsa, 1991.

Testemitsanu, N. A., E. P. Popushoi, and V. A. Ioksa. *Vidnye vrachi Moldavii* (Moldavia's celebrities in medicine). Chişinău: Shtiintsa, 1985.

About the Author

Andrei Brezianu is an independent scholar and researcher, and the author of several books of essays and studies in cross-cultural communication. A resident of Washington, D.C., he has worked as a publicist and international broadcaster with the Voice of America since 1986. In 1984, he was nominated Fellow of Churchill College, Cambridge, by Professor George Steiner. In 1985, as Fellow Commonor of that college, he was granted M.A. status by the University of Cambridge. He holds a Ph.D. in intellectual history and comparative literature from the University of Bucharest and has written extensively on subjects ranging from European history and the history of ideas to comparative literature, art, politics, and the media. His main research interests over the past years have included the history of Moldova as part of European culture and Moldovan authors Demetrius Cantemir and Costache Conachi. Earlier in his career, he taught at the University of Bucharest and Catholic University of America, and served as senior consultant with the Center for Applied Linguistics in Washington, D.C. As a guest of the Free International University of Moldova, he taught courses on the media, the public sphere, and European formation at that university's 1998 and 1999 Summer School. Andrei Brezianu's published works include four original books and over 1,500 pages of published translations.